SELF-MOTION

SELF-MOTION

FROM ARISTOTLE TO NEWTON

Edited by

Mary Louise Gill and James G. Lennox

PRINCETON UNIVERSITY PRESS   PRINCETON, NEW JERSEY

Library of Congress Cataloging-in-Publication Data

Self-motion : from Aristotle to Newton / edited by Mary Louise Gill
and James G. Lennox.
p. cm.
Includes bibliographical references and index.
ISBN 0-691-03235-1 (alk. paper)
1. Aristotle. 2. Movement (Philosophy) I. Gill, Mary Louise,
1950– . II. Lennox, James G.
B491.M6S45 1994
116—dc20 93-45882 CIP

David Furley's essay, "Self-Movers," is reprinted by permission from
Aristotle on Mind and the Senses, ed. Geoffrey Lloyd and Gwil Owen
(Cambridge: Cambridge University Press, 1978).

This book has been composed in Sabon

Princeton University Press books are printed on acid-free paper and
meet the guidelines for permanence and durability of the Committee
on Production Guidelines for Book Longevity of the Council
on Library Resources

Printed in the United States of America

1 3 5 7 9 10 8 6 4 2

Contents

Chapter 11. Ockham, Self-Motion, and the Will

Chapter 12. Natural Motion and Its Causes: Newton on the "Vis Insita" of Bodies

Preface

THE PAPERS in this volume originated in a conference (of the same name), held February 23–25, 1990, celebrating the expansion of the Program in Classics and Philosophy at the University of Pittsburgh into the Program in Classics, Philosophy, and Ancient Science. As the conference progressed, it became clear that the papers told a remarkably unified story of the development of the concept of self-motion from Aristotle, through Hellenistic and medieval philosophy, to Newton's natural philosophy. It was also clear that the commentators had gone far beyond their assigned roles, offering alternative, sometimes complementary, interpretations to those of the speakers. The conference organizers, Mary Louise Gill, James G. Lennox, and Steven K. Strange, therefore decided to ask both speakers and commentators to contribute papers, based on their presentations, for inclusion in a volume devoted to the conference theme. This volume is the result.

Neither the conference nor this volume would have been possible without the support of many, and it is a pleasant responsibility to thank them. The conference was generously supported by the Center for Philosophy of Science (with the help of funding from the R. K. Mellon Foundation), and the Departments of Classics, Philosophy, and History and Philosophy of Science at the University of Pittsburgh. The conference ran smoothly because of the incomparable organizational skills of Linda Butera, ably assisted by Katherine Nolan and John Quilter. Ann Himmelberger Wald, Philosophy Editor at Princeton University Press, has been supportive and encouraging from the outset. We are grateful to Sherry Wert, our copy editor, and to Beth Gianfagna and Colin Barr and the members of the staff at the Press for their assistance. The readers for the Press, David Sedley and Sarah Broadie, provided valuable comments, both on the volume as a whole and on the individual contributions. Oxford University Press, Cambridge University Press, and Blackwell's allowed us to use material published by their presses. To all of these individuals and institutions, we the editors say a heartfelt "Thank you."

One final thank-you is in order. During the conference out of which this collection grew, the extent of the influence of David Furley's paper "Self-Movers" became apparent to all. Originally invited as a speaker, he agreed to comment on one paper that took his own as a starting-point. We felt that this volume should begin, as many of the papers on Aristotle did, with his original paper (making this the third occasion of its reprinting!). We were very pleased that he acceded to our wishes. The editors (no doubt on behalf of our contributors as well) delight in taking this opportunity to give thanks for the inspiration, both specific and general, David Furley has given to those working at the interface of classical philosophy and science.

James G. Lennox
Mary Louise Gill

Abbreviations

Works cited in this volume are abbreviated as listed here. Full references to these works and to other texts cited appear in the Bibliography.

Alexander of Aphrodisias	*De anima cum mantissa*	*De an. man.*
	De mixtione	*De mixt.*
Aristoteles Latinus		*AL*
Aristotle	*Categories*	*Cat.*
	De anima	*De an.*
	De caelo	*De cae.*
	De interpretatione	*De int.*
	De iuventute et senectute	*De iuv.*
	De longetudine et brevitate vitae	*De long.*
	De memoria	*De mem.*
	De respiratione	*De resp.*
	Eudemian Ethics	*EE*
	Nicomachean Ethics	*EN*
	Generation of Animals	*GA*
	On Generation and Corruption	*GC*
	Historia animalium	*HA*
	De motu animalium	*MA*
	Metaphysics	*Meta.*
	Meteorologica	*Meteor.*
	Parts of Animals	*PA*
	Physics	*Phys.*
	Posterior Analytics	*Po. An.*
	Prior Analytics	*Pr. An.*
	Protrepticus	*Protr.*
	Rhetoric	*Rhet.*
Aulus Gellius	*Noctes Atticae*	*Noct. Att.*
[author disputed]	*Centiloquium*	*Cent.*
Cicero	*De oratore*	*De or.*
	De inventione rhetorica	*Inv. rhet.*
	De natura deorum	*ND*
Clement of Alexandria	*Stromateis*	*Stromat.*

Diels and Kranz	*Die Fragmente der Vorsokratiker*	DK
Duns Scotus	*Opus Oxoniense*	*Op. Ox.*
	Ordinatio	*Ord.*
	Quaestiones quodlibetales	QQ
	Quaestiones subtilissimae super Aristotelis Metaphysicorum	QSM
	Reportata Parisiensia	*Rep. Par.*
	Vatican edition	Vat.
	Wadding-Vivés edition	WV
Epictetus	*Dissertationes*	*Diss.*
Long and Sedley	*The Hellenistic Philosophers*	LS
Liddell, Scott, Jones, and McKenzie	*A Greek-English Lexicon*	LSJ
Nemesius	*De natura hominis*	*De nat. hom.*
Ockham	*Exposition in libros Physicorum Aristotelis*	*Exp. Phys.*
	Opera philosophica	OP
	Scriptum in librum primum Sententiarum	*Ord.*
	Opera theologica	OT
	Tractatus de praedestinatione	*Praed.*
	Quodlibeta septem	*Quod.*
	Quaestiones in librum quartum Sententiarum	*Sent.*
Petrus Olivi	*Quaestiones in secundem librum Sententiarum*	Olivi *Sent.*
Origen	*De oratione*	*De orat.*
	De principiis	*De princ.*
Philoponus	*In Aristotelis Physica commentaria*	*In Phys.*
Seneca	*Epistulae*	*Ep.*
	Naturales quaestiones	*Nat. quaest.*
Sextus Empiricus	*Adversus mathematicos*	*Adv. math.*
Simplicius	*In Aristotelis De caelo commentaria*	*In Cae.*
	In Aristotelis Categorias commentarium	*In Cat.*

	In Libros Aristotelis De anima commentaria	*In De an.*
	In Aristotelis Physicorum libros octo commentaria	*In Phys.*
Von Arnim	*Stoicorum veterum fragmenta*	*SVF*

Introduction

THE ORGANIZING THEME of this volume, the problem of self-motion, is clearly defined for the first time in Plato's *Phaedrus*, in a passage whose echoes ring throughout Aristotle's physical, metaphysical, and cosmological works:

> All soul is immortal. For that which is always moving is immortal. But that which moves something else and is moved by something else, since it has a cessation of motion, has a cessation of life. Evidently only that which moves itself never stops moving, because it does not abandon itself; and this is the origin (πηγή) and source (ἀρχή) of motion for other things that are moved as well. (245c5–9)

Plato immediately goes on to prove that such a self-moving source of motion can neither be created or destroyed, and he argues that this is the nature of soul, a claim that seems to be flatly contradicted in the *Timaeus*.

Aristotle, as a number of the following essays will argue, agrees with very little of the above argument. But there can be virtually no doubt that it, and similar passages in Plato's *Laws* 10, are at the root of much of his physical theory.

As in so many other areas of science and philosophy, Aristotle dominated the scientific study of motion and its causes through the sixteenth century. Although there were alternative views in the ancient world and intelligent critics among his Greek, Arabic, and Latin commentators, the basic concepts and problems of the field were those that Aristotle posed. At the very center of the Aristotelian approach to the study of motion is the distinction between self-movers and objects moved by others. Aristotle employs and discusses this basic opposition in many different contexts, and it is by no means clear that his various discussions are mutually consistent. So his followers and critics had ample room to develop and apply the distinction in a variety of ways.

A number of classic works in the history of science have made it an orthodoxy that there was a revolutionary replacement of Aristotle's distinction in the seventeenth century, which was represented paradigmatically by Sir Issac Newton's *Mathematical Principles of Natural Philosophy*. This orthodoxy deserves reassessment. Indeed, the last essay in this volume, which treats the thought of Issac Newton, challenges a fundamental myth of the scientific revolution by suggesting that Newton, far from rejecting the problem context of the ancients, was himself deeply immersed in it.

The essays presented in Part I constitute a systematic study of self-motion in Aristotle's natural philosophy, psychology, ethics, and metaphysics. Those in Part II examine how Aristotle's theory was developed, criticized, and transformed by the Stoics, by the scholastic Aristotelians, and finally by Issac Newton.

Our initial question is whether Aristotle admitted the existence of self-movers at all. Although he frequently calls animals self-movers, on several occasions he appears to deny that they are. The first four papers in Part I examine this discrepancy.

A second question is, What types of self-motion did Aristotle envisage? Is self-motion restricted to animals, or are simple inanimate bodies—earth, water, air, and fire—also self-movers? What about the heavenly bodies and their spheres? And the Prime Mover? The consensus among the authors in Part I is that Aristotle's theory excluded the four elements as self-movers, but views differ on the status of celestial objects and the Prime Mover.

A further question is, What types of organic motion does Aristotle treat as self-motion? Is self-motion restricted to locomotion, or does it have a much wider extension? After the opening paper by David Furley, which poses the general question about Aristotle's commitment to self-motion, the papers in Part I examine the various levels of self-motion, which correspond roughly to the types of Aristotelian soul. Thus, the simplest type of self-motion, which is explored by Mary Louise Gill, is that involving nutritive soul, the faculty common to plants and animals, which accounts for the basic life functions of survival and organic development. Next are the functions proper to animals—perception, desire, and locomotion—which depend on perceptive soul. Self-motions involving these functions are discussed in the papers by Cynthia Freeland and Susan Sauvé Meyer. We turn then to the function proper to human beings—reason. Mental self-motion is treated in the papers by Michael Wedin and Christopher Shields. Aryeh Kosman and Lindsay Judson turn finally to the Prime Mover, the cause of all motion, a being whose life is the activity of thinking.

The papers in Part II indicate that later thinkers transformed Aristotle's theory in various ways. Some philosophers believed that even the elements are self-movers. David Hahm argues that the Stoics developed a comprehensive theory of self-motion that included the motions of inanimate objects, as well as the three levels of animate motion discussed in connection with Aristotle. This view of the elements reemerges in the work of Duns Scotus and Isaac Newton, as Peter King and J. E. McGuire show. But a quite different position was also defended by some scholastics prior to Scotus—that self-motion is impossible in the physical world—and these thinkers, who included in their number Thomas Aquinas, claimed Aristotle's authority for their position. Although they excluded self-motion in the realm of physics, some of these thinkers allowed it in contexts involving non-physical causes, such as the will. As we see in the paper on William of Ockham by Calvin Normore, the tradition that the will is a self-mover developed, not from a consideration of Aristotle's arguments for self-motion, but from Plato's argument in the *Phaedrus* and elsewhere that the soul is a self-mover. William of Ockham, at the end of the Middle Ages, argued that the will is a self-mover and that physical bodies depend for their motion on an external cause. As Normore points out, this view set the stage for the early modern distinction between free spirits and inert matter. And although, as McGuire argues, Newton's view that bodies have an internal force, a *vis insita*, hearkens back to Aristotle's theory of self-movers, this was not a part of his theory that subsequent thinkers pursued.

PART I

The volume opens with David Furley's classic paper, "Self-Movers." This essay poses the interpretive question that remains central for any evaluation of Aristotle's theory of self-motion. Aristotle sometimes calls animals self-movers, but in two crucial passages in *Phys.* viii, he appears to deny that they are. Is this apparent inconsistency due to Aristotle's philosophical development, or is his position as a whole consistent? Furley defends Aristotle's commitment to self-movers, and he argues that the conflict between this commitment and the mechanical model in *Phys.* viii reflects, not a change of mind, but a clash of motives. Aristotle wants to preserve the intuition that animals have an internal source of their own movement, but he also sees the risk that the cosmos itself might have originated its own movement on analogy with animals. To avoid this possibility, Aristotle argues in *Phys.* viii that even the self-motions of animals depend on some previous motion. According to Furley, animals are self-movers because they pursue objects in their environment *under certain descriptions*. So the external object of desire, which the animal exerts itself to obtain, cannot be identified independently of the animal's psychic faculty of desire. Because the object of desire is an intentional object, the source of motion can be said to be "inside" the agent.

In "Aristotle on Self-Motion," Mary Louise Gill examines Aristotle's account of self-motion within the framework of his general theory of change and of active and passive potencies, and she focuses her discussion on self-motion in its simplest manifestation—organic survival and development controlled by nutritive soul. She argues that the discrepancy, to which Furley called attention, disappears if we recognize that Aristotle is asking two sorts of question. First, why is an animal's motion of a particular sort and sustained in a particular direction? And second, what triggers the motion, and why is it sometimes impeded? Gill argues that all living things are self-movers because they have an active source of change, which is internal. But because this source is an unmoved mover, it cannot account for the initiation of motion. To explain why motions start, Aristotle appeals to factors in the organism's environment, which are themselves explained by the motions of the heavenly spheres, and ultimately by the Prime Mover.

Cynthia A. Freeland, in "Aristotle on Perception, Appetition, and Self-Motion," treats the next higher level of self-motion, involving perceptive soul, and she offers another response to the problem posed by Furley. Freeland defends Aristotelian self-motion, not by appeal to the intentionality of animal perception, desire, and action (as Furley suggests), but by appeal to the objective goal-directedness of animal motions. She presents a general account of the teleology of animal movements and shows that self-motion is not restricted to animals capable of imagination but is also displayed in the behavior of simpler organisms. According to Freeland, the periodic movements of cicadas, which Furley claimed Aristotle would explain mechanistically, exhibit an objective goal-directedness. She further argues that the self-motion of animals, although explained teleologically, is also compatible with causal determinism by efficient causes.

Susan Sauvé Meyer, in "Self-Movement and External Causation," looks again at the fundamental question of whether self-motion is possible, given Aristotle's claim that animal motion requires an external cause. Whereas Freeland solves the problem by appeal to the objectively teleological nature of animal perception and appetite, Meyer examines the relationship between two types of efficient causation—that by an unmoved mover within the animal, and that by external moved movers. Meyer contends that although external causes precipitate animal movement, such factors do not undermine the animal's claim to be a self-mover, because they are accidental rather than intrinsic causes of its motion. An accidental cause, such as an object that enters an animal's visual field, may trigger a response in the animal, but it does not explain why the animal responds in the way that it does. The origin of animal movement is an intrinsic cause, which Meyer identifies as the specific dispositions of the animal. The intrinsic cause, whose causal efficacy is continual, regulates the animal's desires and other capacities. Because external causes trigger some response in the agent, but not a particular response, Meyer can argue that Aristotle's claims about voluntary action are compatible with causal determinism.

The highest and rarest form of self-motion is that possessed by the mind, and it is to the mind's self-motion that the papers of Michael Wedin and Christopher Shields attend. In "Aristotle on the Mind's Self-Motion," Michael Wedin argues that in Aristotle's view, the mind or "noetic system" comprises two levels. Actual thinking emerges at the higher level when, at the lower level, productive mind gives rise to the object of thought in receptive mind. This proposal satisfies one of the basic constraints on self-motion set in *Phys.* VIII.5, that an active part of an object cause change in a passive part. But why, asks Wedin, is thinking up to us? The model of self-motion in *Phys.* VIII seems to conflict with this idea, for it treats mind as a paradigm of things that move unless prevented. Wedin points out, however, that thought differs from the lower-level self-motions—nutrition, perception, and desire—in two relevant respects. First, the object of thought is a product of the noetic system itself, brought about by productive mind in receptive mind. Second, the mover is not, in any sense, external to the mind. According to Wedin, thinking is thus "up to us" in a more unqualified way than is perceiving or desiring, the objects of which are external.

Christopher Shields's "Mind and Motion in Aristotle" starts from the same apparent conflict: Do we think only *if* we wish, or *unless* prevented? And the agreement between Shields and Wedin extends two steps further: both take it that Aristotle is committed to an internal, unmoved source of motion that transforms the possession of knowledge into its exercise; and both take the object of thought to be that source of motion. Shields, however, sees problems with each side of this apparent conflict, even when this much is agreed to. First, if the object of thought is a universal, shared by a number of minds, in what sense is it an *internal* unmoved mover? If, as Aristotle claims, part of the reason why we can think when we wish is that the objects of thought are in us, answering this question is crucial. In Shields's view, the answer is that each individual mind that knows *p* stands in a stable dispositional relation to *p*, and that disposition is internal to it, though *p* itself is common. Second, how can thinking be up to us if minds contemplate their objects unless something prevents them from doing so? Shields avails himself of J. L. Mackie's account of causes in insisting that *Phys.* VIII.4 specifies only that the removal of impediments to thinking is among its relevant necessary conditions. This conclusion is analogous to Michael Wedin's view that *Phys.* VIII.4 provides only a partial model of the mind's self-motion.

If minds are the highest form of self-mover, then something that thinks eternally would seem to be the premier self-mover. But making this claim on behalf of Aristotle's Prime Mover is problematic, because, at least in the *Physics* and the *Metaphysics*, the Prime Mover is an unmoved mover, characterized by an active aspect only. A traditional, developmental solution to this problem holds that Aristotle moves from the view in *De caelo* that the outermost sphere is a naturally moving Prime Mover, to the view in *Phys.* VIII that the Prime Mover is an unmoved source of the movement of the outermost sphere, and finally to that in the *Metaphysics* that the Prime

Mover is a transcendent, eternally active being, imitated by the eternal rotation of the outermost sphere. On this traditional conception, the major shift in Aristotle's thought on the Prime Mover comes between the *De caelo* and the *Physics*.

Aryeh Kosman's "Aristotle's Prime Mover" challenges this developmental account in two respects. First, he argues that both the *De Caelo* and the *Physics* leave room for the Prime Mover to be both an unmoved mover and a self-mover. Second, he argues that the major development in Aristotle's conception of the Prime Mover, if there is a development, occurs in *Meta.* Λ.6–8. This text replaces the negative description of the Prime Mover as "unmoved" with a positive description of it as essentially active being. Even this account, Kosman argues, is prefigured in the physical treatises, in their claims that the outermost sphere is a living thing. This characterization suggests that the Prime Mover is the soul of the outermost sphere, which is therefore the paradigmatic self-mover. Why, then, does Aristotle never say this? The account of the soul in *De an.* II–III describes it as a "first actuality"—a capability—and thus fails to capture the nature of an eternally active being. Nevertheless, in all of Aristotle's discussions of the Prime Mover, argues Kosman, it is the psychic aspect of the outermost sphere of the heaven that he is attempting to characterize.

Lindsay Judson, in "Heavenly Motion and the Unmoved Mover," defends the developmental hypothesis against Kosman's attack. Judson points out that the *De caelo*'s claim that the first sphere is alive need not entail that the sphere's Prime Mover be a soul. The material that constitutes the first sphere is said to move, precisely as the sublunary elements do, by nature. If the motion of the superlunary element, unlike that of the other elements, is due to a psychic mover, it is odd that this difference goes unmentioned. Furthermore, although all the heavenly spheres are said to be alive, Aristotle denies that the inner spheres are self-movers. As for *Phys.* VIII, the gravest difficulty for an account of the Prime Mover as an immanent aspect of the heaven is Aristotle's denial that the unmoved mover is moved even accidentally—for he claims that souls of animate things are so moved. On Judson's view, *Phys.* VIII argues that the Prime Mover is not a self-mover, but rather, on pain of vicious regress, an unmoved mover. Aristotle still needs to provide a positive characterization of its nature, and according to Judson, he does so in *Meta.* Λ.6–8. Here he describes a Prime Mover that is eternally active but thoroughly transcends the world of change. Were such a mover immanent in the eternal, perceptible heaven, as the soul of the first sphere, Judson argues that it would be subject to the analysis of composite substance in *Meta.* Λ.1–5. The Prime Mover is not the form of an eternal body; on the contrary, it is the fully actual, immaterial being that the living heaven strives to emulate. The Prime Mover is not a soul, because it is not the form of any body at all.

PART II

Part II opens with David E. Hahm's paper, "Self-Motion in Stoic Philoso-phy." Hahm argues that the types of self-motion treated by Aristotle were drawn together by the Stoics into a single systematic theory, with one striking addition to Aristotle's scheme: the inclusion of inanimate objects as self-movers. The Stoic extension is reasonable, given their general view of the constitution of corporeal bodies. According to the Stoics, all bodies consist of a passive and an active principle—a passive matter and an active material source called *pneuma*. On this view, even the elements should have an inner active source of their own motion. According to Hahm, the Stoic *scala naturae* comprised four levels—inanimate objects, plants, ani-mals, and human beings—and to each level belongs a proper self-motion. The *pneuma* that activates bodies at each level is the same material stuff but in a different physical state. Although a particular type of self-motion is proper to each level, Hahm argues that bodies at each successive stage display not only their own self-motion but also those characteristic of bodies lower on the ontological scale. The types of self-motion are thus cumulative. Hahm further argues that human beings, who achieve at matu-rity the highest type of self-motion, develop via the simpler levels. Such development involves the interaction of internal self-motions and external stimuli, which results in a series of quantum shifts to a higher physical state. Each state enables a corresponding self-motion.

In "Duns Scotus on the Reality of Self-Change," Peter King argues that Duns Scotus, in defending self-motion, departs from most of his medieval predecessors, who had argued that self-motion is impossible in the physi-cal world. If they admitted self-motion at all, they allowed it only in con-texts involving nonphysical causes, such as the will. All apparent cases of physical self-motion were construed as instances of interaction between an agent and patient that are really distinct. Breaking with this tradition, Scotus constructed an argument for the possibility of self-motion that built into the traditional model of change a number of subtle distinctions. For example, on the simple Aristotelian model, an object can become hot, if it is potentially but not actually hot, and if something acts on it that is actually hot. This scheme seems to exclude self-motion, because the same thing would need to have (as agent) the same property that it lacks (as patient). Scotus argues that self-motion is excluded only in cases of *univo-cal* causation—cases in which the active principle of the agent is the same as that induced in the patient. In defending self-motion, he argues for what he calls *equivocal* causation, in which the agent acts in virtue of a property more "eminent" than that induced in the patient. King shows that Scotus does not restrict self-motion to living organisms. Like the Stoics, he regarded even the natural motions of inanimate objects as self-motions, and he argued that this was the correct interpretation of Aristotle as well. In such cases, the agent and patient are really the same, but the active and passive principles within the object, which enable the change, are distinct.

Calvin Normore, in "Ockham, Self-Motion and the Will," examines William of Ockham's theory of the will against the background of earlier medieval discussion. According to Normore, the early Middle Ages inherited from Platonism a conception of the soul as a self-moving power, and this conception was slowly transformed into a conception of the will as a self-moving power. With the rise of Aristotelianism in the thirteenth century, this conception was temporarily submerged by the thesis (discussed by Peter King) that everything moved is moved by another. But thanks largely to Duns Scotus, whose defense of self-motion in physics was by Ockham's time widely taken for granted, the conception of the will as a self-mover had reemerged. Ockham rejected Scotus's appeal to formal distinctions, so he could not use such a distinction to explain the freedom of the will. Instead he argued that the will is free in the strong sense that it is able to move from potency to act without any "triggering" cause. Though he defended the freedom of the will, Ockham broke with Scotus in denying that bodies are able to move themselves locally. On Ockham's account, local motion always involves an external mover at some point in the causal series. According to Normore, Ockham's view, which treats the will as totally free but the motion of bodies as always determined by external causes, marks an important break with Aristotle and Scotus, and it paves the way for the early modern division between a realm of free spirits and a realm of corporeal objects that are themselves inert.

In his essay, "Natural Motion and Its Causes: Newton on the 'Vis Insita' of Bodies," J. E. McGuire argues that, contrary to common opinion, Isaac Newton's *Mathematical Principles of Natural Philosophy* did not break decisively with the Aristotelian analysis of motion and its causes. Though Newton's First Law of Motion treats motion and rest as primitive states, whose changes are explained by reference only to external forces, his third definition and corollary tell another story. According to this story, a natural body possesses a *vis insita*, an inherent source of its persistence in a state—ideas already clearly present in Newton's *Quaestiones* and *De gravitatione*, written in the 1660s. McGuire traces the concept of the *vis insita* through the widely read Renaissance Aristotelian Zabarella back to the works of Duns Scotus, Albert the Great, Averroes, Philoponus, and the Stoic Chrysippus, all of whom held that even inanimate bodies are self-movers. Zabarella's insistence that the forms of inanimate bodies are internal active sources of change that act upon their matter as subject in turn finds its way into many texts on natural philosophy familiar to Newton. Besides these indirect influences, McGuire cites passages in unpublished manuscripts of Newton in which he transcribes, translates, and comments on passages in Aristotle's *De caelo* and *Physics* that focus on the concept of nature as an inherent source of change. Newton's appeal to a *vis insita* raises a basic puzzle about his dynamics: In a world of inertial mass, momentum, and external forces, where is there room for a *vis insita*? McGuire argues that the *Principia* operates with both a surface and an inner ontology: on the surface, *vis insita* is virtually identified with inertia; but below the surface, the *vis insita* represents the Aristotelian notion of an inherent cause of a natural body's motion.

McGuire's essay is a most fitting conclusion to this volume, finding as it does that Newton was steeped in the traditions explored by the other essays, and exposing the extent to which those traditions shaped the thought of the most influential student of nature in the modern world.

Part I

ARISTOTLE

CHAPTER 1

Self-Movers

DAVID FURLEY

ARISTOTLE sometimes calls animals self-movers. We must try to determine what exactly he means by this. In particular, we must look at this thesis in the light of certain passages in the *Physics* that appear to deny that there can be self-movers. Is this apparent anomaly to be explained genetically? Are we to believe that Aristotle criticized and rejected his earlier thesis that animals are self-movers? Or is his position as a whole consistent? How then are we to explain away the apparent anomaly?[1]

To anyone who reads *Phys.* II a little incautiously it might appear that since nature is declared to be an internal source of change and rest (ἀρχὴ κινήσεως καὶ στάσεως [1, 192b13–33]), anything that has a nature must be a self-mover.[2] For what else is a self-mover but a thing that has *in itself* a source of change and rest? Thus all the things specified at the beginning of *Phys.* II.1 would be self-movers: living things and their parts, plants, and the simple bodies, earth, water, air, and fire.

But this turns out, of course, to be too generous. We are told explicitly in *Phys.* VIII.4, 255a5–10 that the bodies that move by nature up or down cannot be said to move themselves. Three reasons are given: (a) to move itself is a "life property" (ζωτικόν) and confined to things that have souls; (b) if they moved themselves, they would be able to stop themselves, and if it is "in its own power" for fire to move upward, it must likewise be in its power to move downward; (c) nothing that is homogeneous and continuous can move itself.

Clearly, then, things with souls have an ἀρχὴ κινήσεως καὶ στάσεως in themselves in a stronger sense than lifeless natural bodies. The refinement,

This paper is a reprint of Furley 1978.

[1] During the preparation of this chapter I had the opportunity of studying the manuscripts of two books not yet published at that time: Nussbaum 1978 and Hartman 1977. The problem investigated in this chapter is one that has interested me for a long time; but the manner of treating it here is much influenced by these two works. I am also indebted to their authors for comments on an earlier draft.

I am especially indebted to D. J. Allan, Malcolm Schofield, and Richard Sorabji for their comments, which have greatly assisted me in revising the paper for publication.

[2] For a review of this subject, especially in its relations with Plato and the Presocratics, see Solmsen 1960, 92–102.

according to *Phys.* VIII, is a difference in the voice of the verb: the natural bodies, as opposed to things with souls, have a source not of causing movement or of acting (κινεῖν, ποιεῖν) but of being acted on (πάσχειν). In fact, this gives too little to the natural bodies in Aristotle's theory. He should at least stress that they have an internal source of being acted on *in a fully determinate way.* But we do not need to pursue that subject here, and we can also leave aside the difficult question of what is the *active* mover of the natural bodies when they move according to their nature—a question to which Aristotle offers no wholly satisfactory answer.

In chapter 5 of *Phys.* VIII Aristotle starts from the proposition that we can distinguish chains of movers, such that A is moved by B, which is moved by C, and so on. He produces a number of arguments to show that such a series cannot be infinite: it must be stopped—or rather started—by something that is not moved by another but by itself: "If everything that is moved is moved by something, but the first mover, although moved, is not moved by another, it must be that it is moved by itself" (256a19–21).

Initially, Aristotle considers only the possibility that such a series is started by a self-mover, not the alternative that it is started by an unmoved mover. It is something of a surprise that he next (256b3ff.) produces an argument from which he says "these same conclusions will follow," but from which he draws a conclusion in the form of a disjunction. "So either the first thing that is moved will be moved by something at rest, or it will move itself" (257a26–27).

The reason why Aristotle can regard this disjunctive conclusion as the same as the other is clear from its context in chapters 4 and 5, in which the concept of a self-mover is analyzed. As a whole, a thing may be said to move itself; but within the whole it must always be possible to distinguish a mover and a moved. This is argued a priori, on the ground that one and the same thing cannot simultaneously be active and passive, or in a state of actuality and potentiality, in the same respect. The conclusion is expressed in these words:

> Well, it is clear that the whole moves itself not by virtue of having some part such as to move itself; it moves itself as a whole, moving and being moved by virtue of part of it moving and part of it being moved. It does not move as a whole, and it is not moved as a whole: A moves, and only B is moved. (258a22–27)

This conclusion is quite general: for *any* self-mover we can distinguish a part (or aspect—the article with the genitive is as noncommittal as possible) that moves without itself being moved, and a part that is moved.

The same analysis is applied explicitly to living creatures in chapter 4 (254b14–33). There is no doubt, says Aristotle, that there *is* a distinction in this case between the mover and the moved, but it is not obvious how to draw the distinction. "For it seems that as in boats and things that are not naturally constituted, so in living beings also there is something that causes movement distinct from what is moved, and thus the whole animal moves itself." At first sight this explanatory sentence appears to support the statement that there *is* a distinction rather than the nearer statement that there is some difficulty about how to draw it. But Simplicius's interpretation probably gets the right nuance (*In Phys.* 1208.30ff.). It is obvious, he says, that a living being is moved by its soul, but it is not clear how this is to be distinguished from that which it moves—whether it is altogether distinct in nature and place or in some other way. The movement of a living being looks like that of a boat or a chariot, in which the cause of motion is the helmsman and the driver (not, incidentally, the oarsmen or the horses); and these both have a distinct spatial individuality and their own nature. But, he implies, there is doubt about whether the soul is such an individual. Simplicius probably has an eye on *De an.* ii.1, 413a8, where Aristotle writes: "On the other hand, it is still unclear whether the soul is the ἐντελέχεια of the body as a boatman is of a boat."[3]

There is a qualification to be added to the conclusion that a self-mover includes an unmoved mover. What Aristotle has shown is that the first mover in a series must cause motion in some way other than *by* being moved itself. The first mover may be moved incidentally. This is true, of course, of living beings, which are moved by their souls and in turn carry their souls about with them (259b16–20).

Aristotle now faces the suggestion that if animals can initiate motion by themselves from a state of rest, without being moved by anything outside themselves, perhaps the whole cosmos might have initiated motion in itself in this way. He attempts to rebut this argument by showing that, after all, animals do *not* start moving from a state of rest without any external cause.

There are two passages where this point is made: (A) *Phys.* viii.2, 253a11–21 and (B) *Phys.* viii.6, 259b1–16. Aristotle seems to think of A as an outline sketch, the detail of which is to be filled in by B (see 253a20–

---

[3] This very controversial sentence is also discussed by Lefèvre 1978, 22–24. Although it is not strictly relevant to my argument, it may be worth mentioning one or two points on which I differ from him.

(a) Grammatically, this sentence beginning ἔτι δὲ ἄδηλον . . . is coordinate with 413a4: ὅτι μὲν οὖν . . . οὐκ ἄδηλον. It is neither a new beginning, as M. Lefèvre thinks, nor coordinate with 413a6: οὐ μὴν ἀλλά. (On this point see Easterling 1966.)

(b) The boatman–boat analogy is not inconsistent with the ἐντελέχεια theory of soul. The problem raised in this sentence is whether the activity that constitutes soul is *localized* (in the heart, although Aristotle does not mention the heart here); that is what is still unclear. That Aristotle would not have thought localization in itself to be inconsistent with the ἐντελέχεια theory (as Sir David Ross thought, among others) may perhaps be shown by considering the analogies with which he introduces the ἐντελέχεια theory—the analogies of the ax and the eye (412b10ff.). The "soul" of these is the ἐντελέχεια of the whole, but in both cases it is localized—the chopping power of the ax in its edge, and the seeing power of the eye in its pupil, or wherever it may be.

21). But in fact each passage contains some details omitted from the other. There is some significance both in the differences and in Aristotle's attitude to them; so we shall have to look at them in detail. I number the points in A; B can be divided into three sections, in the middle one of which I number the correspondences with A.

A

But this [sc. that animals move from a state of rest, having been moved by nothing external to them] is false. [i] We always see one of the connatural parts of the animal in a state of motion, and [ii] it is not the animal itself that is the cause of the motion of this, but perhaps (ἴσως) its environment. [iii] In using this expression, that a thing moves itself, we speak not of every [kind of] motion but only of locomotion. [iv] So nothing prevents—perhaps rather it is necessary—that many motions come about in the body because of the environment, and some of these move the mind (διάνοια) or desire (ὄρεξις), and the latter then moves the whole animal—[v] as happens in sleep, for when there is no perceptive motion present, but there is *some* motion, animals wake up again.

B

[a] We see that there plainly are things that move themselves, such as the class of things with souls, and animals; and these suggested that it may be possible for motion[4] to arise in something from total nonexistence, since we see this happening to them (being immobile at some time, they are then put into motion, as it seems).

[b] Well, we must note this, [iii] that they move themselves with *one* motion, and this not strictly; for the cause is not in themselves, but [i] there are other natural motions in animals, [ii] which they do not have because of themselves —for example, growth, decay, respiration, which are motions undergone by every animal while it is at rest and not moved with its own motion. The cause of this is the environment, and many of the things that enter [the animal], such as food; for [v] while it is being digested they sleep, and while it is being distributed they wake up and move themselves, the first cause being outside themselves.

[c] Hence they are not always being moved continuously by themselves. For the mover is another, which is itself moved and in change with respect to every self-mover.[5]

We shall return to discuss these two passages shortly. Before doing so it may be as well to look around elsewhere in *Phys.* VIII to see the extent of the disharmony in Aristotle's attitude to self-movers.

---

[4] Motion in general, not *a* motion.

[5] For analysis of these two passages, see especially Solmsen 1971. I am not wholly convinced, however, either that these passages attack particularly the Platonic notion of a self-

Aristotle does not *reject* the concept of self-movers in *Phys.* VIII. Chapters 4 and 5 are sometimes regarded as amounting to the rejection of the concept. Chapter 4 contains the sentence "It is clear, then, that none of these moves itself" (255b29), which has been taken as a general rejection of *all* self-movers.[6] But it is not. The reference of the pronoun is to inanimate natural bodies only—"the light and the heavy" (255b14–15). Nothing is said or implied about animals. Nor does the *analysis* of self-movers into a moved part and a moving part imply that there is no such thing as a self-mover. It is evidently quite legitimate, in Aristotle's view in these chapters, to call the whole a self-mover, provided that the moving part is itself unmoved, except accidentally.

But passages A and B seem to deny that proviso and hence, taken together with chapters 4–5, to reject the possibility of self-movers. Yet Aristotle clearly does not want such a conclusion. Even at the end of B he continues to speak of self-movers ("the cause of its moving itself by itself": 259b17). Even in his final argument for the existence of an eternal unmoved mover he continues to allow the possibility of noneternal unmoved movers, and although he does not say so, commentators generally take him to mean animal souls (258b12, b20, b32). The *De motu animalium* summarizes the position reached in the *Physics* thus: "Now, that the ἀρχή of other motions is that which moves itself, and that the ἀρχή of this is the unmoved, and that the first mover must necessarily be unmoved, has been determined previously" (698a7–9). Self-movers here are still allowed the role of ἀρχή for other movements: he still has in mind the distinction between inanimate natural bodies, which have an ἀρχή of *being* moved, and animate beings, some of which have an ἀρχή of *causing* movement (*Phys.* VIII.4, 255a5–10). He has neither rejected this distinction nor provided different criteria for drawing it. In *EE* II.6 and *EN* III.5 he insists that a man is the ἀρχή of his actions. There is a class of actions that are voluntary, and one of the criteria for picking them out is that the ἀρχή is *in* the agent himself (*EN* III.1, 1111a22).

The tension in Aristotle's thinking about this subject is set up by a clash of motives. He clearly wants to preserve the commonsense intuition that the movements of animals, and especially the actions of human beings, are not brought about by external agents in the same way that the movements of inanimate beings are. Yet he sees a danger that *all* the movements in the cosmos might be thought explicable on this principle of the self-movement of autonomous parts, and so insists that even this self-movement presupposes some external changes that are independent of animal movements.

moving soul or that passage B interrupts the "triumphant progress of the thought" in the rest of ch. 6.

[6] For example by Seeck 1965, 151; and Guthrie 1939, xxix. Guthrie interprets the cross-reference at *De cae.* 311a12 in the same sense.

What is particularly striking about the argument of passages A and B is the way in which it assimilates intentional action to mere mechanical movements. What moves the animal is διάνοια or ὄρεξις, but what moves this is the physical metabolism that goes on all the time in the animals, and what moves this is in the first place food and so forth, which enters from the environment. This is a pattern of explanation that one might think suitable, perhaps, for the movements of the periodical cicada of the eastern United States (*magicicada septemdecim*), which lies dormant in the earth until it emerges, noisily, and with all its millions of congeners, every seventeen years (next in May 2004). It seems thoroughly inadequate for explaining the action of a man signing a contract or even of a bird building a nest.

Passage B does not even mention ὄρεξις. Passage A does (iv), but instead of treating it teleologically, as Aristotle does in *De anima* and *De motu animalium*, it reduces it to a simple mechanical response. Even food is not something the animal moves to get (an ὀρεκτόν), but only something that "enters from the environment" and eventually causes the animal to move when it wakes up from its postprandial sleep. The reason why Aristotle puts it this way is surely the nature of his argument. He has an a priori argument in *Phys.* VIII.1 to show that both time and motion have no starting-point. Observation of animals suggests that they do function as starting-points for motion. All Aristotle needs to show is that their motions do not provide an example of a beginning of a motion in a system in which *no* motion took place before, and that they could not be explained at all on the assumption that no motion took place before. It does not matter to his argument *how* the previous motion is related to the alleged beginning of motion, so long as it is a necessary condition for it. So he uses the simplest possible mechanical model: A is pushed by B, B by C, and so on.

The same oversimplified model seems to be in his mind in *De an.* III.10. "There is good reason for the view that these two are the causes of motion, ὄρεξις and practical intelligence; for the object of ὄρεξις causes motion, and because of this the intelligence causes motion, because its ἀρχή is the object of ὄρεξις" (433a17–20). The pronouns are slightly ambiguous; but presumably the sense is that the object in the external world that is desired stimulates the practical intelligence to search for means to get it and thus to put into practice the steps needed to get it.

"What causes motion would be one in form, the ὀρεκτικόν as such, but the first of all would be the ὀρεκτόν, since this moves without being moved, by being the object of thought or imagination (νοεῖν or φαντάζειν), although the causes of motion would be many in number [sc. because desires can oppose each other]" (433b10–13). Again, the unmoved mover of animals in this is the *object* of desire.

If we distinguish three items in a case of motion—(*a*) that which causes motion but not by virtue of being moved itself, (*b*) that which causes motion by virtue of being moved by *a*, and (*c*) that which is moved by *b* without necessarily moving anything—then the role of *a* is played by the external object of ὄρεξις, that of *b* by the faculty of ὄρεξις in the soul, and that of *c* by the animal (433b13–18).[7] Here again the unmoved mover is not the soul or any "part" of the animal but something external to it—the object of ὄρεξις, here identified with the πρακτὸν ἀγαθόν. At the end of this section Aristotle sums up: "In general, then, as has been said, it is as appetitive (ὀρεκτικόν) that the animal is such as to move itself (ἑαυτοῦ κινητικόν)" (433b27–28). As in the *Physics*, we have both an account of an external mover and a claim that the animal is a self-mover.

The picture is not essentially different on this point in *De motu animalium*: "The first cause of motion is the object of ὄρεξις and of διάνοια" (700b23–24). "ὄρεξις and the ὀρεκτικόν cause motion by being moved" (701a1). "According to the account that states the cause of motion, ὄρεξις is the middle item, which causes motion by being moved" (703a4–5).

This oversimplified model produces at first sight a very blatant clash with *De an.* I.3–4, where it is explicitly denied that the soul is moved. The ὀρεκτικόν is certainly part of the soul or an aspect of it; in III.10 it is described, deliberately, emphatically, and repeatedly, as a *moved* mover; yet in these early chapters of the *De anima* Aristotle has claimed that the soul is not moved. In a justly famous passage (408b1–18) he argues that the habit of saying that the soul is pained, pleased, encouraged, terrified, or angered, and that it perceives and thinks, might suggest that it is moved; but this, he says, does not follow. It would be better—that is, less misleading—to say that the *man* is moved to pity, or to learn, or to think, *with* or *in* his soul (the simple dative): "and this not in the sense that the motion is in the soul but in the sense that [sc. the motion proceeds] sometimes as far as the soul and at other times from it." The cryptic last clause is explained briefly in the next sentence: "Perception, from *these* [sc. objects in the perceptible world]; recollection, from *it* [sc. the soul] to the movements or cessations from movement in the sense organs." We can ignore the second part of this; but what does the first suggest? Perceptible objects, it seems, cause the motion (cf. 417b19–21, 426b29–31), and the motion proceeds "as far as" (μέχρι) the soul, which is not, however, moved by it.

In *De an.* II.5 Aristotle says something about the difficulty of finding the right language to describe the relation between the soul and the objects of perception. αἴσθησις consists in being moved and in πάσχειν (416b33). We first proceed on the assumption that being moved and πάσχειν are the same as ἐνεργεῖν (417a14–16). But we have to distinguish different senses of πάσχειν and ἐνεργεῖν. A man who is ignorant of letters πάσχει some-

---

[7] For more comments on this passage see Skemp 1978. I do not differ from his interpretation.

thing when he learns his letters from a teacher. His ignorance is destroyed, and his potentiality for knowledge is actualized. But this degree of actualization is itself a potentiality for further actualization when the man actually has in mind the letter A. In this latter move the state of potentiality is not destroyed but preserved: hence we ought not to say that the man is changed (ἀλλοιοῦσθαι), or at least we ought to recognize a different kind of ἀλλοίωσις (417b2–16). So with αἴσθησις. To have an αἴσθησις is to pass from the first to the second state of actuality, and what causes the actualization is the object of perception.

So the soul is not *moved* by the objects in the external world in any of the senses enumerated in I.3 (φορά, ἀλλοίωσις, φθίσις, αὔξησις), except that it experiences this highly specialized form of ἀλλοίωσις.[8] Is this qualification sufficient to allow Aristotle to maintain his distinction between the movements of animals and the natural motions of inanimate bodies? It is certainly not sufficient in itself, because he uses the same pattern in his explanation of natural motion (*Phys.* VIII.4, 255a30–b13). In this case too we can distinguish two stages: the change from (say) water, which is potentially air, into air, through an external agency; and then the full actuality of the element in attaining its natural place. Here too Aristotle uses the simile of the man first learning, and then exercising, his skill. So if animals are self-movers but inanimate natural bodies are not, the difference in the explanation of their motions is not to be found in this point.[9]

The problem comes into particularly sharp focus in the *Nicomachean Ethics.* In the *Physics* and the biological works, including *De anima,* Aristotle was concerned with fitting the movements of animals into certain general patterns of explanation. In the *Ethics* he has to find the distinguishing characteristics of a subset of animal movements—namely, human actions for which we hold the agent morally responsible. It now becomes crucial for him to decide whether a man is really a self-mover, and in what sense, and when. The notion that the object of desire is what moves a man to action becomes a challenge to the whole concept of moral responsibility.[10]

Suppose someone says that pleasant and good objects are compulsive, since they exercise force upon us and are external to us. Then [1] everything would be compulsive on such a theory, since these are the objects for which everyone does everything. Moreover, [2] people who act because they are forced, involuntarily, do so with pain, whereas those who act because of anything pleasant and good do so with pleasure. But [3] it is absurd to blame external objects,

---

[8] Aristotle nevertheless freely uses the term ἀλλοίωσις of sense-perception in *MA* (701a5, b17–18) and elsewhere.

[9] This is explored further by Carteron 1923, 142ff.

[10] I have examined Aristotle's theory about this at greater length in Furley 1967, pt. 2: "Aristotle and Epicurus on Voluntary Action."

rather than oneself as being too easily caught by such attractions, and to take the credit for one's good behavior but blame pleasant objects for one's bad behavior. (*EN* iii.1, 1110b9–15)

The third point in this passage is the only one that gives an idea of *how* Aristotle proposes to rebut this challenge: the responsibility lies in the man's character and cannot be shifted to an external object of desire. "A man is the source and originator of his actions as he is of his children" (1113b17). We cannot go back to ἀρχαί beyond those that are in us. Aristotle considers a possible objection: perhaps our feeble moral character is itself given to us by nature and is out of our control:

> But perhaps he is the kind of man *not* to take care. No; people are themselves responsible for having become men of this kind, by living in a slack way. They are responsible for being unjust or over-indulgent, by cheating or by spending their lives drinking, and so on. In every field of action, actions of a certain kind make a corresponding kind of man. This is clear from the case of people who practice for any sort of contest or similar activity—they practice by continually repeating the action. (*EN* iii.5, 1114a3–9)

He raises a similar kind of objection a little later, this time in a form more directly relevant to our present theme:

> Suppose someone were to say that everybody desires what *appears* good (φαινόμενον ἀγαθόν) but is not master of the appearance (φαντασία)—the goal appears to each man in accordance with the kind of man he is. But [against this] if each of us *is* somehow responsible for his disposition, he will be somehow responsible for this appearance; otherwise no one is himself responsible for acting badly, but does these things through ignorance of the goal, believing that he will achieve what is best for himself by these means. And the desire for the goal is not a matter of choice, but it is necessary to be born with a natural faculty of sight, as it were, by which one will judge well and choose what is really and truly good; in that case, to be born well will be to have a good natural faculty of this kind. . . . Well, if this is true, how will virtue be any more voluntary than vice? To both alike, the good man and the bad man, the goal is presented and established by nature or however else it may be; and they both act in whatever way they do act by referring all the rest to this. So, whether the goal is presented to each man, in whatever form it may be presented, not by nature but with some dependence on the man himself, or the goal is natural but virtue is voluntary because the good man performs the actions leading to the goal voluntarily, in either case vice must be no less voluntary than virtue. (*EN*, iii.5, 1114a31–b20)

This passage suggests—admittedly in a very sketchy way—an important modification of the theory of desire set out in the *Physics*. In the latter, "the object of desire" (ὀρεκτόν) was presented as if it were simply an object in the external world. But people desire things in the external world, and exert themselves to get them, *under certain descriptions*, and their actions cannot be explained without some notion of what each of their goals means *for them*. The ὀρεκτόν cannot be identified as such independently of the ὀρεκτικόν, and in this sense the ἀρχή of action produced by desire is "inside" the agent.[11]

Does Aristotle recognize that the ὀρεκτόν, as the unmoved mover of human action, is always an intentional object? He does not say so explicitly. At first sight he appears to hedge his answer somewhat in the passage just quoted: "whether the goal is presented . . . not by nature but with some dependence on the man himself, or the goal is natural but virtue is voluntary because the good man performs the actions leading to the goal voluntarily." One might think that Aristotle meant to suggest here that the goal, being natural, moves a man to action in some way that does not involve how it appears to him, by the properties inherent in the nature of the external object that constitutes the goal. But clearly that is not what he meant. He was still thinking rather of the nature of the *agent*. The suggestion is just that one's *perception* of the goal may be in some sense natural— the same suggestion that has just been rejected in the preceding twelve lines. Probably he revives it again here to forestall a possible objection that *some* human goals do after all have a claim to be called natural— εὐδαιμονία itself, for example. Even in that case, he suggests, virtue and vice would be equally voluntary, because the subordinate goals depend on moral character, which is in our power.

The answer is given more clearly in *De an.* III.10. Aristotle begins the chapter by observing that there are apparently two causes of motion, either ὄρεξις or νοῦς, "if one lays it down that φαντασία is a kind of νόησις" (the latter proviso is to take care of the case of animals that have no νοῦς). But these are not put forward as alternative causes of motion, as it seems at first sight: ὄρεξις is always involved, whether or not νοῦς or φαντασία is involved. Aristotle continues: "Now νοῦς is always right, but ὄρεξις and

---

[11] "Systems to whom action can be attributed have a special status, in that they are considered *loci* of responsibility, centres from which behaviour is directed. The notion 'centre' seems very strongly rooted in our ordinary view of such systems, and it gives rise to a deep-seated and pervasive metaphor, that of the 'inside'. Beings who can act are thought of as having an inner core from which their overt action flows. . . . What is essential to this notion of an 'inside,' however, is the notion of consciousness in the sense of intentionality' (Taylor 1964, 57–58). Taylor quotes (68–69) Merleau-Ponty, *Structure du comportement* and *Phénoménologie de la perception*, for an extension of this notion to include the goals of nonhuman animals.

Stuart Hampshire explains Aristotle's position thus: "The reason for an action has been given when the agent's conception of the end has been explained together with his calculation of the means to it. We then see the fusion of the thinking, which is an inhibited discussion of the desired end and the means to it, and the mere wanting. The reason for the action is a fusion

φαντασία are both right and wrong. Hence, although what causes motion is the ὀρεχτόν, this may be the good or the seeming good" (φαινόμενον ἀγαθόν: 433a26–29). Does this suggest that νοῦς is an alternative to φαντασία in this case and that either one or the other apprehends the object of desire? The same may be suggested by 433b12, where he says that the object of desire moves either by νοηθῆναι or by φαντασθῆναι. This would appear to be a consequence of Aristotle's regard for linguistic usage as a guide to the truth. When we are clear and in no doubt about something, we do not say "it appears so" (φαίνεται: 428a14), and hence we do not want to say there is a φαντασία in this case.[12] But it is awkward to use two different terms for what is evidently the same faculty according to whether it gets something right or possibly wrong. At the end of the chapter, in his summary, Aristotle lets νοῦς drop out of the picture: "In general, as has been said, an animal moves itself in that it is capable of ὄρεξις; and it is not capable of ὄρεξις without φαντασία. Every φαντασία is either rational (λογιστική) or perceptual (αἰσθητική). Animals other than man have a share of the latter too" (433b27–30). The discussion in *De motu animalium* repeats this point: "The organic parts are put into a suitable condition by the πάθη, the πάθη by ὄρεξις, and ὄρεξις by φαντασία; the latter comes about either through νόησις or through αἴσθησις" (702a17–19).[13]

This line of thought will give Aristotle most of what he wants in order to defend his distinctions in *Phys.* VIII and to make a consistent whole of the theses announced there. Animals are clearly distinguished from inanimate natural bodies in that although both require external things to explain their movements, only animals require external things perceived (or otherwise apprehended) as having significance *for them*. Note that this is not just a difference in the complexity of the response to a stimulus, but a difference in kind. Only a being with a soul can move in this way. An animal is correctly described as a self-mover, because when it moves, its soul moves its body, and the external cause of its motion (the ὀρεχτόν) is a cause of motion only because it is "seen" as such by a faculty of the soul.[14] There must *be* an external object, however, and hence the movement of an animal does not provide an example of a totally autonomous beginning of motion

---

of these two elements, because the representation to myself in words of an object desired modifies the direction, and sometimes the intensity, of the original, blind appetite" (Hampshire 1959, 167).

[12] See Schofield 1978, 99–140.

[13] There is an excellent discussion of φαντασία and its role in action in Nussbaum 1978.

[14] There is no reason to think it is an internal *image* of the object that moves the animal, rather than the object itself, perceived in a particular way. Dr. Nussbaum has discussed this fully (1978), and has persuaded me that some of what I wrote (Furley 1967, pt. 2) about "mental pictures" was at least too hasty.

(as noted earlier, Aristotle thought that if such an example could be produced, his cosmology would be in danger).[15]

The suggestion made in this paper is not that Aristotle was ready with an articulate theory of intentionality to defend his view of animals as self-movers. It is that he was sufficiently aware of the intentionality of objects of desire to want to retain the notion that animals move themselves, in spite of finding that they are moved by the objects of desire. I think therefore that the apparent inconsistencies in his texts on this subject are not to be explained genetically but rather as coming from two different approaches that he has not fully articulated. I think they could reasonably well have been made into a consistent theory that would have required him to do only a little rewriting.

Although he could plausibly retain the proposition that animals are self-movers, I am not sure that it would be worth struggling to retain the concept of the animal soul as *unmoved* mover. The point is that external objects are not in themselves sufficient causes for the voluntary movements of animals. But they do have some effect on the soul, and it would be obstinate of Aristotle to deny that the effect can be called a movement.

There is one conspicuous loose end in the theory that the ἀρχή of human actions is "in" the agent. Aristotle maintains that people are moved to act by what appears desirable to them, that what appears desirable depends on their character, and that their character in turn depends on their actions and is *therefore* "in their power." His theory needs some explanation of these character-forming actions and of how it is that they are not caused by external pressures but proceed from an ἀρχή in the agent himself.

---

[15] What about delusions, hallucinations, etc.? Aristotle could reply that although animals may on occasion move in pursuit of a purely imaginary goal, these cases are parasitic on genuine cases. They would not pursue the imaginary goal unless there were similar goals in reality.

CHAPTER 2

Aristotle on Self-Motion

MARY LOUISE GILL

In book viii of the *Physics*, Aristotle discusses self-motion in order to show that particular changes caused by one body acting on another can be explained without citing an infinite number of previous changes. In *Phys.* viii.5 he argues that an explanatory regress can be avoided because ordinary changes are caused, either directly or indirectly, by something that moves itself, and self-motions by an unmoved mover within the self-mover. Typical changes thus finally depend on a mover that is not itself changed and so requires no further cause. This solution must be questioned, however, because in the very next chapter, *Phys.* viii.6, Aristotle suggests that animals—the paradigmatic self-movers—do not after all initiate their own motions but derive that impetus from features in their environment (259b1–16).[1] In what sense, then, are animals self-movers, and how does their dependence on external factors affect the proposed solution in viii.5?

In explaining animal motion, Aristotle seems interested in questions that expect two types of answer. First, when an animal moves, why is its motion of one sort rather than another, why is the motion sustained in a particular direction, and why does it stop at a certain limit? To answer these questions he appeals to an unmoved source within the animal. This internal principle legitimates calling the animal's motions self-motions. Second, what triggers the motion, and why is it sometimes impeded? An unmoved mover cannot explain why motion starts in a body at rest or why it stops prematurely in a body in motion, because if it could, the mover would itself be moved in providing the impetus or obstruction. Although an unmoved

This paper was first published in Judson 1991. I read a version of the paper at a conference on self-motion held at the University of Pittsburgh, and I presented parts of it at a seminar at the University of California at Berkeley. I thank those audiences for their helpful questions. I am particularly grateful to David Furley for his challenging commentary on the paper at the Pittsburgh conference, to Lindsay Judson for his perceptive objections, which caused me to rethink my argument at a number of points, and to James Lennox for many valuable criticisms. I am also indebted to Susan Sauvé Meyer, Heike Sefrin-Weis, and Steven Strange for suggestions on particular points.

[1] Cf. *Phys.* viii.2, 253a11–21. For solutions to the conflict, see esp. Furley's paper reprinted in this volume; and Nussbaum 1978, essay 2. On Aristotle's theory of self-motion and its role in the argument of *Phys.* viii, see Waterlow 1982, chap. 5.

mover can be moved accidentally (κατὰ συμβεβηκός) when it is carried along with the body it moves,[2] such a mover cannot be moved in itself (καθ' αὑτό) and still be an unmoved mover. Aristotle appeals to independent triggering factors to avoid two unacceptable alternatives. On the one hand, if an unmoved mover could supply a sufficient reason for motion to start on a given occasion, it would need to alter from a previous state to furnish the stimulation, and would thus fail to be unmoved. On the other hand, if the object moved could respond to an unmoved source without an impetus, the response would be uncaused, and Aristotle would be forced to accept a thesis that he firmly rejects, that motion can start *ex nihilo*.[3] Except for the motions of the heavenly spheres, which are eternal, and so require no instigation and suffer no interruption, all others originate or digress on account of external factors. But if so, how do the self-motions of animals differ from enforced changes caused by one body acting on another? And how can Aristotle escape an explanatory regress of movers?

In the main part of this paper, I shall spell out Aristotle's general theory of change, involving a distinct mover and moved, and show why he thinks that ordinary motions can be explained by a self-motion, and self-motion by an unmoved cause. The discussion of first causes will also establish his justification for distinguishing self-movers from other objects that experience motion, and hence his reason for thinking that animals are responsible for their own behavior. Unlike most interpreters who address the problem of self-motion in Aristotle, I shall focus on first movers as efficient causes.[4] The final cause—often specified as an object of desire—though central to his account in *Meta.* Λ and relevant to his discussion of intentional action in *De motu animalium* and *De an.* III.10, plays no explicit role in his analysis of motion in *Phys.* VIII or *De caelo.* My aim is to determine how a first mover operates in contexts that do not involve desires.

In focusing on first movers as efficient causes, I am not suggesting that such movers are causally efficacious, injecting new forces into a causal chain. I have already indicated that an unmoved mover cannot play such a role and be unmoved. It is a mistake in any case to assume that every Aristotelian efficient cause brings about its effects, because Aristotle distinguishes first movers from instrumental causes,[5] and as examples of first movers he regularly cites the form of the agent or the art that informs the agent's soul.[6] Since he also designates such movers as unmoved,[7] their causal role will be of some special type. Thus part of my task will be to

---

[2] *Phys.* VIII.6, 259b16–20.

[3] *Phys.* VIII.6, 259b1–16; cf. *Phys.* I.8, 191a23–31; GC I.3, 317b11–18.

[4] For a similar perspective, see Sauvé 1987, and Meyer's paper in this volume.

[5] See, e.g., *Phys.* VIII.5, 256a21–b3, 256b14–27; *De an.* II.4, 416b20–27.

[6] See, e.g., *Phys.* II.3, 195b21–25; *Meta.* Z.7, 1032b21–23; Λ.4, 1070b28–35.

[7] GC I.7, 324a26–b14.

explain what it means to class such entities as moving causes. This under-standing should, in addition, help to clarify the nature and role of the final cause, or goal, in nonintentional contexts. Although I shall largely ignore the problem of intentional action, I shall offer some preliminary sugges-tions about how Aristotle's analysis of motion might apply to this case.

The last part of my discussion will treat the initiation of animal motion, and I shall argue that even though one can trace the origin of such motions to features in the environment, this fact does not lead to a regress of the sort Aristotle tried to avoid in *Phys.* VIII.5 when he appealed to an unmoved mover. On the contrary, it indicates that all motions, including the self-motions of animals, depend on the eternal rotation of the heavenly spheres and ultimately on the Prime Mover.[8]

One final preliminary concerns my use of the term "self-motion." In *Phys.* VIII Aristotle focuses mainly on locomotion, or change of place, and in VIII.6 he suggests that animals move themselves in only one way—and, indeed, not strictly even in that way. He is thinking of locomotion.[9] Yet he typically treats changes (κινήσεις) as occurring in three categories—quantity, quality, and place—and as examples of self-motion he sometimes mentions quantitative and qualitative changes, for instance, a doctor cur-ing himself.[10] Thus, though he regards locomotion as the proper self-motion that animals display in respect of their perfected natures,[11] he evidently envisages other self-motions as well, especially those enabled by certain acquired capacities. In addition, self-caused motions seem to be of two general types: first, those, like the ones we have just been discussing, that lead the animal into a new location or state, which I shall call strictly "self-changes"; and second, those that express a state that the animal has already acquired or naturally possesses and that, instead of leading it into a new condition, preserve or perfect the one it is already in. Aristotle typ-ically calls such motions ἐνέργειαι, or "activities," and as we shall see, such motions are presupposed by other typical changes. I shall use the term "self-motion" as a generic expression to apply to both self-changes and activities.

1. PASSIVE AND ACTIVE ΔΥΝΑΜΕΙΣ

Changes—both enforced and self-changes—involve a mover and a moved, each characterized by a special sort of δύναμις, or potency. In *Meta.* Θ.1 Aristotle describes the δύναμις that causes change as "the source of change

---

[8] Cf. the interpretation of Simplicius, *In Phys.* 1258.7–1259.4.

[9] Although the reference to locomotion is not explicit at *Phys.* VIII.6, 259b6–7, it is explicit in a parallel passage at VIII.2, 253a11–21.

[10] See *Phys.* v.1, 255b7–9; and *MA* 5; for the example, see *Phys.* II.1, 192b23–27.

[11] *Phys.* VIII.7, 260b30–32, 261a13–26; *MA* 4, 699b31–32.

in another thing or [in the thing itself] qua other" (ἡ ἀρχὴ μεταβολῆς ἐν ἄλλῳ ἢ ᾗ ἄλλο) (1046a10–11), and *Meta*. Δ.12 specifies the δύναμις more precisely as an active source, an ἀρχὴ μεταβλητική (1019b35–1020a6). The δύναμις responsible for a change thus typically belongs to an entity other than the object changed or, in the special case of self-change, as when a doctor cures himself, to the moved itself considered as other. Aristotle characterizes the δύναμις of the moved as a source of passive change (ἀρχὴ μεταβολῆς παθητικῆς) by another thing or by the thing itself qua other.[12] How should we understand these two principles?

First, a δύναμις, whether active or passive, is always directed toward a definite end or actuality. When a δύναμις is such that its realization requires a change, the actuality is a particular state of an appropriate object. For example, a doctor has an active, an invalid a passive δύναμις for health; and these δυνάμεις differ from those of a teacher and student, which are directed toward a particular type of knowledge. Second, as these examples suggest, pairs of active and passive δυνάμεις correspond in their goal: both members are directed toward a particular state to be realized in the passive object.[13] A doctor's active δύναμις for health enables him to cause health in a suitable patient; and an animal's passive δύναμις for the same state enables it, when properly affected, to become healthy.

Although corresponding active and passive δυνάμεις coincide in their goal, they nonetheless differ in being active or passive. We need to consider in what this difference consists. Let us begin with Aristotle's familiar discussion of the levels of passive δύναμις in *De an*. II.5.[14] We are told that an individual has knowledge potentially in one way if, although lacking the expertise, the individual is the sort of being that regularly does have knowledge. By means of a change she can acquire the positive state. An individual has knowledge potentially in a higher way if, having learned, she can use her ability when she wishes if not prevented. This second-level δύναμις enables an entity to engage in certain activities, and we can ignore it for the moment, since we are presently concerned only with changes. A change is the gradual realization of a first-level passive δύναμις—a subject's transition from lacking the property for which it has the δύναμις to possessing the property.

Because an object's lack can be rectified by means of a change, the

---

[12] *Meta*. Θ.1, 1046a11–26; Δ.12, 1019a20–23.

[13] In *Phys*. III.3 Aristotle speaks of the goal of the agent as a "deed" (ποίημα) and that of the patient as an "affection" (πάθος) (202a22–24), but the two goals are evidently identical, despite the difference in description, because he later objects to the idea that doing and suffering are two distinct motions that occur in the patient on the ground that there would then be two alterations of one thing to one form (εἰς ἓν εἶδος) (202a31–36).

[14] Cf. *Phys*. VIII.4, 255a30–b5. For discussions of the passage in *Phys*. VIII, see the papers in this volume by Wedin and Shields.

privation is not just any state other than the goal, but one on a path leading to it. The healthy comes to be from the sick, the white from the black or gray, and so forth: the privation and form must be properly opposed on a range falling under a common genus within one of the categories of quantity, quality, or place—as black and white under color, or sweet and sour under flavor.[15] Furthermore, according to the passage in *De an.* II.5, the deprived object must belong to a kind whose members sometimes possess the form. For example, a man is potentially musical because human beings are sometimes musical, and he is potentially healthy because living things are sometimes healthy. A final point is clarified by our passage in *Meta.* Θ.1. A passive δύναμις is described as "the source, in the very thing that suffers, of being passively changed by something else or [by itself] qua other" (1046a11–13). A passive δύναμις depends for its realization on a source external to the passive object or, in the case of self-change, within the object itself considered as other. Accordingly, an object has a first-level passive δύναμις for some property φ, if it belongs to a kind whose members sometimes have the property, if it is presently not-φ, and if its privation can be rectified by something else or by itself qua other. As we shall now see, in turning to the active δύναμις, the realization of a passive δύναμις requires a form whose identity corresponds to the goal of the passive object, and thus one opposed to its initial lack.

On several occasions Aristotle describes movers responsible for changes. In *Phys.* III.2 he says: "The mover will always bring a particular form, either substantial, qualitative, or quantitative, which will be the source and cause (ἀρχὴ καὶ αἴτιον) of the change, when it produces change; for instance, a man in actuality produces a man from that which is a man potentially" (202a9–12). And in VIII.5 he says: "The mover is already in actuality, for example, the hot thing heats and generally that which has the form generates" (257b9–10). In natural contexts the changer possesses the form that it produces: a man replicates his form in matter that potentially has the form; similarly, a hot object induces heat in an object that is potentially hot. In artificial contexts, the form imposed is present in the agent's soul. For instance, a builder who constructs a house has the form of a house in mind.[16] According to *GC* I.7, the properties that enable an agent to act and a patient to suffer are like in kind but contrary and unlike in form: one body is affected by another, one flavor by another, and so on (323b29–324a5). By means of a change, the agent assimilates the patient to itself (324a10–11). Thus, once the change has been accomplished, the

---

[15] At *Phys.* I.5, 188a35–b3, Aristotle denies that something white can come to be from something musical, except in the incidental sense that something not-white happens also to be musical.

[16] *Meta.* Z.7, 1032a32–b6, 1032b11–14.

agent and patient are not only like in kind but also like in form. The agent guides the patient from a state unlike its own to one like its own.

Despite the sameness in content between the productive form of the agent and the resulting form of the patient, these forms, too, still typically differ in being active or passive. What distinguishes one form as active and another as passive, when their content coincides? Though the form of the agent enables its own replication and so is somehow responsible for the agent's action, that induced in the patient, though it sometimes—as in organic reproduction—transforms the patient into a new agent, often merely adapts its possessor to respond to its surroundings in particular ways. For instance, the person who has become healthy usually cannot duplicate his health;[17] nor can a house reproduce itself. The acquired form is both a first-level passive actuality, as the goal of the patient's change, and a second-level passive δύναμις. As such, it equips its possessor to behave in certain ways in response to stimulation but does not enable its own reproduction.

Passive forms are not movers but depend for their expression on an active source. Consider an artifact, such as an ax. Let us specify the form of an ax as its function, its capacity to chop. When a craftsman produces an ax, this function, which informs his soul and which he aims to embody, guides his choice of materials and tools, and the organization that he imposes. Once the ax has been completed, the artifact and its maker are like, because the ax has the capacity to chop, which the smith had in mind in carrying out his project. But the form in the artisan's mind is active, whereas that possessed by the ax is passive. Not only can the ax not duplicate its form, it cannot even perform its function without someone who knows how to use an ax. In a telling passage in *De an.* II.1, Aristotle contrasts the form of an ax with that of an animal:

> Suppose that some instrument, such as an ax, were a natural body. The being for an ax would be its substance, and this would be its soul. And if this were removed, there would no longer be an ax, except in name. As it is there is an ax. For the soul is not the essence and formula of such a body, but of the sort of body that has in itself a source of motion and rest. (412b11–17)

If an ax were a living organism, its form would be a soul—an active δύναμις—and the ax would be destroyed if the soul were removed. In fact, however, the "soul" of an ax belongs, not to the ax, but to the person who uses it, and this "soul" can be removed and the ax remain intact. The form of an ax is a passive δύναμις, an ability to respond in certain ways if acted upon by an appropriate agent. The survival of the ax depends only on the retention of this passive capacity. On the other hand, since the active δύ-

[17] See *GC* I.7, 324b14–18.

ναμις belongs to the handler and not to the artifact, the ax depends for the exercise of its capacity, and hence for the full realization of its being, on an external mover.

An active δύναμις, by contrast, is a source of motion and rest. Aristotle describes such a source in *Meta.* Z.7: "The maker (τὸ ποιοῦν) and that from which the motion of becoming healthy begins (ὅθεν ἄρχεται ἡ κίνησις τοῦ ὑγιαίνειν), if [the production] is artificial, is the form in the soul" (1032b21–23). The active δύναμις—the "maker" (τὸ ποιοῦν)—is the form of health that guides the doctor's production. How is such a form productive? I have already explained that a first mover, if unmoved, cannot inject forces into a causal chain. And although the active δύναμις determines the goal to be achieved, it is not simply a final cause, because, as we have seen, the outcomes of many changes, though comparable in content with their active source, are passive rather than active forms. So the active δύναμις as source of motion, though it may include the final cause, is evidently something more.[18]

De an. II.4 offers some clues about how we should understand the productivity of an active form. In discussing nutrition and growth, Aristotle first takes Empedocles to task for suggesting that such operations are fully explained by material factors. According to Empedocles, the roots of plants grow downward because earth naturally tends in that direction, and their stems and branches grow upward because fire naturally tends in that direction. Aristotle protests: Why, if this explanation of growth is correct, do plants not fly apart, their roots in one direction, their stems and branches in another? What prevents this dissolution? It is prevented, he claims, because soul is the cause of nutrition and growth. Next he remarks that some people regard fire as the simple cause of these proceedings. To this proposal he responds,

> [Fire] is in a sense the helping cause (συναίτιον), but it is certainly not responsible without qualification. Rather the soul [is responsible]; for the growth of fire is unlimited (εἰς ἄπειρον), as long as there is something that can be burned. But all things constructed naturally have a limit (πέρας) and proper proportion (λόγος) of magnitude and growth. And these things are [the responsibility] of soul, but not of fire, and of the formula (λόγος) rather than matter. (416a13–18)

Although the soul is the cause of nutrition, there is no indication that it initiates the activity. These passages propose that the soul takes an active role in nutrition and growth by regulating the motions of the simple materials so that they serve a higher purpose. Aristotle suggests that the mate-

---

[18] Note that Aristotle sometimes says that formal, final, and moving causes can coincide; see *Phys.* II.7, 198a24–28; *De an.* II.4, 415b8–12.

rials, if left to themselves, would realize their own δυνάμεις and so destroy the objects they constitute. Earth and fire would move off to their own places, earth toward the center of the cosmos, fire toward the periphery of the sublunary sphere, and so dissolve the compound. And fire would burn indefinitely as long as it had stuffs to consume. But if their natural motions are adapted to a particular end, fire and other materials can help to bring about the positive outcome.

An active form does more than preserve an object composed of simpler stuffs. Passive forms, too, integrate material constituents into objects of greater complexity. The passive form that makes an object an ax, or one that makes an inorganic material iron, unifies the ingredients into a compound with properties distinct from those of the components. As long as the passive form survives, the object remains intact. Furthermore, such forms, as we shall see later when we discuss the four elements, can account for some simple types of behavior. What a passive form cannot do, and thus what distinguishes an active form from it, is to direct motions that replicate the form in a suitable passive object, or to coordinate distinct, and often successive, motions toward a goal whose realization depends upon that coordination, as in an organism's nutrition and growth.[19]

In his biological works, Aristotle appeals to physical mechanisms, such as heating and cooling, to explain the generation of animals and their parts, but he insists that these mechanisms cannot explain why a process yields a particular outcome, for instance, flesh or bone,[20] or why flesh or bone is formed by the application of heat to an appropriate material, at an appropriate time, and in an appropriate place.[21] The nature of the product and the sequence of interactions that yields it are determined by an active δύναμις—by the soul of the male parent during the early stages of embryonic development and later, once the central organ (the heart or analogous part) has been articulated, by the fetal soul, which is located in the heart.[22]

---

[19] In his theory of animal generation, Aristotle attributes an active δύναμις to the male, and a passive δύναμις to the female (GA 1.2, 716a4–7; 1.20, 729a9–11). A new animal is generated when the directive powers of the male, transmitted by the semen at conception, coordinate motions that take place in materials contributed by the female (GA II.3, 737a18–22; II.4, 739b20–30). The situation is more complicated than this, however. The female, too, has active, as well as passive, nutritive powers that enable her to process food for her own maintenance and development; it might therefore seem that she, too, should be able to reproduce her form. Aristotle recognizes this problem for his theory and points out that females of some species are to a certain extent reproductive: they can generate wind eggs. But because wind eggs lack the soul principle contributed by the male, they never become animate beings (GA II.3, 737a27–34; cf. 1.21, 730a4–32; II.5, 741a13–32). Apparently, then, the active δύναμις of the female, though adequate for her own purposes, is simply too weak to be successfully reproductive (GA II.5, 741b2–7).

[20] GA II.1, 734b27–735a5; cf. Meteor. IV.12, 390b2–14.

[21] GA II.6, 743a1–26.

[22] GA II.1, 735a12–21; II.4, 740a1–9, 740b18–741a3. I thank James Lennox for insight into this topic.

Given its regulatory role, we might compare the active δύναμις to a list of instructions that determines the materials and tools needed to realize a particular end, and the order, timing, and extent of operations that are carried out by the instrumental materials.[23]

I have argued that an active δύναμις determines the proper ordering of motions but cannot, as an unmoved mover, introduce new forces into a causal chain, whether by initiating a causal sequence or by imposing physical constraints. Since such a δύναμις does not originate the behavior that it directs, the impetus must derive from other factors inside the organism or in its environment.

Does the account of active and passive δυνάμεις that I have described apply only to low-level organic behavior, like nutrition and growth, whose origin Aristotle explicitly attributes to external factors,[24] or does it also explain psychic involvement in such high-level motions as intentional actions?[25] In his discussion of voluntary action in the *Nicomachean Ethics*, Aristotle locates the ἀρχή of action within the voluntary agent, and he arguably thinks that an internal ἀρχή (such as a choice) originates a causal series.[26] Although Aristotle's theory of intentional action must be a topic for another occasion, some doubts about the scheme's flexibility can be removed, because there is evidence that he extends his model to at least one type of mental activity—contemplation. In this situation the active δύναμις appears to play a role analogous to that in the contexts on which we have focused. Let us, then, briefly consider this topic.

In a short and tantalizing chapter, *De an.* III.5, Aristotle divides the rational soul into two components, identifying part of the intellect as active—a "maker" (ποιητικόν)—and part as its passive material (430a10–15). One might initially think that the productive intellect is introduced as ἀρχή (430a19) to explain why thinking starts on a given occasion, but this is not the question that Aristotle asks. The question that motivates the distinction between active and passive mind is why the mind sometimes fails to think (III.4, 430a5–6). The failure is due, not to the active intellect, which always thinks (430a22), but to the passive intellect, which is subject to change.[27]

The active intellect cannot initiate an act of thinking in the passive mind because to do so would require providing a sufficient reason for the activity to start. Since the active mind is described as ἀπαθής (430a17–18, 430a24), it should be immune to variation, and so unqualified to activate the thinker to episodes of thinking. Aristotle uses several analogies to

---

[23] Cf. the role assigned to an animal's nature at *MA* 10, 703a29–b2.

[24] *Phys.* VIII.2, 253a11–13; VIII.6, 259b8–16.

[25] This question was put to me by David Furley and Lindsay Judson.

[26] See, e.g., *EN* III.1, 1111a22–24. This position was defended by David Furley in a commentary on my paper at the University of Pittsburgh.

[27] *De an.* III.5, 430a10–11, 430a14–15, 430a24–25.

clarify the ἀρχή, comparing it to a state, like light, that makes colors actually visible (430a15–17), and to a craftsman's art (430a11–14). An art, as we have seen, is an unmoved mover that, by establishing the aim of an artistic production, regulates motions toward its achievement. If this analogy is apt, the active mind, too, should be an unmoved mover, determining the object of contemplation and controlling the mental response to it. Since the active mind cannot explain why thinking is intermittent, the passive mind is also required. Because the passive intellect is subject to change, it accounts for the fact that the response sometimes occurs and sometimes does not.

If the active mind cannot originate a causal sequence, does the passive mind do so by means of a choice or some other mental event? If Aristotle's theory of rational activity accords with his physics, he should reject this possibility, because it would involve creation *ex nihilo*. Any event must be caused, even if only by an accidental trigger. If rational activity is episodic, some change in the animal or in its environment must trigger the response.

This synopsis of *De an.* III.5, though only sketching a reading of that difficult chapter, shows that Aristotle applies his scheme of active and passive δυνάμεις to psychic functions besides the nutritive, and so suggests that actions involving intentions may admit a similar analysis. For example, given the treatment of active νοῦς as ἀρχή in contexts of contemplation, it seems likely that the internal ἀρχή involved in voluntary action is an active δύναμις, which directs the activity, rather than an uncaused origin of it.[28] Furthermore, since uncaused events are excluded by Aristotle's physics, mental events, like choices, even if they appear to initiate an intentional activity, should themselves be triggered by factors inside the person or in his environment.[29] So although my discussion of self-motion is confined to its simplest manifestation, I suggest that Aristotle's scheme of active and passive δυνάμεις will also help to explain self-motions involving higher parts of the soul.

[28] In his discussion of voluntary action in *MA* 9, for instance, Aristotle identifies the soul as the ἀρχή of action and locates it in the heart.

[29] At *Meta.* Θ.5, 1048a8–15, Aristotle claims that desire or choice will be the deciding factor in contexts in which an agent could, in the circumstances, take either of two courses of action (for instance, when a doctor in treating a patient could improve or aggravate the condition). But Aristotle does not say that the choice between the alternatives is uncaused, and in *EN* III.3 he treats choice as the result of a process of deliberation (1113a2–12). Pushing the question back, one can ask what initiates the deliberation or the desire that motivates the deliberation. *MA* 8, which spells out the steps that lead to animal motion, locates the ἀρχή that originates the process in the object of pursuit or avoidance, which the animal perceives in its environment (701b33–35). Desire results from imagination, which in turn results from thought or perception (702a17–19). The process thus seems to originate either in the appearance of an external object that triggers the agent's perception or in some internal event that triggers the agent's thought.

2. ENFORCED CHANGE AND SELF-MOTION

Enforced changes involve a distinct agent and patient characterized by correlative active and passive δυνάμεις, and the states of the two objects are like in kind but unlike in form. A change occurs, which replaces the patient's privation with the positive form, if (barring interference) the two objects come into contact. Since all motions, including those caused by an unmoved mover, involve some sort of contact, let us now consider this aspect of Aristotle's theory.

In *GC* I.6 Aristotle introduces a strict notion of contact requiring that mover and moved be discretely located magnitudes that have their extremities together (322b32–323a12). When contact occurs in this sense, the two objects are physically contiguous, and the agent not only acts on the patient but also experiences a reaction caused by the body acted upon. For instance, a knife that cuts is blunted by the object cut, and something that heats is cooled by the object heated. He then loosens the conditions for contact to account for further examples. First, there are cases of action and passion, such as teaching and learning, in which the agent and the patient, though discretely located magnitudes, normally perform their transaction without having their extremities together. Even so, there must be an appropriate relation between the mover and moved such that the one acts and the other responds (323a23–25).[30] He then extends the notion still further to provide for cases in which the mover is entirely unaffected by its contact with the moved. It is possible, he says, for that which causes a motion only to touch what it moves, but not to be touched in return; for instance, a grieving man "touches" us but we do not "touch" him (323a28–33).[31] This final type of contact characterizes the relation between an unmoved mover and moved.

Enforced changes often involve a series of movers, the last of which undergoes direct physical contact with the object moved and the first of which is unmoved. In *GC* I.7 Aristotle discusses such an example. In treating a patient, a doctor often uses an instrument, such as bread or wine, to effect his cure. Such instruments, designated as "last" movers, actually touch the patient and so are themselves reciprocally changed. The doctor,

---

[30] Commentators do not usually distinguish this type of contact from the first (see, e.g., Joachim 1922, 147; Williams 1982, 117–19). Elsewhere (Gill 1989, 195–98) I argue that contact of this sort, which typifies the relation between an intentional agent and the object it moves, differs significantly from the other two types. Nothing turns on this distinction for my purposes here.

[31] Although the touching in this example might seem to be merely metaphorical (see, e.g., Joachim 1922, 147–48), according to Aristotle's theory of the emotions (πάθη), the visible form of the grieving man is impressed upon us and thus affects us. For a helpful discussion of such "one-sided relationships" in Aristotle, see Williams 1982, 118–19.

too, is a moved mover, whose action depends on a first cause—the art of medicine, or the source of health—which informs his soul. The doctor and the invalid experience a relational contact (the second type I mentioned earlier); and the first mover and its objects experience a contact that is one-way, such that the objects are affected while the first mover remains wholly immune.

Aristotle describes this type of chain in *Phys.* VIII.5, when he argues that all changes have their source in a self-motion, and that self-motions are ultimately caused by an unmoved mover. Many self-motions themselves involve such a sequence. For instance, a doctor who cures himself—thus acting on himself qua other—is both agent (as doctor) and patient (as invalid). His instruments, such as bread or wine or his medical tools, are last movers, which produce the cure, and the first cause is the art of medicine, which informs his soul. But even if there is such a series, Aristotle argues that a self-motion requires only the first pair in the sequence. He says, "That which moves itself must contain something that causes motion but is unmoved and something that is moved but need not move anything else, and either both components are in contact with each other or one with the other" (258a18–21); in the next line he affirms the second alternative: between the unmoved mover and moved the contact is one-way (258a21–22).

Consider such a self-mover, for instance, a doctor who responds to his medical art—his knowledge of health. We are here ignoring the doctor's possible relation to an ailing patient, whether himself or someone else, and so are disregarding the change that his motion may cause. Instead, we are considering only the motion displayed by the doctor (as moved) in response to his active δύναμις (as mover). This motion is not a change, because it does not lead to a new condition; it is an activity that expresses the state that the doctor is already in. When such motion occurs, the active and passive δυνάμεις are not initially opposed and unlike, but like.

In *Meta.* Θ.8 Aristotle modifies the account of δύναμις offered in Θ.1 to accommodate these special motions. He says,

> I mean by δύναμις not only the one that has been defined, which is called an active source of motion in another thing or [in the thing itself] qua other, but generally every active source of motion and rest. For nature (φύσις) is also in the same genus as δύναμις; for it is an active source of motion—not, however, in another thing but in the thing itself qua itself. (1049b5–10)

The crucial claim is that a δύναμις can be a source of motion in the thing itself *qua itself*. A δύναμις can operate not only on a body qua other, as when someone cures himself, but also on a matching passive δύναμις, as like on like. The situation can be compared to that of a person who uses an ax, where user and implement share the same active and passive capacities, except that this situation involves a pair of capacities that informs a single individual. Although Aristotle's mention of a φύσις suggests that he is primarily concerned with natural contexts, the same configuration should occur in the case of some acquired capacities.

A doctor possesses not only an active δύναμις—his knowledge (a first-level active actuality)[32]—which enables him to control his bodily and psychic motions to serve his action, but also a second-level passive δύναμις (or first-level passive actuality), which determines the physical and mental organization that promotes such activity. The motion (traditionally called a second-level actuality)[33] is the mutual realization of these active and passive capacities. This motion does not yield a new organization, but rather secures, and often improves, the one that is already there. In De an. II.5, in contrasting this motion with a typical change involving the replacement of a previous state, Aristotle says that it is "rather a preservation (σωτηρία) of what is in potentiality by what is in actuality and like it, in the way that potentiality is [like] actuality" (417b3–5).[34] Activity, the motion caused by an active δύναμις on a comparable passive δύναμις, as like on like, preserves the state that the agent is already in. The activity involved when a doctor responds to his medical art does not alter the agent, but rather maintains his capacity (both active and passive) for such activity. On this view, the final cause—the goal to be achieved—is the activity that expresses and thereby preserves the agent's current condition.

The following picture emerges. Enforced changes, such as a person's recovery of health, result—often through a sequence of intervening motions—from a self-motion that is an activity of an unmoved mover and moved. Aristotle thinks that this account avoids an explanatory regress involving an infinite chain of typical movers, because the unmoved mover proper to the self-moving agent can explain why the change, though typically composed of distinct components, displays a sustained direction and terminates at a certain limit.

With this understanding of self-motion, let us now turn to the question I raised at the outset. If self-motions, as well as other motions, depend on an impetus in order to start, does this dependence result in an explanatory

---

[32] De an. II.1, 412a10–11, 412a19–28. Aristotle does not explicitly distinguish actualities as active or passive, as I am doing, but such a distinction indicates whether we are redescribing an active δύναμις or a second-level passive δύναμις.

[33] For Aristotle's distinction between levels of actuality, see the texts cited in the previous note. He refers to the soul (an active δύναμις) as a first actuality at De an. II.1, 412a27–28 and 412b4–6.

[34] For a defense of the claim that the "preservation" describes the activity rather than the switch to activity (as often assumed), see Gill 1989, 222–26. For the other view, see esp. Kosman 1969, 54–56; 1984, 129–32.

regress, and does it subvert the status of animals as genuine *self*-movers? Moreover, how does this dependence affect Aristotle's thesis in *Phys.* VIII.5 that motions are ultimately caused by an unmoved mover?

3. SELF-MOTION, HEAVENLY MOTION, AND THE PRIME MOVER

One of these questions seems easily answered. Even if self-motions fail to be fully explained by appeal to an internal cause, self-movers merit their special status because they contain an active source—a principle of motion and rest—and so, unlike commonplace objects that experience motion, they can sustain and direct their own, often intricate, behavior. Even so, since the internal active principle cannot trigger the motion, the impetus derives from the creature's environment. Does this reliance on external factors undermine Aristotle's argument in *Phys.* VIII.5?

I think not. Aristotle can preserve the main point of that argument by appealing to the mechanics of the cosmos as a whole. He locates the continuity and variety of sublunary changes in the motions of the heavenly spheres, and particularly in the twofold motion of the sun (*GC* II.10, 336a31–b15).[35] The sun's daily westward rotation with the sphere of the fixed stars and yearly eastward motion along the ecliptic, resulting in longer and shorter days, translates itself down to the sublunary sphere in the elemental change observed in seasonal variation.[36] Without the sun's distinctive motion, the four common elements would be permanently sorted into layers; all the earth would be settled in a ball at the center and surrounded by all the water, then by all the air, and finally by all the fire (*GC* II.10, 337a7–15). There would be no coming-to-be and passing-away.[37] As it is, there is abundant activity, with portions of the elements dislodged from their places and undertaking to regain them again. In their attempt to sort themselves out, they frequently interact, and such interaction sometimes results in the transformation of one element into another, and sometimes in the combination of elements into uniform compounds, such as minerals, natural metals, and various liquids.

In their continuous cyclical transformations, the four elements are said to "imitate" the eternal circular motion of the heavens, and these transformations guarantee the continuity and diversity of sublunary changes (*GC* II.10, 337a1–7). So an animal is constantly subject to stimulation, whether by simple climatic reversals caused directly by the sun's motion or

[35] Cf. *Meta.* Λ.6, 1072a9–17; *Phys.* VIII.6, 258b26–259a6.

[36] On the mechanics of this process, see *Meteor.* I.3, 341a13–32; cf. *De cae.* II.7, 289a28–34.

[37] *Meta.* Λ.6, 1072a10–12; *De cae.* II.3, 286b1–9; *GC* II.10, 336a31–b10.

by other changes that the sun regulates more indirectly, such as animal generation itself (*Meta.* Λ.5, 1071a14–16) and length of life (*GC* II.10, 336b10–15).[38] An animal responds to some stimulants and not others because of its nature (φύσις)—its inner active principle—which should also determine how the response is manifested.[39] Therefore, in explaining why an animal starts moving on a particular occasion, one need not track down an infinite number of previous changes; instead one can appeal, first, to the animal's nature, which determines why a stimulus of a particular sort arouses a response of a particular kind, and second, to the sun's motion, which accounts for the patterns of interaction in the sublunary region.

Having elevated the explanation of animal motion to the superlunary realm, we should now ask what accounts for the sun's distinctive course. Unfortunately, Aristotle says relatively little about the mechanics of celestial motion, and his claims sometimes seem inconsistent. In particular, he appears to vacillate on the question of whether the heavenly spheres are self-movers or not. In *De caelo* he asserts that the heaven is alive (ἔμψυχος) and compares the motions of some of its parts to those of animals.[40] In *Meta.* Λ.7 he claims that the Prime Mover causes motion by being desired or loved (1072b3). If the spheres are moved by their desire, they should be ensouled. These claims suggest that the spheres resemble ordinary self-movers in possessing both internal active and passive sources of motion.

Yet on several occasions Aristotle insists that the mover responsible for the eternal rotation of the outermost sphere is external to it,[41] and *De motu animalium*, after arguing that the heaven is moved by an external unmoved mover, contrasts the heaven with animals, which require, in addition to an external unmoved factor, an internal unmoved component as well (700a6–11).[42] Since the author applauds certain theorists who deny that any part of a rotating sphere can remain fixed and gives as his reason that otherwise the whole sphere would have to remain still or be deprived of its continuity (699a17–20), he apparently thinks that one cannot attribute to the heav-

---

[38] Cf. *GA* IV.10, 777b16–778a9. I thank Allan Gotthelf for calling this passage to my attention.

[39] On the role of an animal's nature in establishing its length of life, see *GA* IV.10, 777b6–8; cf. *De long.* 5, 466a17–b4. A creature's nature also controls its response to external factors, for instance, whether it lives or dies in air or water; see *De resp.* 14, 477b31–478a4; 16, 478a29–35; 19, 479b8–13. I thank James Lennox for calling my attention to these passages.

[40] *De cae.* II.2, 285a29–30; II.12, 292a18–b25. But see note 44 below.

[41] *Phys.* VIII.10, 267b6–9; *MA* 3–4; *Meta.* Λ.7, 1073a3–5.

[42] Nussbaum (1978, 3–12) has argued for the authenticity of this treatise. Even if one questions its genuineness, the text is presumably an early Peripatetic work and the main tenets Aristotelian.

enly spheres both internal moving and moved components without undermining their intrinsic unity.[43] These claims suggest that the sphere of the fixed stars, and perhaps the lower spheres as well, has only an intrinsic passive source of motion.[44]

The motions of the heavenly spheres might therefore be better compared to the natural motions of the four sublunary elements than to the self-motions of animals.[45] According to *De caelo*, the spheres are composed of a fifth element, aether.[46] Like the simple bodies in the lower region, whose natures enable them to move upward toward the sphere of the moon or

[43] Cf. *Phys.* VIII.4, 255a12–18. Although this passage primarily concerns the four sublunary elements, whose natural unity and continuity prevent the distinction between moving and moved components—which would enable their classification as self-movers—Aristotle extends the claim to other continuous bodies as well. This passage, together with the one in *MA*, suggests that the continuity of the heavenly spheres prevents them from being self-movers.

[44] The thesis in *Meta*. Λ.7, that the spheres are moved by their desire, might accord with this possibility, because Aristotle views the faculty of desire as a passive capacity of soul—a moved mover that responds to an unmoved mover (*De an.* III.10, 433b13–18; *MA* 6, 700b32–701a1). The crucial question is whether the account in *Meta*. Λ requires that the spheres resemble animals in possessing an internal active δύναμις as well. Since *Meta*. Λ does not mention an internal active principle, it could be that Aristotle regards the spheres as ensouled, in virtue of their special passive capacity, yet not as self-movers, because they lack an internal directive δύναμις. One might object that Aristotle's silence in *Meta*. Λ tells against rather than for this suggestion, since the proposed disanalogy between the spheres and animals is sufficiently important to merit clarification. But since the disanalogy is mentioned in *MA* 4 (700a6–11, cited above), it seems more likely that *Meta*. Λ is silent because such internal ἀρχαί are not part of the theory. The passages cited above from *De caelo* can also be reconciled with this proposal. From the claim in II.2 that the heaven is alive and has an inner source of motion, Aristotle concludes that it has various parts (upper and lower, right and left). This inference suggests that οὐρανός here refers to the cosmos as a whole rather than to the outermost sphere (cf. *De cae.* I.9, 278b9–21, on the various meanings of οὐρανός). If so, this passage does not bear on our question about the spheres (though it is quite Platonic in suggesting that the whole cosmos resembles an animal). The passage in II.12 is not about the spheres either, but about the heavenly bodies. The claim that they partake of action and life (292a18–22) does not conflict with the proposal that the spheres have only passive souls. Furthermore, the analogy between the planets and animals (292a20–b25) concerns only the number of motions required for them to attain the good; nothing is said about the presence of an inner active principle.

For alternative views of Aristotle's treatment of celestial motion, see the papers by Kosman and Judson in this volume.

[45] For this proposal, see Bogen and McGuire 1986–87, 387–448.

[46] Although Aristotle says a good deal about the fifth element in *De caelo*, he is curiously reticent about it in *Phys.* VIII and *Meta*. Λ. Even so, the heavenly spheres are made out of some material, and *Meta*. Θ.8 carefully distinguishes the incorruptible matter of the heavenly bodies, which enables them to move from one location to another (πόθεν ποῖ), from the matter of bodies in the sublunary region, which accounts (among other things) for their perishability (1050b6–28). A similar distinction occurs at Λ.2, 1069b24–26. In addition, Λ.8 mentions τὸ κύκλῳ σῶμα, which is eternal and unresting (1073a31–32). Given these passages, I assume that the doctrine of a fifth element, which naturally rotates, is presupposed in the relevant discussions in the *Physics* and *Metaphysics*.

downward toward the cosmic center, the celestial element naturally rotates around the center (*De cae.* I.2). The nature of aether apparently accounts for the circular motion of the heavenly spheres in the way that the natures of earth, water, air, and fire account for the natural motions of these bodies. Before pressing the analogy further, however, we need to untangle Aristotle's account of elemental natural motion, which is itself problematic.

In *Phys.* VIII.4 Aristotle denies that the elements are self-movers, arguing that although they possess a passive source, which accounts for why, if unimpeded, they move in one direction rather than another, they lack an internal active principle (255b29–31). The active source lies outside. *Phys.* VIII.4 lists various items responsible for elemental natural motion, including that which generates the element or removes an impediment to its natural progression, but these causes are rightly identified as accidental (255b24–29), because they merely trigger the motion but do not explain why it is sustained in a particular direction or why it terminates at a certain limit. We are left asking what serves as the active principle of elemental natural motion comparable to that in other typical changes.

De cae. IV.3 takes up the question again,[47] and here Aristotle says that even more than things that change on their own in response to slight stimulation, the elements seem to possess an internal principle. Yet he does not reject the conclusion of *Phys.* VIII. Instead he makes a remarkable claim: the elements appear to possess an internal source because, he says, "their matter is closest to substance" (310b31–33). If my earlier suggestion is granted, that an active principle integrates distinct, and often successive, events into a complex motion that promotes a higher goal, the elements should need no internal active source because they display only a single simple behavior, which requires no coordination. Elemental matter is "closest to substance" because the elements, if unimpeded, automatically exercise their δύναμις in seeking their proper places.[48] They are not genuine substances, however, because, in lacking an internal active source, they cannot limit their natural motions at their natural termini. Fire is not programmed to stop at the periphery—it would proceed upward indefinitely if it were not confined by the sphere of the moon;[49] and water would progress downward indefinitely were it not eventually stopped by the heavier mass of earth below.

Aristotle claims in *De cae.* IV.3 that the motion of an element to its proper place is motion "to its own form" (310a33–b1); and he identifies the boundaries—the periphery and the center—as in some sense the form

---

[47] At the end of the chapter (311a9–12), Aristotle mentions the accidental causes listed in *Phys.* VIII.4 and refers to his earlier discussion.

[48] *Phys.* VIII.4, 255b5–12.

[49] Recall Aristotle's claim in *De an.* II.4 that fire would burn "without limit" as long as it had stuffs to consume.

of the body contained at that location (310b7–12). He further states that
the adjacent body above stands to the one below "as form to matter"
(310b14–15). These pronouncements suggest that whatever limits an element's natural motion—the center in the case of earth, the sphere of the
moon in the case of fire, and the accumulated mass of the adjacent element
in the case of water and air—counts as the element's form, and thus plays
the limiting role of an active δύναμις for the simple bodies.

I have suggested that the aetherial spheres may be only natural movers,
like the four elements, rather than self-movers. If so, they possess an inner
passive source, which accounts for their rotation, but the governing principle lies outside the sphere that it directs. A passage in *Phys.* VIII.6 supports
this proposal. Aristotle claims that the ἀρχαί of the heavenly bodies that
experience more than one motion are moved accidentally by something
else, whereas those of perishable things alone are moved accidentally by
themselves (259b28–31). This division excludes the ἀρχή of the outermost
sphere, because the stars display one motion only; and Aristotle has already argued that the first mover responsible for the eternal motion is
unmoved even incidentally (259b20–28). Since the first mover is immune
even to accidental motion, it lies outside the entire rotating system. In *Phys.*
VIII.10 Aristotle locates the first mover on the circumference of the cosmos
(267b6–9). Although the location of the ἀρχαί of the lower spheres is more
problematic, this passage at least establishes that the principle of each
sphere is situated within the rotating system but outside its proper sphere.
For if the lower spheres each possessed an internal active source, that
source would be moved accidentally by itself, like that of animals, because
it would be carried around with its own sphere. Since Aristotle claims
instead that the principle in each case (excepting the stars) is moved accidentally by something else, the ἀρχή must inhabit some sphere (to be
moved accidentally), yet not the sphere of which it is the active principle.
The ἀρχαί of the lower spheres could be located in the sphere of the stars
(and so be carried around with it),[50] or, more likely, the principle of each
sphere could occupy the next sphere above.[51] Either way, the active principle is external to the sphere it moves.[52]

[50] Aristotle thinks that all the spheres exhibit the motion of the outermost sphere as well as
their own; see *Meta.* Λ.6, 1072a10–17; cf. Λ.8, 1073b25–26 (on Eudoxus's theory). Cf.
Simplicius *In Phys.* 1261.17–19.

[51] I owe this suggestion to Steven Strange.

[52] Since the ἀρχή occupies a sphere other than the one it directs, it is accidental to the
sphere in which it resides (because it is not part of its defining account). For the idea that an
active principle can be present in matter accidentally, we might usefully compare Aristotle's
account of the transmission of soul in animal generation. Although the semen and then the
inseminated female material serve as vehicles of soul, the soul is not the actuality *of* these
materials. (Only once the heart of the new creature has been articulated is there a body to
which the soul belongs per se.) On this topic, see Code 1987, 56–58.

On this interpretation, the celestial spheres resemble the four sublunary elements, with their simple rectilinear motions, in moving in simple concentric circles around the earth. The apparently complex motions of the sun, moon, and planets are explained by a combination of homocentric spheres, each rotating in a westward or eastward direction around its own axis.[53] Since Aristotle attributes an ἀρχή to each sphere, not to the luminary whose motion is the product of several spheres (*Meta.* Λ.8, 1074a14–16), the active δύναμις does not coordinate motions but needs only to determine the inclination of a sphere's axis, its proper orientation (to west or east), and the speed of its rotation. To control these factors, the ἀρχή of each sphere should be located in the next above, at the point at which the axis of the lower sphere makes contact with its higher neighbor. The Prime Mover, located outside the rotating system, should account for the axis of rotation of the outermost sphere, its westward orientation and period.[54] But as we shall see, the Prime Mover must also perform a more vital role.

Although the evidence strongly suggests that the celestial spheres are natural movers rather than self-movers, for my general argument the decision one way or the other is not crucial. Since the motion of the celestial spheres persists eternally, the phenomena can be explained by treating the spheres either as animals, whose active δύναμις is internal, or as inanimate objects, like the four elements, whose active source lies outside. On either conception, however, a sphere's rotation should be an activity—an ἐνέργεια—the mutual expression of a mover and moved whose active and passive δυνάμεις are like.[55] In rotating, a sphere does not acquire a new

---

[53] Aristotle's account in *Meta.* Λ.8 appears to transform a geometrical theory of homocentric spheres, which Eudoxus and Callippus used to explain the motions of the sun, moon, and planets, into a mechanical system of spheres in contact with one another. According to Aristotle, Eudoxus and Callippus invoked a set of spheres to explain the motion of each heavenly body and included in each case the sphere of the stars. Aristotle claims that additional counteracting spheres are required if all the spheres combined are to explain the phenomena (1073b38–1074a1). The additional spheres are thus introduced to establish a mechanical system; they counteract the motion proper to each planet so that the motion of the outermost sphere alone is transferred to the heavenly body below. On this topic I have profited from reading Heath 1981, 190–224; and Kuhn 1957, 55–59.

[54] For the dependence of the outermost heaven on the first mover, see *Meta.* Λ.8, 1073a23–25.

[55] Waterlow (1982, 249–57) is concerned that eternal rotation fails to satisfy Aristotle's definition of change in *Phys.* iii.1 (recalled at viii.1, 251a9–10, and viii.5, 257b8–9), because such motion is a complete rather than an incomplete actuality. She argues that it is a change nonetheless because it has a distinct agent (254–55). On my view, the distinction between change and activity does not turn on the presence or absence of a mover: both require a mover, and in either case the mover can be internal or external. So, for instance, when an ax is used to chop, its behavior is an activity even though the mover is external. If this analysis is correct, Waterlow's criterion is inadequate to establish eternal rotation as a κίνησις. Of course, such motion need not satisfy the definition of change if, as I am suggesting, it is an ἐνέργεια. On this topic, see Bogen and McGuire 1986–87, 417–22.

location, but moves continually from and to the same location.[56] By means
of this constant activity, the spheres maintain their positions within the
cosmic hierarchy. If in fact Aristotle thinks that the active principles occupy
their own spheres, the celestial self-movers will independently guard their
proper places within the system. The question, then, is why these autonomous agents adapt themselves to a cooperative venture that benefits the
cosmos as a whole. The Prime Mover will play this organizational role. If
instead, as I have argued, each sphere depends for its orientation on the
next sphere above, the nested spheres are parts of a mechanical network.
But on this construction, too, the Prime Mover is needed to explain why the
celestial spheres are so adapted to foster the continued life and interaction
of bodies in the lower region.

In *Meta.* Λ.10 Aristotle asks whether the good of the whole lies in the
order of its parts or in something separate by itself—whether, as in an
army, the good lies in its organization or in its leader. He claims that the
good lies in both but more in the leader, because the order depends on him
(1075a11–15).[57] The Prime Mover must integrate the proceedings into an
organized system that promotes the good of all its members (1075a16–
25). Like an animal's active δύναμις, which regulates simpler motions to
serve a higher purpose, the Prime Mover, too, is an efficient cause, controlling the motions of the universe as a whole for the sake of the whole
operation. On this interpretation, the good of the cosmos—its οὗ ἕνεκα—
lies both in the Prime Mover himself, whose power is expressed in his
eternal activity, and in the functioning system, whose order and continuity
he maintains by means of the regular motions of bodies acting according to
their natures.[58]

---

[56] *Phys.* viii.8, 264b9–19; *De cae.* i.4, 271a19–22.

[57] Cf. *GC* ii.10, 337a16–22.

[58] This double meaning of οὗ ἕνεκα to specify, on the one hand, the good for the sake of
which (τὸ οὗ ἕνεκα τινός), and on the other, the beneficiary for the sake of which (τὸ οὗ ἕνεκα
τινί), is pointed out by Aristotle on several occasions; see *Meta.* Λ.7, 1072b1–4; *De an.* ii.4,
415b2–3, 415b20–21; *Phys.* ii.2, 194a35–36.

CHAPTER 3

Aristotle on Perception, Appetition, and Self-Motion

CYNTHIA A. FREELAND

ARISTOTLE clearly believes that animals are self-movers. In the *De anima* he describes the capacity for locomotion as a defining power of animal souls. In his biological works he writes at length about exactly *why* animals move in relation to their ends and environments; about their *means* of motion, via a diverse range of appendages including scales, claws, fins, legs, wings, feet, and flippers; and about their *variety* of motions—walking, flying, swimming, jumping, bending, stretching, creeping, crawling, undulating. Humans, too, are self-movers—in this regard we humans count as special cases of animals. Our capacity for self-motion is closely related to our capacity for moral agency.

Certain remarks Aristotle makes in a theoretical discussion of motion in *Phys.* VIII suggest, however, that animals are not genuine self-movers. Aristotle wants to defend the thesis that everything that is moved is moved by something else. Yet animals seem to originate their motion from rest, or from being unmoved. So Aristotle admits that animal motion presents "a particular source of perplexity" (253a7–8). In a study of this problem, "Self-Movers," reprinted as Chapter 1 in this volume, David Furley has emphasized that Aristotle's worry is that, should animals be able to initiate self-motion without being moved by anything outside themselves, "perhaps the whole cosmos might have initiated motion in itself in this way."[1]

To resolve his difficulty, Aristotle notes that self-movers may be divided into a moved and a motion-causing part. He preserves his basic thesis by arguing that the part that causes the motion of the whole self-mover must also itself be moved. This part originating the movement can be said to be moved incidentally in the sense that it gets moved as a part of the whole that it puts into motion (*Phys.* VIII.5, 257b12–22). Aristotle seems to apply this analysis to the self-motion of an animal; here the motion-causing part

I thank Susan Sauvé and Anne Jaap Jacobson for their generous and detailed written comments on an earlier draft. I also received useful criticisms from a publisher's reader and from Mary Louise Gill.

[1] Furley 1978; reprinted in this volume, 3–14.

would be its soul. In a relatively unproblematic sense, an animal's soul can be said to be moved accidentally when the animal as a whole moves, because it is somehow located "in" the animal (*De an.* 1.3, esp. 406a30–b8).

But in *Phys.* viii.2 Aristotle hints that the soul of an animal may also be moved in a nonaccidental way by objects in the animal's environment. This seems to be what he has in mind when he writes:

> So it may well be the case—or rather we may perhaps say that it must necessarily be the case—that many motions are produced in the body by its environment, and some of these set in motion the intellect or the appetite, and this again then sets the whole animal in motion. (253a15–18)

The implication here, that an animal is moved by objects in its environment when it comes to desire them, seems to conflict with the *De anima*'s account of the animals as self-movers (*De an.* iii.10). Perhaps this passage is not decisive, but Aristotle makes the point quite clearly later on, in *Phys.* viii.6, saying, "Well, we must understand this: that they move themselves with one motion only, and that not strictly (οὐ κυρίως); for the reason (αἴτιον) is not from themselves" (259b6–8).

The threat to animal self-motion in *Phys.* viii mostly concerns local motion, not change in general.[2] For Aristotle's purposes it would suffice to interpret the passage from 253a15–18 quoted just above as the weak claim that animal motions always presuppose some motion in the surrounding environment—that no animal can originate motion in a vacuum. Furley sees Aristotle as recognizing this point, but as making it in the *Physics* in a misleading way by using "the simplest possible mechanical model: A is pushed by B, B by C, and so on" (8 above). Even in the *De anima*, Furley points out, Aristotle sometimes speaks of such direct, "mechanical" causation of the "motions" of the soul:

> There is good reason for the view that these two are the causes of motion, appetite (ὄρεξις) and practical intelligence; for the object of appetite causes motion, and because of this the intelligence causes motion, because its starting-point (ἀρχή) is the object of appetite. (433a17–20)

Furley maintains, however, that an account citing a straightforward chain of efficient causes resulting in animal motion misrepresents Aristotle's real view of animal self-motion. True, in the *De anima* Aristotle admits that an animal's perceptions and desires are responses to the envi-

---

[2] In the continuation of the passage just quoted, Aristotle also remarks that animals do not have such natural motions as respiration or growth through themselves. Sometimes instead he seems to have in mind a distinct point about the physics of animal motion, as when in *MA* 4 he mentions the need for two parts in a moving animal, one moving, the other staying at rest to serve it as a sort of fulcrum (700a6–11).

ronment: animals react in certain ways to things in the outside world that they perceive. Perhaps the problem (or self-contradiction) here stems from intricacies (or inadequacies) in Aristotle's account of perception and desire. Notoriously, though he treats perceiving as an affection (πάθος) of some kind (suggesting that the soul "suffers" or is moved in perceiving), Aristotle is hard pressed to explain exactly what kind of affection it is; he ends up describing perception as an alteration (ἀλλοίωσις) only in a very special sense (*De an.* II.5; see Furley, 9–10 above). This means, as Furley sees it, that Aristotle wishes significantly to qualify the claim that external objects "move" animal souls. Animals perceive external objects under certain descriptions—as goods. They have the capacity of imagination (φαντα-σία), the ability to see things as objects of desire, or as relevant to their practical goals. (This is what is really involved in Aristotle's description of perception as only a qualified type of alteration.) Thus, according to Furley, Aristotle maintains that animals are self-movers because objects of desire "cause" animal motion only under certain descriptions. Without attributing to Aristotle a well-developed theory of mental representation and consciousness, Furley says that he "was sufficiently aware of the intentionality of objects of desire to want to retain the notion that animals move themselves" (14 above). Thus a more satisfactory answer to the question of how *Phys.* VIII leaves room for animals to be self-movers is that they have intentionality. I shall call Furley's proposal the "Intentionality Escape." (It is an "escape" because it frees Aristotle from the apparent contradiction between his view in *Phys.* VIII that animal motions are caused and the *De anima* account of how animals are self-movers.)

As Furley remarks, the proposal he has made to get Aristotle off the hook bears similarities to elements in Martha Nussbaum's account of the intentionality of animal perceptions, developed in her commentary on the *De motu animalium*.[3] In *MA* 6 Aristotle appears to confront the same general issue he does in the *Physics*: he says that the Prime Mover might account for ("cause") all other sorts of motion. In *MA* 1 in his treatment of the causes of animal motion, he writes that animals are *not* in the unqualified sense self-moving (698a7–14; on this see Nussbaum 1978, 114–21). Nussbaum interprets Aristotle as reasoning that, if animal motion is to occur within the overall framework of Aristotle's physical theory, it must be consistent with various tenets, such as the supposition that elements have particular natures that behave in characteristic ways; that there is no motion without a background of rest or an unmoved mover; that there is some general overall purpose for motion; and that the spheres are themselves self-movers of a sort, animate and motivated by their awe, knowledge, or worship of God. Nussbaum interprets Aristotle as concluding that "the animal is not

---

[3] Nussbaum 1978, 117.

self-moving because . . . its motions must be explained with reference to an external object of desire, which is an 'unmoved mover'" (120).

In the *De motu animalium*, Aristotle does more than in *Phys.* VIII to fill in the details of the causal chain extending from external objects in the animals' environments to the resulting action. The chain, rendered simply, leads from an external object to a perception, then to an imagination and a desire, and finally to a movement (*MA* 6–8). Aristotle seeks to offer a materialist account of each step of this chain—including the imagination and the desire. So Nussbaum confronts on Aristotle's behalf the same difficulty Furley dealt with from the *Physics*, the implication that animals are not self-movers.[4] Like Furley, she argues that animals are self-movers because of peculiarities in these causal chains. The step from the external object to the desire is "special" somehow because of the intervention of imagination, an intentional state. This means that although Aristotle could explain the entire chain as a sequence of efficient causes, given his thoroughgoing materialism, nevertheless a reductionist account leaves something important out—the fact that the animal acts or moves itself because it perceives an external object as a good.[5] This perceiving-as becomes the crucial factor that accounts for self-motion in the animal. Thus, like Furley, Nussbaum places the theoretical weight of Aristotle's defense of animal self-motion on intentionality itself.

Although the Intentionality Escape seems promising, it suffers from several serious defects. For example, the emphasis on intentionality leads Furley in particular to draw distinctions among animals' capacities for self-motion that do not reflect Aristotle's own views. In discussing what he takes *Phys.* VIII to be insisting on, some fixed chain of efficient/mechanical causes, Furley writes:

> This is a pattern of explanation which one might think suitable, perhaps, for the movements of the periodical cicada of the eastern United States . . ., which lies dormant in the earth until it emerges, noisily, and with all its millions of congeners, every seventeen years. . . . It seems thoroughly inadequate for *explaining the action* of a man signing a contract or even of a bird building a nest. (8 above; emphasis mine)

Furley's contrast here between insect behavior and that of humans or higher animals implicitly invokes a distinction between what we might call "actions" and "mere movements." That is, he seems to say that when periodic cicadas emerge for their foraging, they exhibit not genuine self-motion but mere reflex movement. Or in other words, the cicadas' movements stem from instinct and fail to be genuine actions with meaning *to* the creatures themselves. This general view has contemporary defenders who

---

[4] See ibid., essays 1 and 5.
[5] See ibid., essay 1, "Aristotle on Teleological Explanation," 74–76, 85–88, and 92.

similarly draw distinctions between true purposive behavior of higher animals and evolutionarily explained instincts, drives, or tropisms characteristic of insects or worms.[6]

But it is problematic to suppose that Aristotle would accept this distinction, or that he would not regard periodic cicadas as self-movers in a sense as genuine as humans or doves. Despite the fact that he exhibits some uncertainty about the nature of insects' imagination (*De an.* III.11), he believes that individual insects are capable of actions that exhibit purposiveness.[7] The social behaviors of ants and bees are among his favored instances of purposive animal motion.[8] I see no reason to deny that he would regard mass movements of groups of insects as involving self-motion. Of course, the problem Furley probably has with such cases is that in them self-motion seems not to involve a relevant attribution of intentionality.[9] What thoughts and aims can we plausibly ascribe to the individual ant or cicada?[10]

Another risk of the Intentionality Escape is that it may misrepresent Aristotle's difficulty in more contemporary philosophical terms. I mean that it sets up the puzzle posed by *Phys.* VIII as, in effect, a problem about causal determinism and free will. An animal will not be "determined" to pursue, say, food in its environment unless it perceives it *as* food.[11] Intentionality serves, then, as a means of inserting a gap within the deterministic chain of efficient causes. So Furley sees Aristotle's problem of determining "whether man is really a self-mover" as coming "into particularly sharp focus in the *Nicomachean Ethics*." And in the *Nicomachean Ethics* Furley finds, at least in sketchy form, "an important modification of the theory of desire set out in the *Physics*" (10–12 above).

Though intentionality may thus seem to "bracket" the animal's behavior, detaching it from the chain of efficient causes leading up to it, I do not think that Nussbaum and Furley explicitly advance the Intentionality Escape as a defense of indeterminism. (This would have involved more ex-

[6] For a contemporary philosopher who relies on such distinctions, see Dretske 1988, 89, 93–95, and 122–27. See also Gould 1977, for an explanation of the periodicity of cicada and other species in terms of evolutionary adaptations.

[7] See, e.g., *Phys.* II.8: "If then it is both by nature and for an end that the swallow makes its nest and the spider its web . . . it is plain that this kind of cause is operative in things which come to be and are by nature" (199a26–30).

[8] See, e.g., his discussion of bees in *HA* v.22, and of wasps in v.23.

[9] This is exactly at the root of Dretske's (1988) distinction.

[10] It is worth noting that Aristotle treats cicadas a few chapters later (*HA* v.30), and one comment makes clear he attributes at least some intentionality to them: "If you present your finger to a cicada and bend back the tip of it and then extend it again, it will endure the presentation more quietly than if you were to keep your finger outstretched altogether; and it will set to climbing your finger; for the creature is so weak-sighted that it will take to climbing your finger as though that were a moving leaf" (556b12–21).

[11] For example, see Nussbaum 1978, 87, on animals' selective perception.

plicit attention to Aristotle's own views on necessity and chance.) Rather, they maintain that intentionality is an essential feature of adequate *explanations* of animal self-motions. For example, Furley writes that animal actions "cannot be explained without some notion of what each of their goals means for them" (12; compare Nussbaum 1978, 67–80, 92, and essay 5). When Furley says that objects of desire only serve to *explain* animal motion under certain descriptions, this raises the question whether he means to assert that these same objects serve as *causes* under descriptions. Is the Intentionality Escape a claim about causal explanation or about the causal order? When in *Phys.* VIII Aristotle says that animal motions result from causal influences exerted on them by the external environment—a view he reiterates in the *De anima* and *De motu animalium*—this sounds like a metaphysical thesis, a claim about the causal order.[12] Though at times Furley seems to write as though he realizes Aristotle must block just such a causal claim, he does not clearly distinguish these two options, when he writes, for example, that in animal motion there is "not just a difference in the complexity of the response to a stimulus, but *a difference in kind*. Only a being with a soul can move in this way. An animal is correctly described as a self-mover, because when it moves, its soul moves its body, and the external cause of its motion (the ὀρεκτόν) is a cause of motion only because it is 'seen' as such by a faculty of the soul" (13; emphasis mine). In the first sentence Furley suggests that the causal chain is altered in some important way when intentionality enters the picture. But the third sentence shifts the force of this point back to issues about description or explanation.

Some scholars might regard my question about the Intentionality Escape as unintelligible, because they hold that Aristotle's four causes just are four types of explanation.[13] On this view, problems about the existence and operation of final causes are to be treated as problems about the applicability of teleological explanations. I have argued elsewhere that this reading fails to do justice to Aristotle's causal realism.[14] He maintains that there are distinct, objective causal relations of four types in the world. From this there follows an explanatory realism; that is, Aristotle would also say that causal explanations of various types must refer to just these objective causal relations. Explanations, in other words, are dependent upon facts about the world, rather than vice versa, as some scholars have argued.[15]

In my view, the real problem facing Aristotle in *Phys.* VIII, and in related texts such as *MA* 6, concerns the compatibility of final causation and

[12] Here I am in agreement with remarks made by Cooper (1987, 273–74).

[13] See Moravcsik 1974; Annas 1982; Sorabji 1980; and Fine 1987. Further references may be found in Freeland 1991.

[14] Freeland 1991.

[15] E.g., Graham 1987.

efficient causation. I shall argue that Aristotle holds that animals are self-movers, despite the fact that there are efficient causes of their motions, just insofar as their motions have final causes, or aim at some good. The goal-directedness of animal motions, rather than the intentionality of animal perceptions and desires, is crucial for the definition of animals as self-moving. Of course, I shall have no reason to deny that some animals can and do manifest intentionality, or that this is relevant to causal accounts of how they move themselves. Animals we might regard as lacking intentionality (like Furley's cicadas) can nevertheless act in goal-directed ways, thus qualifying as self-movers.

An adequate understanding of Aristotle's defense of animal self-motion must begin by clarifying how teleology governs all animal motions. In the next section I shall present a general account of the teleology of animal self-motions. My suggested account can be applied at all levels of Aristotle's psychology, from the perceptions and appetites of primitive animals to the movements of higher animals, and from the voluntary behavior of humans to the necessary and eternal revolutions of the spheres. On my model, self-motion depends upon the existence of something I call "objective goal-directedness." (Hence my proposal could be called the "Final Cause Escape.") It will be helpful to show that Aristotelian teleology, which has literally cosmic applications, can be represented by a unified model, one that describes the basic causal relations and explanatory structures applicable to a human's or a dove's deeds, as well as the periodic mass movements of cicadas, or the social behavior of ants and bees.

In subsequent sections, focusing on examples of self-motion exhibiting intentionality, I shall defend my thesis that intentionality is less basic than objective goal-directedness. In section 2 I shall discuss the self-motions of higher animals with complex sensory abilities and forms of imagination. Here I shall further explain why it is anachronistic to view Aristotle's problem in *Phys.* VIII as a problem about determinism and free will. In section 3 I shall defend my account of Aristotelian teleology against two obvious objections. The first objection suggests that even the elements turn out to be self-movers on my account. The second objection reasons that self-motion cannot be defined as always directed toward an objective goal, because there clearly are instances of misguided, evil, or self-destructive human behavior. I conclude with some brief remarks about relations between self-motion, indeterminism, and chance.

1. A UNIFIED MODEL OF ARISTOTELIAN TELEOLOGY

In this section I begin developing a schema to represent the structure of Aristotelian teleology. I have adapted this schema from one proposed by

Andrew Woodfield in his book *Teleology* (1976).[16] In the conclusion of his book, Woodfield lays out four fundamental schemata analyzing distinct types of teleological description. Woodfield describes the common element unifying these four schemata as follows: "It can be seen that together the essence of teleology lies in welding a causal element and an evaluative element to yield an explanatory device" (206). Though they share these central features, teleological accounts may differ according to whether intentionality comes in—that is, whether, as Woodfield puts it, a mind is required "to weld the elements." This factor of mind is important, for it accounts for why we have two "quite different conceptions of what an end is" (211). In one conception we could call the end an "objective" good; in the other it is "subjective," in the sense that it is a good conceived as such by a percipient being.

Woodfield explicitly faults Aristotle for conflating these two distinct notions of ends, objective and subjective goods. But in my view, this was not a conflation; rather, Aristotle deliberately proposed a unified account of teleology. Although his model permits us to describe the pursuit of subjective (or apparent) goods as purposive, it takes tendencies toward objective or real goods as more fundamental. Mention of these objective goods is basic for teleological analysis, and any account of objective goods must be grounded, according to Aristotle, in an account of things' natures. The good of an animal is the good of the species to which it belongs. A species-relative account is in turn subsumable under an account explaining why animals in general are self-movers. In sum, Aristotle's teleological account of why animals are self-movers, that is, why they have the particular capacity for self-motion, must be grounded in a general description of the nature of animals and of their respective goods.

Consider, for example, why hummingbirds have the capacity to hover in flight. Intuitively, we would say that this enables them to use their long bills to glean flower nectar. Hovering enables hummingbirds to get their food, and food, of course, is, in general, an animal good, because it is in the nature of animals to nourish themselves. Aristotle will explain the actions of an individual animal as instances of purposive behavior directed toward the good for that animal's kind. Thus the explanation of why a particular hummingbird is hovering near a hibiscus is that it aims to use its bill to glean the flower nectar.

Let me now turn to my suggested account of the structure of Aristotelian teleology. Schematically, a teleological account of an animal kind K's having a particular capacity C might go as follows:

Animal kind K has capacity C for the sake of G =
K has C because C causes or level-generates G, and G is good.[17]

[16] Woodfield 1976.
[17] Adapted from Woodfield 1976.

Several points of commentary on this proposal are in order before I can proceed to lay out Aristotle's own teleological account of why animals in general have the power of self-motion.

1. *Goods* are species defined and objective. That is, Aristotle believes that a quasiscientific study of animals will reveal what their activities typically tend toward, and that this would indeed be their good.[18]

2. Aristotle holds that *capacities* are closely related to, indeed are defined in terms of, their respective activities. A capacity is related to a good, then, because it makes action toward that good possible.

3. The notion of *level-generation* is borrowed from Woodfield, who explains it as follows: "Roughly speaking, act *A* level-generates act *A'* when the agent does *A'* by or in doing act *A*" (137). With appropriate modifications to substitute "capacities" for "acts," this formula can readily be adapted to the Aristotelian context.

4. The most problematic aspect of this schema is the interpretation of the "because" on the right-hand side. There is in addition a potential scope ambiguity here in the right side; I suggest a subjunctive conditional reading: "If either {*C* did not cause *G* or *G* were not good}, then *K* would not have *C*."[19]

According to the schema I have just suggested, it ought to be possible to explain why animals in general have the capacity for locomotion by showing that locomotion causes or contributes to something that is good for animals. Aristotle does propose such an explanation of animal motion in the *De anima*, but to understand it requires some backtracking, because locomotion is not in and of itself the fundamental capacity that distinguishes all animals. Rather, it is sensation that qualifies something as an animal.[20] Some animals that do have sensation do not move. Aristotle says that nature does not leave out what is necessary, so we can know that these lower animals lack even the capacity for movement, since they are not

---

[18] On this, see Irwin 1980.

[19] In a contemporary version of a similar account, like that of Dretske (1988), the relevant "because" in cases of animal behavior will cite an evolutionary tale. This, of course, is not the kind of explanation available to Aristotle, since it proceeds by citing efficient causes rather than purposes, whereas Aristotle thinks that nature has designed the animals in certain ways *in order to* promote their goods. Dretske draws another important distinction between animals with purposive behaviors that involve fixed reactions and those that permit learning. Evolution may have favored the development of a behavior that, in certain circumstances, leads an animal toward harm rather than good. In such cases, he says, the animal engages in the behavior in question *because of* its evolutionary history and not *because* it will achieve a good thereby. This is another distinction Aristotle cannot avail himself of. Below I will allude to how he would handle a similar distinction, in discussing cases of misguided or self-destructive behaviors.

[20] "It is the possession of sensation that leads us for the first time to speak of living things as animals" (413b1–2). Aristotle first describes the particular nature of animal souls as part of his initial characterization of the kinds of soul in *De an.* ii.2–3. Later in book iii he returns to

provided with organs to realize this capacity. If locomotion had been a good for the lower animals, they would have been provided with the organs for it (legs or whatever; see 432b21–26). (Aristotle makes exactly the same point about the stars, on the basis of their spherical shape, in *De cae.* II.8, 290a30–32.) The capacity for sensation is either identical to, or always accompanied by, the capacity for appetition: "If sensation, necessarily also imagination and desire (ὄρεξις); for, where there is sensation, there is also pleasure and pain, and, where these, necessarily also appetite (ἐπιθυμία) (413b22–24).

Much the same explanation is offered in *De an.* II.3:

> If any order of living things has the sensory, it must also have the appetitive (τὸ ὀρεκτικόν) [viz. psychic power or δύναμις]; for appetite (ὄρεξις) is the genus of which desire (ἐπιθυμία), passion (θυμός), and wish (βούλησις) are the species; now all animals have one sense at least, viz. touch, and whatever has a sense has the capacity for pleasure and pain and therefore has pleasant and painful objects present to it, and wherever these are present, there is desire, for desire is appetition of what is pleasant.[21] (414b1–6)

It thus turns out that Aristotle's explanations of the good afforded by animal capacities are not as clear as one might wish. For example, one passage seems intended to offer a teleological account of animals' possession of the capacity for sensation (I number sections for ease of reference):

> [1.] Animals must be endowed with sensation, since nature does nothing in vain. Every body capable of forward movement would, if unendowed with sensation, perish and fail to reach its end, which is the aim of Nature; for how could it obtain nutriment?

> [2a.] Stationary living things, it is true, have as their nutriment that from which they have arisen; but it is not possible that a body that is not stationary but produced by generation should have a soul and a discerning mind without also having sensation. (Nor yet even if it were not produced by generation.)

> [2b.] Why should it not have sensation? It would have to be better either for the soul or for the body; but in fact it is neither—for the absence of sensation

---

the topic of animal natures in a slightly different context, focusing primarily on imagination and desire. Animals are described in the earlier passages as living beings with the power of sensation. At the opening of *De an.* III.9, Aristotle writes that animal souls are characterized by two capacities, the capacity for "discrimination" (κριτικός) (he must mean sensation) and the capacity for originating local movement (432a15–19). Also within this chapter Aristotle appears to list imagination as a third and separate capacity of animals, but his views on this are a little unclear (432a31–b3). Despite the remark quoted above from 413b22–24, he vacillates about whether all animals have imagination and whether they all have desire (ὄρεξις), strictly speaking, rather than mere undifferentiated appetite (ἐπιθυμία).

[21] Cf. *De sensu* 1, 436b18–437a1.

will not enable the one to think better or the other to exist better. Therefore no body that is not stationary has soul without sensation.

[3.] But if a body has sensation, it must be either simple or compound. And simple it cannot be; for then it could not have touch, which is indispensable. (434a30–b9)

Part 1 of the passage is odd, because Aristotle argues here as if his goal is to explain only why certain animals, namely, those with the capacity for locomotion, require sensation. For them, it contributes to the good of obtaining food. As the passage continues, he persists in writing as if his topic is why moving animals—rather than animals in general—have a need for sensation.

Next, in part 2a, Aristotle grants that some living things remain stationary and yet manage to survive without sensation—namely, plants. In part 2b he argues that sensation can contribute to two animal goods: it helps the mind think (a point of little relevance to most animals!), and it helps the body survive. But both of these points are still restricted to instances of moving animals.

At the conclusion of this little argument in part 3, Aristotle finally does zero in on why nonmoving animals are endowed at least minimally with the sense of touch. Touch is necessary, he suggests, for an animal's very being. (The other senses, like locomotion itself, function toward both the being and the "well" of an animal.[22]) Plants, which presumably also need some means of taking in the appropriate nourishment, lack the capacity for sensation, as is demonstrated by their simple bodies. (But of course, that their bodies are simple in precisely the relevant sense—lacking the ability "to take in form without the matter"—may only be inferred from the fact that they do not need sensation.) How does Aristotle know that plants do not perceive? Granted, they do not move around to pursue food or avoid enemies; but they do appear to respond to features in their environment, such as nutrients, water, or sunshine.[23] Besides, Aristotle admits that some animals are fixed, like plants, and do not move. What is different about them, then? Aristotle must believe that even stationary and lower-level animals manifest rudimentary approach/avoidance behaviors that are somehow more complex than those of plants. Though such simple animals, like sea anemones for example, may remain spatially fixed, he believes that their ability to sense provides them with a broader repertoire of

[22] Gotthelf (1989a) argues against placing any important theoretical weight on the difference between "the good" and "the well" in such contexts. See his section 2. In other respects my own emphasis on the evaluative element in teleological descriptions disagrees with the thrust of his argument.

[23] See the interesting examples and discussion of plant behavior in Dretske 1988, 11, 47, and 89–90.

behavior (what we would call stimulus-response behavior) than plants have.[24] We can imagine he thinks either that plants would be destroyed under similar circumstances, or that they can get by with more automatic reactions to the surrounding environment, for example, to sunlight, water, or nutrients they need. On Aristotle's behalf we can say two things: his knowledge of anatomy was primitive, and of course he knew nothing about nerve cells and the nervous system; further, he did explicitly recognize that it is hard to decide whether certain creatures should count as animals or plants.[25]

In sum, the primitive animals' possession of the lower-level senses of touch and taste serves the good of animal survival.[26] Aristotle says:

> An animal is a body with soul in it: every body is tangible, i.e., perceptible by touch; hence necessarily, if an animal is to survive, its body must have tactual sensation. All the other senses, e.g., smell, sight, hearing, apprehend through media; but where there is immediate contact the animal, if it has no sensation, will be unable to avoid some things and take others, and so will find it impossible to survive. (*De an.* iii.12, 434b12–19)

In this passage the senses of touch and taste are distinguished as immediate or contact senses from the other three senses whose operation involves a medium. Possession of these higher sense-capacities goes along with the capacity for locomotion.[27] Aristotle believes that whereas the senses of taste and touch enable an animal to live minimally, that is, to survive by obtaining food, the distal senses together with locomotion contribute to an animal's well-being—presumably to its doing better at finding food, as well as at other animal goals, such as evading predators or finding mates. He emphasizes this contribution of the higher senses at the very conclusion of the *De anima*:

> Animals have all the other senses, as we have said, not for their being, but for their well-being—for example, sight, which, since [an animal] lives in air or water, or generally in what is transparent, it must have in order to see, and taste because of what is pleasant or painful to it, in order that it may perceive

[24] Sometimes he looks at anatomy as well as behavior; see Freeland 1992.

[25] A remarkable fact cited in *De an.* ii.2 is that, just as certain plants cut into parts seem to acquire multiple souls through their new multiple sources of (re)generation, when certain animals (insects) are divided in two, each segment possesses both sensation and local movement (413b17–20).

[26] For the purpose of differentiating food in the environment, taste and touch suffice. Aristotle argues that these two senses are always found together; this has led some commentators (e.g., Sorabji 1980) to say that he does not have effective arguments distinguishing the two senses; I have explained the basis for my disagreement elsewhere (Freeland 1992).

[27] Discussing this same topic in the *De sensu*, he similarly says that the three other senses— the three distal senses of smelling, hearing, and seeing—belong to animals with the capacity for locomotion (436b18–437a1).

these qualities in its nutriment and may be set in motion by desire, and hearing that it may be communicated with. (435b19–25)

At this point it seems appropriate to modify the basic sketch of an account I suggested earlier in the following way:

> Animal kind K has the capacity of *sensation* for the sake of survival = Animal kind K has the capacity for sensation because sensation promotes nutrition and hence survival, and this is good for all animals.

> Animal kind K' has the capacity for *locomotion* for the sake of survival or living well = Animal kind K' has the capacity for locomotion because locomotion promotes finding food, avoiding enemies, attracting and discovering mates, etc., and these either are necessary or improve the quality of life of animals of kind K'.

Sensation and motion serve an animal's being and its well-being; but again, the exact structure of Aristotle's teleological explanation is unclear. Does he reason from the need to the organ, or from the organ to the need?[28] How does this general teleological account work out for details in specific cases? In practice, teleological explanation of why animals possess the capacities they do is complicated by the fact that Aristotle treats sets of capacities as working together to serve the animals' good. He observes that in nature there are quite specific correlations between animals' sensory and locomotive capacities: the eagle flying high up in the air has extremely acute vision, enabling it to detect its prey below, whereas the mole burrowing under the earth is practically blind, but compensates through excellent hearing and smell, and so on. This suggests amending the schema above to read:

> Animal kind K has a particular capacity for sensation s along with a particular capacity for locomotion l for the sake of G = Animal kind K has s *and* l because together s *and* l contribute to certain activities that are either necessary for survival or raise the quality of life of animals of kind K.

Even this general sketch of the explanatory pattern of teleological explanation may clarify the difficult cases of Furley's cicadas or the social movements of bees and ants. The schemata just above mention an animal capacity—perception—that may involve intentionality, and they purport to explain why animals have this capacity in terms of the animals' good. But there is no crucial reference to the role of minds as "welding together" the causal with the evaluative elements of the analysis. Instead, these sche-

---

[28] His account of the connections between sense perception and locomotion is complicated by the fact that at least two steps of some sort intervene between an animal's perception and its self-motion: imagination and appetition. I will consider these links separately in section 2 below.

mata state that the animal's perceptions and movements are *actually* linked to things in its environment that are good for it. It would be inappropriate to amend either schema above as follows, to conform with a specifically intentional teleological description:

Animal kind *K* has a capacity *c* for the sake of *G* = Animal kind *K* has *c* because animals of this kind *think that c* causes or level-generates *G*, and *G* is good.

Animal kind *K* has a particular capacity for sensation *s* along with a particular capacity for locomotion *l* for the sake of *G* = Animal kind *K* has *s* and *l* because together animals of this kind *think/perceive that s* and *l* cause *G*, the animals' survival or their flourishing.

Aristotle holds that in all cases, the perceptual or locomotive abilities of animals serve their good. To do so, these abilities must place animals in reasonably correct relation to relevant features of their environments. The link between sensation and appetite presumes a basically appropriate processing of information from the environment: helpful stimuli are perceived as pleasant and are pursued, harmful ones are perceived as painful and are avoided. Even in cases of stationary animals, capacities of perception and appetite direct them to eat or avoid certain objects in the environment. The locomotive abilities of higher animals enable them to pursue or avoid relevant objects around them in more complex ways related to their well-being, in addition to their being. Actions of individual animals exemplify the goal-directedness belonging to the species as a whole: if a particular wolf chases a rabbit, it is because smelling and then chasing rabbits serves a good end for wolves—nourishment and survival. Similarly, when ants and bees construct farms or hives, tend queens, or store food, these are self-movements that serve the species' survival and well-being. The same would be true, presumably, for mass periodic foraging of Furley's cicadas.

2. PERCEPTION AND IMAGINATION IN ANIMALS' BEHAVIORAL ECONOMIES

In this section I shall examine in more detail Aristotle's account of how perception and imagination function within an individual animal's behavioral economy. My focus here will be on the higher animals, those possessing distal senses and a fairly complex repertoire of behavioral responses to the world. Recall that earlier I hypothesized that Furley adopted the Intentionality Escape because he was worried that if animal movements are all "mechanical" in the way he thinks the cicadas' movements are, there will be little room for voluntary self-motion for animals. In holding that

(higher) animals are self-movers "because" they manifest intentional properties, Furley emphasizes that animals' perceptions, appetites, and actions
involve some sort of consciousness or internal representation of the external world. The intuitive idea here is that imagination somehow frees animals from the deterministic operation of efficient causes. It introduces an
element of free play; the animal has a complex repertoire of responses.
Furley presumably is inclined to call the dove building a nest a self-mover
because in some important sense it initiates its own motions: it chooses
how, where, and from what to construct its nest. The dove has a goal and is
a conscious agent, not an automaton, as a Cartesian dove would be. (By
contrast, Furley seems to think of the cicada that emerges for its brief life of
foraging as, in effect, an automaton.)

As I said earlier, Furley agrees with Nussbaum's interpretation of Aristotle's views on animal self-motion in her commentary on *De motu animalium*. Nussbaum emphasizes that an animal does not desire things in its
environment merely after perceiving that they are red, smooth, or whatever; it desires what it has an image (φάντασμα) or selective perception of
as food.[29] A berry does not "cause" a bird to eat it by simply being there in
the bird's environment, or even by being seen by the bird. It can only enter
into a causal story about the bird's behavior if the bird sees this round red
shiny thing as food. For this, imagination is required.

In Furley's and Nussbaum's accounts, then, φαντασία or imagination
carries most of the weight of supplying animals with intentionality.
Nussbaum emphasizes passages in which Aristotle contrasts the capacities
for perception and imagination by calling them the same but different
in being (εἶναι; Nussbaum 1978, 234–35). She interprets Aristotle as
strongly contrasting the two faculties, emphasizing that sensation is passive, whereas imagination is active. Commenting on Aristotle's remark that
sensation is always right, but imagination can be false (428a11–12), she
explains that "it emphasizes the mechanical, reproductive side of *aisthēsis*
on Aristotle's theory" (256). By contrast, imagination seems active: it
accounts for the agent's "selective fastening on certain aspects of its environment" (257–58).[30] Aristotle even says that, in contrast to opinion
(δόξα), imagination is in our power (427b19–20; cf. Nussbaum 1978,
256). Unlike Furley, Nussbaum asserts that this is true for all animal

[29] See Nussbaum 1978, 230–34. Nussbaum discusses movement in relation to thought
(265). She distinguishes two types of imagination, deliberative and perceptual (261), arguing
that imagination and desire are jointly necessary conditions for animal motion. Imagination
is a necessary condition for desire: see 433b26–30. It is also said to "prepare" desire: see *MA*
8, 702a18-21. For a summary of Nussbaum's view, see 1978, 140–42, and the whole of essay
5 there.

[30] Nussbaum is careful not to go too far with a modern copy or "image" view of the
imagination (ibid., 225–27; cf. 228–30 for a discussion of "seeing-in").

movers, even the most primitive—all possess the capacity for imagination
(236–37).[31] Intuitively, all of Nussbaum's remarks about imagination suggest that an animal with the capacity for imagination has some kind of
voluntary power to view and classify the world around it. This is why I have
described the Intentionality Escape as setting up the problem about self-
motion in terms of freedom and determinism.

In a recent book, Deborah Modrak argued that Nussbaum over-
emphasized the passivity of sensation as well as the activity of imagination.[32] On Modrak's interpretation, perception itself is intentional in an
important sense. Even though Aristotle does think of sensation as a kind of
"registering" of external sense-objects, this need not be construed mechanistically or nonmentally. Modrak thinks that quite complicated background conditions of knowledge and experience may be brought to bear on
animal perceptions. She discusses the example of an animal selecting a
particular berry (1987, 96–97). Perception, imagination, and desire are
all, in a sense, modes of taking in reality, that is, modes of being affected by
external objects. But Modrak concludes,

> The complexity of the cognitive activity involved in voluntary motion attests
> to a broad conception of the powers of the perceptual faculty. The animal sees
> the berry as pleasant-for-him-at-this-moment; this complex cognition takes
> account of his present situation (that he is hungry) and his past experience
> with berries of this sort. Always in the case of animals and frequently in the
> case of humans, such complex cognitions are a function of the perceptual
> faculty.[33] (98–99)

Notice that Modrak sees Aristotle generalizing this point so that even low-
level animals (like cicadas) could be said to exhibit intentionality in their

[31] There has been considerable debate about this point. Some writers disagree with
Nussbaum and think that Aristotle restricts the scope of imagination to the higher animals.
See, e.g., Wedin 1988, 42 n. 21; Labarrière 1984, 23–24; and Labarrière 1990. Since the
lower-level animals possess only primitive sensory capacities and have no capacity for self-
motion, Aristotle himself wonders whether they have imagination (De an. III.11). He writes
that though the lowest animals may have appetite (ἐπιθυμία), they do not have desire (ὄρεξις),
for they have no images; and he remarks that entities capable of perceptual states are not
automatically entities capable of images. Then again, he also insists at least once that all
animals have imagination (see De an. II.3, 415a10–11 and III.3, 428a9–11; on these passages, see Wedin 1988, 41 n. 18; and Nussbaum 1978, 234).

[32] Modrak 1987, 99–107. See also Wedin (1988) on this topic; he emphasizes that there is
something like a judgment here (35). On his interpretation, sensations (αἰσθήματα) figure as
ingredients in episodes of perception; they are nonmental items that play a role in the story of
perceptual awareness.

[33] Of course, it seems that perceptions would be more directly caused by the proper objects
of each sense. That is, the bird perceives red because the berry is red, it perceives the scent
because the berry really has it, and it even perceives its shape because the shape affects its
common sense. But the berry is what Aristotle would call an incidental object of perception.

perceptions. But in any case, I argue that intentionality in itself is not the critical factor in self-motion.

I can now suggest how the teleological schema I supplied above to account for animal capacities subsumes an individual case of animal self-motion. Let me return to the example of a hummingbird hovering near a hibiscus, extending its bill into the flower. What exactly does Aristotle consider relevant to an account of this bird as a self-mover? He describes the object of desire as an unmoved mover (see, e.g., *De an.* III.10, 433b13–17). Clearly the bird responds to the hibiscus; what prevents our saying that the hibiscus "causes" the hummingbird to move? On the Intentionality Escape we must emphasize the importance of the fact that the hummingbird perceives this flower as food. The bird's own perception or imagination is what causes it to move. On my proposal also this is true. But I believe that Aristotle would instead identify two other factors as crucial for defining the bird as a self-mover. Intentionality alone cannot suffice. A "scientific" bird might exhibit intentionality in its complex classification of flowers without necessarily moving itself as a result. Intentionality is relevant for self-motion only when it figures into the perception of objects as ends or goals. Pursuit of particular goals is built into an animal's very nature, just in case those goals are part of its good. So the first factor required for the action of the hummingbird to be self-motion is that its movement be directed toward a goal that is objectively good for hummingbirds. In this example, that something is flower nectar, which is good for hummingbirds because it is, in fact, their food.

Second, since not all goal-directed motion is self-motion according to Aristotle, I must add a qualification: namely, that what actualizes the hummingbird's capacity for self-motion be something present in the bird itself, not outside it. To say that the flower causes the bird to hover near it is a misrepresentation, despite the fact that the flower moves the bird's faculty of desire. What actualizes the bird's capacity to hover is the hummingbird's own soul, a principle within it. How does its soul move the hummingbird?

Modrak disputes Nussbaum's claim that Aristotle assigns perception of the incidental objects of sense to imagination. Through a special sense, he maintains, an animal perceives particular objects of that sense—color for sight, scents for smell, etc. Common sense has as its objects motion, number, and figure. Objects of imagination are harder to spell out. This distinction is laid out, for example, at 424a21–24, where Aristotle remarks that sensation (αἴσθησις) is not affected by what we call the thing but by its qualities. Nussbaum in her discussion of this passage reads it in a fairly natural way, using as an example seeing a rose. When we see a white rose, we do not actually *see* it as a white rose, or as a rose; what we *see* is some white, or a white. It requires more of an intellectual or conceptual grasp to relate the white thing seen to a rose; recall that for Aristotle, perception is of the particular, knowledge of the universal. (See Nussbaum 1978, 258–59.) Aristotle maintains that through a particular sense, we perceive or are perceptually made aware of sensory features of things in the world, of what he calls the "proper" objects of sensation.

By an informed conception of the particular goal of food, in this case, flower nectar. There is, undoubtedly, an efficient causal chain like that traced in *De motu animalium* between the flower, perception of the flower, desire, and action. Further, I acknowledge that intentionality is a factor in the relevant causal chain. Nevertheless, as this second requirement emphasizes, it is the animal's own soul that has the power to actualize its capacity to move. Unlike the simple elements (earth, air, fire, and water), an animal sets and pursues its own goals. The elements are actualized or put into motion by something outside themselves, their natural places. (I shall have more to say about this contrast in section 3 below.)

Within Aristotle's discussion of how animals move, he compares animal sensations and comments on their accuracy. In each case he emphasizes the links between the animals' perceptions, appetites, and natural ends. That is, the two factors I have identified, objective goal-directedness and actualization from within, are always relevant. This becomes especially clear when he contrasts two methods for assessing and comparing the accuracy of the senses in *GA* v.2. He says that accuracy means "in one sense to perceive as accurately as possible all the distinctions of the objects of perception, in another sense to hear and smell far off" (781a14–16). For example, animals with long nostrils (such as the Laconian hound) or long ears perceive things that are far off much better than humans do. But even so, Aristotle emphasizes that they scent things only in relation to their appetites. In the *De sensu* again, appetite and pleasure are at the forefront of his account of perceptual accuracy. In those cases where humans have sensory superiority to other animals, it serves the good end for humans of obtaining accurate knowledge about the world for its own sake. So despite the fact that we perceive a limited range of scents, and have a less keen sense of smell than many animals, we perceive smells in and of themselves more accurately, that is, more objectively and less in relation to our desires. This point is again stressed in what Aristotle says about our superior vision, for example, in *De sensu*. Our vision is superior, despite its limitations vis-à-vis the eagle, the cat, etc., because for us vision does not just provide a means of preservation; it also brings in tidings of many distinctive qualities of things, from which knowledge, a human end, is generated.[34]

My point in this section has been that the Intentionality Escape goes amiss in construing Aristotle's problem about animal self-motion as a problem about freedom versus determinism; hence the Intentionality Escape fixes upon intentionality as the source of animal free will (or responsibility). Aristotle wants to defend natural teleology, which extends to include the purposive self-motions of animals, alongside what could amount to a complete causal determinism in the order of efficient causes.

---

[34] Freeland 1992 contains a fuller discussion of these issues.

This is a matter of ontology, not epistemology or pragmatics. We should not let our own doubts about the success of Aristotle's causal dualism (or pluralism) interfere with our construal of his intentions. It is helpful here to recall what Aristotle says about the cooperation of natural teleology with (material) necessity in other passages, such as *Po. An.* II.11 or *Phys.* II.8 and 9. He maintains that something can come about both of necessity and for a purpose. In the case of a house being built, for example, a variety of efficient causes contributes to production of the completed structure. But there is also something in reality directing these efficient causes toward their goal. In the case of a house, this goal is posited by its builders. But nature posits its own goals. When the spider spins its web, it works toward an end; it is self-moving because this is an end posited by its very own nature, and because its motions are actualized by a principle from within the spider's own soul.

3. THE SPECTRUM OF SELF-MOTION

Having discussed requirements for the self-motion of higher animals and humans, I now address two difficult problems for my claim that Aristotle analyzes self-motion in terms of objective goal-directedness. Below I shall consider an objection that begins by noticing cases in which animals or people make mistakes and do things that can harm them. But first I discuss whether my proposed schema for Aristotelian teleology offers too broad a characterization, implying that all natural things, even the elements, are self-movers.

As an alternative to the Intentionality Escape, I have proposed the "Final Cause Escape": in other words, what is crucial for defining animals as self-movers is that their behavior exhibit some underlying objective goal-directedness, not simply that they have consciousness, or that their perceptions and desires exhibit intentionality. Elements, too, have natures that direct them toward specific ends; they have tendencies to move or change in specific ways under specific conditions. So it is not surprising to read in *Meteor.* IV.12 that elements may be described as having attenuated goals. Plants seem to have an even stronger claim to count as self-movers, for they naturally send out roots "downward" and grow leaves "upward"—thus apparently moving toward their natural goals of water and sunlight.[35] But Aristotle denies that elements are self-movers, as he denies that locomotive capacity can belong to plants (*De an.* II.3, 414a32–33); it is surely relevant here that neither elements nor plants have the power of perception.

---

[35] For an interpretation of self-motion in Aristotle that would permit plants to be self-movers in virtue of their nutritive souls, see Gill's paper in this volume.

Thus intentionality may quite naturally seem to be the key differentiating factor.

How does Aristotle explain that not all cases of natural movement are cases of self-movement? He raises this problem explicitly concerning the elemental motions in *Phys.* VIII.4. Clearly the elements do have some sort of natural principle of motion, yet Aristotle gives a number of reasons for denying that they are self-movers (255a5–10).[36] He proposes to determine which things are self-movers by asking whether a thing is moved by itself or by outside forces. More specifically, he asks whether the principle that actualizes the thing, its end or goal, comes from within the thing or from outside it. He struggles to explain why the elements are not true self-movers by supplying a complex discussion of the sense in which elements have potentials, and of exactly what sorts of things actualize these potentials (255a24–b31). Air, for example, has the potential to rise, so it is light, not heavy; but it may not actually rise if something acts as a hindrance (think, for instance, of steam pushing against the lid of a pan). In one sense, Aristotle says, something that removes the hindrance actualizes the air's potential to rise, but in a truer sense it is a region, the region of "up," that does so. Hence Aristotle concludes about the elemental motions, "So it is clear that in all these cases the thing does not move itself, but it contains within itself the source of motion—not of moving something or of causing motion, but of suffering it" (255b29–31).

By contrast with the elements, which have a source of suffering motion, animals are self-movers because they have within themselves a principle that can actualize their own capacity to move. On the Intentionality Escape, though the actualizer is an external object, the animal can be said to move itself because it responds to, or sees, this object as its goal. Intentionality places primacy on the role of subjective goods in prompting animal motions. I have emphasized instead that the soul of an animal has the power to (efficiently) cause the animal's motion and to direct it toward a final cause, that is, toward something that is in fact an objective good for that kind of animal. This is why Aristotle emphasizes that thought alone cannot cause animal motion, because desire must also enter in: presumably thought is itself intentional (an animal conceptualizes an object of thought somehow), yet desire is additionally necessary, and desire is for something *good*. If the animal were not acting in pursuit of a good or a goal, then its actions would not be self-movements; they would instead be

---

[36] Curiously, plants are omitted from this discussion. Probably this is due to the fact that the discussion is focusing on movement (κίνησις) not as change in general but as local motion. A separate question could be raised about whether plants are self-movers given a broader conception of movement, and given the qualification on self-motion that Aristotle is about to provide.

random or chance spasms. I shall have more to say on this point just below, in my response to the second objection.

My account, emphasizing objective goal-directedness rather than intentionality, can be made stronger by considering the celestial spheres, which Aristotle insists have life.[37] There is a close, indeed a necessary, relation between the good for these spheres (a good related to the good of the universe as a whole) and their simple motions. As Charles Kahn, in a recent discussion of this topic, explains, "love" cannot apply literally to the living beings that are the aethereal spheres (199).[38] Having no sense-organs or limbs, these beings have no perception or imagination, and nothing like our human kind of desire; yet they *are* agents of some sort. They must, accordingly, have some altogether distinct, superior form of intentionality; not only do they act to obtain something they conceive as a good, but this is a part of their very being. In a sense they are not free, but are determined by their being, to pursue precisely the one path they do; this is because they can make no mistakes in conceptualizing or realizing their goal. Hence these beings at the higher levels of the cosmos manifest less variety of motion than lower beings like humans or animals, as Aristotle explains in the *De caelo*:

> For it is plausible that the best-conditioned of all things should have its good without action, that that which is nearest to it should achieve it by little and simple action, and that which is farther removed by a complexity of actions. We must, then, think of the action of the stars as similar to that of animals and plants. For on our earth it is man that has the greatest variety of actions—for there are many goods that man can secure; hence his actions are various and directed to ends beyond them—*while the perfectly conditioned has no need of action, since it is itself the end, and action always requires two terms, end and means.* The lower animals have less variety of action than man; and plants perhaps have little action and of one kind only. For either they have but one attainable good (as indeed man has), or, if several, each contributes directly to their ultimate good. One thing then has and enjoys the ultimate good, other things attain to it, one immediately by few steps, another by many, while yet another does not even attempt to secure it but is satisfied to reach a point not far removed from that consummation.[39] (*De cae.* II.12, 292a20–b12, emphasis mine)

For the spheres, in other words, movement always, necessarily, and directly reaches its end. The goal is built into the being of the spheres—it is an

---

[37] See references supplied by Nussbaum 1978, 133, and her discussion, 133–42.

[38] Kahn 1985a.

[39] On this passage, see ibid., 192.

actuality always actualizing. In the immediacy of this link and the simple unity of their motions, the highest living beings turn out to be surprisingly similar to the lowest ones, plants. Action in both cases leaves perception and imagination out of the picture. Plants lack perception and local motion, but their nature actualizes their goals for other kinds of self-change (growing and reproducing). But this passage should help make it clear that animals and self-movers differ from both higher and lower beings not so much because they manifest intentionality as because there is a gap between their natures and the corresponding goals.[40]

I turn now to the second objection to my account of Aristotelian teleology. My proposal explains animal self-motion as motion caused by the animal's own soul when it actualizes the animal's capacities to move toward something that is good for an animal of that kind. It is crucially important, on my interpretation, that this good be objective and not subjective. Aristotle is well aware of the vast range of sensory and locomotive abilities distributed among animals; he acknowledges that there may be a great deal of complexity in relations among animal behaviors and goals. But in all the various arrangements he surveys, he stresses that animals possess their special varieties of perception, and hence appetite, because these are for the most part effectively directed toward ends that are in fact good for the animal. This is not to deny that animals, like nature itself, can make mistakes. Aristotle explicitly admits as much in *Phys.* II.8. But this admission appears to generate a problem for my account, because in cases of mistakes it seems that animal motions are directed toward merely subjective goods, that is, toward ends that are not really good, that may in fact be harmful to them.

For example, in Houston every fall migrating cedar waxwings indulge in pyracantha berries, and tend to get drunk on the fermented fruit.[41] Subsequently, they fly poorly and may have tragic accidents. (Local newscasters advise homeowners to keep their cats indoors at this time.) Or again, fiercely territorial hummingbirds sometimes break their necks by crashing into plate-glass windows when they attack their own reflections, perceiving them as rivals. I want to say that Aristotle would hold that the waxwings eat the berries because they want food, and the hummingbirds attack their reflections because they wish to chase off rivals. And in general, getting food and fending off rivals are objective goods or natural ends that birds pursue.[42] To put the point another way, were we to reconstruct the relevant

[40] See Nussbaum 1978, 120 n. 21, for a discussion of consequences of this distinction between animals and the spheres.

[41] Linda Mourelatos and Cynthia Koch independently confirmed this for me.

[42] See Gould 1982, on the evolutionary reasons for scattered cases of maladaptive organs or behaviors as stemming from the "beanbag nature of the gene" (e.g., 17–44).

practical syllogism leading these birds to their actions, we would find that they operated with a sensible (or true) major premise, but made a perceptual mistake, giving them a false minor premise. For example, here is a reconstruction of the hummingbird's practical syllogism:

> Fending off rivals is my goal.
> (Perceiving its own image:) There's a rival!
> I'll fend him off.[43]

In other words, Aristotle would maintain that mistaken cases of animal behavior are nevertheless cases of self-motion when they can be explained in terms of a general and true teleological account, one mentioning a goal that birds in general have, such as eating berries or chasing off rivals.

Woodfield criticizes Aristotle for generating the problem I have just described for my account, objecting that he fails to offer enough distinctions here, thus "conflating" natural teleology with intentionality. Woodfield focuses on a passage from the *Physics*, commenting:

> In *Physica* Book II, 3, he says that final causes are "causes in the sense of the end or the good of the rest; for 'that for the sake of which' means what is best and the end of the things that lead up to it. (Whether we say the 'good itself' or the 'apparent good' makes no difference.)"[44] Except for the sentence in brackets, this thought could almost serve as a motto for my account. (Woodfield 1976, 206)

After criticizing Aristotle's "conflation" represented in this passage, Woodfield remarks that people continue to be confused about this matter. One source of the confusion, he diagnoses, is our "tendency to peel off intensional operators in conversation":

> We get confused, for instance, about the differences between a thing's being good, our thinking it good, and someone else's thinking it good. Hence we fail to distinguish between (a) a thing's having a purpose antecedently, before anyone thought it was good for anything, and (b) a thing's having a purpose for someone antecedently, before we thought of it as being good for anything. These and similar confusions, resulting from careless use of intensional operators, are the source of the teetering between different meanings of "in order to." (Woodfield 1976, 212)

[43] For construals of animals' practical syllogisms, see Nussbaum 1978, essay 4, 165–220; and Cooper 1975.

[44] Woodfield (1976) adds a footnote referring to *Phys.* II.3, 195a24–26 and *Meta.* Δ.2, 1013b25–27.

The passage Woodfield quotes from the *Physics* is certainly not anomalous in the Aristotelian corpus. Woodfield cites a parallel in the *Metaphysics*, and Aristotle also writes in much the same way in *De anima*:

> Now thought (νοῦς) is always right, but desire (ὄρεξις) and imagination (φαντασία) are both right and wrong. Hence, although what causes motion is the desired object (ὀρεκτόν), this may be the good or the seeming good. (ii.10, 433a26–29)

Other similar passages can be cited (e.g. *MA* 6, 700b23–29); Aristotle repeatedly says that it will not matter whether we talk of the good or of the apparent good.

How should these passages be construed? Does Aristotle place emphasis on the "apparent" or on the "good" in such passages? I want to say it is the latter. Notice how Aristotle himself puts the point in *MA* 6:

> The first mover is the object of desire and also of thought . . . in the sphere of things that can be done. *So it is a good of this sort that imparts movement*, not everything noble. For insofar as something else is done for the sake of this, and insofar as it is an end of things that are for the sake of something else, thus far it imparts movement. *And we must suppose that the apparent good ranks as a good*, and so does the pleasant (since it is an apparent good). (700b23–29, emphasis mine)

The hummingbird is a self-mover because it aims at something that is in fact a good for hummingbirds, fending off rivals. Another way to make this point is to consider the grounds on which Aristotle would *deny* that an animal is a self-mover. On the Intentionality Escape, the threat to self-motion is external efficient causation. An animal fails to move itself if it is efficiently caused to move by the external object—here, the hibiscus blossom. This is why I have said that the Intentionality Escape sets up Aristotle's problem as a problem about determinism by efficient causes. And the Intentionality Escape does not really offer a satisfactory escape from this deterministic causal series; instead, it insists on the need to look at this series in a different light, or on a different level, to explain animal motion. But on the Final Cause Escape, the interpretation that I think better captures Aristotle's view, the hummingbird would fail to be a self-mover if its flying and hovering were aimless and random, that is, if they lacked purpose. Notice how this case would be different from the case of a mistake about the good, even where such a mistake could be deadly (the bird might, for instance, die of malnutrition because it kept drinking from a feeder put out by an ignorant person who sweetened the liquid with saccharine). Even in such an extreme case, the bird's movements are still directed toward its natural end, food. But a hummingbird that has lost its senses of smell and taste, and as a result its desire for food, and that flies randomly about without trying to eat or drink, exhibits behavior with no purpose or direction. My inclination is to say that Aristotle would regard this bird as an automaton; it fails to be a self-mover because it cannot pursue its own good.

My response to the second objection has thus far focused on cases in which animals either make mistakes about or cannot pursue the good. I suggested that if an animal makes a mistake, it is still a self-mover rather than an automaton, because it is pursuing the objective good for its species. But this response might seem open to question concerning the actions of people. Aristotle surely recognizes that the distinction between the real good and the apparent good has special relevance in the context of ethics. Perhaps he even thinks that certain mistakes are ethically accountable or blameworthy. In *EN* III.4 Aristotle discusses the topic of wish (βούλησις), which he has defined as desire for the good, and he raises the very question with which I am concerned: *Should* wish be defined in this way, as desire for the good? Would it not make a difference for ethics to acknowledge that sometimes people seem *not* to desire the good? Whether because they are ignorant and confused, or perverted and evil, they may not desire the real good, but only the apparent good.

Aristotle's discussion of the problem in this passage is dialectical, making it somewhat tricky to discern his own view. He writes that on the one hand, if desire (wish) is genuinely directed to the good, "that which the man who does not choose aright wishes for is not an object of wish (for if it is to be so, it must also be good; but it was, if it so happened, bad)" (*EN* III.4, 1113a16–18). But on the other hand, if it is only the apparent good that is the object of wish, then "there is no natural object of wish, but only what seems so to each man. Now different things appear so to different people, and, if it so happens, even contrary things" (1113a21–22).

I take it that Aristotle clearly wants to reject the second horn of this dilemma, because he thinks that there *is* a natural object of human wish and desire; remember that the opening of the *Nicomachean Ethics* refers to the good as "that at which all things aim" (*EN* I.1, 1094a2–3). A final end for humans structures all our desires and choices. But can Aristotle accept the first horn of the dilemma—that if this is so, that is, if all wish or desire is really for the good, then we must somehow discount or redescribe the desire of the confused or evil person? Aristotle's resolution of this problem is hard to understand. He writes:

> If these consequences are unpleasing, are we to say that absolutely and in truth the good is the object of wish, but for each person the apparent good; that that

which is in truth an object of wish is an object of wish to the good man, while any chance thing may be so to the bad man, as in the case of bodies also the things that are in truth wholesome are wholesome for bodies which are in good condition, while for those that are diseased other things are wholesome? (*EN* III.4, 1113a23–29)

Aristotle seems to be saying that humans do indeed fit into the overall teleological scheme of things by having a species-end. This is the good that a healthy person, a person with a clear mind and a good character, will naturally pursue. When an unhealthy person pursues something else, that end may be bad in itself for humans, and good only in relation to his diseased nature. Aristotle himself remarks:

Each state of character has its own ideas of the noble and the pleasant, and perhaps the good man differs from others most by seeing the truth in each class of things, being as it were the norm and measure of them. In most cases the error seems to be due to pleasure; for it appears a good when it is not. We therefore choose the pleasant as a good, and avoid pain as an evil. (*EN* III.4, 1113a32–b1)

For example, the healthy athlete enjoys and pursues strength through practice and good performance, but the diseased athlete enjoys and pursues the results of steroid injections. And the honest stockbroker enjoys and pursues clear thinking about a deal, whereas the evil broker enjoys plotting details of a shady takeover. In other words, when people pursue something (especially some sort of pleasure) as good that is not in fact good, for us to explain why it is not good requires placing it in relation to the good person's selection of a true good. These human cases can be analyzed in much the same way I suggested earlier for the cases of self-harming bird behavior, as cases involving false or mistaken minor premises of practical syllogisms. The hummingbird's attack on its reflection was purposive because it was an instance of the behavior pattern of fending off rivals, so it could be related to an actual hummingbird good. Similarly, the athlete and the stockbroker aim at real human goods, physical strength or professional success, but in mistaken ways.

If we could not similarly describe vicious or misguided human behavior as directed toward *some* human good, it would appear self-destructive to the point of purposelessness.[45] Consider, for example, a person who has a

---

[45] Compare Anscombe's (1969) discussion of the limits on what we can accept as a person's claim about what he wants—whether, for instance, we can understand someone who claims to "want a saucer of mud" (70–72). I think Aristotle would similarly dismiss a person's claim to be aiming at unhappiness as the goal of life.

certain compulsion, a behavioral tic or a seizure. Perhaps it is true that without desiring it, finding it pleasant, or thinking of it as good in any way, an autistic child bangs its head against the wall. Would Aristotle countenance calling such behavior self-motion? I want to answer no, because we have passed beyond a certain limit here. Such behavior fails to satisfy either of the two requirements I described for self-motion. Clearly the end to which it is directed is not a human good. Moreover, what I have tried to get at by calling this behavior compulsive, Aristotle would probably indicate by saying that it was done through force, rather than by the child itself. Having no final cause, it is random and purposeless; it does not manifest the child's own capacity for self-movement.

Still, there are other cases that may be problematic. In the next chapter of the *Nicomachean Ethics* (III.5) Aristotle argues against the view that no one is in control of the appearing (1114a32–b25). Thus, whereas presumably the cedar waxwings I mentioned earlier do not get drunk on purpose, some humans might. Because the humans bear more responsibility for forming character, and have more capacity to realize what they are doing, Aristotle blames them in a way he would not blame the birds.[46] Might not a person be wicked in the sense of pursuing something bad as an explicitly formulated end? For purposes of ethical evaluations, it would seem critically important to be able to assert that wicked or conflicted people are worse than people who merely make mistakes or who are damaged so that they cannot desire the good. People who deliberately choose things that are evil nevertheless must be self-movers, for otherwise they would have no responsibility for their actions. Aristotle finds such a conclusion repugnant and seems concerned with warding it off and arguing that people are not compelled by what they desire: "It is absurd to make external circumstances responsible, and not oneself, as being easily caught by such attractions" (*EN* III.1, 1110b13–15).

Nevertheless, I believe that Aristotle says things that qualify this conclusion. For one thing, he seems to think that there is a serious sense in which the actions of a person who has established a vicious character are not strictly speaking that person's *self*-motions, because they are no longer under his control.[47] In addition, a wicked person goes wrong by failing to recognize the nature of the real human good. Even wickedness is a kind of mistake,[48] a falling away from natural good rather than a pursuit of some

---

[46] Nussbaum (1978, 245) has also discussed problems raised by the *Nicomachean Ethics* discussion.

[47] *EN* III.5, 1114a15–21. On this point, see discussion in Freeland 1982, esp. 19.

[48] Another way to put this is to say that the wicked person has a false minor premise about what constitutes happiness.

natural, objective evil as an alternative goal. Notice how Aristotle puts this point in *EN* vii.8: "For virtue and vice respectively preserve and destroy the first principle, and in actions the final cause is the first principle."[49]

I have argued that for Aristotle, animals are self-movers only when they are caused by their own souls to act for the sake of something objectively good. There is no doubt that animal motions occur within a broader context of efficient causes, and that these motions may be influenced by external environmental as well as internal physiological factors. Surrounding efficient causal chains also include special occurrences in animal souls, the experiencing of goals or purposes, and these are phenomena exhibiting intentionality. But intentionality, at least as Furley conceives it in his article "Self-Movers," does not suffice to account for self-motion, because Furley writes as if some animals lack it. In addition, intentionality cannot account for goal-directedness, because it could easily enough be present (in perception, for example) but unrelated to perception or thought about goals in particular. I have argued that animal intentionality alone cannot account for the important facts that objective goals do exist and operate within Aristotle's universe, and that animal movements are effectively directed toward their natural ends.

Supporters of the Intentionality Escape, I have suggested, want to say that animals may be regarded as self-movers because the factor of intentionality (which amounts in essence to their having imagination) somehow frees them from the deterministic operation of efficient or mechanical causes. It does so, supposedly, by enabling the animals to see certain things *as* goals or goods. It seems probable that proponents of the Intentionality Escape view think that the efficient causal chain is the only one possible, and that intentionality somehow, mysteriously, interrupts it. (Recall quotes I cited above suggesting that imagination permits a "free" response.) This amounts to saying that self-motion introduces indeterminism into the causal order.[50] On my view, however, the issue of self-motion in *Phys.* viii really concerns the compatibility of final with efficient causation. If we interpret the Intentionality Escape as making the somewhat weaker claim

---

[49] ἡ γὰρ ἀρετὴ καὶ μοχθηρία τὴν ἀρχὴν ἣ μὲν φθείρει ἣ δὲ σῴζει, ἐν δὲ ταῖς πράξεσι τὸ οὗ ἕνεκα ἀρχή (1151a15–16).

[50] In *Meta.* E.3 Aristotle argues against the view that the outcomes of all human acts are determined in advance. On a reasonable construal of this passage, Aristotle's worry turns out to be about whether everything we do is determined by *final*—and not *efficient*—causes; see Frede 1985. Thus Aristotle's point in this chapter of the *Metaphysics* provides a complement and support for my construal of self-motion as objective goal-directedness.

that we must utilize a distinct kind of *explanation* to understand animal self-motion, this leaves unanswered questions about what *in the real world* necessitates multiple kinds of explanation—or about how explanations, especially teleological ones, make contact with reality.[51]

[51] This is without prejudging the issue of how final causes are "real" in Aristotle's metaphysics; a variety of proposals have been made in the recent literature. See Cooper 1982, 1987; Gotthelf 1989a, 1989b; and Kahn 1985a.

CHAPTER 4

Self-Movement and External Causation

SUSAN SAUVÉ MEYER

ARISTOTLE maintains that we are the origins of our voluntary actions (*EN* III.1, 1111a22–24; *EE* II.6, 1222b19–20). I would like to consider a challenge to this claim that calls into question his account of self-movement in the *Physics*. Aristotle's response shows that his conception of voluntary action is defensible within the general framework that he invokes to explain change in the natural world.

1. ORIGINS AND EXTERNAL CAUSES

In *EE* II.6, Aristotle indicates that being the origin of an action involves more than simply playing a role in the sequence of causes that brings it about. The causal role an origin plays must not be subordinate to that of any other cause. He makes this point by drawing an analogy with "causation" in geometry:

> If the fact that a triangle contains two right angles entails that a quadrilateral contains four, then the cause (αἴτιον) of this [namely, that the quadrilateral contains four right angles] is clearly the fact that the triangle contains two right angles. . . . And if nothing else is the cause of the triangle's being like this, then this [namely, the triangle's having two right angles] is a kind of origin (ἀρχή) and cause of what comes after. (1222b31–41)

Aristotle here states an instance of the general principle: if *A* is the cause (αἴτιον) of *B*, but *C* is the cause of *A*, then *A* is not the origin (ἀρχή) of *B*. His example invokes formal rather than efficient causes, and he does not indicate here exactly how the principle applies in the domain of efficient causation, where human beings are the origins of actions. His account of self-movement in *Phys.* VIII shows us how it applies to efficient causation.

A self-mover is a kind of efficient cause, for "mover" (κινοῦν) is one of

I would like to thank Sarah Broadie and Mary Louise Gill for helpful comments and advice.

Aristotle's ways of referring to the efficient cause (*Phys.* ii.7, 198a19, a24). Only a self-mover can properly be called the origin (ἀρχή) of an outcome:

Indeed, if we had to investigate whether the cause (αἴτιον) of the movement—that is, the origin (ἀρχή)—is what moves itself or what is moved by something else, everyone would say the former is. (*Phys.* viii.5, 257a27–30; cf. vii.1, 241b34–37)

A self-mover has this special causal status because, unlike a moved mover, it does not cause movement (κινεῖν) by itself being moved to do so by anything else:

The stick moves the stone and is moved by the hand which is moved by the man. But he does not do so by being moved by anything else (τῷ ὑπ' ἄλλου κινεῖσθαι). (*Phys.* viii.5, 256a6–8; cf. a21)

In other words, a self-mover is properly called the origin of its movement because it is the efficient cause of that movement, and nothing else is the efficient cause of its causing that movement.

Aristotle proceeds to indicate that the aspect of the self-mover playing this crucial causal role fails to be moved by anything else because the moving (κινεῖν) it does is not itself a movement:

So, of the whole, one aspect must be unmoved (ἀκίνητον) and another will be moved. Only in this way can there be something that is self-moved. And since the whole moves itself, the one aspect will move (κινήσει) and the other will be moved (κινήσεται). (258a1–4; cf. vii.2, 243a14)

The aspect of the self-mover that is "unmoved" (ἀκίνητον) moves (κινεῖν) the aspect that is moved. This "unmoved mover" (ἀκίνητον κινοῦν, 258a7, a9) moves the moved aspect by means of a third thing (ᾧ κινεῖ) (256b14–15, cf. b20), which is a moved mover (256b16–20).

Let us identify these three aspects of the voluntary agent offered as an example of a self-mover at the beginning of *Phys.* viii.5 (256a6–8, quoted above). The man is the self-mover, and his hand is the aspect in which he is moved. At *De an.* iii.10, 433b13–18, and *MA* 6, 701a1, Aristotle tells us that the man's desire is "that by means of which he moves himself" (ᾧ κινεῖ). These chapters also indicate that the object of desire (ὀρεκτόν [*MA* 6, 700b23–24]) or "practical good" (πρακτὸν ἀγαθόν [*De an.* iii.10, 433b15–16]) is the unmoved mover. It is not immediately obvious how the object of the man's desire is an aspect of the self-moving agent. An aspect of the agent to which it is clearly related, however, is the disposition (ἕξις) of the various faculties of desire, which in the case of rational agents is their state of character (ἠθικὴ ἕξις). (The object of desire is intimately related to this disposition because the object of a desire is the agent's goal [τέλος], and our ethical dispositions determine our goals [*EN* vi.2, 1139a31–35;

vi.13, 1145a4–6; *EE* ii.11, 1227b12–38].) In *EN* ii.5, while defining states of character as dispositions of our capacities for desire,[1] Aristotle implies that these dispositions are the unmoved mover. Though our faculties of desire are capacities for being moved, our states of character are not respects in which we are moved:

> In addition, according to the feelings, we are said to be moved, while according to the virtues and vices we are not said to be moved, but rather disposed in a certain way (διακεῖσθαί πως). (1106a4–6)

Given that an unmoved mover is something that causes change without itself being subject to change, it would not be unreasonable of Aristotle to claim that such a disposition is an unmoved mover of the agent's faculty of desire. An ethical disposition clearly has causal efficacy over the agent's faculties of desire; it determines at what objects and to what extent they will be exercised. Just as clearly, its efficacy is not of the sort that is exerted in a movement or change. A disposition of a set of capacities is not a further capacity added to the set, which then sets about regulating the exercise of the capacities in the way that, for example, the conductor regulates the activities of the different musicians in an orchestra. Rather, the disposition is a capacity of a higher order than those of which it is a disposition. It is more like that acquired by two violinists, a violist, and a cellist when they become a string quartet. This disposition is not acquired by adding a fifth member, but by accustoming the capacities of the individual members to be exercised as an ensemble. It is acquired by the four musicians by playing together. Similarly, the disposition that is a state of character is acquired by exercising, in a particular way, the capacities of which it is a disposition— the capacities for feeling and desire. The disposition of a set of capacities is a standing condition that exercises its causal efficacy over these capacities whenever they operate in their normal and unimpeded way. The disposition of an agent's capacities for feeling and desire is "at work" whenever the animal is awake. It does not move (κινεῖν) the particular occurrent desires, by means of which the animal moves itself, by producing a separate motion (κίνησις) that precipitates the desire. Rather, its causal efficacy is continual, both when a particular capacity for desire is exercised and when it is not.

Let us therefore proceed on the assumption that the aspect of the self-moving agent that is the unmoved mover is this disposition. We are now in a position to articulate the challenge to Aristotle's claim that we are the origins of our actions.

---

[1] Aristotle explicitly says here that they are dispositions of our faculties for feelings (πάθη), but he offers the list of these faculties in enumeration of the capacities of the soul he initially introduces in *EN* i.13, 1102b30 as the faculty of desire.

2. A PROBLEM FOR ARISTOTLE'S CLAIMS ABOUT SELF-MOTION

In claiming that we are the origins of our actions, Aristotle implies that we are self-movers, and this in turn implies that nothing external to us moves us to have the desires by means of which we move ourselves. He seems to think that our moral character (the set of the various dispositions of our faculties of desire) constitutes the internal aspect that causes these desires. Hence he is committed to denying that external objects cause our characters to cause them. But how, given Aristotle's own conception of states of character, can he consistently deny this? On his view, a moral character is a fully determinate disposition to act and react in certain ways in certain circumstances. For example, it determines at what objects one will become angry, how angry one will get, and what, if anything, one will do as a result of being angry.[2] So the presence of an object toward which one is disposed to be angry in a particular way is sufficient to precipitate that particular manifestation of anger. It is natural, in English, to refer to these objects as the things that "make" us angry,[3] and Aristotle uses an equivalent locution in Greek: these objects of anger are the ἐμποιοῦντα (inducers) of our anger (EN ιν.5, 1125b30). Given the causal influence of these external objects, how can Aristotle deny that they move us to have the desires on which we act?[4]

One way out of this problem would be for Aristotle to withdraw the claim that voluntary agents are self-moved. There are a number of passages in the De anima, the De motu animalium, and the Physics where Aristotle appears to some commentators to renege on this claim, and to allow that animals (and hence voluntary agents) are in fact moved by the external objects that precipitate the occurrent desires on which they act. So let us first turn to consider these passages, which, on closer examination, will turn out to make no such admission.

In MA 6, 700b24–29, and De an. ιιι.10, 433a17–21, Aristotle identifies the unmoved mover of the animal's voluntary movement as the object of desire (ὀρεκτόν). But in so claiming, he does not allow that an external

---

[2] EN ιι.5, 1105b25–28; ιν.5, 1125b31–1126a3. The latter passage, which includes the activity χαλεπαίνειν (to be violent or difficult) in the domain of the exercise of anger, indicates that the disposition concerning anger determines what actions one does while angry, not simply how angry one feels. Aristotle generally includes both feelings and actions in the domain of the exercise of the capacities for feeling.

[3] Or make us sad, or move us to pity.

[4] My discussion of self-movement is greatly indebted to David Furley's "Self-Movers" (reprinted in this volume). The solution I offer to the problem of self-movement is in certain respects quite similar to his. The significant difference is that my solution shows why Aristotle is entitled to deny that the self-mover is moved by external objects, whereas Furley (14) suggests that Aristotle had best abandon this denial.

perceptual stimulus moves the self-mover to have a particular desire,[5] for such a stimulus is not the object of desire. Consider the scenario in which, for example, an unlucky lamb wanders into the visual field of a lion, thereby triggering in the lion the desire to pursue and eat it. The object of the lion's desire (ὀρεκτόν) is not the lamb, but eating the lamb. The object of the desire is its goal (τέλος [cf. *MA* 6, 700b15, b25–29; *De an.* III.10, 433a15–17]), which is a future state of affairs desired by the lion. Though the external object, the lamb, may be the object of the lion's pursuit, it is not the object of the lion's desire.[6]

Second, there are two passages in *Phys.* VIII where Aristotle appears to allow that external objects move (κινεῖν) the self-mover's desire.[7] In *Phys.* VIII.2 Aristotle claims that animal self-locomotion is preceded by bodily changes that are due to external factors, and he explicitly claims that these bodily changes move (κινεῖν) the animal's faculty of desire:

> It appears that the animal moves itself from a state of rest with nothing from the outside having moved it. But this is false. For we see that there is always in movement some natural part of the animal, and the cause of this movement is not the animal but presumably the environment. And we do not say that the animal moves itself with respect to every movement, but only in respect to locomotion. So nothing prevents, and presumably it is necessary, that many movements are engendered in the body by the environment, and some of these move (κινεῖν) the animal's thought or desire, which in turn moves the whole animal. This is what happens, for example, in sleep. There occurs in the body some movement, although it is not a perceptual movement, and the animal wakes up. (253a9–20)

Aristotle here allows that changes in the animal produced by external factors can move (κινεῖν) the faculty of thought and desire, which is the faculty by means of which the animal moves itself (a17–18).[8] But he insists

---

[5] So Furley (8–9) interprets these passages.

[6] We are misled into identifying the object of desire as the lamb, rather than eating the lamb, because of the spatial metaphors for desire, in particular the metaphors of the hunt and the archer. But it is just as misleading to call the lamb the object of the lion's desire as it is to call the target the object of the archer's desire. The archer desires not the target, but rather to hit the target. The temptation to identify the prey and the target as the ὀρεκτόν is considerably lessened if we pay attention to the fact that Aristotle says the ὀρεκτόν in these cases is the πρακτὸν ἀγαθόν (*De an.* III.10, 433b16). A πρακτόν is something that can be done. Although we may be misled by the metaphor of the hunt to think the lamb is the ὀρεκτόν (object of desire), it is not so easy to think that it is the πρακτὸν ἀγαθόν. Though the lamb is something that we might colloquially say the lion desires, it is certainly not something the lion can do.

[7] Furley discusses both passages in detail.

[8] *De an.* III.10, 433a10–30, indicates that thought along with desire is involved in self-movement.

(a19) that these changes are not perceptual changes. They are the changes that go on during sleep, and that can cause the animal to wake up (a19–20).

In *Phys.* VIII.6, in a context that refers back to the present passage (259b1–7), Aristotle describes these changes in more detail:

> We must note that animals move themselves with respect to only one motion, and even this one not strictly (οὐ κυρίως). For the cause is not from the animal itself. Rather, there are other movements natural to animals that are not due to themselves: for example, growth, diminution, and respiration. Animals are subject to these movements when they are at rest and not experiencing self-motion. And the cause of this is the environment and many things that enter from the outside. For example, the cause of some of these movements is food. When it is being digested animals sleep, but when it is distributed they wake up and move themselves. The first origin is from the outside. (259b6–14)

The external changes that affect the animal are those associated with, for example, digestion. Digestion, when it is completed, wakens the animal. Wakening is the activity that Aristotle in *Phys.* VIII.2 calls moving (κινεῖν) the animal's desire (253a17). But to move (κινεῖν) the animal's desire in this way is simply to activate the animal's perceptual and conative capacities. This "movement" of desire differs from the movement of desire whereby the lion is moved to pursue the lamb. Aristotle cites an external cause only for the fact that the animal's faculty of desire is active at all—that is, for the animal's being awake. He does not mention the changes that subsequently precipitate the awakened animal to form a particular occurrent desire that causes a particular self-movement. Aristotle does *not* claim that the lion is moved by an external cause to have the particular occurrent desire that moves it to pursue the lamb.

Aristotle denies here that animals move themselves strictly (κυρίως; 259b7) because, as in the corresponding passage in *Phys.* VIII.2, he is concerned to defend a very general principle about change that is important to his overall argument in *Phys.* VIII. This is the principle that, for any change that begins at some point in time, there must have been some prior change that brought about the conditions sufficient for it—for example, by bringing the active and passive powers into proximity so that they necessarily interact to produce the change in question (*Phys.* VIII.1, 251a23–b10; VIII.7, 260b1–4; cf. VIII.2, 253a2–3). This is one of the principles to which Aristotle appeals in his arguments for the eternity of change. His denial that animals move themselves strictly simply reflects his view that self-movement is not a counterexample to this principle. Self-movement, like any other change, presupposes prior change.

Aristotle does not, in these passages, undermine or withdraw his claim that animals are self-movers. He does not allow that an external object of perception that precipitates a particular occurrent desire is the mover of that desire. But these passages do not enlighten us any further about how Aristotle can consistently deny this claim. Indeed, we might formulate the objection by appeal to the very principle about change that he defends in these passages. The principle must apply to all noneternal changes—including the occurrent desires that, according to the account of self-movement, are the movements by means of which the animal moves itself. So we can ask, of the occurrent desire that moves the lion to pursue the lamb, what prior change accounts for the fact that at time t_1 this desire was not occurring, but at time t_2 it was? The answer, presumably, is: the change whereby the unlucky lamb entered the perceptual field of the lion. How then, we must ask Aristotle, can it fail to be the case that the lamb (or at any rate, something external to the lion) moves (κινεῖν) the lion to desire the lamb?

3. SELF-MOVEMENT AND CAUSAL DETERMINATION

The Aristotelian exegete Alexander of Aphrodisias suggests a solution to this problem—at least for rational agents. Aristotle insists that a self-mover's actions must be up to it to do and not to do (cf. *Phys.* VIII.4, 255a7–10). In his *De fato* (XI–XV), Alexander offers an account of what it is for an action to be up to us in this way. He attributes to Aristotle the view that only the actions of rational agents are up to them, because unlike nonrational animals, they need not yield to perceptual impressions, the impulses to action induced in them by external objects (Alex. *De fato* 183.32–184.1). The capacity for reason allows us to deliberate about whether to act in accordance with such externally produced impulses (178.17–25, 179.8–12, 180.4–7). In exactly the same circumstances, both internal and external, it is possible for a rational agent to choose the opposite of what his deliberation actually decides upon (179.12–18, 180.20–21, 181.5–6, 185.8–9). Alexander's interpretation in effect allows that the disposition of our nonrational desires is perfectly determinate, but denies that the disposition of our rational capacity for making decisions is. Our decisions are caused by our faculty of reason, but there is no set of conditions sufficient to determine whether that faculty will opt for or against a given alternative.

Alexander appears to arrive at this interpretation by connecting Aristotle's account of deliberation (*EN* III.3; *EE* II.10) with a distinction he introduces in *Meta.* Θ.2, 1046b4–24, between one-sided and two-sided capacities. According to Aristotle, fire's capacity to heat and its capacity for upward travel are one-sided capacities. Examples of two-sided capacities include skills such as medicine, which, though it is a capacity for causing health, enables the doctor to cause both sickness and health (1046b6–15). Unlike fire's capacity to heat, which makes fire able only to heat, not also able not to heat, the possession of a two-sided capacity makes one able to do opposites (1046b23). At *Meta.* Θ.5, 1048a3–7, Aristotle says that when the possessor of a one-sided capacity is in the conditions appropriate for the exercise of its capacity, it is necessary that that capacity be exercised. By contrast, he claims that when the possessor of a two-sided capacity is in the conditions appropriate for the exercise of its capacity, it is not necessary that the capacity be exercised (1048a5–10). What is needed in addition is the desire or decision, and when these are added, it is necessary that the capacity be exercised in the way desire or decision indicates (1048a10–15). These remarks of Aristotle indicate at most that he thinks a capacity is two-sided if its exercise is contingent on the exercise of the agent's capacity for desire or decision. They imply nothing about how the agent's desire or decision is determined. According to Alexander, however, the decision that determines how the capacity will be exercised is itself the expression of a two-sided capacity,[9] and he takes this to imply that its exercise is not determined by preexisting causes. But this goes well beyond what Aristotle's account of two-sided capacities says or implies.

Alexander's proposed solution to the problem of self-movement denies one of the premises that generate the apparent difficulty. He attributes to Aristotle the view that the external stimuli of desire do not in fact precipitate the desire with which the rational agent moves himself; our states of character, together with the circumstances in which we act, do not completely determine our actions. Although the evidence to which Alexander appeals does not support his interpretation, one might still suppose that something very much like his interpretation must be correct. One might suppose that, in claiming that the self-mover is not moved to cause itself to move, Aristotle must mean that there are no preexisting conditions sufficient to bring about the act of self-movement. Call this the indeterminist interpretation of the unmoved mover.[10] It runs into serious difficulty if we consider it in the light of one of the uses to which Aristotle puts the distinction between unmoved and moved movers.

The central claim of Aristotle's physical and biological works is that the nature of an organism is its form, more than its matter (*Phys.* II.1, 193b6–7). He defends this thesis in a variety of ways, sometimes by claiming that the formal cause of the organism is its unmoved mover, whereas its material

---

[9] For a detailed discussion of whether decision is the exercise of a two-sided capacity, see Freeland 1982.

[10] Alexander insists that his view does not entail that there be uncaused change (ἀναίτιον κίνησιν [*De fato* 185.9]). The agent's decision is not uncaused, he claims, because it is caused by the agent. But in insisting that the preexisting causes (προκαταβεβλημένας αἰτίας [180.27–28]) leave open both the decision and its alternative, he is committed to the view that there is no cause for the particular decision the agent makes. For this reason, I classify his view as indeterminist.

causes are only its moved movers.[11] In making these claims, Aristotle expresses the view that the natural changes in an organism, like an animal's self-locomotion, are cases of self-change. The distinctive feature of natural change, Aristotle insists, is that it is internally caused.[12]

Once we see that the distinction between unmoved movers and moved movers applies to the distinction between form and matter, the indeterminist interpretation of the unmoved mover runs into a serious difficulty. The problem arises from the fact that form and matter are relative notions for Aristotle (*Phys.* II.2, 194b8–9). The matter of a bed is wood (II.1, 193a9–12), but the property of being wood is itself formal relative to its elemental constituents (193a17–22). This relativity of form and matter holds for both artifacts and organisms. For example, the powers that a bodily part has insofar as it is a hand are formal relative to the capacities of its immediate constituents; but the powers that it has qua hand are material relative to the form of the whole organism of which the hand is a part.[13] Given the relativity of matter and form, the same particular capacity can be both material and formal. If, as Aristotle claims, formal capacities are unmoved movers, and material capacities are moved movers, then the indeterminist account of unmoved movers has the unhappy consequence that the exercise of certain capacities of an organism would both have sufficient antecedent conditions (insofar as the capacity is material) and lack sufficient antecedent conditions (insofar as the capacity is formal). But this consequence is impossible. We therefore have good reason to be skeptical of the indeterminist interpretation of the unmoved mover. Aristotle's claim, that the agent is unmoved in causing himself to move, does not mean that there are no preexisting causes sufficient to precipitate that activity.

4. SELF-MOVEMENT AND AGENT CAUSATION

A different interpretation that proposes to solve the problem takes Aristotle's account of self-movement to concern what I will call "agent

[11] Form as unmoved mover: *Phys.* II.7, 198a33–b4 and *GC* I.3, 318a1–8; matter as moved mover: *GC* II.9, 335b29–31, 336a1–12. I defend this interpretation of these passages in Sauvé 1987, 176–77.

[12] In the contexts in *Phys.* VIII where Aristotle describes the external antecedents of self-locomotion, he appears to endorse the denial that natural changes, such as growth, nutrition, and respiration, are self-motions (253a14–15, 259b6–7). These denials, however, are simply *ad hominem*. Aristotle addresses opponents who think animal self-locomotion is a case of change originating *ex nihilo*, but do not take this view of natural processes. At *Phys.* VII.1, 241b35–38, he allows that something is a self-changer if it has in itself the origin of its change, which is the definitive feature of a natural thing identified in *Phys.* II.1 (192b13–32). In *De an.* II.1, he defines a living thing as what is nourished, grows, and diminishes "through itself" (δι' αὑτοῦ [412a14]).

[13] *GA* I.1, 715a9–11; cf. *Meta.* H.4, 1044a15–25; *GA* II.1, 731b18–27; *Phys.* II.1, 193a17–21.

causation." This interpretation focuses on the fact that in cases of self-movement, Aristotle claims that a substance causes an event. In the example of self-movement described at the beginning of *Phys.* VIII.5, the man (a substance) causes his hand to move (an event), and this event in turn causes a sequence of events: the movements of the stick and the stone. At the beginning of this sequence there is a cause that is not an event but a substance—the man. According to the theory of agent causation, substances do not exercise their causality in events, and this is why their causality is not due to antecedent events. If Aristotle's account of self-movers is an account of agent causation, then it attributes to agents causal powers of a kind completely different from those at work in the rest of nature. In the rest of nature, events are causes, but in cases of agency, a substance, not an event, initiates a sequence of events.[14]

An immediate problem for the interpretation of Aristotelian self-movement as agent causation is that, for Aristotle, efficient causes in general are substances rather than events. In his general account of efficient causation, his examples of efficient causes are almost invariably substances: the father, the advisor, the sculptor.[15] In the example of self-movement that opens *Phys.* VIII.5, not only the self-mover but also all the moved movers are substances. The man moves his hand, his hand moves the stick, and the stick moves the stone. Since all the movers in the sequence are substances, Aristotle cannot think the self-mover has the special causal status it does simply because it is a substance.

Moreover, contrary to the doctrine of agent causation, Aristotle does not deny that the causal activity of a substance is an event. An efficient cause is identified in terms of its capacity for causing change (cf. *Phys.* II.3, 195a6, 195b21–25). This capacity (δύναμις) is an "origin of change in something else or in some other aspect of itself" (*Meta.* Δ.12, 1019a15–20), and it is by exercising this capacity for causing change that the efficient cause produces the thing of which it is the efficient cause. For example, the builder (οἰκοδόμος) is the efficient cause of the house (οἰκία) in virtue of possessing the capacity of housebuilding (οἰκοδομική), and produces the house by exercising that capacity (*Phys.* II.3, 195b16–21). The exercise of a capacity is an event. Therefore, insofar as a self-mover is an efficient cause, we should expect it to exercise its causality in an event—the event that is the exercise of the capacity in terms of which it is identified.

Of course, the defender of agent causation will point out that the self-

---

[14] This view is developed by Chisholm ([1964] 1982), who calls causation by a substance "immanent causation" and causation by an event "transeunt causation." He explicitly takes Aristotelian self-movement to be an instance of immanent causation (30).

[15] *Phys.* II.3, 194b30–32, 195a21–22, a32–35, II.7, 198a25–27; *Meta.* Δ.2, 1013a30–32. Occasionally he refers to events as efficient causes: the invasion is the cause of a war (*Po. an.* II.11, 94a37; *Phys.* II.7, 198a19–21), an insult the cause of a fight (*Meta.* Δ.1, 1013a10). In the latter examples, Aristotle refers to the causal activity of the substance that makes it the efficient cause. For different views on this question, see Fine 1987 and Annas 1982.

mover's causation of its desire is, on Aristotle's view, not a movement (κίνησις). This feature distinguishes the causal action of the self-mover from that of the other efficient causes in the sequence, which cause movement (κινεῖν) by being in movement (κινούμενον) themselves. So, the defender of agent causation may conclude, self-movers, unlike moved movers, do not exercise their causality in events; therefore the bothersome question about the cause of their causal action does not arise.

But would it follow from the fact that the act of self-movement is not a movement or change (κίνησις) that it is not an event? Aristotle regularly distinguishes between two kinds of exercise or actuality (ἐντελέχεια) of a causal power: a change or movement (κίνησις) and an activity (ἐνέρ-γεια).[16] In denying that the actuality of the unmoved mover is a movement or change (κίνησις), Aristotle presumably implies that it is an activity (ἐνέργεια). But clearly the act of self-movement, even if it is an "activity" rather than a movement or change, is the exercise of a causal power, and for this reason it would seem to count as an event. And if it is an event, presumably we may ask what change precipitated its occurrence. A defender of the agent-causation interpretation might respond that Aristotle, in claiming that everything that is in motion is moved by something (*Phys.* VIII.4, 256a3), does not claim that every activity (ἐνέργεια) is caused by something, but only that every movement or change (κίνησις) is. This response is unsatisfying, however, for it does not explain why the features that distinguish an activity from a movement should exempt "activity" (ἐνέργεια) from the principle that everything that happens happens as the result of the causal activity of something. Although Aristotle in *Phys.* VIII states the principle in a form that applies explicitly only to movement or change (κίνησις), the very general thesis about change that he defends[17] seems to commit him to the stronger view that something must be responsible for the fact that at one time the agent is not exercising this faculty, and at another time he is. Call this exercise something other than change if you will, but the principle surely implies that some change preceded its occurrence. Agent causation therefore fails to provide a satisfactory model for understanding Aristotle's account of self-motion.

5. ARISTOTLE'S DISTINCTION BETWEEN CAUSES

The problem about self-motion that we have been considering is generated by the assumption that if there is a set of antecedent conditions sufficient for the exercise of a capacity, such as the agent's capacity for desire, then we

---

[16] *Meta.* Θ.1, 1045b34–1046a6; *De an.* II.5, 417a21–b28.

[17] The principle that, for any change that begins at some point in time, there must have been some prior change that brought about the conditions sufficient for that change (*Phys.* VIII.1, 251a23–b10; VIII.7, 260b1–4; cf. VIII.2, 253a2–3).

must accept that the capacity has been moved by something in those conditions. Both the indeterminist and the agent-causation interpretations accept, and indeed are motivated by, this assumption. They propose to solve the problem by in effect denying that such sufficient antecedent conditions exist. An alternative approach to the problem would be to challenge that assumption. This is what the ancient Stoics did. They were rigorous determinists; yet they insisted that our actions are up to us. They defended this conclusion by making a distinction between causes.

In response to the claim that external stimuli cause our actions in a way that makes our actions not up to us, the Stoic Chrysippus drew a distinction between two types of cause. There are on the one hand, he claimed, "perfect and principal" causes, and on the other hand, "auxiliary" causes. The external stimulus that "makes" the agent have a particular occurrent desire is only the auxiliary cause of his action, whereas the agent is the perfect and principal cause. Only if the external stimulus were the perfect and principal cause of the agent's response would it follow that his action is not up to him. Chrysippus illustrates the point of this distinction by appealing to the different reactions a cone and a cylinder would have to the same push from an external force: the cylinder rolls in a straight line, whereas the cone rolls in a circle. The external push is only the auxiliary cause of the cone's or cylinder's activity; the nature of the cone or cylinder is the perfect and principal cause. Similarly, the external object (e.g., a pot of gold) whose perception "makes" the vicious person decide to steal it will not have this same effect on the virtuous person. Hence it is only the auxiliary cause of the vicious person's theft, whereas the person's vice is its perfect and principal cause.[18]

Does Aristotle have a distinction between causes to which he might appeal in a similar argument? He does. In his natural philosophy he regularly distinguishes between intrinsic (καθ' αὐτό) and accidental (κατὰ συμβεβηκός) causes (e.g., *Phys.* II.5, 196b24–29). An accidental cause is not properly attributed causal responsibility for a result.[19] But not every set of conditions sufficient to precipitate a given result contains an intrinsic cause. For example, the creditor and debtor who meet in the marketplace, when neither intended this result or had any knowledge that it would occur, meet by accident; the meeting has no intrinsic cause (*Phys.* II.5, 196b33–197a14). Aristotle explicitly applies the distinction to the case of agency, indicating in *EN* v.8 that the voluntary agent is the intrinsic cause of his action, not simply its accidental cause (1135a17–28). So perhaps Aristotle might appeal to this distinction to defend his claims about self-

[18] Cicero *De fato* 40–43; Aulus Gellius *Noct. Att.* 7.2.6–13.

[19] *Po. An.* I.4, 73b10–16; *Phys.* II.3, 195b3–4; VIII.4, 255b24–27; *Meta.* Δ.30, 1025a25–27. I discuss in more detail the application of this distinction to Aristotle's claims about moral responsibility in Meyer 1994, chs. 4 and 6.

movement. Perhaps he thinks that the external antecedents of the self-mover's activity are only its accidental causes, and for this reason denies that the self-mover is moved to act by these external factors. In the final section of this essay I will evaluate whether such an argument can respond to the problem about self-movement. But first I will argue that we have reason to attribute such an argument to Aristotle.

Aristotle nowhere claims explicitly that the external antecedents of desire are only the accidental causes of the desires they precipitate. His discussion of the causes of elemental motion in *Phys.* VIII.4 gives us reason to think, however, that such an assumption underlies his claim that the self-mover is not moved by external causes. Aristotle discusses at length the causes of the natural movements of the elements because he thinks these movements present an apparent counterexample to his thesis that everything in motion is moved by something (254b33–256a3). The natural upward movement of fire and the natural downward movement of earth appear to be counterexamples because they are not self-motions (255a1–18); yet, at the same time, it is not clear that these elements are moved by anything else (255a31–33), for they will be subject to these motions as long as nothing impedes them (255a33–b13). Aristotle solves the apparent difficulty by claiming that the elements are moved by whatever removes the impediment. But the remover of the impediment, he insists, is only accidentally the cause of the elemental movement:

> What removes the support or the impediment is in one way the mover but in another way not. I mean, for example, the person who removes the pillar, or who removes the stone from the wineskin in the water. For he causes the movement accidentally (κινεῖ κατὰ συμβεβηκός). (255b24–27)

Aristotle here distinguishes two ways in which one thing can be said to move (κινεῖν) another: accidentally and nonaccidentally. The external entity, which brings about the change that precipitates the elemental movement, is only the accidental cause of the elemental movement, and hence is not really its efficient cause in the proper sense of "cause" (*Phys.* II.3, 195b3–4).[20]

Phys. VIII.4 is not the only place where Aristotle appeals to the distinction between accidental and nonaccidental causation in order to defend the claim that the origin of something is in one entity rather than another. He makes a similar move in *Meta.* E.3. The chapter is notoriously difficult,

---

[20] Why does Aristotle go to the trouble to point out that such external causes are only accidentally responsible for the elemental motions? Presumably because he would find it hard to defend his claim that such movements are natural (VIII.4, 254b12–23, 255a18–23) if he allowed that they have nonaccidental external causes. For the distinctive feature of natural change is that it is due to an origin that belongs to the natural entity nonaccidentally (II.1, 192b8–32).

and its interpretation disputed, but I think that at least the following things are clear.[21] The chapter defends the thesis that not every occurrence is the result of a nonaccidental cause. After introducing the thesis (1027a29–32), Aristotle proceeds to indicate that if it is false, then the causal chain of anything that happens can always be traced indefinitely far back into the past (1027a32–b7); but that if it is true, then some causal chains go back only so far—to an origin that cannot be traced back to anything else (1027b11–12). Such an origin is one for which there is no cause of its coming into being (1027b13–14). But the accidental is what lacks an origin of coming into being.[22] As in *Phys.* VIII.4, Aristotle here defends the claim that *X* is the origin of something by claiming that *X*'s causal antecedents are only its accidental cause.[23]

These two passages give us reason to suppose that Aristotle would defend his thesis that we are self-movers by arguing that external objects, although they induce in us the desires on which we act, are only the accidental causes of our decisions and actions. So let us now turn to evaluate the success of this response to the problem about self-movement.

6. SELF-MOVEMENT AND NONACCIDENTAL CAUSES

Aristotle routinely identifies the nonaccidental efficient cause of a result in terms of a causal power that "naturally produces" it. For example, the skilled builder (οἰκοδόμος) who builds the house (οἰκία) is the nonaccidental cause of the house (*Phys.* II.5, 196b24–26; *Meta.* E.2, 1026b6–10) because he exercises a causal power (οἰκοδομική) that is productive (ποιητική) or "naturally produces" (πέφυκε ποιεῖν) such a result (*Meta.* E.2, 1026b10, 1027a1). Aristotle often explains what makes the nonaccidental cause "naturally productive" of an outcome with the claim that the cause produces it "always or for the most part" (*Meta.* Δ.30, 1025a14–19; E.2, 1026b27–37). I take such claims to mean that the nonaccidental cause produces the result by exercising a causal power that will succeed in producing something of this type unless it is impeded.[24] An accidental cause of

---

[21] I follow Sorabji's interpretation of this chapter (1980, 7–11), although I disagree with his contention that Aristotle there denies determinism. The thesis of necessity that Aristotle here claims would be true if his thesis about accidents is false is not that of causal determinism, but is a much stronger thesis.

[22] *Meta.* E.2, 1026b22–24; cf. Δ.30, 1025a28–29; and E.3, 1027a29–30.

[23] *De int.* 9 admits of a similar interpretation. There Aristotle rejects a thesis of necessity quite similar to that of *Meta.* E.3, on the grounds that it entails, among other things, that (a) nothing happens accidentally, and (b) human deliberation is not the origin of action. I propose that (a) and (b) are related in the way the analogous claims are related in *Meta.* E.3. Aristotle is not claiming that the outcome of deliberation is by chance, but rather that its external antecedents are only its accidental causes.

[24] I defend this interpretation in Meyer 1992.

a result, by contrast, exercises a causal power that, in its normal and unimpeded exercise, is no more likely than not to produce a result of the type in question.

We can see why Aristotle thinks the voluntary agent is the nonaccidental cause of his voluntary action. Such an agent acts on a motivation that is reliably productive of actions of this type. Let us now consider why Aristotle would think that the external antecedent of the occurrent desire on which the voluntary agent acts is only the accidental cause of that desire. Let us consider the example discussed in the previous section, in which a vicious person sees an untended pot of gold and decides to steal it. This external object, given the agent's dishonest disposition, precipitates in the agent the occurrent desire to take the gold.[25] But is the pot of gold the sort of thing that reliably precipitates such desires in agents? Considered in itself, does it have the power that, if unimpeded, will reliably induce in agents the desire to steal it? Clearly not, for it will only induce such a desire in agents with a particular vicious disposition. In itself, it is no more a cause of desires for stealing than of desires for not stealing. Which sort of desire results from perceiving the gold depends on more than the unimpeded exercise of the causal powers of the gold. Hence the gold is only the accidental cause of the desire to steal, and hence of the theft.[26]

One might object that although the pot of gold does not have the capacity reliably to produce in human agents the desire to steal, it still is reliably productive of such desires in agents of this type. That is, it has the power, if unimpeded, to induce, in agents with the disposition to steal if they can get away with it, in situations in which they can get away with it, the occurrent desire to steal. Just as the shoemaker has the power, if unimpeded, to turn nails and leather into a pair of shoes, the pot of gold has the power to turn such situations with such agents in them into situations in which the agent has the desire to steal.

Aristotle agrees that any request for an explanation—that is, any search for a cause—asks why one thing belongs to another (*Meta.* Z.17, 1041a10–b9). On the objection we are considering, the external object of perception is nonaccidentally responsible for the fact that the agent, who is disposed to pursue such objects if she perceives them, has the additional property of actually desiring to pursue the object. But is this explanandum

---

[25] It does not matter whether this desire issues from deliberation or from simple perception. If it results from deliberation, it is still a result of the agent's deliberative disposition, and hence is "triggered" by the external object in a way relevantly similar to the triggering of the desire unmediated by deliberation.

[26] By contrast, an external object of perception that is the nonaccidental cause of a desire it precipitates would be an object that any human being would react to in the same way. The naturally fearful things that any sensible person would fear (*EN* III.7, 1115b8–10) would be examples of external causes that do move the agent to have the desire or feeling they "make" (ἐμποιεῖν) him have.

the same as the one assumed by Aristotle's claim that the agent is the origin of his action? In claiming that the vicious agent is the origin of the theft, surely Aristotle is thinking that the agent is responsible for the fact that, in a situation in which such an external object is present, the object is stolen rather than not. While we may be able, with sufficient ingenuity, to specify some situation involving the agent for which an external perceptual stimulus is the nonaccidental cause, it is not within our power of stipulation to make the external object the nonaccidental cause of the explanandum that is relevant to the claim that the agent is the origin of the action.

Aristotle can appeal to the distinction between nonaccidental and accidental causes to support his claim that the agent's desire is not moved by an external object. The external object is only the accidental cause of that desire, whereas the agent's character is its nonaccidental cause. Aristotle therefore can defend his claim that voluntary agents are self-moved without subscribing to either indeterminism or agent causation. His claims abut self-movement are defensible without attributing to agents causal powers discontinuous with, or radically distinct from, those he thinks are at work in the rest of nature.

CHAPTER 5

Aristotle on the Mind's Self-Motion

MICHAEL V. WEDIN

EVERYONE KNOWS that Aristotle's animals are self-movers, and almost everyone knows that Aristotle has a problem explaining this. If, for example, everything that is moved is moved by something else, then nothing will move itself. And how can a thing move itself, if movement is just the actualization of a potentiality to be moved (*Phys.* VIII.5, 257b6–9)? For what effects the actualization must be something already actual (τὸ κινοῦν ἤδη ἐνεργείᾳ [257b10]). These worries extend to a special, and distinctively human, brand of animal movement, namely, thinking. And it is with this sort of movement that I shall be concerned in the present essay. So I am interested in self-movers insofar as they are thinkers, and I shall accordingly restrict myself to the role of self-motion in the Aristotelian mind (νοῦς). I will sometimes refer to this as "noetic self-motion."[1]

There is little doubt that in the psychological writings Aristotle regards persons as capable of noetic self-motion. In *De an.* II.5, for instance, he says at one point that the person who possesses a certain bit of knowledge is able to think it whenever he wishes (ὁ δ' ὅτι βουληθεὶς δυνατὸς θεωρεῖν

Some of the material in this paper was presented at a conference on Aristotle's thought at the University of California, San Diego, in December 1989. A more direct ancestor was read at the University of Chicago and at the Pittsburgh Self-Motion Conference. On each of these occasions I benefited greatly from the comments of a number of people, but I particularly wish to thank Julia Annas, David Charles, Ian Mueller, and my commentator at Pittsburgh, Christopher Shields. For help in the final stages, I am indebted to Mary Louise Gill and to James Lennox, who provided written comments, as well as to a referee for the press.

[1] This paper promotes a particular sort of interpretation of Aristotle's views on thinking. The interpretation itself, which has affinities with what is now called cognitivism, has been developed and defended at length in Wedin 1985; 1988; and 1989. These studies used, but left relatively unanalyzed, the notion of noetic self-motion. The present paper aims to remedy this omission. It turns out that what Aristotle says on the topic, in passages from the *Physics* to the *Eudemian Ethics*, is congenial to a cognitivist approach. So in turning here to such texts and to the topic of self-motion, I hope not only to shed light on Aristotle's theory of noetic self-motion, but also to secure additional lines of support for my overall interpretation of his account of mental activity.

[417a27–28]), provided nothing external prevents this; at another point, he says that thinking is up to us, whenever we wish (νοῆσαι ἐπ' αὐτῷ, ὁπόταν βούληται [417b23–24]). Indeed, one of the questions that opens *De an.* III.4 and guides its discussion of thought—"How will thinking come about?"—asks for an account of the cause of episodes of thinking, and the answer is to be given in terms that satisfy a model of thought sketched by Aristotle at 429b5–9. The model (which I below call the "Canonical Model") requires that the answer explain how an agent can exercise the capacity for thought by himself (δύνηται ἐνεργεῖν δι' αὐτοῦ [429b7]). This voluntary or autonomous feature of thinking counts as a kind of self-motion. *Phys.* VIII.4, for example, reports that only living things are capable of acting by themselves (αὐτὰ ὑφ' αὐτῶν). Such things are capable of self-motion. That is, says Aristotle, they must be capable of moving themselves (αὐτὰ ἑαυτὰ κινοῦσιν) and stopping themselves (ἱστά-ναι αὐτὰ αὐτά). This, in turn, is equivalent to saying that such a thing can act and refrain from acting by itself (ἐπ' αὐτῷ). And this is just the idiom that *De an.* II.5 applies to thinking.

Nothing I say is meant to deny that, properly, thinking (νόησις) is an activity. Rather, my account presumes that some sort of movement, or something like a movement, is involved in the activity's coming about. To revert again to *De an.* II.5, when the accomplished mathematician exercises some part, k, of his knowledge, a change, or something like a change, occurs. Aristotle describes this as a change from the mathematician's potentially$_2$ knowing k to his actually$_2$ knowing k.[2] It is to this switch that *De an.* III.4's opening question is directed.

In fact, two questions open *De an.* III.4. The first—"What distinguishing mark will it (the mind) have?"—is answered at 429b21–22, where νοῦς is characterized as a capability for grasping objects insofar as they are separate from matter. So it is clear that Aristotle intends to provide answers to his questions. The question of immediate interest, how the mind comes to think, calls for a theory of the mind's internal mechanisms. *De an.* III.4 has little to say about this, although it has a good deal to say about the features of thought that these mechanisms are rung in to explain. In my view, the silence of *De an.* III.4 gives way to *De an.* III.5's noisier distinction between productive and receptive mind. For these I construe to be structures or mechanisms countenanced in order to explain the transition from potential$_2$ to actual$_2$ thinking.[3]

---

[2] Subscripts mark Aristotle's so-called "first" and "second" potentialities and actualities. These are worked out at 417a21–b16, where Aristotle distinguishes three grades of knower and two kinds each of potentiality and actuality: (K1) S is a knower$_1$ ↔ S is the sort of thing that is capable$_1$ of developing into a knower$_2$; (K2) S is a knower$_2$ (an actual$_1$ knower) ↔ S is capable$_2$ of knowing$_3$; (K3) S is a knower$_3$ (an actual$_2$ knower) ↔ S is contemplating a particular object of thought.

[3] A fuller account of this is available in Wedin 1989.

1. TWO VIEWS

De an. III.4's concern about how actual$_2$ thinking occurs is not addressed until the following chapter, where the need for a cause of episodes of thinking leads Aristotle to countenance the so-called active or agent intellect (what I prefer to call "productive" mind). The accomplished geometer, for example, is able to entertain the thought that the diagonal of the square is incommensurate with the side. His doing so presupposes that he has already acquired the component thoughts (νοήματα) and is able to use them in thinking the complete proposition. If the first condition calls for receptive mind, the second calls for productive mind. For he can be said actively to think the proposition only if his mind can be said to possess resources sufficient for him to produce, on his own, the required thought(s). So the productive part of the mind is a requirement of its autonomy.

The precise role productive mind plays in this story is, of course, subject to intricate and ongoing debate. This essay does not pretend to do justice to the details of this discussion.[4] I would, however, like to sketch at the outset two *kinds* of accounts of productive mind's role in thinking. They will be in the background of much of what I say. One of these I call "Spring Theory," the other "Surge Theory."

Spring Theory is so called because it sees productive mind as part of the internal mechanism that subserves thinking, as part of the springs of thought. Roughly, the idea is that productive and receptive minds are not distinct intellects within the Aristotelian soul. Rather, they are structures needed to account for the function of thought. As part of the internal mechanism required for agents to produce thoughts autonomously, from a ready stock of concepts, they are to be thought of as occurring at a lower level of cognitive organization in the noetic system. Acquired or potential$_2$ thoughts are housed, as it were, in receptive mind and brought to actuality$_2$ by occurring in actual$_2$ episodes of thought. For this to happen autonomously, the mind itself must be able to initiate thinking. In short, what is called for is a productive factor, proper to νοῦς itself, that operates episodically. Thus, productive mind enters on the strength of its role in individual acts of thinking.

Surge Theory holds that productive mind is always thinking all objects of thought. Alexander of Aphrodisias, the founding father of Surge Theory, identified productive mind with the cosmic mind of the unmoved mover. Latter-day Aphrodisiasts tend to promote a weaker relation. Charles Kahn, for example, comes down in favor of isomorphism between productive mind and the cosmic mind.[5] The received fact that agents think sometimes

---

[4] For more, see Wedin 1985; 1988; and 1989.

[5] See Kahn 1981 and 1985b. Surge Theory has made an even more recent appearance in Lear 1988 and, possibly, in Joseph Owens's "The Problematic of the Active Mind's Causation

one thing, sometimes another, and often appear to be thinking nothing at all, is not explained by an additional discrete act, or acts, by which productive mind initiates, or plays a causal role in initiating, actual episodes of thinking. Rather, it is explained by a variety of "external" factors that interrupt or, as sometimes in the case of sleep, entirely shut off the noetic flow. The thoughts that agents are aware of are those that surge through.[6]

The main testing-ground for these two views is, of course, *De anima*'s discussion of νοῦς and νοεῖν. One cannot, however, balance the claims of Spring Theory and Surge Theory simply by focusing on *De an.* III.5, because productive mind must play its role within the account of the mind (νοῦς) that is offered in *De an.* III.4. That is, it must find its place within the model of the mind as a full faculty of the soul. This model, the "Canonical Model," plainly borrows from Aristotle's discussion of cognitive capacities and their exercises in a section of *De an.* II.5 that deserves to be called the "Framework Passage."[7] The model is given at 429b5–9:

> When the mind has become each thing (ἕκαστα) as one who actually₁ knows (ὁ ἐπιστήμων ὁ κατ' ἐνέργειαν) is said to be—and this happens when he can actually₂ exercise his potentiality₂ by himself (ὅταν δύνηται ἐνεργεῖν δι' αὑτοῦ)—it is still in some sense a potentiality₂ but not in the same way as before it learned or discovered [i.e., not as a potentiality₁]. Then it is capable₂ of [actually₂] thinking itself (αὐτὸς δὲ αὑτὸν τότε δύναται νοεῖν).

The Canonical Model guides *De anima*'s discussion of the mind and its operations, so it serves as a constraint on the interpretation of noetic self-motion. This is hardly surprising. Where else but in the psychological works would one look for authoritative guidance? Nonetheless, there are good reasons for beginning the discussion of noetic self-motion by looking at *Phys.* VIII and *EE* VIII.

2. *PHYSICS* VIII: THINKING AS ΠΑΣΧΕΙΝ

At *Phys.* VIII.4, 255a33–b5, Aristotle appears to give us a more extensive but considerably less well-known version of the Canonical Model. There

---

in Aristotle, *De anima*, 3.5," read to the eighth annual SSIPS/SAGP conference. Reservations regarding Kahn's account are detailed in "The Alleged Isomorphism of Productive and Divine Mind," section 4 of chap. 6 of Wedin 1988. For some worries about Lear's view, see note 41 below.

[6] Associated imagery for each might be: on Spring Theory, the noetic light switches on and off; on Surge Theory, the light is always on.

[7] The Framework passage—roughly 417a21–b16—gives an account of a faculty and its functions that is meant to apply generally in the psychology. It does this by distinguishing three grades of knower and two kinds each of potentiality and actuality. See note 2 above.

are several reasons for beginning here. One is that it occurs in the midst of Aristotle's discussion of self-motion and so, perhaps, we can expect some enlightenment on the topic of the mind's self-motion. Another reason is that it is one of the passages in the eighth book of the *Physics* that is easily taken to favor Surge Theory, and this is a theory I wish to reject. For reasons soon to be apparent, I shall say that this passage contains the "Partial Model":

> One who is learning a science potentially$_1$ knows it in a different sense from one who, while already possessing the knowledge, is not actually$_2$ exercising it (ὁ ἔχων ἤδη καὶ μὴ ἐνεργῶν). Whenever we have something capable of acting and something capable of being correspondingly acted on, in the event of any such pair being in contact (ἀεὶ δ', ὅταν ἅμα τὸ ποιητικὸν καὶ τὸ παθητικὸν ὦσιν) what is potential becomes at times actual (γίγνεται ἐνεργείᾳ τὸ δυνατόν): e.g., the learner becomes from one potential$_1$ something another potential$_2$ something: for one who possesses knowledge of a science but is not actually$_2$ exercising it knows the science potentially$_2$ in a sense, though not in the same sense as he knew it potentially$_1$ before he learned it. And when he is in this condition (ὅταν δ' οὕτως ἔχῃ), if something does not prevent him (ἐάν τι μὴ κωλύῃ), he actively$_2$ exercises his knowledge (ἐνεργεῖ καὶ θεωρεῖ): otherwise he would be in the contradictory state of not knowing. (*Phys.* VIII.4, 255a33–b5)

At first glance, this passage seems to support an interpretation much along the lines of the Canonical Model. It appears, for instance, to take the capacity for doing something of a cognitive nature—say, asserting or entertaining a proposition—as criterial for possession of a concept. But the matter is not so straightforward. For Aristotle immediately goes on to say that the case is similar (ὁμοίως) with respect to natural bodies. Because air is generated from water, one might say that something light (namely, air) is potentially in something heavy (namely, water). But air itself, he says, is actually light and will straightaway (εὐθύς) realize its activity unless something prevents it. And the activity (ἐνέργεια) of what is light is to be in a place, namely, up.

Aristotle's purpose in this section of the chapter (beginning at 255a24) is to explain why it is difficult to grasp the source of natural movement. This requires that he clarify different senses of potentiality. The distinction he wishes to make emerges most clearly in the case of psychological faculties, above all in the case of knowledge. It is Aristotle's favorite example, and the one he leans on most heavily in developing the framework for cognitive faculties in *De an.* II.5 and III.4's Canonical Model. So, admittedly, it is tempting to read back into *De anima* as a whole lessons gleaned from examination of the Partial Model (contained in the passage cited above) and Aristotle's commentary on it.

What are these? For a start, we are encouraged to think of air, when unseparated from water, as potentially$_1$ light and air, and when separated from water, as actually$_1$ or potentially$_2$ light. The latter, Aristotle says, immediately realizes its activity or actuality$_2$, *unless* it is prevented from doing so (ἂν μή τι κωλύῃ [*Phys.* VIII.4, 255b10–11]). Suppose we represent this as

[1] S is a potential$_2$ φer & nothing hinders S's φing → S φs.

I am happy to grant that proposition [1] covers certain physical phenomena. One might even grant that it covers certain psychological faculties. Unless something prevents me (sleep, visual blinders, or physical impairment), it is plausible to suppose that I will straightaway see what is in my visual field. As Aristotle suggests at 255b4–5, this would be part of what is involved in the claim that I am a potential$_2$ perceiver. Common to both cases is a certain inevitability about the exercise of the potentiality$_2$: other things being equal, there is no question that air will rise and, other things being equal, there is no question that I will perceive what is in my visual field.

The last point suggests a corollary to [1]:

[1a] (S is a potential$_2$ φer & nothing hinders S's φing → S φs) → S's φing
     is not up to S.

Now proposition [1a] is arguably satisfied by the perceptual faculties. As Aristotle says in *De an.* II.5 and elsewhere, perception is not up to us. What about νοῦς ? Well, the *Physics* (VIII.4, 255b3–4) does appear to extend proposition [1] to thought, and it does so in language that later is applied to air as a potentiality$_2$. Both potential$_2$ air and potential$_2$ knower realize their proper activities unless something prevents them (ἐάν τι μὴ κωλύῃ). The first case appears congenial to Surge Theory—air *will* rise if left to itself. So it is tempting to bring thought as well under Surge Theory. But did Aristotle do this?

Not quite, I think. For one thing, it is difficult to see how thinking could be "up to us," if it is covered by proposition [1a]. Since Aristotle says it is, the operation of νοῦς would seem to fall outside the scope of [1a].[8] Only

---

[8] Some (for example, Hamlyn [1968]) are of the opinion that, Aristotle's view aside, νοῦς ought to be brought under the scope of [1a]. Commenting on *De an.* II.5, Hamlyn points out (102–3) that what Aristotle in fact asserts is that if x knows y, then x's thinking y is up to x. This prompts the criticism, first, that Aristotle wants to distinguish knowledge and perception in terms of whether they are "up to us," and second, that this forces Aristotle to switch the subject matter from knowledge versus perception to thinking versus perception because, says Hamlyn, "knowledge is, just as much as perception, dependent on its object (you cannot know what does not exist or what is not the case)." For some reasons why Hamlyn's criticism fails, see Wedin 1989, 72.

the Canonical Model is explicit on the point that thinking is "up to us." Nevertheless, the similarity between it and the Partial Model will suggest to some that the Partial Model is meant to provide for the autonomy of thought and that only Aristotle's commentary on the model invites us to bring thinking under proposition [1a].

But this is too easy. For notice that the Partial Model says simply that the person who potentially$_2$ knows something *will* actively exercise this potential$_2$ knowledge. Missing here is the Canonical Model's rider "by himself" and *De an.* II.5's "whenever he wishes." Moreover, the omissions are not inadvertent. For Aristotle goes on to link thought to a general principle:

> The case where something of a certain quality changes to being in activity is similar, for the knower will straightaway theorize unless something prevents it (εὐθὺς γὰρ θεωρεῖ, ἐὰν μή τι κωλύῃ). (*Phys.* VIII.4, 255b21–23)

This, in turn, appears to leave no room for the mind's self-motion:

> It is, then, clear that in none of these cases does a thing move itself; but it has a principle of movement, not of moving or doing, but of being affected (ἀλλὰ κινήσεως ἀρχὴν ἔχει, οὐ τοῦ κινεῖν οὐδὲ τοῦ ποιεῖν, ἀλλὰ τοῦ πάσχειν). (255b29–31)

These remarks make it clear that the Partial Model characterizes thought as a purely passive affair. What is capable only of being affected can be brought to activity only by the agency of something external to it. Hence, the Partial Model excludes noetic self-motion and, with that, the autonomy of thought itself. It thus seems impossible to avoid the conclusion that Aristotle has saddled himself with a contradiction in putting forward both the Partial Model and the Canonical Model.

At this point one might attempt to downplay this worry by pointing out that the "nothing prevents" proviso in proposition [1] is ambiguous between

[1′] S is a potential$_2$ φer & nothing *external* hinders S's φing → S φs

and

[1″] S is a potential$_2$ φer & nothing *external or internal* hinders S's φing → S φs,

and then insisting that, although [1″] does entail [1a], [1′] does not.[9] So if proposition [1] of the Partial Model is read with [1′], there will be no contradiction after all between it and the Canonical Model. This is because the Canonical Model appears to be committed to something like [1′]. After

---

[9] I am indebted to Christopher Shields for impressing on me the need to address this ambiguity.

all, at *De an.* ii.5, 417a27, Aristotle says that the potential$_2$ thinker is able to theorize whenever he wishes so long as nothing *external* (ἔξωθεν) prevents this. Of course, I may be prevented from thinking about the Pythagorean Theorem, even though I wish to, because I have dropped the large Liddell-Scott on my toe or because my neighbor has forced me at knife point to talk to her about Derrida. But, according to Aristotle, none of this detracts from my noetic autonomy because it is all caused by something external. That is, the Canonical Model's analogue to [1'] would be

[CM1'] S is a potential$_2$ φer & S wishes to φ & nothing *external* hinders S's φing → S φs.

There will be cases in which an internal hindrance (say, a throbbing headache) is the result of external factors (say, a slapshot to the forehead). Here propositions [1'] and [1″] are equivalent. But not all internal factors are like this. Thus, [1] would not appear, after all, to entail [1a], because a thinker may be prevented from thinking about the Pythagorean Theorem by his or her free choice to think about, say, the Gödel Theorem. Notice, however, that this presupposes that the Partial Model includes the *choice* or *wish* to think about the object of thought. But, as we have seen, the Partial Model has nothing corresponding to the second condition in [CM1']. It says only that the potential$_2$ thinker will think provided nothing prevents this. It also lacks the "nothing *external*" proviso and, thus, appears open to the stronger reading [1″]. So, perhaps, the Partial and Canonical models are incompatible after all.

Such a prognosis is premature, however. It does not even follow, for instance, that in *Phys.* viii.4 Aristotle denies the possibility of noetic self-motion. It is certainly possible to exclude a certain property from consideration of a given process (or object) without thereby denying that the process has the property. Some properties—even those characteristic of the process—may simply be irrelevant to its use in the model. So we may think of *Phys.* viii.4 as containing a partial model of thought because it contains only those properties of thinking required by the task at hand, namely, explaining the natural motion of physical phenomena such as air and fire.[10]

What is this property of thought that is so useful for modeling physical phenomena? We know that it cannot be the property of self-motion, for Aristotle explicitly restricts this to living things (255a5–7). So it will be the property of natural motion, understood along the lines of proposition [1]. I have some idea what this amounts to for the upward movement of air.

---

[10] Use of the notion of a partial model allows us to read the remark in *Phys.* viii.4, 255b29, that "none of these moves itself" to include animals (*pace* Furley 1978) without denying that they are self-movers, *contra* Guthrie 1939.

Other things being equal, actual$_2$ air will be at its natural place, namely, someplace high up. So when it occurs free, that is, as a potentiality$_2$, air moves to its natural place unless constrained by something external. The nature of natural movement is unclear because, as Aristotle puts it, the upward movement in a way is and in a way is not caused by removal of the external constraint (255b24–25).

It might be suggested that in the case of the mind, natural motion just is self-motion. But it is still difficult to see how thought can be a kind of natural motion, let alone how it is an especially transparent case of it, for this would seem to require that whatever has the potentiality$_2$ to think will naturally think simply in virtue of having the potentiality$_2$. Though Surge theorists might find this unobjectionable, it seems to me only slightly less odd than saying that whoever has acquired the potentiality$_2$ to sing opera will straightaway do so. Of course, this is an acquired potentiality$_2$, whereas the potentiality$_2$ to think is something we come by naturally. Nonetheless, this will suggest to some a way of understanding the mind's alleged natural movement.

So consider again proposition [1]:

[1] S is a potential$_2$ ϕer & nothing hinders S's ϕing → S ϕs,

and a modified version of it:

[1*] S is a potential$_2$ ϕer & S's potentiality$_2$ is activated by an object O & nothing hinders S's ϕing → S ϕs.

Version [1] appears to cover the upward movement of air because the only causal factor required, in addition to air's "natural striving," is removal of an external constraint. This might be called a privative causal factor— Aristotle says it is a cause incidentally (κατὰ συμβεβηκὸς κινεῖ [255b27]). Version [1*] goes beyond this and requires a proper causal factor that activates the potentiality$_2$ to be (become) high up. But nothing in the *Physics* texts indicates that the latter is required to explain the natural movement of air. Thus, to the extent that thought provides the model for such movement, the movement of the νοητικόν from potential$_2$ to actual$_2$ thought would not appear to require a proper causal factor. On this view, the mind, like air, is always straining to be in activity. So movement toward its being in activity automatically follows upon removal of constraints. If this "noetic striving" is explained as productive mind's "always thinking," then we have a view congenial to Surge theorists. I suppose this makes some sense if one thinks of sleep and other forms of general unconsciousness as hindrances and if there is some sort of underlying activity that surges forth at restoration of consciousness. Something like this appears to happen in perception insofar as it just comes about when one awakens.

But what is left without explanation is how this "suppressed" activity can be the same as the intentional activity one is later aware of in actual₂ thought, in particular how it is even relevant to the need for intentional objects. What Surge Theory leaves out is the causal role of the object of the faculty's exercise. Certainly, for perception, the object perceived is the cause of the episode of perceiving.[11] So we appear to at least need something like [1*]. To this it might be objected that *on just this point*, namely, the causal role of the object, thought diverges from perception, and that this explains why Aristotle constructs the Partial Model using thought. Here there is no proper causal factor that effects the switch from potential₂ to actual₂ thinking. I think this view is wrong, but not because the object of thought has a straightforward role. The story is rather more complicated. We may begin by looking at what Aristotle says about psychological states—the internal causal correlates of the objects.

3. *PHYSICS* VII.3 ON PSYCHOLOGICAL STATES

Aristotle begins *Phys.* VII.3 with a pair of related claims: Whatever undergoes alteration (ἀλλοίωσις) is altered by sensible objects (ὑπὸ τῶν αἰσθητῶν), and alteration can occur only in what can be said to be properly affected by such objects (καθ' αὐτὰ πάσχειν ὑπὸ τῶν αἰσθητῶν). States of the soul are not such things. This is because they just consist in the obtaining of a certain relation to something (ἐν τῷ πρός τι πῶς ἔχειν). Things of this sort—Aristotle calls them relatives (τὰ πρός τι)—are not subject to alteration in their own right. The elements on which these states primarily depend may be subject to alteration, but the states themselves are not.

This is also true for mental states. When Aristotle explicitly turns to the noetic soul at *Phys.* VII.3, 247b1, he reports that (i) states of this part of the soul (αἱ τοῦ νοητικοῦ μέρους ἕξεις) are not themselves alterations (ἀλλοιώσεις), nor is there any generation (γένεσις) of them. This is because (ii) knowing just consists in the obtaining of a certain relation (τὸ ἐπιστῆμον ἐν τῷ πρός τι πῶς ἔχειν), and (iii) there is no generation of things of this sort. The ἐπιστῆμον or knowing in (ii) is, or at least involves, the state or ἕξις of the actual₂ knower, the Canonical Model's man who is thinking by himself (ἐνεργεῖν δι' αὐτοῦ). So the knowing just is the possession of a relative, namely, the particular knowledge.

There is a familiar sense of ἔχειν according to which someone can have, but not employ, an item of knowledge. It is in this way that the potential₂ knowledge of the knower₂ is had. It is unlikely, however, that Aristotle imports this sense of ἕξις into (i), for these states result from the presence to

---

[11] See, for example, *De an.* II.5, 417b20–22, where the objects of perception are said to be the productive causes of the activity (τὰ ποιητικὰ τῆς ἐνεργείας).

the mind of something particular and thus will surely be actual₂ states of knowledge₃. This, at any rate, is what Aristotle goes on to say at 247b4–7:

> For what is knowing potentially (τὸ κατὰ δύναμιν ἐπιστῆμον) comes to be actual₂ knowing (ἐπιστῆμον)[12] not by being moved itself but by the presence of something else (οὐδὲν αὐτὸ κινηθὲν ἀλλὰ τῷ ἄλλο ὑπάρξαι γίγνεται ἐπιστῆμον); for when it encounters the particular (γένηται τὸ κατὰ μέρος), it somehow knows the universal in the particular (ἐπίσταταί πως τὰ καθόλου τῷ ἐν μέρει).

In *Meta.* Λ.7 Aristotle makes important use of the thesis that the mind is actual when it possesses the object of thought (ἐνεργεῖ δὲ ἔχων). This thesis, given at 1072b22–23, appears to be what is intended in (ii). So the ἕξεις of (i) would appear to belong to the first sort of ἕξις discussed in *Meta.* Δ.20. That is, as opposed to a disposition (διάθεσις), it will be "a sort of activity of the haver and of what is had" (οἷον ἐνέργειά τις τοῦ ἔχοντος καὶ ἐχομένου), "something like an action or movement" (ὥσπερ πρᾶξίς τις ἢ κίνησις).[13]

To make the point transparent, Aristotle immediately adds: "Again (πάλιν), there is no becoming (γένεσις) of the use (χρήσεως) or activity (ἐνεργείας) of these [potential₂ noetic states], unless it is thought that there is a becoming of touch and sight, for the use (χρῆσθαι) and activity (ἐνεργεῖν) is similar to these" (*Phys.* VII.3, 247b7–9). (Note that Aristotle then turns to the original acquisition [λῆψις] of knowledge and construes this as a *contrasting* case.[14])

In *Phys.* VII.3, or so I would like to suggest, the style of causation involved in thinking is what might be called "levels causation." Here, roughly, is the idea.

[LC] To say that a psychological state, *m*, comes to exist at *t* is at least to say that, while *m* itself is no proper part of a standard causal process, there exists at *t* a nonpsychological state, *s*, that is such a proper part and *m* exists because *s* exists.

---

[12] With Hardie and Gaye in the Oxford translation, I take the second ἐπιστῆμον to mark, not the acquisition of potential₂ knowledge, but the switch to the actual₂ exercise of such potential knowledge.

[13] Of course, *Phys.* VII.3 sometimes regards states or ἕξεις as potential₂ as opposed to actual₂ states of the soul. But these are not alterations in their own right, nor is their acquisition to be described as an alteration or a becoming (γένεσις), in the proper sense of those terms.

[14] *Phys.* VII.3, 247b7–9, might, by itself, be thought troublesome, if taken to entail that no causal factor is involved in the switch from potential₂ to actual₂ thinking. The case of sight rules this out, however. We know that actual₂ seeing is caused by the object of sight, and yet, as *De sensu* 6, 446b3–6, points out, actual₂ seeing can occur without coming to be (εἰσὶν ἄνευ τοῦ γίγνεσθαι). So, in any case, the entailment fails.

Thesis [LC] is meant to express a causal asymmetry between psychological states and their lower-level causes and to catch the idea that a caused state is emergent with respect to the causal process because it is not a proper part of the process. Roughly, we might say that if B results from a causal process involving A and if B shares a material base with A, then B is a proper part of the causal process beginning with A. A statue shares a material base with the marble whence it came, so thesis [LC] does not apply to its production. Because there is no such base for the object of thought, its production satisfies [LC].

Aristotle appears to give two grounds for [LC]. One appeals to the "relational" nature of the psychological states themselves, and the other to the distinction between such states and the things they are realized in. Let us begin with the first ground. At *Cat.* 7, 7b15, Aristotle contrasts relatives that are simultaneous by nature (τὰ πρός τι ἅμα τῇ φύσει εἶναι) with those that are not. The first is exemplified by the pairs, double–half and slave–master. Such items, he explains later (14b27–29), "reciprocate with respect to implication of existence and neither is in any way the cause of the other's existence" (ἀντιστρέφει μὲν κατὰ τὴν τοῦ εἶναι ἀκολούθησιν, μηδαμῶς δὲ αἴτιον θάτερον θατέρῳ τοῦ εἶναί ἐστιν). We might put this as follows.

[SYM]   x and y are simultaneous relatives ↔ x and y are relatives & □(x exists ≡ y exists) & (y is not the cause of x & x is not the cause of y).

The contrasting case, exemplified with pairs such as knowledge and the knowable, appears to look like this:

[ASYM]   x and y are nonsimultaneous relatives ↔ x and y are relatives & ~□(x exists ≡ y exists) & (y is the cause of x ∨ x is the cause of y).

Of these, only [ASYM] is even a candidate for catching the asymmetry claimed for psychological states and their causes. For, to take the case of perception, the object of perception (τὸ αἰσθητόν) both exists independently of perceiving (αἴσθησις) and is the cause of it. Nonetheless, it is doubtful that [ASYM] gives us the asymmetry we want. For the *Phys.* VII.3 account of psychological states parallels the account of bodily states (e.g., 246b2). These states (health is the favorite example) exist in virtue of a certain relation (τῷ πρός τι πὼς ἔχειν). But rather than a relation *to* something external to the physical system, as with the object of perception, these states are said to exist in virtue of a certain relation holding *among* other elements in the system (αὐτῶν πρὸς αὐτὰ τῶν ἐντός). (So here we get the second ground for [LC].) Aristotle likens this to the way form (εἶδος) and shape (μορφή) come to exist as a result of genuine alterations occurring among elements, such as the hot and cold or whatever the things are, in which a given state is *primarily* realized (ἐν οἷς τυγχάνουσιν οὖσαι πρῶτοις [246b17]).

This causal asymmetry is intrasystemic and makes use of the notion of levels of explanation. A property or feature, a form or shape, emerges at one level in virtue of certain causal relations holding among items at the next level down.[15] (So I take the force of πρῶτοις in 246b17.) Suppose we think of this causal asymmetry as a kind of levels asymmetry. At 246b20 Aristotle appears ready to extend causal asymmetry to psychological states, including, at 247b1, mental states. Thus, a certain occurrent mental state will exist in virtue of a certain relation holding among items at a lower level in the noetic system. In a passage from *Phys.* VII.3, cited above, Aristotle indicates that such items will be particulars.[16] Elsewhere, principally in *De an.* III.8 and *De memoria*, the particulars suited to play the central causal role in thought are identified as images. Indeed, the mind is characterized as that which thinks its objects, forms, in images (τὰ εἴδη τὸ νοητικὸν ἐν τοῖς φαντάσμασι νοεῖ [431b2]). In the idiom of *Phys.* VII.3, we may say that such forms exist in virtue of a certain relation holding among images. Moreover, in *De an.* III.7, occurrence of an image, in appropriate conditions ("apart from perception" and so on), is sufficient to move the mind (ἐκτὸς τῆς αἰσθήσεως, ὅταν ἐπὶ τῶν φαντασμάτων ᾖ, κινεῖται [431b4–5]).

The causal role of images in production of the object of thought involves the fact that they are a certain representation or exemplar of the object. So we might say, following *De memoria*, that forms, the objects of thought, exist in virtue of an image playing its representational role in the noetic as opposed to, say, the mnemonic or perceptual subsystem.[17] So the existence

[15] Thus, for both [ASYM] and intrasystemic causal asymmetry, what is said to be a relative is emergent with respect to its realization. This feature, registered in [LC] above, appears to be echoed at *EN* I.4, 1096a21–22, when Aristotle reports that the relative appears to be an offshoot and accident of being (παραφυάδι γὰρ τοῦτ' ἔοικε καὶ συμβεβηκότι τοῦ ὄντος).

[16] *Meta.* M.10 also gives particulars an explicit role in actual₂ thinking. The relevant passage is discussed in Wedin 1988, 202–8.

[17] How this works is fairly complicated. Part of the story, argued at length in Wedin 1988, is that φαντασία is not a full faculty of the soul but a general representational capability that *subserves* such faculties by providing the devices, namely, images, that proper faculties use to represent the objects of their various proper functions and exercises. I called this the "functional incompleteness" of imagination, to reflect the fact that imagination has neither a proper exercise nor a proper object (Aristotelian faculties being defined by their proper objects). Wedin 1988 focused primarily on the relation between imagination and thought; hence, it gave preference to imagination insofar as it figures in thought. It has subsequently been objected, in a pair of reviews—Labarrière 1991 and Franks 1992—that the argument of Wedin 1988 neglects certain crucial passages from *De motu animalium* that threaten the functional incompleteness of imagination. Though right about the neglect, they are wrong about the threat. The crucial passages are, I believe, the following: 700b19–22: for both

of an actual mental state, m, is explained not as the result of processes or states that m itself undergoes, or of the mind that possesses m, but as the result of processes or states that occur at a lower or underlying level. When such processes occur, the object of thought emerges, and because this amounts to the presence of mental content, we say that the object of thought causes actual$_2$ thinking.[18]

Notice that [ASYM] and levels asymmetry complement each other in the following way. The object of perception (τὸ αἰσθητόν) causes the primary physical state on which a given perceptual state depends. It does so by initiating a process (involving, for example, transmission of movement from the outer medium to the medium in the eye) that yields the primary state. In the case of thinking, it is more difficult to separate [ASYM] and levels asymmetry because the mechanisms of thought are internal to the noetic system. The object of thought (τὸ νοητόν) that brings the mind to activity must, as Aristotle says in De an. II.5, be somehow in the soul. It is for this reason that use of levels of explanation is even more crucial in the account of how we think.

On the Partial Model, thought is construed as purely passive. Because it is not designed to accommodate the autonomy of thought, I have insisted, literally, on the model's partial status. I have also urged (and will later argue) that Aristotle assigns the object of thought a causal role in the account of actual$_2$ thinking. But it is unclear how the problems facing the Partial Model can be avoided by giving the object of thought causal force, even when this is interpreted as levels causation. For the Causal Thesis, as I call the thesis that the mind is brought to activity by the very object it

---

imagination (φαντασία) and perception (αἴσθησις) are in the same space as thought (τὴν αὐτὴν τῷ νῷ χώραν ἔχουσιν) because all are discriminative (κριτικά), but they differ in ways we have discussed elsewhere; 701a29–33: for whenever a thing is actually exercising perception (ἐνεργῇ σῇ τῇ αἰσθήσει) or imagination (τῇ φαντασίᾳ) or thought (τῷ νῷ) toward its object (πρὸς τὸ οὗ ἕνεκα), it does at once what it desires . . . "Here is drink," says perception or imagination or thought . . .; 702a17–19: for the affections suitably prepare the organic parts, desire the affections; and imagination the desire; and imagination comes about either through thought or through perception (αὕτη δὲ γίνεται ἢ διὰ νοήσεως ἢ δι' αἰσθήσεως). Now 700b19–22 appears to put imagination and perception in the same space as νοῦς because all are discriminative. But the passage also calls for a difference and refers, arguably, to De an. III.3, which gives no role for imagination as a discriminative faculty. More troublesome is 701a29–33, which might be taken to put imagination on a par with perception and thought with respect to the object of desire. But so far from picking out a proper object for imagination, this simply registers the familiar fact that each has a role to play in action without saying anything more fine-grained about the role. Indeed, this suggestion gains plausibility in the light of the more complex picture at 702a17–19. For when Aristotle gets to the detailed account, he is careful to say that φαντασία comes about through thought or through perception. This need indicate nothing more than its functional incompleteness and strictly representational role.

[18] For more on this, see Wedin 1989.

thinks,[19] is consistent with a purely passive characterization of thinking—depending on how one construes the causal role of the object. Perceiving, for example, is purely passive because it occurs when the perceptual faculty is affected by an object of perception. But the purely passive character of perception is tied to the fact that its objects are external. The same appears true of the Partial Model, for what causal factors it does countenance (it eschews all proper causal factors, including anything analogous to the object of perception) seem to be external. Removal of the constraining condition on a potentiality$_2$ is an incidental cause of the natural exercise of the potentiality$_2$ precisely because it is extrinsic to the system realizing the potentiality$_2$.

The Partial Model can afford to neglect the object of thought because it aims to model what naturally occurs once a potentiality$_2$ has been activated. For this purpose it simply does not matter how a noetic potentiality$_2$ is activated. Moreover, such activation just amounts to actual$_2$ thinking. So in the case of the mind, what follows activation of a potentiality$_2$ is just its being in activity. Because thought happens all at once, there is no additional movement, natural or other. This is why it is especially suited for explaining the source of natural movement. The point can be sharpened by considering two ways to think of removal of the constraining condition, namely, as (a) removal just of what blocks the onset of movement, or as (b) removal of the block plus the stages through which the natural body must move. On (b), the constraining condition is operative throughout until the body has finally reached its natural place or achieved its natural activity. Because (b), in effect, includes the natural movement itself, (a) is a more likely candidate for the *cause* of natural movement. But (b) does suggest an interesting reason for Aristotle's taking thought to be a model for natural motion. What is light moves to its place, says Aristotle, because it is naturally a certain sort of thing (αἴτιον δ' ὅτι πεφυκέν ποι [*Phys.* VIII.4, 255b15]), namely, a thing that is up (τὸ τῷ ἄνω). Notice that Aristotle does not say that the nature of light things is an *upward tendency* or tendency to *become* up. Though it is true that air has an upward tendency, this fact is not explanatory. The upward motion of air is to be explained, rather, by its natural propensity to *be* up. Indeed, this would explain as well the upward tendency of air. Suppose now that Aristotle thinks of an object in natural motion as encountering resistance along its path and, further, that absent such resistance nothing would prevent the object from immediately being at its natural place.[20] One who held this might think that in principle there is little difference between our two cases; only the contingent fact that it meets intermittent resistance prevents a "liberated" natural body from

---

[19] In Wedin 1989.

[20] Steven Strange first drew my attention to this suggestion. He, in turn, deflects credit to Tim Maudlin.

immediately realizing its potentiality$_2$, that is, from being at its natural place. Because it is unconstrained by such intermittent factors, actual$_2$ thought has achieved, straightaway, the status that air's natural movement strives for.

One problem with the suggestion, however, is its attribution to Aristotle of at least the conceptual possibility that a body could traverse a distance at a moment. Aristotle does, of course, allow for instantaneous changes. The transparent, for example, is activated as a whole and all at once, and forms may come to exist without undergoing a process of coming into existence. But these cases do not involve *local* movement of a body, a wave, or anything else. Natural motion does. The presence of the intermittent medium is, moreover, no simple contingent fact. For processes that occur in time, there must be some such medium in order to account for the notion of being in a place at all. Of course, the upward movement of air is just such a process. Nonetheless, were there (counterfactually) no such intermittent medium, neither would there be a process occurring in time. The last condition is satisfied by thinking, and so, perhaps, this counterfactual reading is the best we can do by way of explaining how thought models natural motion. Note that this holds equally of the last section's two versions of natural movement, version [1] and version [1*]. The Partial Model simply has no need for this distinction.

In the psychology, however, the situation is different. Here we need an account that fits our intuitions about human agency, particularly those concerning acts that are up to us.[21] *De an.* II.5 gives the external nature of the object of perception as the reason that perceiving is not up to us. Thinking, on the other hand, is up to us because its objects are not external. They are "somehow" in the soul itself. These remarks might suggest that the psychology can keep the Causal Thesis and save the autonomy of thought by distinguishing between external and proper internal causal factors. The idea would be that because it is properly internal to the noetic system, the object of thought can bring the system to activity without threat to the system's overall autonomy. (In earlier terms, this would allow us to honor the entailment from [1*] to [1a] for perception and its objects but to reject it for thought and its objects.) Although this suggestion will turn out to be quite fruitful, as formulated it is too vague to be of much use. We need a more illuminating account of the internal causal mechanisms. I propose to approach this by looking at an interesting, but rather overlooked, passage in *Eudemian Ethics*. The passage is useful because it explicitly presses the question of what in the soul is the source of movement (ἀρχὴ τῆς κινήσεως), including noetic movement, and argues firmly

---

[21] The difference between the two models is underscored by the fact that from the point of view of the Canonical Model, both [1'] and [1''] are false.

against one kind of answer. So it yields clues as to what sort of account Aristotle would find adequate.

4. THE *EUDEMIAN ETHICS* ON THE ΑΡΧΗ OF THOUGHT

At *EE* viii.2, 1248a15, Aristotle has just considered an argument that proves not that luck fails to be a cause of anything, but that luck is not a cause of all the things it seems to be. The burden of proof is borne by the case of the man who desires what he ought to desire, when he ought to desire it, without having deliberated—indeed, by doing what is contrary to the dictates of knowledge and reason. Though this appears to be a case of luck, it is not really so. For because the desire is natural (presumably, as Woods [1982] says, because it is naturally directed at the good), it is not without reason (οὐ ἀλόγιστον). Hence, the good fortune following on this desire is not assignable simply to luck. Then, at 1248a18–19, Aristotle turns to the actual desiring and asks whether *this*, the desiring of p at t, is caused by luck. The question is immediately generalized: "Will luck similarly be the cause of everything?" An apparent advantage of the generalization is that it would make luck the cause of thinking and deliberating (αἰτία τοῦ νοῆσαι καὶ βουλεύσασθαι). This is an advantage because it would block something even less palatable, namely, a vicious regress concerning the start of thinking. There is, however, another solution, one that Aristotle prefers. This solution, that there is an intrinsic starting-point of movement in the soul, is of considerable interest to us. For because the passage can be considered independently of the general discussion of luck, it provides some direction on the topic of noetic self-motion.

The passage in question, *EE* viii.2, 1248a18–29, divides into three parts. The first sets a puzzle concerning the starting-point of thinking, the second issues conditions on its solution, and the third identifies something that meets the conditions.

A
He who is deliberating has not already deliberated and in turn deliberated prior to that, but there is a certain starting-point (ἀρχή τις); nor has he who thinks already thought prior to thinking (οὐδ' ἐνόησε νοήσας πρότερον νοῆσαι) and so on to infinity (καὶ τοῦτο εἰς ἄπειρον). Thought, then, is not the starting-point of thinking (οὐκ ἄρα τοῦ νοῆσαι ὁ νοῦς ἀρχή). (1248a18–21)

B
Or is there a certain starting-point with no other outside it (τις ἀρχὴ ἧς οὐκ ἔστιν ἄλλη ἔξω), being essentially the sort of thing that is capable of doing this (αὕτη τοιαύτη τῷ εἶναι τὸ τοιοῦτο δύναται ποιεῖν)? What we seek is thus a

certain starting-point of movement in the soul (τίς ἡ τῆς κινήσεως ἀρχὴ ἐν τῇ ψυχῇ). (1248a22–25)

C

It is then clear that as god [is the starting-point of movement] in the universe, so it is in the soul, for somehow the divine element in us moves everything (κινεῖ γάρ πως πάντα τὸ ἐν ἡμῖν θεῖον). The starting-point of λόγος is not λόγος but something superior, and what could be superior to knowledge and thought (νοῦς) but god (θεός). (1248a25–29)

Let me begin with the puzzle. Section A concludes with the remark that thought (νοῦς) is not the starting-point of thinking (νόησις). This is apparently an undesirable result. Why? One reason is this: if νοῦς is not the starting-point of thinking, then how can thinking be up to us? That this is of concern to Aristotle is suggested by the first line of section B, which, in effect, gives us the following dichotomy.

> [2] (a) νοῦς is the starting-point of thinking v (b) something outside νοῦς is the starting-point of thinking.

Proposition [2] assumes that there is an ἀρχή or starting-point of thinking. Some (for example, the Surge theorists) might argue that this assumption is false, at least for productive mind. Hence, one way of dealing with the dilemma would be to reject the assumption underlying proposition [2]. I shall propose, on the other hand, that Aristotle adopts some version of (a). He clearly cannot adopt (b), at least not without sacrifice to the autonomy of thought, and this is a price he would be unwilling to pay. It must, then, be possible to understand (a) in a way that does not generate section A's regress (the "EE-regress").

The EE-regress depends on the following proposition.

> [3] νοῦς is the starting-point of thinking $\rightarrow$ $(x)(T)(x$ thinks $T \rightarrow$ $(\exists T')(T \neq T'$ & T' occurs prior to T & x thinks T' & x's thinking T' causes x's thinking $T))$.

Notice that proposition [3] appears to assume that for νοῦς to be the start of an episode of thinking is just for this episode to be caused by another episode of the same type.[22] That is,

> [3a] νοῦς is the starting-point of thinking$_k$ $\leftrightarrow$ thinking$_j$ is the starting-point of thinking$_k$,

for some thinking$_j$, where j and k are same level. Of course, the text does not rule out the possibility that *sometimes* one episode of thinking may cause a second episode. What it rules out is that this *always* happens. Also,

---

[22] Here I am in agreement with Woods 1982, 182.

we need to understand proposition [3a] as excluding the possibility that a complete thought is its own cause. Otherwise, it will be irrelevant to the regress yielded by proposition [3]. In any case, this is clear from *EE* viii.2, 1248a27–28, where the thought (νοῦς) that is declared unfit to be the starting-point of thinking is the actual₂ episode of thinking, because here Aristotle formulates the point by saying that λόγος cannot be the starting-point of λόγος (λόγου δ' ἀρχὴ οὐ λόγος). So the ἀρχή of thinking cannot be a thought that is combined or propositional in nature.[23]

When Aristotle begins section B, then, he is posing an alternative to the reading of νοῦς in [3a]. Let us suppose, for the moment, that the interrogative character of B is a point of style only. Where (a′) is a generalization of (a) in [2] above, the following holds of whatever is the starting-point of thinking.

> [4] (a′) x is the starting-point of an episode, T', of thinking → (c) x causes T' & (d) there is no z outside of x in virtue of which x causes T' & (e) x is essentially capable of causing T'.

One might take the expression ἧς οὐκ ἔστιν ἄλλη ἔξω ("outside of which there is no other") to mean that the starting-point of thinking can in no way be outside of the mind. This is certainly true—after all, *De an.* ii.5 insists that thinking and perceiving differ just on the point that the objects of the first, but not the second, are in the mind. But this makes (d) irrelevant to the question of what, if any, internal mechanisms are required for the mind to think by itself. Moreover, this would fail to avoid the regress generated by propositions [3] and [3a]. That regress concerned whether one mental item could always be caused by another mental item. So of

> (d1) There can be no starting-point for thinking outside of the mind,

and

> (d2) There can be no starting-point for an episode of thinking outside of the episode,

it must be the second that Aristotle intends in (d) of [4].

In urging (d2) on Aristotle, I am not just saying that a particular episode of thinking is its own starting-point. Though this may be true, it does not articulate Aristotle's concern here. A given episode of thinking is the result of, or is associated with, a change, namely, the change from being a potential₂ thinker to an actual₂ thinker. So when Aristotle asks for the starting-point of thinking, he is asking for the starting-point of actual₂ thinking. As he says at *EE* viii.2, 1248a25, we are seeking a starting-point of movement

---

[23] The propositional nature of λόγος is arguably attested at 1247a13–15, where having a λόγος for φing entails being able to say why (εἰπεῖν διὰ τί) one φed.

in the soul. If this is just the actual₂ thinking itself, then we are left without an explanation of the change. So within the constraints of (d2), we need to find room for the ἀρχή that is the cause of actual₂ thinking.

5. CONSTRAINTS ON NOETIC SELF-MOTION

I proposed that the regress argument of *EE* VIII.2 provides clues as to what the ἀρχή of acts of thinking might be. It must be something that does not lie outside the act it initiates and that is still able, by its very nature, to initiate thinking. If what I have said so far about the *EE*-regress is at all correct, then the ἀρχή itself cannot be propositional. Strictly speaking, this means, as Aristotle says, that νοῦς cannot be the ἀρχή of thought because *as a faculty* νοῦς is actual only insofar as it thinks a complete thought, and this is just what needs to be explained.[24]

The *EE*-regress concerns what might be called "synonymous" or, better, "same-level" causation. One thing is caused by a prior thing that is or was an actual thing of the same kind. Often this style of causation is harmless, as in the case of persons begetting persons. But where my ability to author my thoughts is in question, the causal regress is vicious because it is an explanatory regress. The *explanation* of an ability can hardly consist in citing a same-level exercise of the ability. The ἀρχή of thought can be the cause of acts of thinking, in a theoretically satisfying way, only if the causation operates at a different level from the combined or propositional thoughts it explains. On a view I have argued elsewhere, and continue to advance here, this involves clarifying the role of *De an.* III.5's productive mind in levels causation.[25]

The *EE*-regress provides two further clues to the identity of the ἀρχή of thought. It is said to be divine or the divine in us or, at least, to be linked to something like this. And it is said to be or, more accurately, to involve some kind of capability. Let me first say something about the ἀρχή's divinity, a trait shared by *De anima*'s productive mind, and then turn to the more difficult question of the kind of capability required by the ἀρχή.

Aristotle shows surprising confidence about the ἀρχή's divine status. Concluding discussion of the *EE*-regress in section C, he says it is clear (δῆλον δὴ ὥσπερ) (i) that as god is the principle of movement in the universe (ἐν τῷ ὅλῳ θεός), so is it in the soul. And he argues for (i) on the basis of (ii) that it is the divine in us that moves everything in the soul (κινεῖ

---

[24] This does not exclude that the faculty may be an ἀρχή of something other than thinking. It may, for example, play some such role in action.

[25] See references in note 1. The *EE*-regress may, then, give new and independent support to what is proposed in these works.

πως πάντα τὸ ἐν ἡμῖν θεῖον). As it stands, (i) could be taken in at least two ways. It might mean that god is the principle of movement in the universe and also the principle of movement in the soul;[26] or it might mean that the starting-point of motion, mentioned in the previous phrase, moves in the soul in the way that god moves in the universe. But because (ii), the sufficient condition, is most naturally read as

[5] x is moved & x is in the soul → ($\exists z$)(z is the divine in us & z moves x),

nothing is called for that is any stronger than

[6] (x is the principle of movement in the universe → x is god) → (z is the principle of movement in the soul → z is divine).

Hence, there is no need to suppose that Aristotle intended anything more than analogy in linking the god that drives nature with the ἀρχή that moves all things in the soul.[27] The point of the analogy, I suggest, concerns the style of movement in each case. In the domain of nature, god moves solely as an unmoved mover. So, in the soul, noetic movement must be initiated in the same way, and the ἀρχή is somehow responsible for this.

This last point is connected with the final clue yielded by the *EE*-regress, that the ἀρχή is a capacity of a certain sort. It is, as Aristotle reports, "the sort of thing that is essentially capable of doing this," namely, of causing acts of thinking without need of anything external to the act. In the light of the above paragraph, we can now say that the style of causation involved here will be like that of an unmoved mover. In the next section I will turn directly to this style of mental causation and, in particular, to its connection with the activity of productive mind. But first a rough spot needs some attention.

The *EE*-regress implicitly attributes the following characteristics to the

---

[26] With Alexander and certain neoaphrodisiasts.

[27] Here I agree with the suggestion attributed to Verdenius that the crucial sentence be translated, "It is clear that this starting-point is analogous to the part which God plays in the universe, where he moves everything" (Van der Ejik 1989). Van der Ejik objects that this severs the connection with what follows because he thinks that "the ἀρχή sought is not τὸ ἐν ἡμῖν θεῖον (which is the νοῦς) but ὁ θεός (which is κρεῖττον τοῦ νοῦ)" (30 n. 17). That is, he thinks the ἀρχή is not the divine in us, which he takes to be νοῦς, but god, which he takes to be what is more authoritative than νοῦς. But this fails. Granted, elsewhere Aristotle says that νοῦς is the divine in us (τὸ ἐν ἡμῖν θεῖον [*EN* x.7, 1177a13–16 and b27–31; *Protr.* B108–10 (Düring 1961)]). But these texts have no need to raise, let alone resolve, the question as to which part of νοῦς is responsible for the divinity of the whole. The *EE*-regress, on the contrary, requires this. Further, the remark that god (ὁ θεός) is more authoritative than νοῦς (κρεῖττον τοῦ νοῦ) may serve simply to underscore the claim that τὸ ἐν ἡμῖν θεῖον is superior to the faculty of νοῦς as a whole. It does not, in any event, require identification of ὁ θεός and τὸ ἐν ἡμῖν θεῖον, but calls only for a weaker gloss, something like, "Because, in general, god is superior to νοῦς, the divine in us is superior to our νοῦς."

ἀρχή of thought: (1) it cannot be a "propositional" cause; (2) it cannot be a same-level cause; (3) it must be a certain kind of unmoved cause (that is, a divine or quasi-divine cause); and (4) it is a sort of capability. The rough spot is that Surge Theory appears to remain afloat, at least as far as characteristics (1), (2), and (3) are concerned. Because on Surge Theory thought is always ongoing, (3) appears to be satisfied and (1) and (2) seem only to concern the structure or complexity of this ongoing thought. Characteristic (4) is more difficult, however, because it clashes with the Surge Theoretic principle that thought is always ongoing. For, in general, Aristotle holds that whatever enjoys some measure of potentiality need not, and so over the long term will not, always be in activity. It will not do to respond that the thought that is always ongoing is sometimes rendered unconscious by external factors but never stopped. For on mainline Surge Theory, this durable ongoing thought is just productive mind. But if *De anima*'s productive mind is the *Eudemian Ethics*'s ἀρχή of thought, then productive mind will *not* always be thinking, and Surge Theory would appear to be in trouble.

Finally, the *EE*-regress suggests (5) that the ἀρχή is a *productive* cause of thinking (δύναται ποιεῖν [*EE* viii.2, 1248a23–24]). The Partial Model of *Phys.* viii.4 recognizes (255b26–31) a principle of noetic movement (ἀρχὴ κινήσεως), but it is a principle of being affected only (οὐ τοῦ κινεῖν οὐδὲ τοῦ ποιεῖν ἀλλὰ τοῦ πάσχειν). So the *Eudemian Ethics* is calling for something more. This productive feature of thought is closely related to characteristic (3), for a principle of movement that operates in the manner of an unmoved mover could hardly be said to be a principle of *being affected*. So we can say that the ἀρχή will somehow be or involve an unmoved productive cause of thinking.

6. PRODUCTIVE MIND AND THE ΑΡΧΗ OF THOUGHT

The positive proposal I wish to defend is that the *Eudemian Ethics*'s characterization of the ἀρχή of thought fits, in a surprisingly close way, *De anima*'s productive mind. Obviously, the divine nature of the *Eudemian Ethics*'s ἀρχή favors linkage with productive mind insofar as *De an.* iii.5 makes much of the latter's divine status. At first glance, at least. But we can also develop in some detail the admittedly deflationary suggestion that the *EE*-regress presumes that the ἀρχή of thinking must somehow be unmoved because this is the mode of divine causation.

One place to begin is by noticing that Aristotle makes considerable use of Anaxagoras's views in developing the account of νοῦς in *De an.* iii.4. In particular, Aristotle makes explicit a dilemma that is implicit in his predecessor's views and, hence, uses them to fashion a theory that avoids the dilemma. Thus, Aristotle will share certain Anaxagorean doctrines but will show how to make them safe for thought.

At *De an.* III.4, 429a18–20, Aristotle mentions, and even appears to endorse, the Anaxagorean view that the mind is unmixed (ἀμιγῆ). This property appears for a second time at 429b22–23, under the description "having nothing in common," along with the property of being simple (ἁπλοῦν) and that of being unaffected (ἀπαθές). These three properties lead to a problem with a familiar look. For what began the chapter as an apparently straightforward question has, by the chapter's end, been transformed into a dilemma (I shall call it the "End Dilemma"):

> If the mind is simple (ἁπλοῦν), unaffected (ἀπαθές), and has nothing in common with anything (μηθενὶ μηθὲν ἔχει κοινόν), as Anaxagoras says, how will it think if thinking is a kind of being affected (εἰ τὸ πάσχειν τί ἐστιν)? (429b23–26)

The End Dilemma is left unresolved in *De an.* III.4.[28] We leave that chapter without a positive account of the switch from potential₂ to actual₂ thinking. The following chapter's distinction between receptive and productive minds is needed to explain this and so fully to resolve the dilemma.

Again, the Anaxagorean account will prove useful. Now several things are clear about Aristotle's dilemma. For example, because of the Causal Thesis, it is clear that thinking is, at least, something like a kind of being affected. So one obvious suggestion for resolution is ruled out, namely, dropping the πάσχειν condition completely. It is also clear that Anaxagoras recognizes all three of the End Dilemma's properties. At *De an.* I.2, 405a13–19, for example, Aristotle reports that the Anaxagorean mind is simple (ἁπλοῦν), unmixed (ἀμιγῆ), and pure (καθαρόν). The last two, we may suppose, are equivalent to having nothing in common (μηθενὶ μηθὲν ἔχει κοινόν) and being unaffected (ἀπαθές), respectively. (In any case, these are added at 405b19–21.) Further, it is clear from 405b19–22 that being unaffected and having nothing in common are sufficient for the End Dilemma:

> Anaxagoras alone says that the mind is unaffected (ἀπαθῆ) and has nothing in common with anything else (κοινὸν οὐθὲν οὐθενὶ τῶν ἄλλων ἔχειν). But if it is like this (τοιοῦτος δ' ὤν), how will it think (πῶς γνωριεῖ) and by what cause (διὰ τίν' αἰτίαν)?

---

[28] This is not quite correct. Aristotle offers at the end of *De an.* III.4 to meet the dilemma by appealing to the thesis that the mind in activity is the same as its object. But this amounts to little more than a nominal solution. In particular, we are given no indication of how the mind must be organized in order to accomplish what the nominal solution requires. (For an extended discussion of this proposal, see Wedin 1988, especially "*De anima* III.4 and the 'Paradoxes' of Thought," 195–202.)

So despite the fact that he calls the mind the principle of movement (at 405a17–18 it is reported to be the ἀρχή of knowing and movement), the Anaxagorean cannot account for the cause of thinking. *Phys.* VIII.5 gives us a nice way to see this dilemma. At 256b16–24, Aristotle considers three components of movement: the thing moved (τὸ κινούμενον), the thing that moves (τὸ κινοῦν), and that by which the movement occurs (τὸ ᾧ κινεῖ). The first must be in motion, the third both moves and is in motion, but the second must be unmoved. Then Aristotle says,

> For this reason Anaxagoras speaks correctly when he asserts that the mind is unaffected (ἀπαθῆ) and unmixed (ἀμιγῆ), since he makes it the principle of movement (κινήσεως ἀρχὴν αὐτὸν εἶναι ποιεῖ), for it could move in this way only by being unmoved (οὕτω γὰρ μόνον ἂν κινοίη ἀκίνητος ὤν). (256b24–27)

This suggests a useful formulation of the End Dilemma. The properties that in *Phys.* VIII.5 entail that the mind move as an unmoved mover are the very same properties that in *De an.* III.4 call into question how the mind can think at all. Thus, *De an.* III.4 also appears to call into question how the mind can move as an unmoved mover, because this is the crucial condition in explaining how the mind can be a self-mover. For a system is self-moving only if it contains something that is capable of initiating movement without being moved (ὃ κινεῖ ἀκίνητον ὄν [*Phys.* VIII.5, 256b24]). In the domain of action, it might be sufficient simply to count the mind as this unmoved feature. But where the domain is already restricted to thinking, the unmoved mover must be located *within* the mind itself. This is why the Anaxagorean proposal finally cannot explain *noetic* self-motion and why *De an.* III.4 worries about how thinking can come about.[29]

Notice that the property of simplicity is not mentioned in *Phys.* VIII.5's version of the End Dilemma; nor is it mentioned along with the other two Anaxagorean properties at the outset of *De an.* III.4. So why does Aristotle include simplicity when he formulates the End Dilemma at the chapter's end? Well, one reason is that it provides a bridge to *De an.* III.5. It would not be enough, for example, simply to add that, as well as a sort of being-affected, thinking is also a sort of producing. For if the mind were simple, we would still require external causation. If, then, we are to provide for self-motion and thus secure the autonomy of thought, the mind cannot be simple. Hence, Aristotle gives us the property that must be relinquished, if self-motion is to be saved.

---

[29] It will not do to suppose that the *Phys.* VIII.5 discussion concerns a different sense of movement. There and in *De an.* III.4, Aristotle is concerned about the moving cause of individual acts of thinking. For the *Phys.* VIII.5 discussion is governed by VII.2's opening remarks that the first movement of a thing is not the "for the sake of which" but the source of motion, that is, ἡ ἀρχὴ τῆς κινήσεως. So here, as in the *EE*-regress and *De anima*, Aristotle's concern is with how the mind can switch from potential₂ to actual₂ thinking.

The suggestion that the End Dilemma concerns the possibility of noetic self-motion and that its resolution involves giving up simplicity as a property of the mind will come as no surprise to students of Aristotle's physics. At *Phys.* VIII.5, 257a31–33, in announcing a fresh start, Aristotle says: "If something moves itself, how and in what manner does it move (εἴ τι κινεῖ αὐτὸ αὐτό, πῶς κινεῖ καὶ τίνα τρόπον)?" It is, he says at 257b2, impossible that a thing move itself as a complete whole (ἀδύνατον δὴ τὸ αὐτὸ αὐτὸ κινοῦν πάντῃ κινεῖν αὐτὸ αὐτό). Rather,

> What moves itself must have in it that which moves but is unmoved (τὸ αὐτὸ ἑαυτὸ κινοῦν ἔχειν τὸ κινοῦν ἀκίνητον) and that which is moved (τὸ κινο-ύμενον) . . . and these must be in contact with each other or at least one with the other (ἁπτόμενα ἤτοι ἄμφω ἀλλήλων ἢ θατέρου θάτερον). . . . It moves itself as a whole (ὅλον κινεῖ αὐτὸ ἑαυτό), being moved and moving (κινού-μενόν τε καὶ κινοῦν) in virtue of having in it something that moves and something that is moved (τῷ αὐτοῦ τι εἶναι τὸ κινοῦν καὶ τὸ κινούμενον). (258a18–25)

Far from denying the possibility of self-motion, this passage attempts to explain it. Self-motion of a whole is allowed, but it must be explained by appeal to certain causal relations among the parts of the whole. So nothing that is simple could move itself. In mentioning simplicity in the End Dilemma, then, Aristotle gives us the key to the dilemma's solution and points ahead to *De an.* III.5's distinction between a part of the mind that is such as to produce all things in the mind and a part that is such as to become all things. These are just productive and receptive minds.

But there is more to the story than this. For according to the Causal Thesis, νοῦς is moved to thought by the object of thought (τὸ νοητόν), and it is unclear how this is related to productive mind's activity. The situation is further complicated by the fact that we must preserve the divine style of the mind's thinking. So the production of thought must preserve the unmoved character of the cause of thinking. My suggestion is that Aristotle, in effect, adopts the following principle.

> [PROD] Productive mind produces the object that, without being moved, moves the mind to actual$_2$ thought.

From the *EE*-regress we know that whatever productive mind produces, it cannot be "propositional" in nature—not, at any rate, if it is to bring νοῦς as a whole to activity$_2$. So productive mind will have to produce something nonpropositional. Roughly, the idea is that it produces objects of thought, the νοητά. Woods suggested (1982, 182) that the *EE*-regress could be stopped if we were to give up the supposition that "each mental act is initiated by another of the same type." In effect, I am proposing just this on Aristotle's behalf, because productive mind's producing of the νοητόν is equivalent to the switching of νοῦς, as a whole, from potential$_2$

to actual$_2$ thinking, and though the thinking itself may be propositional, the switch is not.

Some might worry about this use of the *EE*-regress. In particular, they might challenge use of the *EE*-regress to support the claim that the ἀρχή of thought is nonpropositional in a way that bears on noetic self-motion, in a way, that is, that involves some kind of nonpropositional noetic event. One source of worry might be the fact that surrounding texts contain a number of claims that may be difficult to reconcile with my proposal, including: (a) one can have success without reason (*EE* VIII.2, 1247a13–16); (b) certain impulses (ὁρμαί) operate without reason (1247b18–20); (c) certain agents lack reason and yet succeed because they have a starting-point that is superior to thought and deliberation (1248a29–34). Now (a), (b), and (c) appear to entail that, when Aristotle asserts in the *EE*-regress passage that the starting-point of λόγος is not λόγος, he means that the starting-point is impulse. Thus, how can it be appropriate to use the *EE*-regress as support for the thesis that the start of actual thinking is some sort of nonpropositional noetic event?

Despite some initial plausibility, the objection can be met. For one thing, I have already indicated that, on the points of interest to us, the text containing the *EE*-regress can be considered pretty much on its own. So the appeal to flanking passages would not be conclusive anyway. Notice, in any case, that the ἀρχή mentioned in objection (c) can operate independently of reason, whereas the ἀρχή sought in the *EE*-regress passage is explicitly said to be the start of *thinking*. It is the ἀρχή τοῦ νοῆσαι. So despite the fact that both are said to be "superior," the one to thought (νοῦς) and deliberation (βούλευσις), the other to thought (νοῦς) and knowledge (ἐπιστήμη), the two starting-points are importantly different. Indeed, mention of deliberation in the first case may indicate that there Aristotle is concerned with the starting-point of action only.

Let us suppose, nonetheless, that the starting-point of thought is something like an impulse. It will, then, still be nonpropositional, perhaps, something like an impulse to act or to do something. But now it is unclear how this is even relevant to the *EE*-regress, for the *EE*-regress concerns thought only. Perhaps, it might be suggested, there is some sort of "quasi-impulse" that initiates thought. Still, this will have to be strictly noetic. So where we are concerned with thinking in the proper sense of the term, that is, with thinking that does not serve action or production, the starting-point will still have to be a nonpropositional *noetic* event. But this is virtually what has been proposed here. Finally to arrive at our interpretation, as opposed to a Surge Theory account, we need a provision for the self-moving nature of thinking. This, in effect, is [PROD].

It is important to be clear on what [PROD] is claiming. It is not, for example, claiming that Aristotle countenances some sort of "nonpropositional" thought that the *person* engages in. When I think something, I do so in virtue of the faculty of mind (νοῦς). At the outset of *De an.* III.4, this faculty is described as "that whereby we know and reason," and these arguably are propositional functions. But my exercising such a function *autonomously* requires that from a ready stock of concepts I can produce the thoughts I wish, when I wish. This calls for the further distinction between receptive and productive minds. Because they are merely subsystems of the faculty of mind, neither operates on its own. Thus, we do not find ourselves in the position of having to explain how two supposedly autonomous faculties, each with their unaccountably distinct objects, are related, but only how the subsystems together subserve the function of thought, that is, the grasping of universals—the mind's proper objects. Take, for example, the proposition P, that the diagonal is incommensurate with the side of the square. To think the proposition is ipso facto to think of the objects the thought is about, say, diagonality D, and incommensurability I. Certainly, I am aware of thinking P, but I am not aware of producing D and I. Yet produced they must be. According to [PROD], they are produced by productive mind and, because productive mind is a lower-level subsystem, there is no need for me to be aware of the producing. So the thinking that I do in virtue of having the faculty of mind is pretty certainly propositional, but the lower-level functions that cause it need not be. It is, I think, no accident that *De an.* III.6 goes on to discuss uncombined thoughts, for these are precisely what would be involved in productive mind's production of a nonpropositional object of thought.[30]

Not everyone will regard [PROD] as intuitively compelling.[31] So it is important to clarify the exact nature of the concerns about it. The source of at least some of the worries can be traced to the fact that [PROD] is not a simple thesis but, in fact, contains subtheses that appear to raise problems for [PROD] itself. In particular, concern might be directed at the following:

[PROD₁] Productive mind produces the object(s) of thought.

[PROD₂] The object of thought produced by productive mind is not moved.

---

[30] This is discussed at greater length in Wedin 1988. Christopher Shields has alerted me to the need to address the worry that [PROD] runs afoul of the quite plausible claim that causes relate events and explanations relate propositions. But the worry can be allayed. First, S's coming to think something at t might be said to be caused by (a) something propositional occurring at t, or by (b) something nonpropositional being produced at t. Both causes are events, but only (a) contains a propositional entity as constituent; (b), which [PROD] entails, does not. Second, where Aristotle is concerned with the fine structure of the causal mechanisms, it will typically be the object figuring in the event that is assigned primary causal agency. That is, not the event of the hammer's moving downward, but the hammer itself is what makes contact with the spike. In the case of thought, it is the object of thought that moves the mind to actual₂ thinking (see below and Wedin 1989).

[31] In this and the following couple of paragraphs I am, again, indebted to worries and suggestions put by Christopher Shields.

[PROD₃] The object of thought produced by productive mind moves the mind to actual₂ thought.

I shall argue that, when properly understood, these subtheses are not subject to the worries in question and that, perhaps, such resiliency is to be taken as an additional mark in favor of [PROD].

The first objection (call it the "Production Problem") focuses on the style of production involved in [PROD₁]. If the object of thought is produced in the standard way, that is, in the way that a couch is produced by a couch maker, then it would appear to be moved after all; hence, one of the *EE*-regress's constraints on the ἀρχή of noetic self-motion will be violated, namely, the requirement that the ἀρχή provide for an unmoved cause of thinking. A first response to the Production Problem is to point out that it assumes that the production of the object of thought is like production of an artifact. If we reject this assumption, as I think we should, then we must deal with the question of the nature of production that is supposed to be involved in [PROD₁]. The quick answer to this is that the production in question is what I earlier called levels causation. More needs to be said about this, but first it will be useful to consider a second, and related, concern.

The second concern is that [PROD₁] and [PROD₂] may not be consistent and, thus, that [PROD] itself may be incoherent. Here is one way to put the Coherence Problem, as I shall call it. [PROD₁] says that the object of thought is produced by productive mind, and [PROD₂] requires that this object itself be unmoved. If the production mentioned in [PROD₁] is a kind of being moved, then [PROD] appears to harbor a contradiction, namely, that the object of thought is both moved and unmoved.

But this consequence can be avoided, for [PROD₂] might mean either

[PROD₂ₐ] The object of thought produced by productive mind is not moved *in coming into existence*,

or

[PROD₂ᵦ] The object of thought produced by productive mind is not moved *in its role in bringing the mind as a whole to actual₂ thought*.

For the moment, I will grant what both the Production Problem and the Coherence Problem assume, that the producing done by [PROD₁] is a kind of being moved. So, provisionally, I am willing to count [PROD₂ₐ] false. But this is compatible with the truth of [PROD₂ᵦ], and it is [PROD₂ᵦ] that is crucial to [PROD] itself. In short, that the object of thought is moved as a result of its being produced does not entail that the *produced* object is moved in its role as the cause of thinking. After all, objects of perception result from production, but no one would conclude from this that they are moved in their role as the cause of episodes of actual$_2$ perceiving.

As with the Production Problem, this response to the Coherence Problem generates the need for a finer account of the style of production involved in [PROD]. One way of approaching this is to put renewed pressure on [PROD$_1$]. What sort of production is to be attributed to productive mind? One suggestion would be that it is possible for an object of thought T to be an unmoved mover, even though there are antecedent conditions that are sufficient for T's existence, that is, conditions that yield T. Represent this as

[DET] T is an unmoved mover (of thought) → (There exist certain conditions c & (c obtains → T obtains)).

We may, then, specify a second, perhaps indeterministic, account by denying the existence of such antecedent conditions.

[INDET] T is an unmoved mover (of thought) → ~(There exist certain conditions c & (c obtains → T obtains)).

At first glance, [INDET] would appear to command some allegiance. After all, the unmoved causal role of the object of thought must be squared with Aristotle's insistence that thinking be up to us, and [INDET] at least avoids the appearance of noetic determinism. On the other hand, in insisting that persons are able to think *what they wish*, *when they wish*, Aristotle requires that what a subject thinks be (in some sense) under his control. This goes beyond [INDET], which appears to allow that a subject's thoughts be purely random.

What is attractive about [INDET], and certainly worth retaining, is the idea that our thoughts are not caused by anything outside us. But this does not rule out their being caused internally, so long as this preserves the overall self-moving character of thinking. An interpretation of [DET] along these lines could provide an account of [PROD], but only if the antecedent conditions, c, are not external and do not yield T by an ordinary causal process. For an ordinary causal process holds between items that touch *each other* and so are reciprocally moved.

Above I provisionally allowed that in being produced by productive mind, the object of thought might in some sense be moved. But if [LC], the principle of levels causation, applies to this producing, then it will not count as any sort of standard causal process. Thus, let c, the antecedent conditions mentioned in [DET] and [INDET], be something like the supervenient basis for the object of thought, T. Then, although the existence of c is sufficient for the existence of T, T is not a proper part of the causal processes involving c. Rather, T simply emerges at the level of the mind itself. So there can be antecedent conditions sufficient for T's occurrence, and yet we need not allow that *T* itself is moved in any standard way. By the same token, *T* is not moved in bringing Smith's mind to active thought: for *T* to be produced at *t* is just for *T* to emerge as the content of Smith's mind at *t*, whether the content be *T* itself or a proposition about *T*.[32]

This is what one would expect in the light of the *EE*-regress, which requires that the cause of thinking not be a same-level entity or process. As a kind of levels causation, we are to conceptualize production of *T* as production occurring at a lower level of organization in the noetic system. When, at that level, a νοητόν is produced, then, at a higher level of organization, the mind as a whole is brought to activity. From this point of view— that is, from the point of view of a multileveled system—what is produced, and so in some sense moved, at one level may act as an unmoved mover at another level. So insofar as the mind as a whole is concerned, the object that brings the mind to activity, that is, the object that the thought is about, is both actual$_2$ and unmoved *relative to that act of thinking*. And because the object is produced internally, the thinking it causes is up to us.

Some will argue that the switch from potential$_2$ to actual$_2$ thinking does not involve a causal factor, certainly nothing like the object of thought. In effect, this challenges the need for [PROD$_3$]. But the evidence tells a different ent story. The thesis that the object of thought enjoys a causal role (the Causal Thesis) is one that Aristotle holds to.[33] In fact, the causal role of the object of thought is critical to Aristotle's theory. In particular, it is essential that the νοητόν, the proper object of thought, be the *proper cause* of actual$_2$ thinking. In part, this reflects Aristotle's insistence on what might be called the Proper Cause Thesis, namely, the thesis that the proper object of a faculty's exercise be the very object that causes the exercise. No doubt one motivating factor here is epistemic reliability: If a cognitive faculty is by nature reliable,[34] and if a subject's actual$_2$ cognitive state is caused by the object of the faculty's function, namely, its proper object, then it is hard to motivate interest in skeptical worries. So, at least, might Aristotle have reasoned.

In the present context, however, Aristotle's insistence on the Proper Cause Thesis may have a more interesting source, for it can be used to thwart a regress, at the level of productive mind, analogous to the *EE*-regress. That is, not only is the νοητόν that causes my (propositional)

---

[32] Because I believe it undesirable to attribute to Aristotle so-called "nondiscursive" thought (see Wedin 1988, 128–32), I prefer the second alternative. The important point here is that, as the object that brings the mind to activity, *T* must be nonpropositional.

[33] For a full defense of attribution of the Causal Thesis to Aristotle, see Wedin 1989, 72–73; and Wedin 1993.

[34] In *Rhet.* I.1 we get a crisp statement of faculty reliabilism. Of the faculty (δύναμις) whose domain is truth and falsity, Aristotle says that men have a natural capacity sufficient for truth (πρὸς τὸ ἀληθὲς πεφύκασιν ἱκανῶς) and in most cases attain it (1355a14–17).

thinking not propositional, but it is also not caused by another non-propositional νοητόν, and so on. For the νοητόν, which is the proper cause, will be emergent with respect to certain lower-level and, perhaps ultimately, physical processes. The Proper Cause Thesis is crucial at this lower level as well, for it protects noetic autonomy against the effects of lower-level causal determinism. Thus, suppose that c, the supervenient basis for the object of thought T, is caused by a prior state c_1, and that c_1 determines c. Suppose further that this pattern of determination continues indefinitely. Were one to say that c *properly* caused T, then nothing would prevent our saying that c_1 caused T, and so on. This is avoided by insisting that, at least in the case of the mind, the proper object of a faculty's exercise is also the proper cause of the exercise. But because T is simply an offshoot or concomitant of c (recall [LC] here),[35] Aristotle is free to install T as the proper cause of thinking without threat from whatever causal regress may attach to the primary state that gives rise to T.[36]

If the object of thought is the first mover of actual₂ thinking, then it must satisfy what I shall call the Immediacy Constraint, a condition contained in the opening lines of *Phys.* vii.2:

> That which first moves (τὸ πρῶτον κινοῦν), not as that for the sake of which (τὸ οὗ ἕνεκα) but rather that from which we get the start of motion (ὅθεν ἡ ἀρχὴ τῆς κινήσεως), is together with what is moved (by "together" I mean that there is nothing between them [οὐδέν ἐστιν αὐτῶν μεταξύ]). (243a32–34)

It seems to me that we cannot take the Causal Thesis seriously without taking seriously the Immediacy Constraint. The constraint takes the first thing that moves to be that *from which* (ὅθεν) the start of motion (ἡ ἀρχὴ τῆς κινήσεως) ensues. This will be the object that moves without being

---

[35] Again I appeal to the idiom of *EN* I.4 mentioned in note 15 above. See now also Sauvé (1987), whose general account of unmoved movers seems to support, in certain respects, the specific account given here. The Proper Cause Thesis may prove especially attractive to functionally or cognitively minded interpreters. Because they are the *proper* causes of noetic episodes, objects of thought are in principle invariant with respect to their supervenient bases. Thus, occurrence of a given object of thought could be, or could have been, subserved by a different physical base. So the theory appears open to the multiple realizability favored by functionalists. For more on this, see Wedin 1993.

[36] Gill (1989, 225 n. 29) has objected that a first mover, to initiate motion, must provide an impetus, and that unmoved movers cannot do so. Thus, the object of thought cannot be both unmoved and the cause of actual₂ thinking. But it is hard to see how this squares with the claim at *De an.* II.5, 417b19–26, discussed above, that the *activity* of perception is caused by external objects (τὰ ποιητικὰ τῆς ἐνεργείας ἔξωθεν) and that of thinking by something internal, not to mention the claim at *Meta.* Λ.7, 1072a30, that the mind is *moved* (κινεῖται) by the object of thought. Though this is not the entire story, it is clear that objects of thought are conceived of as proper unmoved causes. (I note, however, that Gill takes a rather different line from mine on the *De an.* II.5 passage.)

moved. If the Immediacy Constraint is meant to apply to thinking, then we would expect to find Aristotle holding that, when νοῦς as a whole is caused to think by the νοητόν, nothing lies between them. They must be in contact, as it were. As it turns out, precisely this is recommended in *Meta.* Λ.7. At 1072b19–24, the mind is characterized as that which is capable of receiving the object of thought. It is active$_2$ when it possesses the object, and it becomes active by coming into contact with the object.[37]

How are we to think of this noetic contact? As a rule, Aristotle appears to hold that one object can move another by push or by pull. The first case covers standard causal processes, that is, processes in which x moves y by physical contact. But in such cases, x itself is moved. So push causation, as we might call it, will not work for thought because here Aristotle needs a notion of contact that does not result in T, the νοητόν that moves the mind, being moved in turn. Given this, it is tempting to turn for help to the second style of object causation, pull causation. In particular, it is tempting to appeal to the way the object of desire "pulls" or moves the soul, and thus the animal, to action.

I suppose one might think of the mind's being moved by the object of thought as a kind of attraction to an object of desire, perhaps to an object of "noetic desire." But the comparison is imperfect. First, unlike the object of thought, the object of desire is a particular that exists independently of the agent. Second, though in the case of action the attraction or pull may come to operate at a moment, it gets played out over time, until completion of the action. In noetic acts, on the other hand, occurrence of the object of thought is ipso facto occurrence of a complete thought. Third, unlike the animal that is moved by desire, the mind is nothing until it thinks (recall *De an.* III.4, 429b30: ἀλλ' ἐντελεχείᾳ οὐδέν, πρὶν ἂν νοῇ). Because it has no organ, the mind is not the actualization$_1$ of any set of physical structures. So unlike other faculties, the mind is nothing other than the potentiality$_2$ to grasp objects of thought (and pretty abstract ones at that, namely, universals). For it to be actual$_2$ is just for it to grasp such an object. For this to happen, the object must be produced, and this is just for certain mental content to occur, namely, content that amounts to representation of the object. And because, absent such content, there is nothing actual to count as the mind (as opposed to the actual thing that has noetic potentiality$_2$), the occurrence thus of T is equivalent to the mind coming into existence *as a mind thinking T*.[38] So it is a corollary of the theory that νοῦς itself "materializes" when a νοητόν is produced.

[37] For more on this, see Wedin 1989.

[38] This underlies what in Wedin 1988 was called model *M*: At t, a thinks something P if, and only if, at t, a's mind not only produces P but also produces itself by producing P. The relation suggested here between mind and mental content also fits Aristotle's thesis that the mind in activity is the same as its object (what I call the Sameness Thesis in Wedin 1989). See further Wedin 1993.

Moreover, the noetic causation featured in the theory counts as a kind of contact. After all, nothing lies between the object of thought and the mind it brings to activity. Furthermore, although the object moves the mind by contact, it remains itself unmoved, because this is not a case of reciprocal contact. It is, rather, the one-way contact described at *Phys.* VIII.5, 258a18–25, where only one member of the mover–moved pair is in contact with the other. Thus, the νοητόν makes contact with the mind without suffering contact in return. Indeed, given Aristotle's theory, this alternative cannot arise. Because occurrence of the νοητόν just constitutes actual$_2$ thinking, it counts as something like a limiting case of contact. And because the mind is nothing until production of the νοητόν brings it to actual$_2$ existence, there could be no reciprocity in such contact.

We are advised again to bear in mind that the causation involved in this story is levels causation. Just as the object of thought emerges given the occurrence of certain lower-level primary states, so also does the mind itself. Underlying this is the conviction that there is no Cartesian-like mental substance that engages directly in full mental acts. Indeed, early on in *De anima*, at 408b5–17, Aristotle cautions that we should say not that the mind thinks, but that the person thinks in virtue of his mind. This I take to be a recommendation to replace agency talk with subsystems talk.[39] That is, rather than saying that the *mind* thinks *T*, we ought to say, when speaking carefully, that I think *T* in virtue of a capacity$_2$ for representing the object of thought *T*. And this is just a capacity$_2$ for occurrence of a certain psychological state. Productive mind is just part of the mechanism that subserves this capacity, part, that is, of what enables the occurrence of mental content about or involving *T*.[40]

Notice, finally, that it is not productive mind itself but the νοητόν it produces that is the primary source of movement. Productive mind is, rather, the enabling mechanism. So for productive mind, at one level, to produce an object of thought is ipso facto for νοῦς, at another level, to come into contact with the object and, thus, for the noetic system as a

---

[39] Not all commentators share this view. For a defense see Wedin 1988, 10–11, and Wedin 1993, "Appendix I: Levels Causation Revisited."

[40] There is more to the story than this. Of particular importance is the fact that production of the νοητόν amounts to a kind of representation. Thus, we might say that productive mind produces the object of thought by producing a representation of it. This will be the νόημα. The representational role of the νόημα is in turn explained by the occurrence at a yet lower level in the system of an appropriate image (φάντασμα). It is worth observing that [LC], the principle of levels causation, will apply at each level of organization. The presence to νοῦς of an object of thought, produced by productive mind, puts the noetic system, or mind as a whole, into an internal state (whatever state it is in when it is active$_2$), and this state is emergent with respect to the properties and entities countenanced at the level of productive and receptive minds. These in turn will be emergent with respect to images, and so on. The way thoughts and images enter the story is, thus, quite complicated. I cannot go into that here, but see Wedin 1988; 1989; and 1993.

whole to be brought to activity.[41] When this happens, the person thinks—
or, perhaps better, when the person thinks, this is what happens.[42]

For Aristotle, noetic self-motion is among the received facts of human
psychology. But given his theoretical commitments, it is a puzzling fact,
resisting straightforward attribution either to persons or to their minds. It
is, rather, a phenomenon to be saved by theory. The theory conceives of the
mind as a complex, multilevel system, within which productive mind plays
an essential role in providing for the autonomy of thought. So productive
mind is essentially a creature of theory. Its acceptability rests on the theoretical adequacy of the system of which it is a part, namely, the noetic
system of *De anima*.

A virtue claimed for the interpretation offered in this paper is that it
provides an integrated account of a number of Aristotle's pronouncements
on the mechanisms of thought. Among these were the following:

1. Thinking is up to us.
2. The start (ἀρχή) of thinking is not (propositional) thinking.
3. The cause of thinking must operate as an unmoved mover.
4. Actual$_2$ thinking is caused by the object of thought.
5. The object that brings the mind to activity must be actual$_2$.
6. What moves the mind to think does so by contact.
7. Something can move itself only insofar as it has parts of a certain sort.

In sketching a theory adequate to these seven features, I have given prominence to [PROD], the thesis that productive mind produces the object that,
without being moved, moves the mind as a whole to think. It should be
clear by now how [PROD] fits an account that explains all seven features.

---

[41] Lear (1988, 135–41) has a rather different account of productive mind, one friendly to
Surge theorists. He insists that its "making" is not any sort of productive activity, but rather is
"explicable in terms of the causal responsibility of form at the highest level." One advantage
claimed for our account was its ability to wed productive mind to Aristotle's causal claims on
behalf of the object of thought, that is, the claims that νοῦς is moved by the νοητόν and that
νοητά are the ποιητικά that cause the switch from potential$_2$ to actual$_2$ knowing. For Lear, on
the other hand, productive mind has an essentially metaphysical role. By its "causal responsibility," he means that "in being understood the form rises to its highest-level actuality: it
now is mind thinking the form" (137). I do not see how this could amount to much more than
redescribing the problem, whatever it is. In any case, it has the consequence that all natural
forms depend on the mind. Thus, a frog's natural form exists, when thought, in a richer way
than when enmattered in froggy stuff. Predictably, this leads Lear away from a scientific
account of productive mind and toward its identification with god.

[42] Because the object produced by productive mind is nonpropositional, and because what
persons think is propositional, an account needs to be given of how propositional thinking
occurs. Aristotle himself says very little about this, appearing to be content with the remark at
De an. III.6, 430b5–6, that νοῦς is able to combine thoughts. See further Wedin 1989.

Nonetheless, a few summary remarks might be useful. Feature 1, of course, is the principle explanandum because it is equivalent to, or at least entails, the possibility of noetic self-motion. Feature 2 is a constraint taken from the *EE*-regress, and feature 3 is from the *EE*-regress's assertion that the ἀρχή of thought must be something divine. The unmoved style of causation, coupled with the prohibition on same-level causation, suggests feature 4, which is also independently attested. Feature 4 can be maintained in the face of feature 1 only if the object of thought is not external. But the internal status of the object of thought will not save feature 1 if the *source* of the object lies outside. Thus, productive mind enables the system itself to produce, at a lower level of organization, the object that, at a higher level of organization, moves the mind itself to think. This enables us to account for feature 5, because from the point of view of νοῦς as a whole, the νοητόν that causes thinking is actual$_2$. It is also, as feature 6 requires, in immediate contact with the mind because it is just what our thought is about. Finally, feature 7 issues a general constraint on any system capable of self-motion. For noetic systems, it is met by distinguishing the productive and receptive parts of the mind.

A final word on the divinity of νοῦς. *EE* viii.2 promotes the divine nature of the ἀρχή of thought. On the deflationary reading suggested here, this is a claim about the *way* in which the ἀρχή initiates thinking—more specifically, that it is a call for an unmoved cause of thought. In *Phys.* viii.2, 253a11–21, and viii.6, 259b1–16, Aristotle voices a worry about animals starting movement from a complete state of rest, without any external cause. For might not, then, the entire cosmos have moved itself in this same way? Aristotle blocks this potential embarrassment by declaring that, in fact, most of these movements come about because of factors present in the external environment. Two cases are of interest here. On the one hand, there are nonperceptual or nonintentional movements that are subject to external factors. Typically, these are bodily movements of which we are unaware, which therefore are not up to us. Such movements can, prompted by external factors, result in restoration of intentional states—as when animals awaken. So this is a movement that is not up to us. On the other hand, there are certain intentional movements that are up to us but are not completely independent of external factors. For example, πρᾶξεις or actions are up to us, and so they must be self-moved in some sense. But Aristotle is not entirely persuaded that actions are cases of pure self-motion. This uncertainty is reflected in the complicated nature of *De an.* iii.10's account of the producer of action. It is the faculty of desire as such (τὸ ὀρεκτικὸν ᾗ ὀρεκτικόν), but primarily, he says, it is the object of desire (πρῶτον δὲ πάντων τὸ ὀρεκτόν).[43]

It is at least clear that Aristotle's account of human action gives an

---

[43] For more on this, see Susan Sauvé Meyer's contribution to this volume.

essential causal role to the object of desire. On our interpretation, the object of thought has a parallel role in Aristotle's account of thinking. But there is a major difference. In both thought and action, the first thing that moves is an unmoved mover, the νοητόν and the ὀρεκτόν, respectively. In action as in perception, however, what causes the action will be or will involve an external object or state of affairs. But, unlike perception, acting is still up to us. So why is it not divine, like thought? Put another way, why is φing's being up to us only a necessary condition for its divinity? The answer is to be sought in the causal role played by the object of φing. Acting is up to us because, in principle, we have final say on whether we pursue, avoid, or refrain from a given course of action that presents itself. In a sense, it is up to us which objects or states of affairs we allow to move us to action. Nonetheless, if action is to ensue, certain external circumstances must obtain, including, typically, the presence of the object. This suggests that thought's claim to divinity is tied to the fact that the object of thought is *in no way* external. Now, I think it is true that this permits the divinity of noetic causation. But it does not establish it. After all, neither νοῦς nor any of its parts would rate divine status were the νοητά that bring it to activity implanted or induced by Martians, or even by god. For, strictly speaking, this would not count as self-motion. So what makes νοῦς divine must be that it produces the very objects that bring it to activity. This is also what makes νοῦς capable of self-motion; and because it produces the objects, credit for the mind's divinity ultimately goes to productive mind.[44] For this reason also, productive mind alone fits the *Eudemian Ethics*'s requirement that the ἀρχή of thought be τὸ ἐν ἡμῖν θεῖον.

[44] The deflationary account of productive mind's divinity is matched by a deflationary account of its separability. Additional support for the first is found in Wedin 1988, chap. 6. On the question of separability, see chap. 5, sec. 5 there, "The Attributes of Productive Mind."

CHAPTER 6

Mind and Motion in Aristotle

CHRISTOPHER SHIELDS

> The actuality of perception is spoken of as similar
> to contemplation. There is, however, a difference.
> (*De an.* ii.5, 417b19–20)

IN HIS DISCUSSION of νόησις in the *De anima*, Aristotle allows that an individual with an established, articulated conceptual repertoire can think at will, or, as he says, "Having [so] wished, one is able to contemplate (βουληθεὶς δυνατὸς θεωρεῖν)" (*De an.* ii.5, 417a27–28). Similarly, Aristotle holds that knowledge apprehends universals, whereas sense perception senses individuals (*De an.* ii.5, 417b23; cf. *Po. An.* i.31, 87b37–88a7), and that consequently we can move ourselves to think in a way we cannot move ourselves to perceive. "Universals," he says, "are in a sense in the soul itself—that is why thinking is up to one, whenever one wishes (νοῆσαι μὲν ἐπ' αὐτῷ ὁπόταν βούληται)" (*De an.* ii.5, 417b23–24). This much may seem phenomenologically apt. If one knows the paradox generated by the Russell set, one can call it forth to consciousness at will: part of what it means to possess a concept is to stand in some intentional relation to it such that one can apply or employ it in appropriate circumstances and at will.

Although by itself plausible, the claim that one can think at will is in need of qualification. After all, how could Aristotle regard it as a necessary condition of actually knowing some proposition *p* that one can actually contemplate *p* (or apply concept *c*) whenever one wishes? One might wish to contemplate the Russell set but be precluded from doing so because one is too hungry to think, too busy preparing lecture notes, or otherwise engaged expounding the liar paradox. Aristotle is himself aware that some such qualification is necessary; indeed, he explicitly notes that his view must be modified: "Whenever someone is in this condition [namely, of

I thank Paul Saalbach and James Lennox for provocative written comments on an earlier draft, and Michael Wedin, who helped alert me to some of the problems I discuss. Although my interpretation of noetic self-motion differs in some ways from Wedin's, it is nevertheless indebted to his chapter in this volume.

possessing some set of concepts], he actively exercises his knowledge and contemplates, so long as nothing prevents him (ἐάν τι μὴ κωλύῃ)" (*Phys.* VIII.4, 255b3–4). Here Aristotle allows, as he should, that it is possible for us to be in possession of some concept even though we are hindered or prevented from actively using that concept, so that our willing may in some cases be ineffectual. He holds, then, that intellectual agents are noetic self-movers—that we can bring about our own intellectual activity so long as we are not hindered from doing so.

Aristotle approaches the issue of concept possession with the right sort of caution. On the one hand, he recognizes what must be a minimal adequacy condition of concept ascription:

> *S* has a concept *c* if and only if ($\exists R$)(R is a propositional attitude and *S* stands in *R* to proposition p [...*c*...]).[1]

Still, he insists that it is possible to have concepts that we may not be able to access at will. As he notes, it seems a datum of experience that we are sometimes hindered in using the concepts we possess. We would therefore be mistaken to insist, without qualification, that possessing concept *c* is sufficient for applying it at will. The minimal adequacy condition Aristotle recognizes falls short of any such commitment, since it does not require of intellectual self-movers that they be in a position to make their propositional attitudes occurrent at will.

---

[1] Aristotle sometimes suggests that nondiscursive thought is possible, where this would include thinking of a concept nonpropositionally. See, e.g., *Meta.* Θ.10, 1051b27–1052a4, and *De an.* III.6, 430b26–31. Several commentators have doubted the cogency of this position as well as the textual evidence in Aristotle. See esp. Sorabji (1982) and Lloyd (1969–70). By contrast, I believe that Aristotle does commit himself to the possibility of nondiscursive thought and that there is nothing philosophically suspect about this commitment. If I am right, however, Aristotle cannot be committed to this minimal adequacy condition as stated: nondiscursive thought allows for the possibility of standing in an intentional attitude to a simple intension unembedded in any proposition. Hence, in the case of nondiscursive thought, *S* can have a concept without satisfying a necessary condition of the minimal adequacy condition. This complication should be noted, but need not undermine our attributing the minimal adequacy condition to Aristotle: (1) we can regard it as obtaining in all but nondiscursive cases; or more directly, (2) we can emend it to read:

> *S* has a concept *c* if and only if ($\exists R_i$) ($\exists R_p$)((R_i is an intentional attitude and *S* stands in R_i to *c*) and (R_p is a propositional attitude and it is possible for *S* to stand in R_p to proposition p [...*c*...])).

This will have the effect of allowing for nondiscursive thought without abandoning the force of the minimal adequacy condition. The revised condition simply allows that one could stand in an intentional relation to some intension without its being embedded in a proposition, while insisting that *S* has the right sort of acquaintance with that intension only if *S* can employ that intension in propositions. It therefore captures the purport of the minimal adequacy condition, and allows Aristotle a commitment to nondiscursive thought compatible with the reasonable minimal adequacy condition he evidently accepts elsewhere in the *De anima*.

This seems correct.[2] When one knows the paradox generated by the Russell set, then one knows it whether or not one happens to be thinking about it at the moment. We are inclined to say that one knows in different senses when one is thinking about it and when one is otherwise occupied: we fasten on a distinction between dispositional and occurrent knowledge, and so implicitly think that different senses of "know" are required for describing one's knowledge before and during actual contemplation. Aristotle agrees, but explicates the distinct senses of "know" in terms of first and second actualities:

> When the intellect has become each thing in the way [that] one actually knowing is said to (this occurs whenever one is able to exercise [his ability to know] through himself), even then he is in a way in potentiality, but not in the way he was before learning or discovering. (*De an.* iii.4, 429b5–9)

One can actually know something, but nevertheless remain "in potentiality in a way" (δυνάμει πως), since one can know something without actually contemplating it at the moment. In such a case, Aristotle holds, a person is in a state of first actuality (actuality$_1$). When one who actually$_1$ knows begins contemplating, one actually knows in the sense of a second actuality (actuality$_2$). Presumably someone who actually$_2$ knows is no longer in any way in potentiality (qua knower of the proposition in question); at least the contrast drawn at *De an.* iii.4, 429b8–9, would seem to have this import.

Aristotle must think knowledge is an especially clear case of his distinction between first and second actualities, since he readily uses it as an illustration of other initially more obscure cases (for example, of the way in which the soul is the first actuality of the body, at *De an.* ii.1, 412a20–25). He may be right: our distinction between dispositional and occurrent knowledge appears to map fairly cleanly onto Aristotle's distinction between first and second actuality, and insofar as we have a handle on this

---

[2] When Aristotle accepts as a necessary condition of concept possession that one must be able to employ the concept in relevant circumstances by making appropriate discriminations, he embeds his analysis of concept possession in the larger context of his capacity-based approach to philosophical psychology. From this perspective, Aristotle's account very closely resembles Gareth Evans's treatment of Russell's Principle (roughly, that someone cannot make a judgment about an object without knowing which object the judgment is about [Russell 1912, 58]). As Evans develops and defends Russell's Principle, a necessary condition of mental reference is having "discriminating knowledge" (Evans 1982, 90), which in turn requires our employing or relying upon a "fundamental idea" (107) of the object in question. Strikingly, Evans understands the having of a fundamental idea not in the descriptive-theoretic context of complex thoughts structured out of intensions: "I should prefer to explain the sense in which thoughts are structured, not in terms of their being composed of several distinct elements, but in terms of there being a complex of the exercise of several distinct conceptual *abilities*. Thus, someone who thinks that John is happy and that Harry is happy exercises on two occasions the conceptual ability which we call 'possessing the concept of happiness'" (101, italics as found). See also Geach 1957, chs. 5 and 14.

distinction in epistemic contexts, we may be licensed to extend it to analogous phenomena in nonepistemic settings.

To this extent, then, Aristotle's conception of noetic self-motion may seem both phenomenologically apt and theoretically well-founded. The caution he exercises in characterizing concept possession and intellectual willing evidently captures a minimal adequacy condition for concept possession that respects the fact that we are not in every instance at liberty to make use of the concepts legitimately ascribed to us. Even so, Aristotle's attitude is peculiar in several important respects. To begin, he holds two principles that are not obviously compatible with one another. First, he holds a principle of intellectual willing:

[IW] Actual thinking is subject to the will. (*De an.* ii.5, 417a27–28)

But he also suggests that whenever one has satisfied the minimal adequacy conditions of concept possession, actual thinking occurs so long as nothing prevents it. He also seems to hold, then, a principle of intellectual actualization:

[IA] Relative to some context C, an antecedent sufficient condition for S's actively thinking p is S's possessing the concepts constitutive of p.[3] (*Phys.* viii.4, 255b3–4)

According to [IA], intellectual agents move directly toward contemplation once they possess the requisite concepts. *Phys.* viii.4, 255b3–4, states that an intellect in possession of some set of concepts actually thinks "so long as nothing prevents" him (ἐάν τι μὴ κωλύῃ).

1. WILLING CONTEMPLATION

Here Aristotle's account of noetic self-motion takes on a perplexing hue. To begin, [IA] appears perverse in its own terms. One would hardly think that, having acquired the concepts necessary for appreciating the paradox generated by the Russell set, S will necessarily contemplate that paradox unless hindered. This yields a picture of intellectual agents such that they are equipped with a set of concepts whose members each has its own exigency to be the object of present contemplation, a picture where discrete items of actual$_1$ knowledge perpetually war with one another for the coveted actual$_2$ status.

---

[3] Given the possibility of nondiscursive thought, this principle, too, will need to be revised. Like the minimal adequacy condition, [IA] can be admitted with the proviso that *mutatis mutandis* a revised principle will suffice; consequently, this complication can be ignored for the present discussion. For the balance of the discussion I will ignore the issue of nondiscursive thought, and will treat Aristotle's views on noetic self-motion primarily at the level of propositions rather than at the level of concepts.

Proposition [IA] further suggests that the comfortable mapping of Aristotle's distinction between actual$_1$ and actual$_2$ properties and states onto our distinction between dispositional and occurrent properties and states may be ill-advised. Glass is fragile, which means, in part, that glass has the dispositional property of being such that it will shatter when an object of sufficient mass, weight, and velocity collides with it. Similarly, if someone believes that snow is cold, she will likely respond affirmatively if asked whether snow is cold, will dress warmly when she has the desire to stay warm and the belief that she must go out into the snow, and so forth. Although perhaps not occurrently thinking that snow is cold at t_1, we are nevertheless for these reasons justified in attributing to her, at t_1, the dispositional belief that snow is cold. Minds, according to [IA], do not exhibit quite this kind of dispositionality. Minds are more like dammed bodies of water that flow into motion as soon as the barriers are removed. Just as water will flow down a canyon so long as nothing hinders it, so minds actually contemplate so long as nothing prohibits them.

If so, [IA] threatens to remove actual contemplation from the province of the will, and so seems to undermine Aristotle's own reasonable commitment to [IW]. If someone with an articulated conceptual repertoire can think whenever she wishes, she should not, in virtue of her very concept possession, be so situated as to contemplate whenever she is not hindered from doing so. If his conception of noetic self-motion requires that she is, Aristotle will have some difficulty explaining how noetic self-motion is noetic *self*-motion. He will need minimally to explain how intellectual agents differ from naturally constituted entities, which exhibit precisely the propensity toward complete actualization here ascribed to intellects.

I will argue that Aristotle's analysis of concept possession, together with his conception of νοητά as unmoved movers, offers a way of explaining his account of noetic self-motion such that: (1) intellectual agents are appropriately regarded as *self*-movers, because (2) while standing in a suitable intentional relation R to νοητά is not sufficient for actually contemplating those νοητά, R nevertheless provides a causally salient condition for actual$_2$ thinking; consequently (3) Aristotle can consistently maintain both [IW] and a suitably qualified version of [IA]. This suitably qualified version of [IA] also circumvents the perversities implicit in the unrestricted version.

I have identified two problems: first, [IA] seems perverse in its own terms; and second, [IA] threatens any robust or interesting version of [IW]. These two problems are related, and jointly foist a dilemma on Aristotle. The first problem follows from Aristotle's evidently stating a sufficient condition where one expects only a necessary condition. Realizing that one can appropriately be said to possess a concept even when precluded from using it, Aristotle does more than merely note as a proviso that one cannot actually think when hindered. Instead, he rather oddly says something much stronger: he claims that as long as one is not hindered, one contemplates whenever one is an actual₁ knower. The language of *Phys.* viii.4, 255b3–4, seems unambiguous here. Adding the indices for types of actualization, we have: "Whenever one is in this position [of being in actuality₁], if nothing hinders [one], one moves into actuality₂ and contemplates (ὅταν δ' οὕτως ἔχῃ, ἐάν τι μὴ κωλύῃ, ἐνεργεῖ καὶ θεωρεῖ)."[4] Hence, he suggests not only that not being hindered is a necessary condition for moving from first to second actuality, but also that it is sufficient.

It is precisely this sufficiency that notifies us of a problem in Aristotle's thought. In virtue of this commitment, Aristotle seems to make intellectual agents passive spectators of their own cognition. This is not a mere slip on Aristotle's part: in *Phys.* viii.4, he draws a crisp analogy making intellectual agents move toward second actuality the way stones move toward the ground:

> It must be inquired how light things and heavy things are moved to their [proper] places. The reason is that they naturally move towards a certain position; and this is what it is to be light or heavy, the former being determined by an upward and the latter by a downward tendency. As we have said, a thing may be potentially light or heavy in many ways. Thus when a thing is water it is in a sense potentially light, but when it has become air it may still be potentially light; for it may be that through some hindrance it does not occupy an upper position, whereas if what hinders it is removed, it becomes actually [light] and rises ever higher. How something changes into a condition of actuality is similar: thus one who knows contemplates at once, unless something definite prevents [him]. So, too, what is of a certain quality extends itself over a certain space unless something definite prevents [it]. The thing in a sense is and in a sense is not moved by one who moves what is obstructing and preventing its motion—e.g., one who pulls away a pillar or one who removes a stone from the wineskin in the water is the coincidental cause of motion; and in the same way the rebounding ball is moved not by the wall but by the thrower. So it is clear that in none of these cases does the thing move itself, but each contains within itself the source of motion—not of moving something or of causing motion, but of suffering it. (*Phys.* viii.4, 255b13–31)

If in all these cases—including contemplation—one contains a source of motion only in the attenuated sense that one is so constituted to suffer

---

[4] There is, however, a question as to whether Aristotle means to take ἐνεργεῖν and θεωρεῖν transitively. I have translated them intransitively because the text does not supply objects. Still, these may well be implicit. If they are taken transitively, perhaps Aristotle's point will be best paraphrased as: "Whenever one has mastery over some set of concepts, one actualizes and contemplates them so long as one is not hindered from doing so." The force of the verbs will differ, but the problem about self-motion will remain, or become even more pointed. On this account, agents consistently try to contemplate the propositions in their conceptual repertoire, and succeed whenever they are not prevented by some manner of hindrance.

motion (τοῦ πάσχειν) unless hindered, then one is hardly a self-mover. How, then, can Aristotle hold that someone in possession of a set of concepts can think at will? Moreover, how can he differentiate, as he wishes to differentiate elsewhere, ensouled entities from artifacts on the ground that artifacts do not have sources of motion within themselves? For example, after using an ax to illustrate the principle of homonymy in *De an.* ii.1, Aristotle remarks: "But as it is, it is an ax; for it is not a body of that sort . . . [it is not] a natural body of a particular kind, one having a source of motion and rest in itself" (*De an.* ii.1, 412b15–17). In short, if we are noetic self-movers, how can Aristotle maintain in speaking of water, wine, rebounding balls, and minds, all quite generally, "that it is clear that none of these things moves itself (ὅτι μὲν τοίνυν οὐδὲν τούτων αὐτὸ κινεῖ ἑαυτό, δῆλον)" (*Phys.* viii.4, 255b29)?[5]

Why should Aristotle liken concept actualization to processes that he explicitly regards as processes of entities incapable of self-motion? One possibility would be that in the *Physics* Aristotle is worried about self-movers, and especially about the possibility of regarding human intellectual agents as bona fide self-movers that do not depend for their motion on the causal agency of influences outside themselves. This would be a legitimate worry, and one that might induce Aristotle to view himself as having to choose between two equally unattractive horns of a dilemma:

1. Either minds move from first to second actuality by themselves or they do not.

2. If not, then contemplation is not subject to the will, and is not, in any interesting sense, up to us (any more than it is up to a rock to fall when the pillar on which it is resting is moved).

3. If so, minds are noetic self-movers, and must be capable of setting themselves into motion (in which case we have something of a mystery).

4. Hence, either contemplation is not up to us or we have something of a mystery.

This heuristic dilemma charts the options available to Aristotle.

---

[5] Furley (1978, reprinted in this volume) suggests a restriction. Aristotle, he argues, never offers a general rejection of self-motion. "The reference of the pronoun [viz. τούτων at 255b29]," he maintains, "is to inanimate natural bodies only—'the light and the heavy' (255b14–15). Nothing is said or implied about animals. Nor does the *analysis* of self-movers into a moved part and a moving part imply that there is no such thing as a self-mover" (7). Furley's suggestion would be welcome, but it cannot be right: (1) the referent of the pronoun is unlikely to extend as selectively backward as Furley suggests, and there is nothing in the text suggesting the restriction he supplies; (2) although right to claim that the analysis of self-movers as composites does not entail that there is no self-motion, Furley's restriction ignores the protracted comparison between minds moving from first to second actualities and natural bodies whose propensities are realized when hindrances are removed; and so most importantly, (3) Furley disregards Aristotle's commitment to [IA] in the passage.

2. APPROACHES TO THE DILEMMA

Aristotle might want to reject the first horn of this dilemma. We have already seen that, in effect, he can. For although [IA] threatens [IW], there is certainly no formal contradiction between them. It is therefore open to Aristotle to hold both. He can hold, for example, that willing ourselves from actually$_1$ to actually$_2$ knowing is really nothing more than a form of permitting ourselves to be moved from actually$_1$ knowing to actually$_2$ knowing.[6] Willing, on this approach, will then consist in removing those barriers under our control, thereby allowing ourselves to be coincidental causes of our own contemplation, in the way that we would be coincidental causes of wine's pouring out of a wineskin by removing the stone, or of a stone's falling by removing the pillar upon which it rests (cf. *Phys.* VII.4, 255b26). Conversely, we might focus on some concept or set of concepts by setting up barriers to *all* concepts beyond the desired subset; to will the actualization of some concept will consist, then, in stifling all others. Although this may seem at best a misdescription of the actual process of contemplation, and at worst a theory-driven expediency, it would provide for Aristotle a way of denying the first horn of our heuristic dilemma, and would therefore permit him to hold both [IA] and [IW]. It would provide for him a way of denying the first horn by allowing us a role in our own contemplation, a role that rocks, for example, cannot play in their falling. They cannot set up or remove hindrances; we can. Accordingly, although we are not wholly autonomous self-movers—we do not move from first to second actualities altogether by ourselves—we can will our own contemplation. Here we are unlike dammed water in that we can will the floodgates open.

This approach is unacceptable for a series of related reasons. There are, first of all, the reasons already given, namely, that it is both phenomenologically peculiar and expedient in the worst sort of way. More importantly, this approach hardly seems faithful to Aristotle's considered views in the *De anima*. There he wants to hold, for example:

> When the intellect has become each thing in the way [that] one actually knowing is said to (this occurs whenever one is able to exercise [his ability to know] through himself). (*De an.* III.4, 429b5–7)

Here Aristotle seems to suggest not just that one can think by willing oneself into the appropriate context, but that one has the resources in oneself: one can think, as he says, δι' αὐτοῦ—through oneself.[7] It is hard

---

[6] Leibniz is sometimes driven to an analogous point about the divine intellect (de Careil 1854, 22).

[7] Hicks glosses δι' αὐτοῦ as: "without further instruction, unaided" (Hicks 1908, 484). This strikes me as correct but not yet sufficient, since Aristotle will still need to explain the

to see how Aristotle could make it a distinguishing feature of actually$_1$ knowing p that one can—through oneself—actually$_2$ know p, and nevertheless hold that the only way an actual$_1$ knower could prevent herself from actually$_2$ knowing is by constructing barricades of some sort. In holding that one who actually$_1$ knows can bring herself to know in the fullest sense, Aristotle evidently supposes that one can *act* to bring it about that one knows in the fullest sense without merely acting to bring that result about coincidentally by putting oneself in a position to *suffer* in such a way that the result is brought about by forces essentially beyond one's own control. An intellectual agent is more than a rock capable of removing hindrances to its free-fall (cf. *Phys.* VIII.4, 255a7).

Moreover, even if we were willing to acquiesce to the peculiar, counterintuitive account of intellectual willing required by this approach, we would in the end merely have traded the first horn of the dilemma for the second. The account of intellectual willing introduced in the end does require a form of intellectual self-motion, at least insofar as it requires of νοῦς the autonomous ability to set up or remove barricades. How νοῦς could do this, by itself (δι' αὑτοῦ), remains a mystery. Hence, this attempt to rebut the first horn of the dilemma merely invites us to consider the force of the second horn.

Finally, by considering the second horn, we can focus more clearly on [IA], the principle that relative to some context C, an antecedent sufficient condition for S's actively thinking p is S's possessing the concepts constitutive of p. [IA] looks questionable; it seems just to make us passive spectators of our own contemplation. Hence, a rejection of it commends a rejection of the second horn—in other words, a suggestion that we are noetic self-movers. We should therefore look to the second horn of the our heuristic dilemma to see if we can make some sense of our being noetic self-movers.

In short, if it is true that as long as one can think whenever one wishes to think, and if it is true that we have in ourselves principles of motion and rest, then we would do considerable violence to Aristotle by opting to reject the the first horn. He seems rather to want to insist that we are after all self-movers, and that there is an account of self-motion that makes this altogether nonmysterious. As Furley points out,[8] despite the analogy between minds and natural bodies, Aristotle wants to make it a *condition* on self-motion that it pertain exclusively to living things: "It [having one's motion through oneself] is a characteristic of life and of living things" (*Phys.* VIII.4, 255a7).

---

conditions under which one moves from actual$_1$ to actual$_2$ knowledge, even if this occurs without the aid of any instructor.

   [8] Furley [1978], 3, this volume.

3. MENTAL CAUSATION IN THE *EUDEMIAN ETHICS*

As a first approach to Aristotle's rejection of the second horn of our heuristic dilemma, it is worth considering a perplexing passage from the *Eudemian Ethics* in which Aristotle offers a peculiar regress about thinking in the midst of his discussion of the role luck (τύχη) plays in causation. The regress appears rather impressionistically, and in any case is not crisply drawn. It is given in the following passage:

> The question might be raised: is luck the cause of this very thing—of desiring what one should or when one should? Or will luck in that way be the cause of everything? For it will be the cause both of thinking and deliberating; for a man who deliberates has not deliberated already before deliberating—there is a certain ἀρχή. Nor did he think, after thinking already before thinking, and so on to infinity. Intelligence, therefore, is not the ἀρχή of thinking, nor is counsel the ἀρχή of deliberation. So what else is there save luck? Thus everything will be by luck. Or is there some ἀρχή beyond which there is no other, and this—because it is essentially of such a sort—can have such an effect? But what is being sought is this: what is the ἀρχή of change in the soul? It is now evident: as it is a god that moves in the whole universe, so it is in the soul; for, in a sense, the divine in us moves everything; but the starting-point of reason is not reason but something superior. What then could be superior to knowledge and intelligence but a god? (*EE* VIII.2, 1248a15–29)

The dialectical argument to which Aristotle responds (streamlined for the present purposes) seems to be:

1. Every mental event is caused.
2. If every mental event, e.g., every instance of thinking, is caused by another event of that same type, then the causal ancestry of my thinking p at t_n includes my having had some other thought q at t_{n-1}, and so on into infinity.
3. This consequent of (2) is impossible.
4. So, it is not the case that every mental event is caused by another event of that same type.
5. If (4), then some mental events are caused by luck.
6. So, some mental events are caused by luck.

Now, Aristotle rejects (6), but accepts (1), (2), (3), and hence (4); he therefore rejects (5). But his rejection of (5) consists in an affirmation that there is "something divine" in us, and that this something accounts for our being able to originate thought of our own accord.

Although answering to a number of similar passages in Aristotle where we are alleged to have a bit of the divine in us (e.g., *EN* x.7, 1177a13–17, b27–31), this remark seems to trade an *explicandum* for a *res occulta*:

what is the divine in us, and more importantly, *how* does it account for our noetic self-motion? This I take to be the difficult question for Aristotle, and not one I see adequately addressed in the *Eudemian Ethics*.

Even so, the *Eudemian Ethics* does place constraints on the form an adequate solution will need to take. The "divine in us" to which Aristotle appeals in blocking the regress is, I take it, merely analogous to the Prime Mover of the universe and nothing more. So we are left to determine how it is analogous. Here the principal point of analogy would seem to be precisely that the mind *is* a self-mover, and so contains not only an internal ἀρχή of its own motion, but an internal ἀρχή of a special sort, namely, one that is an ἀρχὴ τῆς κινήσεως in a way analogous to the way in which the Prime Mover is an ἀρχὴ τῆς κινήσεως. Hence, any satisfactory account of the mind's self-motion will need to posit an internal ἀρχή of thought (and so, remotely, of intentional action) that is properly regarded as an unmoved mover.

So, the import of the *Eudemian Ethics* regress for Aristotle's account of noetic self-motion seems to me significant but limited: significant, because it carries a reasonably clear commitment to noetic self-motion, but nevertheless limited, because it never specifies how "the divine in us" is to be understood. Aristotle makes no attempt in the context of this regress to characterize our capacity for self-motion, and indeed makes no effort to characterize the way in which we are legitimately regarded as having internal ἀρχαί that are the unmoved movers of human acts.

4. UNMOVING MOVERS

The *Eudemian Ethics* passage just considered is not unique in holding that the Prime Mover is not the only unmoved mover. Aristotle quite regularly holds that contingent beings can be unmoved movers as well. In *Phys.* VIII.5, for example, Aristotle analyzes the causal sequence involving a man's hitting a stone with a stick by suggesting that "the stick moves the stone and is moved by the hand, which is moved by the man, but he is not moved by anything else" (*Phys.* VIII.5, 256a6–8). So the man is an unmoved mover in this causal sequence. Nor is this an isolated instance: in his account of animal locomotion, Aristotle quite regularly posits the existence of contingently existing unmoved movers. Indeed, Aristotle claims quite generally that everyone will say, if asked, that the cause of motion, the ἀρχή, is what moves itself (*Phys.* VIII.5, 257a27–30).

This may seem arresting. Does Aristotle, in so speaking, mean to hold that the sublunar world is populated by an infinite number of discrete origins of motion, by an infinite number of uncaused causes? This might seem analytic: an unmoved mover simply is an uncaused cause—a cause of some event that itself lacks any antecedent sufficient condition. Such an interpretation would treat Aristotle as a radical indeterminist, one whose analogy between minds and God would be quite literal, with the exception that the minds existed contingently rather than necessarily.

This is not his view.[9] "Unmoved mover" does not simply *mean* uncaused cause. Something that moves, a κινοῦν, is not a mover in an intransitive sense, but a cause of motion; something μὴ κινούμενον is not something uncaused, but rather something not *moving*, that is, something not in motion. Hence, when Aristotle says that there are unmoved movers in the sublunar world, he means only to say that there are causes of motion that are not themselves in motion. So, for example, the man moving the rock is an unmoved mover of the causal chain *not* insofar as some one event locatable in him is uncaused; rather, he is a moved mover insofar as some event locatable in him moves without itself being in motion.

We can see, then, how minds can be noetic self-movers: they can be the causes of their own action if they incorporate events that are unmoved movers, that is, events that cause motion even while they are not themselves in motion. Aristotle thus needs to locate this sort of cause in the movement from actual$_1$ knowing to actual$_2$ knowing. This, then, will enable Aristotle to provide an account of the ways in which minds are noetic self-movers, an account that responds to the second horn of our heuristic dilemma by explicating an intelligible version of noetic self-motion. This will also provide a way of understanding our original [IA] in such a way that it does not render us passive spectators, driven to contemplate by factors beyond our control.

5. [IA] RECONSIDERED

The constraints on an adequate response to the second horn of our heuristic dilemma are clear. One needs an account of noetic self-motion such that (1) unmoved movers are internal to the soul, and (2) those same unmoved movers are the ἀρχαί of moving from first to second actualities by being unmoved movers in the sense of being movers that move without themselves moving. An unmoving cause is presumably in a certain way static, capable of imparting motion without itself engaging in motion, even though there may be an antecedent sufficient condition for its existence.

Aristotle provides such a cause in his analysis of νόησις, namely, the universals or νοητά that function as the contents of thoughts. In two important, related passages he claims: "Universals are in a sense in the soul itself—that is why thinking is up to one, whenever one wishes (νοῆσαι μὲν

[9] See Sauvé 1987.

ἐπ' αὐτῷ, ὁπόταν βούληται)" (*De an.* ii.5, 417b23–24); and similarly, "Within the soul the faculties of knowledge and sensation are potentially these objects, the one that is knowable and the other that is sensible. They must be either the things themselves or their forms. The former is of course impossible: it is not the stone which is in the soul, but its form" (*De an.* iii.8, 431b26–29). In each of these cases, Aristotle locates a formal cause of thinking, as "in the soul" (ἐν τῇ ψυχῇ) and as something that therefore should meet our first desideratum. There is, however, a question about this "bold phrase," as Ross calls it.[10] In what sense can νοητά be said to be "in the soul"?

Aristotle hardly seems justified in asserting that νοητά are in the soul. If two poeple both think *that the ball is green,* then the proposition they believe is the one picked out (on Aristotle's account at any rate) by the genuinely referring singular term *that the ball is green.* The νοητόν to which they equally stand in the belief relation will therefore simply be this proposition.[11] Νοητά would therefore seem to be shared or shareable, whereas something's being "in the soul" would seem to entail its being a subjective entity at least in the minimal sense of being indexed to its bearer.[12] In the ontology of the *Categories*, individual bits of grammar are nonsubstance particulars, where this requires minimally that they are indexed to their individual bearers, and so depend upon them for their existence; Socrates' knowledge of grammar is not and could not be Callias's knowledge of grammar, even though they might know the same grammar (*Cat.* 2, 1a29–b3).[13] If νοητά are objective, it is hard to see how they are "in the soul"; yet if νοητά are subjective, it is hard to see how they can serve as propositional contents in the way required of them by the theory Aristotle propounds in the *De anima.*

Aristotle evidently feels this or some similar tension. He does not baldly assert that universal νοητά are in the soul. Rather, he says that universals are "in a sense" (πώς) in the soul, where the πώς fairly clearly serves to qualify the force of his claim (cf. *Meta.* H.6, 1045b21).[14] By flagging the

[10] W. D. Ross 1961, 237.

[11] There is some disagreement among commentators about the ontological status of νοητά in Aristotle's semantic theory, and even about whether he has a semantic theory in any way recognizable by the contemporary philosophy of language. For this sort of doubt, see Irwin 1982, 243 n. 3; and Kretzmann 1974, 7. I assume here without argumentation, and contrary to Irwin and Kretzmann, that Aristotle offers a recognizable semantic theory, and one that should be recognized as such by the contemporary philosophy of language. (Our difference is in part due to disagreements about Aristotle's commitments, but also in part due to competing conceptions of the philosophy of language.)

[12] I have in mind objectivity and subjectivity in precisely the sense employed by Frege (1956).

[13] For a discussion of this topic, see Heinaman 1981.

[14] Hicks (1908, 359, note to 417b23) suggests: "By πώς, as we shall see hereafter, he means

difficulty of claiming without qualification that universals are in the soul, Aristotle seems to want to suggest that they have some existence independent of the intellect, as indeed he should if he thinks that the objects of thought are constituted by forms (*De an.* III.4, 429a27). The force of their independent status can to some extent be inferred from the context in which Aristotle offers judgment:

> Being affected is not simple. In one case, it is the destruction of something by its opposite, but in another rather the preservation of a potentially existing being by an actually existing being which is similar to it, in the way that potentiality can be similar to actuality. For the one having knowledge comes to contemplate, and this is either not an alteration or a different type of alteration (for the development is into itself and into actuality). For this reason it is not right to say that what thinks is altered when it thinks, any more than it is right to say that the builder alters when he builds. Hence, what brings [about a change] from what is potential into what is actual in the one who thinks and exercises judgment is not instruction, but is by rights called by some other name. Whoever learns and receives knowledge [by being brought] from potentiality [into actuality] by someone who is in actuality and is capable of instructing should either not be said to be affected or there are two types of alteration, one a change to states of privation and the other to dispositions (ἕξεις) and [to a thing's] nature. In the case of the perceptive faculty, the first change comes about from the parent; when it is generated, it has perception in the same sense as knowledge, and its actuality is spoken of as similar to contemplation. There is, however, a difference, because what is productive of its actuality is external, the object of sight and of hearing, and similarly for the remaining objects of perception. The reason is that actual perception is of particulars, but knowledge is of universals; and these are in a way in the soul. For this reason, thinking is up to one, whenever one wishes, but perception is not up to one, for the object of perception must be present. (*De an.* II.5, 417b2–26)

The argument suggests that, on Aristotle's view, it is precisely because a νοητόν is universal that it is "in the soul"; its being in some sense shareable is part of what makes it subjective in the requisite sense.

δυνάμει." He cites *De an.* III.7, 431b20–22, where Aristotle claims that the soul is the same as its perceptive and intellective objects. The passage is of minimal help, however, since Aristotle reintroduces the same hedge: "Knowledge is in a sense (πώς) its objects, and sensation its objects." Rodier (1900, 2: 261) agrees with Simplicius (*In de an.* 124.25) in holding that the πώς merely restricts the universals to part of the soul, νοῦς. Rodier thinks this is confirmed by *De an.* III.7, 429a27, but this is unlikely to be the entire explanation. Even if correct as far as it goes, Rodier and Simplicius's view does not respond to the dilemma in the text. Alexander (*De an. man.* 85.11) comes nearer the mark: he notices the πώς, and attempts to explain it in part by suggesting that universals exist in the intellect only as κοινά.

This may seem odd, but the context helps to explicate why Aristotle should think this way. At *De an.* ii.5, 417b12–18, Aristotle distinguishes between two distinct kinds of alteration: (1) to states of privations, and (2) to a thing's stable dispositions (ἕξεις) and to its nature. The second kind of alteration is a perfection or completion of an activity or process. Such "alteration," Aristotle insists, either is sui generis or is simply not genuine alteration at all. This is why a housebuilder serves to illustrate Aristotle's point: although evidently engaging in all manner of changes when going about the business of building a house, a housebuilder does not change qua housebuilder when building.[15] A housebuilder does not change qua housebuilder precisely because he has a stable disposition (ἕξις), which permits him to engage in the activity of housebuilding directly, and at will. By analogy, a thinker does not change, qua thinker, precisely because mastery over some body of knowledge is a stable state of the thinker himself.

If this is correct, then there is a sense in which νοητά are internal to the soul: although a νοητόν, qua νοητόν, is universal and so is shared or shareable, a thinker standing in an intentional relation to a given νοητόν is in a stable state, a state that is appropriately called a state *in* the soul. Two housebuilders can know the same body of propositional knowledge, the body constitutive of housebuilding; nevertheless, each can be said to have that knowledge "in the soul." The sense, therefore, in which a νοητόν is "in a sense in the soul" is this: a thinker standing in an intentional relation to a given νοητόν will necessarily have a ἕξις, a stable state of that individual's soul, essentially indexed by that νοητόν.[16]

[15] I here disagree with Heinaman (1985, 154), who holds that Aristotle's point cannot merely be that housebuilding is an alteration of the second sort, on the ground that "housebuilding is not a change of kind [2] in the housebuilder because it is not a change *to* a state in the housebuilder but the actualization of a state of the housebuilder" (italics as found). I understand the phrase ἐπὶ τὰς ἕξεις καὶ τὴν φύσιν to mean, in paraphrase, a change "concerning a thing's permanent disposition and nature," where the ἐπί need not mean, as Heinaman suggests, a change in the housebuilder from a lack *to* the acquisition of a certain ἕξις. I therefore also disagree with the conclusion he reaches: "The distinctions drawn in *De Anima* ii.5, then, fail to explain why Aristotle says that the housebuilder is not altered when he builds a house." On the contrary, it is precisely his distinction between types of alteration that allows him to hold that housebuilding and, by extension, thinking are not alterations in the primary sense, or, if we wish to legislate that only alterations in the primary sense are alterations, are not alterations in any sense.

[16] Cf. note 2 above. Notice, however, that Aristotle will allow capacities to be individuated by their objects, and so, presumably, the capacities required for individual concept possession will be individuated by their individual concepts. (Hamlyn [1959] doubts whether Aristotle embraces the account of capacity individuation invoked here. Hamlyn's doubts are adequately met by Sorabji [1971].) If this is so, Aristotle mutes the *purely* capacity-based account of concept possession Evans adopts, in favor of a mixed account that preserves the core idea that concept possession requires capacities of certain sorts without identifying concept possession with a bald capacity for discrimination. This seems desirable, since it will permit Aristotle to deploy his account even where concepts are necessarily co-extensive.

Aristotle's claim that νοητά are internal to the soul is, consequently, initially explicable, and helps provide him a way of meeting our first constraint. He can justifiably treat νοητά as, in a sense, internal to the soul. Will the νοητά also count as ἀρχαί and as unmoving movers?

On one reading of Aristotle's semantic theory, the answer to the second question will surely be yes. Νοητά are abstract entities of a definite sort, and as such are not susceptible to motion. They are therefore unmoving. Are they also movers? They are not sufficient conditions of thought. But they may nevertheless be movers in the sense that they are INUS conditions in Mackie's sense (insufficient but necessary components of unnecessary complexes of sufficient conditions).[17] Such conditions are the salient features of causal conditions, such that without them, there would be no effect. What is the relevant effect in our case? A moving from first to second actuality, and so to a state of contemplation. And clearly such conditions are necessary. If we recall our earlier minimum adequacy conditions of concept possession, this becomes clear:

S has a concept c iff $(\exists R)(R$ is a propositional attitude and S stands in R to proposition p [...c...]).

If there is no νοητόν, there is no noetic attitude.

If this is correct, such conditions can be internal ἀρχαί, again not in the sense of being identifiable sufficient conditions. These will necessarily incorporate background conditions and, as Aristotle rightly notes, the removal of hindrances. Still, as the causally salient component of the INUS conditions, the νοητά will be formal causes, and so properly regarded as the sources of motion in noetic activity.[18]

If so, Aristotle can hold that noetic self-motion is possible, and is subject to the will. But he will have to emend [IA]. As introduced, [IA] held that relative to some context C, an antecedent sufficient condition for S's actively thinking p is S's possessing the concepts constitutive of p. Aristotle will need instead to hold a revised version of [IA]:

[IA*] relative to some context C, itself a sufficient condition for S's thinking p, an antecedent necessary condition for S's thinking p is S's possessing the concepts constitutive of p.

---

[17] See Mackie 1965.

[18] Formal causes, as formal causes, are not debarred from being efficient causes as well. Aristotle frequently enough allows the formal, final, and efficient causes to pick out the same state of affairs. See, e.g., *De an.* ii.4, 415b8–12, where Aristotle allows a formal cause also to be a source of motion: "The soul is a cause and principle of the living body. These are spoken of in three ways, and the soul is a cause similarly in each of the three ways already distinguished: the soul is the cause as the source of motion, that for the sake of which, and as the substance of an ensouled body." (See also *De an.* ii.4, 415b21–22; *Meta.* A.3, 983a26–b4; Δ.2, 1013a24–b3; and *PA* i.1, 641a19–34.)

This revised principle is wholly consistent with our principle [IW], that moving from actual$_1$ to actual$_2$ knowing is subject to the will. Incorporating as it does only a necessary condition, [IA*] does not bypass the will, and so allows that thinking is up to us. [IA*] certainly does not explain Aristotle's views on the mechanism of willing. It does, however, provide a place for discussing such a mechanism within the context of Aristotle's theory of intentionality, and in particular within the context provided by his analysis of the role played by formal causation within that theory.

Thinking is up to us, but not entirely up to us. Behind the rather obvious thought that we can be precluded from thinking by all manner of hindrances, both external and internal, lies the less obvious thought that intentional states are essentially relational, and so necessarily tied to objective contents. Even so, because one fastens on objective contents intentionally rather than causally, thinking is up to us in a way that other essentially relational states (including, most notably, αἴσθησις) are not. Aristotle recognizes in the *De anima* that thinking, alone among all essentially relational psychic states, is up to us. Perhaps this recognition comes to nothing more than an awareness of the irreducibly intentional character of mental phenomena. This may be so; but if it is so, it likewise comes to nothing less.

CHAPTER 7

Aristotle's Prime Mover

ARYEH KOSMAN

AT THE END of his lectures on the principles of nature and change, the lectures we know as the *Physics*, Aristotle turns to the question: Is κίνησις—change or, as we often call it, "motion"—perpetual? The turn is not a surprising one. For one central subject of his lectures is nature's essential capacity for what we might call "othering" (what we in fact term in our inkhorn style "alteration") and the manifestation of that capacity in the activity of becoming other; the *Physics* is about the world considered as moveable and in motion, or more generally as changeable and in change. It is natural, therefore, to ask whether motion or change may itself be subject to change, and may have arisen from or be destined for conversion into a state other than itself, the state of remaining the same: rest. Given furthermore that the activity of motion has been revealed to involve that mode of extension we know as "time," it is not surprising that this question is framed in terms that ask whether motion is everlasting. And finally, because motion and change constitute at once a sign of life and an emblem of mortality, it is understandable that Aristotle should inquire whether motion is, as he puts it, "a deathless and unceasing property of what is, a kind of life for everything constituted by nature" (*Phys.* VIII.1, 250b14).

What might seem more surprising, however, is that this turn should so easily develop, as it does in the *Physics*, into a theory of an unmoved mover—an unchanging first principle and source of change. Why should a treatise on motion end with a discussion of a being that is itself unmoving? One answer to this question that is not Aristotle's in any simple sense is the following: since motion is incapable of explaining itself, there has to be something other than motion that explains the existence of motion, and that something is the Prime Mover. It is misleading to attribute this answer to Aristotle without qualification because the existence of motion *in general* needs no explanation on Aristotle's view. Particular motions, like other

This essay is an extensively revised version of the paper I read at the Pittsburgh Self-Motion Conference at which these papers were originally presented. Much of my rethinking has been occasioned by the cogent objections that Lindsay Judson made to earlier arguments of mine in his patient and careful commentary at that conference, for which I am grateful. My thanks also to James Lennox for generous and helpful comments on earlier drafts.

local phenomena, *are* open to explanation; but they can be explained locally, especially with reference to the particular and local self-movers—animals—that Aristotle identifies as paradigmatic substances. We may thus be led to ask: what is the explanatory force of the Prime Mover in Aristotle's discussion, and what is its relation to the self-motion of these lesser substances?

The last book of the *Physics* offers an answer to the first of these questions. The eternity and uniformity of motion introduced at the beginning of that book require, it is argued, a principle that is itself not in motion. This is a different and more recognizably Aristotelian claim than that the *existence* of motion requires such a principle. But it is a claim that still might seem more appropriate to a separate treatise superordinate to the *Physics*; in invoking a step up to a higher explanatory principle, it is as though book VIII were part of a treatise on metaphysics rather than physics.

Perhaps we should not find such a move surprising; recall *Meta.* Λ or *De an.* III.5, where we witness the same turn of argument. There appears to be a pattern in all these works of appeal to a divine principle more appropriate to a superordinate science. But note the difference. In the *Metaphysics*, the discussion of divine being provides an account of a formal principle of substance-being (and therefore of being in general) that divine being constitutes; the divine being of separate substance is a paradigm of that substantial being. Similarly, in the *De anima*, the divine consciousness of book III may be seen as a paradigm of consciousness in general. But what is noteworthy about the *Physics* is that the principle of motion is itself not in motion. There is, of course, no a priori requirement that a principle of motion be in motion, any more than that the monarch of England be English or the form of plurality be plural. But the fact that the first mover is unmoved appears to mark an interesting difference between Aristotle's ontology and psychology on the one hand, and his theory of motion on the other. What the theory of motion seems to lack is a paradigmatic principle, and we may wonder why this is so. If self-movers explain motion as substances explain being, why is the first principle of motion not a divine self-mover, as the first principle of being is a divine substance?

The turn in Aristotle's argument might occasion a further perplexity, rather like that occasioned by the very discussions of the *Metaphysics* and *De anima* just mentioned. If we read Aristotle's naturalism as central to his philosophical vision, it is easy to be bemused by what seems his too-ready abandonment in these texts of a naturalist theology. Why, we may want to know, does he feel the need to introduce this separate and apathetic divine thinker? The account of substance and being in the central books of the

Metaphysics seem quite complete without such an introduction, and the account of human life and thought in the *De anima* as well seems complete without it. So in the *Physics*: the account of motion in the earlier books, and the account of celestial motion in the *De caelo*, seem satisfactory in themselves. Why, then, the introduction at the end of the *Physics* of an unchanging Prime Mover?

To feel this fact more forcefully, recall the picture of celestial motion Aristotle draws in the *De caelo*. There is, according to this picture, an eternal mover that is embodied in the divine outermost sphere of the universe; this sphere moves with a uniform circular motion that is without beginning and without end. The divine and immortal motion that this sphere exhibits is the source and principle of all lesser heavenly motions, and therefore ultimately of all motion.

Here is Aristotle's summary at the beginning of book II of the *De caelo*:

> We may be well convinced that the ancient theories, above all those of our own tradition, are true, that there is something deathless and divine among those things that exhibit motion, exhibiting a motion of which there is no limit, but which is rather the limit of all other motions. For a limit is that which surrounds (τῶν περιεχόντων ἐστί), and this circular movement, being complete, surrounds motions that are incomplete and have limit and cessation. But it itself, having neither beginning nor end but continuing ceaselessly in infinite time, is the source of the beginning of some further motions and contains the cessation of others. Our ancestors assigned heaven and the upper region to the gods, believing it alone to be deathless, and our present discussion witnesses to the fact that it is indestructible and ungenerated, and that it suffers none of the ills of the mortal, and that it involves no effort, since it needs no force of necessity by which it may be prevented from following some other more natural path.[1] (*De cae.* II.1, 284a2–16)

Aristotle's view here may seem marked as an early moment in his thinking; note the clear echoes of his predecessors throughout—the circular completeness of Parmenides (about which more later), the surrounding principles of Anaximander (DK 12A11; *Phys.* III.4, 203b11) and Anaximines (DK 13B2), and above all, the self-moving principle of motion of Plato's *Phaedrus* (245C) and *Laws* (x.895B). But it is a view with a simple power and attractiveness. We may then want to ask: How are the views that we encounter in the *Physics* and in the *Metaphysics* related to this early view in the *De caelo*?

---

[1] This passage is worth citing if only because it provides one example (I shall cite another example in a moment) of what may lie behind Cicero's reference to Aristotle's *suavitas et brevitas* (*Inv. rhet.* 2.2.6) and his description of Aristotle as one of those who are *eloquentes et in dicendo suaves atque ornati* (*De or.* 1.11.49), a testimony that readers of the crabbed and often graceless prose of the *Metaphysics* might find surprising.

Consider the following interpretation. The divine principle of motion described in the *De caelo* is distinguished from the Prime Mover introduced in the *Physics* and described in the *Metaphysics* in several related respects. Perhaps most obvious is the fact that the principle of the *De caelo* is in motion, whereas the Prime Mover of the *Physics* and *Metaphysics* is, notoriously, an *unmoved* mover. But this difference may be seen as the result of a deeper shift in Aristotle's views. In the *De caelo*, the circular motion of the outermost sphere is natural to the aethereal body of which that sphere is composed; it is therefore as self-explanatory as the downward motion of earth or the upward motion of fire. This naturalness of the outer sphere's circular motion may itself differ from what Cicero reports to be Aristotle's view, that the movement of the stars is contrasted to the natural movement of the light and the heavy and said to be "voluntary" (*ND* 2.16.44).[2]

However much these early views may differ, on one point they are in clear, if complex, agreement: on both accounts, the motion of the celestial sphere is a form of self-motion, although perhaps in different senses. In the *De caelo*, the motion is self-motion only in the sense that it is self-explanatory; since the first *mover* is none other than the first *moved*, the *primum mobile* of the outermost starry sphere of the heavens is its own natural source of motion, as well as the principle of all lesser motions. In the *Physics*, however, and subsequently in the *Metaphysics*, it appears that Aristotle no longer views the first motion as self-motion even in this attenuated sense. The motion of the outermost sphere is no longer self-explanatory, but is in need of causal explanation, and that explanation must be provided by an unmoved mover, a being separate from the first moving sphere and the source of its motion and thus of all lesser motions. On this view, the first motion is not a self-motion, for mover and moved are distinguished and indeed actually separate.

Interpretations such as this form part of what I take to be a standard developmental reading of Aristotle's thinking. On this reading (setting aside speculation concerning what Aristotle may have argued in his lost works), there is a radical break between the picture we are given in the *De caelo* of a divine celestial motive principle that is essentially a species of self-motion and that is the principle of all lesser motions, and the picture we are given in book VIII of the *Physics*, and in an elaborated form in book Λ of the *Metaphysics*, of a separate unmoved first principle of motion. A clear

---

[2] It is generally assumed (perhaps on slight grounds) that Cicero is here relying, as in several other attributions to Aristotle later in the *De natura deorum*, on a much earlier work of Aristotle's, his lost *De philosophia*, which Cicero mentions by name earlier at *ND* 1.13.33.

expression of this developmental view can be found in Ross, who summarizes his discussion in these words:

> Thus the belief in an unmoved first mover is not an early belief but Aristotle's last word on the subject; the *De Philosophia*, the *De Caelo*, the *Physics*, and the *Metaphysics* reveal the successive stages in the development of Aristotle's view.[3]

My aim in this essay is to subvert that reading by recommending a different and somewhat more complicated relationship among the representations of the divine principle of motion given in these three works. I shall suggest that the unmoved mover of the *Physics* is in fact closer to the kinetic principle of the *De caelo* than we might be led to suppose, and conversely that there is a more complicated relationship between Aristotle's account of the Prime Mover in the *Physics* and his account of divine being in *Meta.* Λ than we often suppose.

On the reading I shall recommend, therefore, there is a sense in which Aristotle's Prime Mover remains a self-mover. For the unchanging mover of the *Physics* is the principle of the outermost heaven's motion, analogous in ways that I shall suggest to its soul, and the prime motion that is the principle and source of natural change is thus the self-movement of that outermost heaven, the motion whose proximate cause is that principle or soul-analogue. Aristotle's account of the *Physics* differs from that of the *De caelo* in the prominence it accords this principle as explanation of the heaven's self-movement. But despite the significance of this fact, there remain, as I shall argue, important continuities between the views in the *De caelo* and in the *Physics*. In turn, the account of the Prime Mover in the *Physics* and that of divine substance in the *Metaphysics* must be carefully distinguished, for there is a difference between these accounts and between the role that the Prime Mover plays in the arguments of these two works. This difference, I suggest, derives from Aristotle's emphasis in the *Metaphysics* on the priority of *activity* to *motion*—of ἐνέργεια to κίνησις—an emphasis that can be seen throughout his thinking but that is most central to the argument of the *Metaphysics*.

In one sense, then, the strategy of this essay is a modest one of realignment; I want to invite us to see the *Physics* as closer to the *De caelo* and as further from the *Metaphysics* than we are accustomed to do. But more than that, I want to redirect the terms in which we think about Aristotle's account of the divine principle of motion in these works. If there is a development in the course of Aristotle's discussions, I suggest, it is not the simple discovery that the principle of motion does not move, but the more

[3] W. D. Ross 1957, 75. Cf. Guthrie 1939, i–xxxvi; 1933; and 1934.

positive disclosure of the explanatory priority of activity to motion. If anything develops in Aristotle's description of the first principle of motion in the *De caelo*, the *Physics*, and the *Metaphysics*, it is therefore his understanding of the sense in which the Prime Mover constitutes a motive principle that is *prime*.

On the standard account of Aristotle's view, I have suggested, the argument of the *Physics* depends upon his repudiating an earlier belief that the first motion is an instance of self-motion. It is tempting, if we accept this account, to see Aristotle's repudiation as part of an even larger repudiation of the possibility of self-motion in general. For we might imagine Aristotle to be arguing that every putative case of self-motion can be analyzed into mover and moved. But such a general view can hardly be right; for given Aristotle's characteristic comfort with commonly accepted truths that some perspectives make appear paradoxical—truths such as the existence of *akrasia*, or indeed of motion in general—it would be surprising if Aristotle should deny the self-motion of living substances. And as several arguments in this volume show, and as we shall see clearly in a moment, he indeed does not.

But the *Physics* does have rather daunting things to say about self-motion: it appears to argue that natural motion is not self-motion in any obvious sense, and what is more important, it appears, in the argument of book VIII, to deny the possibility of self-motion specifically with regard to the prime unmoved mover. So let us consider first what Aristotle actually says in *Phys.* VIII about self-movers.

The first mention of self-movers occurs early in chapter 2, when Aristotle considers whether the existence of animate self-movers might constitute an argument against the eternity of motion. We can understand why it might be thought to do so; for it may happen with respect to such animate beings as we ourselves are "that when nothing is moving in us, but we are at rest, we nevertheless begin to move, the principle of such motion being in us and nothing outside doing the moving" (*Phys.* VIII.2, 252b18–21). But, Aristotle continues, "if it is possible for this to come about in an animal, what is to prevent it happening in the universe as a whole? For if it comes about in a microcosm, why not in the greater cosmos? And if in the cosmos, why not in the unlimited, if the unlimited is indeed capable of motion and rest as a whole?" (*Phys.* VIII.2, 252b25–29).

Aristotle denies the cogency of this argument, pointing out that it only appears to be true that nothing occasions the animal's self-motion; in fact, changes in what surrounds it—in its περιέχον—are responsible for the initiation of that motion (*Phys.* VIII.2, 253a15). This is a fact to which we shall return in a moment. But for now, note the exact purport of the argument; it concerns not the question of self-motion per se, but the phenomenon of self-motion as a possible (but inappropriate) model, in the context of asking whether motion is eternal, for motion's genesis or initiation, a model for motion as a whole having *come into being*.

At the same time, Aristotle's argument reinforces the reality of self-motion in the case of such beings as animals. This feature of the argument is made even clearer subsequently in the course of *Phys.* VIII, when, in a passage that we shall examine momentarily, Aristotle assures his readers that "there are such beings that move themselves, namely living beings in the genus of animals" (*Phys.* VIII.6, 259a31–b4).

The acceptance of the reality of self-motion in these texts makes understandable the subsequent repeated invocation of self-motion when Aristotle begins to mount his argument for the necessity of a first mover; for the argument concerning first movers is repeatedly cast in terms of the possibility of their being self-movers. In chapter 5, Aristotle concludes an initial stage in the argument for a first mover by noting that "if everything in motion is moved by something, but the first mover is not moved by something else, it is necessary that it be moved by itself" (*Phys.* VIII.5, 256a20–21), and a subsequent argument concludes: "Therefore according to this argument, whatever is in motion must be moved by something that moves itself, or must at some point lead back to such [a self-mover]" (*Phys.* VIII.5, 256b1–3). Later in the same chapter, we read that

> it is therefore not necessary that whatever is moved be moved by something else that is itself moved; the series will therefore come to an end. The first mover will therefore be moved either by something at rest, or it will move itself. (*Phys.* VIII.5, 257a26–28)

And in chapter 6 Aristotle summarizes his argument in these words:

> Positing that everything that is moved is moved by something, and that this is either unmoved or moved, and if moved is moved either by itself or by some other thing, and so on, we proceeded to conclude that the principle of what is moved is, on the one hand, of moving things that which moves itself, but of all things that which is unmoved, and we see clearly that there are such beings that move themselves, namely living beings in the genus of animals. (*Phys.* VIII.6, 259a31–b4; cf. *MA* 1, 698a10–17; and *Phys.* VIII.7, 261a25)

Aristotle immediately reminds us that the existence of such self-movers, as we just noted, can only be illicitly proposed as a model for the possibility of motion as a whole coming into being *de novo*. Moreover, he proceeds to argue that self-movers of this sort—animals—cannot constitute the primary principle of motion needed to explain the eternity and continuity of change, for as earlier noted, such self-movers are in fact moved by other moving agents, and therefore do not exhibit *continuous* self-motion (*Phys.* VIII.6, 259b7–22).

This argument, then, is designed specifically to show that since the soul is moved incidentally by the forces that move the body, it cannot be responsible for continuous motion. It is therefore not an argument against the explanatory power of such self-movers as *would* be capable of continuous self-motion. But a divine self-moving principle such as we find in the *De caelo* is an instance of just such a mover, for it is not, as other self-movers are, subject to the causal agency of a περιέχον, a surrounding environment, for the initiation of its self-motion. Indeed it *has* no περιέχον, for it *is* the περιέχον (*De cae.* 1.9, 279a24, 278b23; II.1, 284a7). The subsequent claim in the *Physics* (VIII.6, 259b20–25) that the first mover is not moved even incidentally may therefore not preclude a sense in which the self-motion of the outermost sphere constitutes precisely such a first mover. If this is true, perhaps there is not as great a difference between the account of the *De caelo* and that of the *Physics* as we had initially supposed.

Surely, however, the self-motion of the first mover of the *Physics* is denied in Aristotle's repeated insistence that the Prime Mover must be *unmoved*. It is indeed this fact, I suggested, that seems most sharply to distinguish the divine self-moving principle of the *De caelo* from the Prime Mover of the *Physics*; the former but not the latter is in motion. And isn't this distinction clear in the passage from *Phys.* VIII.6 that we have just noted, in which Aristotle appears to contrast the self-moving mediate principle of moving things with the unmoved first principle of motion in general?

It is undeniable that in these several contexts and numerous others, Aristotle characterizes the first mover of the *Physics* and *Metaphysics* alike as unmoved. But it does not follow from this fact alone that these contexts contrast substantially with the account we have seen in the *De caelo*; for the *De caelo*'s theory of a first self-moved principle is in fact more complex than our earlier description would indicate, and complex in ways that should, I suggest, blunt the force of the distinction between it and the *Physics*.

The last section of book I of the *De caelo* is devoted to showing that there can be only one οὐρανός, that is, only one heaven and one universe under it.[4] Aristotle's argument is ingenious; first he concedes that there might

---

[4] As Aristotle explains at *De caelo* 1.9, 278b10–22, he means οὐρανός to refer at once to the outermost circumference of the world, to the body next to that circumference, and to the world surrounded by it.

seem to be more than one world, given the distinction between the existence of a particular world (this one) and the form of a world in general; the notion of a form distinct from matter entails the possibility of more than one instance of that form (*De caelo* 1.9, 278a13–16). But since the distinction rests on the possibility of a form instantiated in different matter, a plurality of worlds is possible only if there is matter other than the matter of this particular world, and there is none.

Aristotle asks us to imagine by analogy a single nose or a single human being that possesses all the bones or flesh in existence; in this case there could be only one nose or one human being. So it is with the world; for in fact our world contains all the matter that there is (*De cae.* 1.9, 278a25–b7). Aristotle's argument, in other words, is not that the *concept* of a world entails that there is only one world, as one might argue that the notion of a *universe* contains the notion of uniqueness; there could not be another world simply because there is nothing out of which to make it.

The extramundane poverty of matter on which this argument is based is expressed in Aristotle's remark that "the whole that is surrounded (περιεχόμενον) by the outermost circumference is necessarily composed of all natural and sensible body, for neither is there nor could there come to be any body outside the heaven" (*De cae.* 1.9, 278b22–24). There ensues an argument for this claim, at the end of which Aristotle repeats the conclusion that "outside the heaven neither is there nor is it possible that there should come to be any bodily mass whatever" (*De cae.* 1.9, 279a7–8), and concludes furthermore that as a result there is "neither place nor void nor time outside" (*De cae.* 1.9, 279a12–13).

We might expect that the outermost circumference of the material world thus marks the limit of all being, and that beyond the divine self-moving sphere there is nothing. But in fact Aristotle continues in a different and somewhat surprising manner:

> As a consequence, what is there (τἀκεῖ) is neither begotten in space, nor does time make it age; nor is there any change of any sort in any thing that lies beyond the outermost motion, but changeless and unaffected (ἀναλλοίωτα καὶ ἀπαθῆ), enjoying the best and most self-sufficient life, it continues through all ages (διατελεῖ τὸν ἅπαντα αἰῶνα). (*De cae.* 1.9, 279a17–22)

The fact that the outermost circumference of the heaven is the furthest *body* at the edge of the universe does not therefore mean that it marks the limit of *being*, but only that it marks the limits of *somatic* being.

We might feel uncomfortable about this second stage of Aristotle's argument in relation to the first; for we might be moved to ask why, if there can be a specific being beyond the edge of our world that is immaterial, there could not as well be another *world* that was itself immaterial. One direction in which this question might take us is to a consideration of how place and time figure in the concept of a world.[5]

What is more important, it should reveal to us the respect in which the being "beyond" the outer moving sphere is not wholly independent from the sphere itself. To see this more clearly, note how Aristotle continues immediately after his assertion that there is eternal, changeless, and impassive divine being beyond the outermost circumference, being described as enjoying, throughout all αἰῶνα—all ages—a life like that of the divine mover of the *Metaphysics* (*Meta.* Λ.7, 1072b24–31):

> And this word (αἰῶνα) was a divinely inspired coinage of our ancestors. For the end that surrounds (περιέχον) the time of each thing's life and that cannot naturally be gone beyond, they called the αἰών of each thing. By the same argument the end of the entire heaven as well and that which contains all time even unto infinity is αἰών, taking the name from the words ἀεὶ εἶναι [to be forever], for it is deathless and divine. From it proceeds the being and life of all other things, some more obviously, others more obscurely. And in the popular philosophical works upon the divine, it is frequently made clear by argument that the first and highest divinity is necessarily wholly unchanging (ἀμετά-βλητον), which confirms what we have said. For there is neither anything superior that can move it (for then that would be more divine), nor has it anything bad, nor does it lack anything fair appropriate to it. And it moves with an unceasing motion, as is reasonable. For all things only cease moving when they arrive at their appropriate place, but for the body that moves in a circle it is the same place from which its motion proceeds and in which it ends. (*De cae.* i.9, 279a23–b3)

It is clear in this passage that the eternal and unchanging being that Aristotle has just described, although conceptually distinct from the outermost self-moving sphere that it is said to be beyond, is at the same time not independent of it; Aristotle moves with casual ease from speaking of one to speaking of the other and back again, as though they formed, as it were, the soul and body of a single divine entity.

To be sure, Aristotle nowhere explicitly terms the motive principle of the heaven a "soul," any more than he terms the Prime Mover of the *Physics* or *Metaphysics* a soul. But he clearly states that insofar as the heaven exhibits the mode of motion it does, it may be said to be alive, that is, "ensouled" (ἔμψυχος), and to be so precisely by virtue of possessing a principle of motion: ὁ δ' οὐρανὸς ἔμψυχος καὶ ἔχει κινήσεως ἀρχήν ("The heavenly sphere is ensouled, that is, it possesses a principle of motion" [*De cae.* ii.2, 285a29–30]). The mover of the *Metaphysics*, described in terms equiva-

---

[5] Consider, for example, the role of space and time in the elaborate medieval discussions concerning the creation and eternity of the universe, e.g., Maimonides, *Guide for the Perplexed* 2.13–26 (Pines 1963), and Thomas Aquinas, *Summa theologica* 1.46 (Pegis 1945).

lent to those which describe the *De caelo*'s outermost self-moving sphere and to those which describe the unmoved mover of the *Physics*, is equally said to be alive (*Meta.* Λ.7, 1072b26–31). But it would surely be odd to refer to something as alive that does not in some sense have a soul, just as it would conversely be odd, as Aristotle notes in the *De anima* (1.5, 411a16), to designate something that has a soul as not alive.

The term ψυχή, however, has come to be used by Aristotle exclusively (for reasons we can understand) to refer to the soul as principle of animal life in the earthly zoosphere. There it refers, as the discussion of the *De anima* makes clear, to what he identifies as a first grade of activity (what we standardly call "first actuality"), that is, to a capacity for active functioning that may or may not be realized, a power that may or may not be actively exercised; the soul is, as he puts it, the principle of both sleeping and waking life (*De an.* II.1, 412a24). But the mover of the heavenly sphere does not sleep, nor does it slumber, for the first movement of the heaven is eternal, uniform, and continuous; the force of this fact will be fully appreciated when in the *Metaphysics* we come to recognize the Prime Mover as a being ἧς ἡ οὐσία ἐνέργεια ("whose very substance is activity" [*Meta.* Λ.6, 1071b20]).

It is therefore understandable that Aristotle never explicitly refers to the heavens as having a soul, nor to the Prime Mover as a soul. But that the Prime Mover is importantly *psychic* should be clear from the fact that it constitutes the principle of the living activity of the heaven; we may therefore speak of it as forming with the heaven what is essentially the soul and body of a single divine entity. And what is equally clear in the passage we have just quoted is that this divine entity both moves with an eternal circular motion and is unmoved:

> The first and highest divinity is necessarily wholly unchanging, which confirms what we have said. For there is neither anything superior that can move it (for then that would be more divine), nor has it anything bad, nor does it lack anything fair appropriate to it. And it moves with an unceasing motion, as is reasonable. (*De cae.* I.9, 279a32–b2)

That here in the *De caelo* the prime self-moving principle is described as unchanging may mean only that its motion is uniform. But it may also reflect the fact that every prime mover is said to be unmoved, and that every instance of automotion involves a principle that may be said to be unmoved. If, for example, I walk from Anaheim to Azusa, I am automotive, for my movement is an instance of self-movement. But my soul is unmoved. This does not mean either that there is nothing that we may invoke as the explanation of my self-movement, or that my soul does not, so to speak, accompany me to Azusa, remaining instead among the bright lights and glittering streets of Anaheim and directing my journey by remote control. What it means is that my soul is unmoved qua *mover*; it is not insofar as *it* is in motion that my soul explains my motion, nor need it be in motion to be the principle of such explanation.

To be unmoved in this sense means simply to be first in a chain of causal explanation—to be, in other words, a prime mover. A prime mover such as my soul thus need not move in order to be the principle of further motion; the question of its motion is independent of the question of its explanatory power relative to subsequent motions. But it may move; this is exactly what it means that my soul as prime mover may be in motion incidentally (*Phys.* VIII.6, 259b17–20).

So with the motion of the *primum mobile*; to understand the sense in which its motive principle is unmoved, we need not imagine that as the sphere of the fixed stars makes its daily orbit about the earth, this principle remains immobile, situated at Control Center somewhere in a cosmic Houston and directing from afar that first motion. This description is incorrect in that it suggests the possibility of attributing place to this being, whereas where it is, in the beyond, there is (paradoxically) no place: οὔτε τόπος οὔτε κενὸν οὔτε χρόνος ἐστὶν ἔξωθεν ("There is neither place nor void nor time outside the heaven" [*De cae.* I.9, 279a18]); as Gertrude Stein would say, "There's no there there." And in another sense, the principle of the sphere's first motion may be said to inform the sphere and might therefore be thought to accompany (in a manner of speaking) its motion.

But here is a problem. For in this sense, such a principle might appear to exhibit, like my soul when I journey from Anaheim to Azusa, incidental motion; the unmoved mover would be "carried along" by the motion of that for whose motion it is responsible. If this were true, however, it would suggest that the soul of the first mobile *cannot* be the unmoved mover of the *Physics*, since the latter is said not to be moved even incidentally (*Phys.* VIII.6, 259b22).

This observation affords us the possibility of seeing why the uniform, eternal, and circular self-motion of the divine first mover is not incompatible with its being unmoved. For even in this second sense, the principle of the outermost sphere's motion does not exhibit the incidental motion that my soul might exhibit in the course of my journey from Anaheim to Azusa; for there is, as we have seen, no larger περιέχον, no surrounding environment, in relation to which as a whole it might be said to move *from one place to another*. Its motion, precisely because it is circular, eternal, and continuous (see *GC* II.11, 338a17–b2), is self-contained, and because of its πάλιν ανακαμπτεῖν—its "returning back on itself" (*GC* II.10, 337a7; see *Phaedo* 72B)—it remains at rest in relation to the larger context that it alone defines: "It is the same place from which its motion proceeds and in which it ends" (*De cae.* i.9, 279b2). It is in this sense that the primary motion itself may be termed unmoved—ἀκίνητον; it is a sense, as we shall soon remark, that anticipates the more important sense in which the divine substance that is essentially active is unmoved.

The divine being of the *De caelo*, from one point of view the deathless and unceasing motion of the outermost heaven and from another the unchanging and ageless god "beyond" that heaven, is thus unmoved in a sense nonetheless compatible with its being in continuous and uniform circular motion. In the *De caelo*, that motion is connected specifically with the divine first mover, whereas in the *Physics* it has come to be associated with the *mediate* motion of the *primum mobile*. This fact, however, does not belie the substantial community between the account of the *De caelo* and that of the *Physics*; rather, it reveals the move of conceptual separation between the aspects of the first heavenly motion and the shift of attention that has occurred in the *Physics* in the context of the specific argument of that work.

There is, however, another respect in which we may think of the eternal self-motion of the *De caelo* as unchanging, even if we concentrate on the first self-moving sphere alone; and it is a respect, I shall suggest, that is important for understanding Aristotle's larger strategy. This respect is clearly adumbrated in Aristotle's description of circular motion in the passage we first looked at; it rests upon the sense in which circular motion is an icon of the mode of unmoving being that is at the same time not mere rest, the mode of being that Aristotle describes as ἐνέργεια: activity that is self-fulfilling.

I remarked earlier on the similarity between Aristotle's description in the *De caelo* of the life of divine being "beyond" the heavens and his description in the *Metaphysics* of the life of divine substance. Note further the similarity between the language of Aristotle's description in the *De caelo* of divine circular motion itself and that of his description in *Meta.* Θ.6 of activity in contrast to motion. Divine circular motion is said to have no limit, but to govern those motions that have a limit, and to be complete and to surround those motions that are incomplete (*De cae.* ii.1, 284a5–10). Just so, activity is contrasted to those "actions that have a limit, [none of which] is a completion, but is the sort of thing *relative to* a completion . . . [and so] is not an action or at least not a complete one (just because it is not a completion)" (*Meta.* Θ.6, 1048b19–22).

The parallel should suggest a recognition of uniform circular motion as a mediating figure that is in one sense clearly motion, but in another virtually a mode of the activity that contrasts with motion. Recall that although activity and motion are, in other places and in other contexts, intimately related insofar as they contrast with the indolent rest of inactivity (*Meta.* Θ.3, 1047a30–b2), the contrast of *Meta.* Θ.6 is meant to determine activity specifically as unmoving, that is, ἀκίνητον, and it does so largely in the same terms in which circular divine motion is characterized.

These parallels should equally begin to suggest to us that there is a community of doctrine throughout Aristotle's argument, but that just as Aristotle's emphasis shifts from the *De caelo* to the *Physics*, so it shifts in the context of the argument of the *Metaphysics*. The shift is important, but subtle; it is reflected largely in Aristotle's identification of the Prime Mover as the divine being whose essential nature is activity.

In chapter 6 of *Meta.* Λ, in the context of his discussion of the mode of divine being that may be said to be the principle of substance-being itself, and thus of being in general, Aristotle turns his attention to that substance which he describes as eternal and ἀκίνητον, "unmoved" (*Meta.* Λ.6, 1071b4). The arguments that he gives for the necessity of such a mode of unmoved substantial being are essentially those of the *Physics*; but now, in keeping with the prominent role that activity has come to play in the argument of *Meta.* H and Θ, the discussion immediately moves to an account of divine substance as a being that is essentially active, that is, characterized as ἐνέργεια.

In the remainder of chapter 6, the term ἀκίνητον—"unmoved"—nowhere appears; the argument now centers upon the invocation of activity as the necessary principle of motion and of that eternity of motion which in the *Physics* is explained by the Prime Mover's being unmoved.

> If [eternal substance] is not active (μὴ ἐνεργήσει), there will not be motion; nor if it is active, but its substance is the power to act (ἡ δ' οὐσία αὐτῆς δύναμις); for then there will not be eternal motion. (*Meta.* Λ.6, 1071b17–20)

There must therefore, Aristotle concludes, be a principle that is *substantially* active: ἧς ἡ οὐσία ἐνέργεια (*Meta.* Λ.6, 1071b20). When at the beginning of the next chapter, Aristotle sums up his earlier argument, he does so by noting that it follows from what has gone before that

> there is something that is moving with an unceasing motion, which is a circular motion, . . . and therefore the first heaven must be eternal. There is therefore also something that moves it. But since that which is moved and moves is also intermediate, there is therefore something that is not in motion but moves (οὐ κινούμενον κινεῖ), and it is an eternal substance, which is activity (ἀίδιον καὶ οὐσία καὶ ἐνέργεια οὖσα). (*Meta.* Λ.7, 1072a21–26)

The systematic redescription of *unmoved* substance as *active* substance—the replacement of the term ἀκίνητον by the term ἐνέργεια—is not an abandonment of the requirement that the first mover be unmoved. What it discloses is the sense in which the first mover must be understood in terms of a principle that is unmoved in a deeper and more subtle sense than the simple ἀκίνητον may capture, the sense revealed in recognizing the divine principle of motion and being alike as activity.

Behind this disclosure is the important fact that for Aristotle the concept of motion must itself be understood in terms of this deeper concept of activity, that ἐνέργεια which is prior to motion and which is realized, as Aristotle stresses in the *De anima*, not ἐξ ἐναντίας μεταβαλὼν ἕξεως, but rather ἐκ τοῦ ἔχειν . . . μὴ ἐνεργεῖν δ' εἰς τὸ ἐνεργεῖν: not by a change from one characteristic to another, but by the active exercise of a power that was present but dormant (*De an.* ii.5, 417a32–b1). It is this prior concept of activity in terms of which Aristotle constructs his account of motion: an entity is in motion when its capacity to be other than it is, a capacity dormant when the entity is at rest, is actively exercised, when, that is, the entity is most fully being potentially other (*Phys.* iii.1, 201a27–30). More critically, this sense of activity as the active exercise of a being's nature is what Aristotle invokes in the discussion of *Meta.* Θ.6, where, even though it explains motion, it is contrasted with motion as an activity that is its own perfection. And it is ultimately this sense of activity, a sense prior to the concepts of motion, change, and the family of surrounding notions, which is harnessed by Aristotle in his analysis of substance-being.

Here in book Λ of the *Metaphysics*, where divine substance is invoked as the principle of the being and motion of the cosmos as a whole, its identity as activity is thus particularly relevant to our much earlier discussion. For activity, as the principle of motion in general, is most specifically and immediately figured in *circular* motion, that mode of motion which, since any part of its journey is as much the end as any other, is activity's closest analogue. Circular motion may thus be said to aspire to activity as to a principle, that is, precisely in the way Aristotle describes in his celebrated account of the divine bringing about motion by love and attraction (*Meta.* Λ.7, 1072a25–b3).

In one sense, ἐνέργεια is represented in the axis of such motion, in the still point at the center of the most energetic activity. This image of ceaseless activity made serene by its unmoved center as a figure of the cosmos and its individual modes of activity has deep resonance for Aristotle. Recall in the *Republic* the spinning top's immovable peg, that unwobbling pivot that is a type of the calm and ordered soul at the center of that dialogue's politically active hero (*Republic* iv.436D). And recall the shining, singing axles of the chariot that takes the Parmenidean neophyte to the place of his revelation, a revelation of the Ἀληθείης εὐκυκλέος ἀτρεμὲς ἦτορ ("the unmoving heart of full-circling truth" [Parmenides DK 28B1.29]).

But it is equally the bounding and limiting circumferential motion itself that, in establishing limit and in its steadiness of circuit, expresses that reality. Unless we recognize this intimate tie between activity and circular motion, we risk being seduced into thinking that when Aristotle describes the Prime Mover as unmoved, he means to suggest that it is inert and inactive. The danger is analogous to the more general danger that we shall be led to think of an Aristotelian substance as an inert *thing* rather than as a determinate center of *active being*. These are seriously mistaken, and analogously mistaken, readings of Aristotle's views; just as it is the determinacy and steadiness of a substance's activity that constitute it as an instance of substance-being rather than as merely the fugitive activity of accidental being, so it is the unmoved steadiness of full-circling motion, the unmoved steadiness by which it figures and aspires to activity, that marks it as divine and as the principle of all lesser motion. Recall Dante's description: 'Sì come rota ch'igualmente è mossa / l'amor che move il sole e l'altre stelle" ("Just like a wheel that's uniformly moved, the love that moves the sun and other stars" [Dante, *Paradiso* 33.144–45]).

The notion of a divine first mover is thus no simple concept in Aristotle. At one level, the Prime Mover is the ceaseless encircling motion of the outermost heavenly sphere. We may want to distinguish between this self-moving sphere itself and the principle of its motion, as between the outermost heavenly body and its soul. But given that it is *self*-moving, and given Aristotle's understanding of the soul as nothing other than the active principle and formal being of the living body, it is not surprising that in the *De caelo* the first mover is indifferently thought of as the outermost moving sphere of the heavens itself and as the divine unchanging being that informs that sphere, indifferently thought of, we might almost say, in the two senses of *primum movens*.

The relative emphasis appropriate to each of these beings will depend on larger issues concerning body and soul and concerning economies of ontological theory (compare Spinoza's later exploration of the complex modalities of *natura naturans* and *natura naturata*). It will moreover depend on strategies of explanation and emphasis local to specific contexts; thus in the *Physics*, concerned specifically with the question of the eternity and uniformity of motion, Aristotle stresses the fine structure of motion's explanatory context by focusing attention, with an emphasis lacking in the *De caelo*, upon the first mover as the analogue of heaven's soul. Of equal moment for Aristotle is the fact that the formal principle of this Prime Mover (whether we understand it as the whole of the first heaven or only as that aspect which may properly be called the unmoved mover of the *Physics*) is a divine being whose mode of activity is the explanatory principle of motion in general, and indeed, more basically, of being in general; it is the divine being whose essential nature is more revealingly identified in the *Metaphysics* as ἐνέργεια: self-fulfilling activity.

Aristotle's Prime Mover is thus revealed to be a paradigmatic principle, as we earlier thought it might not be, and to be so in two respects. As self-moving, it is the principle of the motion of all lesser animate self-movers; more significantly, as the exemplar of that mode of self-fulfilling activity identified in the *Metaphysics* as divine ἐνέργεια, it is the formal and on-tological principle of all motion and change, as indeed it is of being in general.

———————

But it may seem that we have left unresolved the central issue; for earlier we thought that the motion of the outermost sphere is in the *Physics* no longer self-explanatory, but is in need of causal explanation by a mover that is *separate* from the first moving sphere. This is indeed why we thought that in the *Physics*, the first motion is not a self-motion, since mover and moved are distinguished, and indeed are actually separate. So now we have to consider this question: Is the prime kinetic principle of the *Physics* and *Metaphysics* indeed separate in a way that it is not in the *De caelo*?

Note the purely metaphysical cast—one might even say the theological cast—that our question must now take. And here (as with most theological questions) we need first to know just what this question—Is the first princi-ple of motion indeed separate from, that is, transcendental to, that which primarily moves?—is meant to ask. Consider this fantastic scenario. Sup-pose that we could transport an ancient student of Aristotle into the pre-sent and show him our picture of outer space (as we now call it). How would he respond? To begin with, he might be interested in the fact that there appears in this picture no outermost sphere, but rather a deep three-dimensional space in which the stars are situated. He should view this fact as part of an astronomy that is quite different from Aristotle's and, assum-ing we could reveal to him the surrounding body of scientific theory needed to provide the proper context, one that he would most likely accept as correct. He would, in other words, recognize that Aristotle's physical as-tronomy constitutes a picture of the physical nature of the universe that is, relative to ours, a primitive one.

But what of metaphysics and theology? Here, I think, the philosophical arguments that might lead an Aristotelian to embrace the theory of an unmoved mover would be seen as unaffected by his conversion to a new scientific theory. For there is no story to be told about philosophical theory analogous to that which we have told about astrophysics. Whatever our visitor might come to think about the correctness of Aristotle's kinetic theory that the great steady motion of deathless and divine heavenly bodies generates those confused and violent motions that govern our poorer and mortal (though perhaps finally more interesting) lives, we should expect that he would continue to insist on the correctness of the metaphysical and theological principles behind such a theory.

Suppose in particular that we were to make the following observation, parallel to our having pointed out that there is no outermost celestial sphere of crystalline aether: "Notice that there is also no Prime Mover other than the movement of these celestial bodies; clearly that part of Aristotle's theory is incorrect as well." Surely in response to this point we should expect from a sophisticated Aristotelian mild amusement, much as we might expect in response to someone's asking exactly where in the heavens Heaven itself is located, or where in the animal is the soul itself. For we clearly would have misunderstood the nature of the ontological import of Aristotle's discourse about the Prime Mover.

Can we translate the question of the transcendence of the Prime Mover in such a way that it is not so foolish, and thus is not so easily dismissed? The proper question, I think, must go like this: Is the circular self-motion of the heavens both explanatory and self-explanatory, so that in giving an account of the world understood as I described it at the beginning of this essay—an account such as we find in the *De caelo* in terms of an eternal principle of circular self-motion—we shall have given a full account of such motion? Here I think the proper Aristotelian answer (the exact words are from *Meta.* H.3, 1043b4, but the strategy is ubiquitous and typical) is τινὶ μὲν τινὶ δ' οὔ; in a sense yes, in a sense no.

For in one sense we shall indeed have given an account of the motions of the heavens, and in so doing we shall have given an account, at some very broad level, of the changes and cycles of change of our sublunary lives. And this is no mean accomplishment; it is the recognition that there is but one comprehensive universe whose cycles and configurations of change are organically connected and importantly related, so that the force that through the heavens drives the chariot of the sun is the same force that through the green fuse drives the flower (and that drives my green age) and so that the cycles of the heavens (as astrology has always to our chagrin proclaimed) both determine and variegate the fabric of our lives. This is the force of Aristotle's discussion at the end of *On Generation and Corruption* (II.11, 338a19–b5), and it is the recognition articulated in the *Metaphysics* (Λ.10, 1075a16) by the words πάντα συντέτακταί πως: all things are somehow ordered together. That recognition is, it seems to me, the realization of an important truth, hardly uniquely Aristotelian, but not therefore insignificant.

To see in addition that the prime and cosmic shaping motions of that universe, the motions that we know in their appearances as the complex periodic cycles of our life—most basically the cycles of day and night and of the yearly seasons—are, as it were, self-motivated and therefore self-explanatory is to see, as thinkers from Aristotle to Newton to Wittgenstein have seen, the *givenness* of the universe, the fact that there is nothing outside its limits.

But Aristotle invites us in addition to recognize, in an invitation that he extends throughout the discussions of the *Physics* and *Metaphysics*, the fact that motion itself is an incomplete form of activity. This is an argument the force of which I neither can nor need to rehearse here, but it is one that explains, it seems to me, the sense in which the Prime Mover of the *Metaphysics* stands behind the Prime Mover of the *Physics* and the *De caelo*.

For as the principle of becoming is being, so the principle of motion is activity, and Aristotle, like Father Parmenides, finds at the heart of all being that which is unmoved but not inactive—that Ἀληθείης εὐκυκλέος ἀτρεμὲς ἦτορ which I earlier invoked; at the heart of the cosmos is that which is full activity. It is for this reason that the Prime Mover, which in the *De caelo* is the self-moving outermost sphere and whose mediate principle is the unmoved mover that is the soul of that sphere, must finally be described as the ἐνέργεια of divine substance whose description we read in the *Metaphysics*, not simply an unmoved mover, but, what is more important, an unflagging activity.

CHAPTER 8

Heavenly Motion and the Unmoved Mover

LINDSAY JUDSON

THIS PAPER is concerned with Aristotle's accounts of the motion of the heavens in *De cae.* I–II, *Phys.* VIII, and *Meta.* Λ. In the *De caelo*, Aristotle's view is that the heavenly sphere moves itself; I shall ask what role, if any, is played by the sphere's soul in this motion. In *Phys.* VIII and *Meta.* Λ, Aristotle introduces the prime unmoved mover. I shall argue against the position of Aryeh Kosman, presented in this volume, and in favor of the traditional view that this unmoved mover is a transcendent entity quite distinct from the heavenly sphere whose motion it causes; and I shall ask in precisely what sense the unmoved mover is a cause of motion.

A brief account of Kosman's dispute with what we might call the "traditional view" of these three works will set the scene.[1] It is common ground between Kosman and the traditional view that *De cae.* I–II, *Phys.* VIII, and *Meta.* Λ represent three different stages or phases in Aristotle's thinking about the explanation of the heavens' motion.[2] The traditional view sees Aristotle in the *De caelo* as tracing the movement of all things back to the motion of the outermost heavenly sphere, and as taking this motion to be entirely self-generated, in the sense that it depends upon nothing else whatever for the production or maintenance of its eternal, circular motion. At some later point Aristotle decided that this sort of self-motion—which we

Earlier versions of various parts of this paper were read at the Pittsburgh Self-Motion Conference, the Aristotelian Reading Group in Oxford, and the University of Padua. I am grateful to all those who participated in the discussions on these occasions, and especially to Michael Frede, Mario Mignucci, and Steven Strange. I should also like to thank Joseph DeFilippo for his comments on the appendix.

[1] Versions of this view can be found in Guthrie 1933; Guthrie 1939, introduction, pt. 2; W. D. Ross 1936, 94–102 (cf. W. D. Ross 1957, 73–75).

[2] There may have been a still earlier phase in Aristotle's thinking, recorded by Cicero in his *De natura deorum* (Aristotle frags. 23, 24, 26 Rose: see Kosman's essay here, 138 and note 2). Kosman seems to doubt that Cicero's account refers to an earlier phase; but the doctrine that the sun, moon, and stars move voluntarily cannot be that of the *De caelo*, which explicitly denies that the stars' motion is voluntary (*De cae.* II.9, 291a22–28), and it can hardly be the doctrine of either of the later two phases, both of which presuppose the same position vis-à-vis the stars. Cicero may, of course, be ineptly confusing the stars with the heavenly spheres that carry them around; but if his report is reliable, it must refer to an earlier phase.

might call "absolute" self-motion—was impossible.[3] The motion of the *primum mobile*, he now thought, had to be caused by something else, which must itself (on pain of merely pushing the problem back a step) be unmoved. And this is the argument of *Phys.* VIII: the motion of the outermost heavenly sphere is not wholly caused by itself, but requires a distinct entity, a primary *unmoved mover*, as well. In the third phase, in *Meta.* Λ.6–10, Aristotle elaborates the notion of the primary unmoved mover by giving a more detailed account of its nature and activity. I would add a yet further stage—the introduction of the doctrine of the plurality of the unmoved movers, elaborated in what is now Λ.8. I have little confidence in chronological arguments, but I feel inclined to agree with Ross's view that Λ.8, written late in Aristotle's life (c. 327–323), is a subsequent addition.[4] This is partly because chapter 8 breaks up an obvious flow of ideas from the end of chapter 7 to the start of chapter 9, and partly because of the character of the other references to a plurality of unmoved movers. The hesitant character of *Phys.* VIII.6, 258b10–12 and 259a3–15, noted by Ross, suggests a phase earlier than that of the dogmatic confidence of Λ.8; and though the reference at Λ.6, 1071b20–22, is suitably dogmatic, it is quite unexpected in its context—nothing in the preceding argument prepares the reader for a plurality of unmoved movers—and it looks like a rather hasty insertion by Aristotle.[5]

The traditional account, therefore, sees the third phase (the main part of

---

[3] This interpretation does not require that Aristotle took *all* forms of self-motion to be impossible. He insists in *Phys.* VIII that animal motion is not absolute self-motion in this sense, since it always depends on external triggering; but that is quite compatible with the view that animals are self-movers in a different sense, and I agree with David Furley, Mary Louise Gill, and Susan Sauvé Meyer that Aristotle holds this view (see the papers by Furley, Gill, and Meyer in this volume).

[4] Ross 1924, 2: 384 (cf. 1957, 73–74). I do not find all of Ross's own arguments for it convincing, however. (1) There is no good reason to date the rest of *Meta.* Λ early, as Ross does—he is too ready here to believe the arguments in Jaeger 1948. (My own feeling is that the rest of Λ is a relatively mature work, written shortly before *Meta.* ZHΘ; but there are no strong arguments for any dating of this work.) (2) The talk of "one mover" in the argument for the uniqueness of the cosmos (1074a31–38) need not be read "monistically" in the sense of implying that there is only one unmoved mover: it only requires that there be only one unmoved mover of each type.

[5] If this view of Λ.8 is right, then *Phys.* VIII.6, 259b28–31, would also have to be an insertion. These insertions need not postdate the composition of Λ.8: Aristotle might have become persuaded of the need for such a plurality, and revised these texts, well before working out the details in Λ.8. I should stress that the considerations I have advanced for a late date for Λ.8 are not decisive. Even if *we* find the placing of chap. 8 between chaps. 7 and 9 intrusive, clearly it did not seem unduly so to Aristotle when he placed it there; and my claim that the reference to a plurality of cosmic movers in Λ.6 *looks* like a hasty insertion may be too subjective: indeed, someone might hold that the very existence of this reference is good evidence for the integrity of Λ.8. We should note also a further reference, at *Phys.* II.7, 198a24–29, quoted below, 166.

Meta. Λ) as an elaboration of the position arrived at in the second, but sees the second as involving a relatively sharp break with the first. Kosman argues that there is no such break: the *Phys.* VIII doctrine, as he interprets it, is an elaboration, and not a rejection, of the *De caelo* doctrine. This is because the ultimate self-mover of the *De caelo* is still present, he argues, in *Phys.* VIII and *Meta.* Λ, since the "soul"[6] of this self-mover is in fact the unmoved mover that is argued for in the *Physics*, and whose nature is discussed in *Meta.* Λ.[7] I shall return to this dispute in section 2; but first I shall turn to the *De caelo*.

1. HEAVENLY MOTION IN THE *DE CAELO*

The disagreement between Kosman and the traditional view focuses on the interpretation of *Phys.* VIII and *Meta.* Λ; both sides agree that in the *De caelo* the heavens are in some way or other self-moving.[8] Nonetheless, the issue of the precise nature of this self-motion, and in particular the question of the role played by the sphere's soul in this motion, is an important question in its own right.[9]

Aristotle's view in the *De caelo* is that the outermost heavenly sphere is intelligent and alive:[10] this is what we would expect, since it is divine and the highest being. But *De cae.* I.2–3 also tells us that the sphere is made of a fifth element, αἰθήρ, which, like the other elements, possesses a natural motion—motion in a circle. The idea that the sphere is made of stuff that naturally moves in a circle is not incompatible with the idea that the outermost sphere is moved by its soul; for it could be that it is the nature of αἰθήρ to move in a circle *when certain other conditions obtain*, and that these conditions are provided by the workings of the soul of the sphere. For

---

[6] Kosman is reluctant to use the word "soul" in this context, using "soul-analogue" instead (139 above), since he thinks that Aristotle himself takes the use of "soul" to be inappropriate. But his argument for this (144–45) is weak; moreover, at *De cae.* II.2, 285a29–30, Aristotle makes a point of saying that the heavens are ἔμψυχος (literally, "ensouled"), and I cannot see the sharp difference that Kosman detects between being ἔμψυχος and having a ψυχή. So I shall keep "soul."

[7] Kosman rightly argues that we must not underestimate the difference between the *Phys.* VIII and *Meta.* Λ phases: the latter's use of the ἐνέργεια/κίνησις distinction represents a major development in Aristotle's thinking (147–51 above). But he is wrong to imply that holders of the traditional view deny this: the traditional view's claim that there is no major difference between these two phases relates only to the doctrine that there is a transcendent Prime Mover.

[8] Kosman's interpretation of the nature of self-motion seems to be just that of W. D. Ross 1924.

[9] For a recent discussion, not confined to the *De caelo*, but not in developmental terms, see Gill [1991], reprinted in this volume, 15–34.

[10] *De cae.* II.2, 285a27–30.

instance, it could be that the soul is required in order to activate αἰθήρ's natural capacity for motion, which would otherwise lie dormant.[11] Indeed, when it comes to *Meta.* Λ, Aristotle probably still thinks that the heavenly spheres are made of αἰθήρ, and, as we shall see, he certainly thinks that each sphere's soul is involved in moving its sphere by desiring the relevant motion.[12] Thus in Λ, at least, we should envisage an account of this sort: the soul's desire for motion activates the αἰθήρ's capacity for motion.[13] In *Phys.* VIII, nothing is said directly as to how the unmoved mover produces motion. But there, too, the requirement of an unmoved mover must mean that the αἰθήρ's capacity for natural motion is insufficient by itself to produce motion, and that it is activated in some way by the unmoved mover, either directly or indirectly via the soul of the sphere (and Aristotle may already have the *Meta.* Λ account in mind[14]).

Thus in the *Physics* and *Metaphysics*, αἰθήρ's capacity for circular motion must be in itself an entirely *dormant* one in the sense that it requires activation by something else: if, *per impossibile*, the αἰθήρ were left to itself, it would not move at all. This conception of how αἰθήρ works produces a sharp disanalogy with the way in which the four sublunary elements possess natural motions: earth, water, air, and fire have no souls, and their natural motion requires no activation by souls or any other sort of agent.[15] Yet in *De cae.* I Aristotle draws a straightforward parallel between aethereal and sublunary natural motions, and he does not mention, let alone offer any explanation of, any such disanalogy. This makes it very hard to avoid the conclusion that in the *De caelo* Aristotle's position is different, and that he takes αἰθήρ's natural capacity for motion not to be a "dormant" one at all, but to be a sufficient explanation of the sphere's rotation. On this account, it would seem, the sphere's soul is simply moved around with the αἰθήρ, and need never be cited in a full account of the sphere's motion.[16]

Someone might object that the only possible function of the soul of the sphere, the only activity in virtue of which it can be the principle of the

---

[11] As Guthrie suggests (1939, introduction, pt. 2).

[12] On the "traditional view," the unmoved mover's role is to activate this desire: see section 3 below.

[13] Though it may do more than this as well: see 159–60 below.

[14] In section 3 below I deal with what is often taken to be a major objection to this idea— the fact that the argument of *Phys.* VIII is conducted in terms of efficient causation, whereas the unmoved mover of *Meta.* Λ is a final cause.

[15] It is true that *Phys.* VIII insists that parcels of the four sublunary elements must be set in motion by the removal of an obstacle; but this is a distinct and much weaker condition than the "activation" condition that the necessity for an unmoved mover imposes on αἰθήρ: for left to itself (i.e., in the absence of any help *or* hindrance), Aristotelian fire will move upward, earth downward, etc.

[16] Cf. Guthrie 1939, introduction, xxxii–xxxiii.

sphere's life, is that it produces motion. But this reply will not do. According to the *De caelo*, the *stars* are also alive and have a function, but they are not self-movers: they are merely carried around by the movement of the sphere.[17] Thus the souls of the stars do not produce motion, and so must have some other function, such as thinking. The soul of the heavenly sphere could also have this function. *De cae.* II.3, 286a9–12, might seem to equate the function of the divine outermost sphere with its motion: "The activity of a god is deathlessness; and this is eternal life. So eternal motion must belong to the god. And since the heaven is of this kind (for it is a divine body), that is why it has its circular body, which by nature moves in a circle forever." But all that Aristotle need mean is that the nature of a divine being requires the eternity of its attributes; since this god—the outermost sphere—is in motion, it must be so eternally, and so must have a body "which by nature moves in a circle forever." Aristotle *may* mean more than this, however; for, as we are about to see, there is a way in which the divine being's activity may be bound up with its motion that does not introduce the troublesome disanalogy with the sublunary elements.

So far the evidence is strongly against any involvement of the soul in the heaven's self-motion. There is one passage in *De cae.* II, however, that suggests a different picture.[18] In the discussion of left/right and above/below in chapter 2, Aristotle contrasts the motion of the heavens with that of the inanimate (ἄψυχα) sublunary elements, and connects it instead with the sphere's being ἔμψυχος, aligning it with the motion of plants and animals.[19] Now it could be that Aristotle does not have a single, well thought-out theory in the *De caelo*, but is developing various different

---

[17] *De cae.* II.12, 292a18–21: the stars have a share of πρᾶξις and ζωή. II.8: the stars are not self-movers.

[18] I share Guthrie's view that two other passages, II.6, 288a27–b7 and 288b22–289a8, are probably later additions, inserted after the composition of *Phys.* VIII: see Guthrie 1939, introduction, xxiii–xxv.

[19] See esp. *De cae.* II.2, 285a27–31: "Since it has already been determined that it is in whatever has a principle of motion that such δυνάμεις [involving left/right, etc.] are to be found, and the heaven is alive (ἔμψυχος) and has a principle of motion, it is clear that it has both above and below and right and left." Gill suggests that "the heaven" (οὐρανός) here means the whole cosmos rather than the outermost heavenly sphere ([1991], reprinted above, 30, note 44): this would remove the problem altogether. But I am unconvinced by this interpretation. It is true that Aristotle begins the chapter by asking whether left and right belong "to the body of the whole" (τῷ τοῦ παντὸς σώματι), and this might suggest that he is thinking of the whole cosmos; but his later remarks make it clear that he has the outermost sphere in mind. In particular, at 285a33–b1 he says of this "whole" that "all its parts are similar and in eternal motion," something true of the sphere but not of the cosmos as a whole; and at the climax of his discussion, 285b16ff., he applies the left/right distinction to "the motion of the heaven": this must be that of the heavenly sphere, because the cosmos as a whole does not move at all, and because he links the motion in question directly to that of the fixed stars, which are carried round by the outermost sphere.

ideas without giving enough thought to how they can be integrated.[20] Or it could be that Aristotle is clutching at straws here in a effort to prove that the sphere has an intrinsic orientation. But it is possible to interpret the passage at *De cae.* II.2 in such a way as to give the sphere's soul a role in its motion without committing Aristotle to the fatal disanalogy between αἰθήρ and the other elements.

First, to say that the soul plays a part in the motion of the sphere is not necessarily to say that it does so by means of a desire. Many of an animal's functions and activities are due to its soul without being the products of desire. Second, the soul can be involved in an activity in more than one way. We have already encountered one form of involvement—in which the capacities of the material are sufficient to explain the activity once those capacities are activated by the soul. But it is also a familiar Aristotelian doctrine that many natural processes and activities (the development of an embryo into a mature organism and the natural behavior of such organisms being the paradigm cases) have complex structures that cannot be fully explained in terms of the object's material nature, nor in terms of the mere activation of that nature by the soul: the essential nature of these processes cannot be understood except in terms of the organism's form—its soul.

Aristotle may have this second type of soul-involvement in mind in *De cae.* II.2. Let us suppose that the analogy between αἰθήρ and the sublunary elements suggested by *De cae.* I does indeed hold: if it were left to itself, in other words, αἰθήρ would still move in a circle. The argument of II.2 may be that, over and above its circularity, the motion of the outermost sphere has a "structure" or form that cannot be explained by reference to the αἰθήρ but that mirrors, and can be explained by, the form of the being whose matter the αἰθήρ is. More precisely, the circular motion possesses a particular direction (which Aristotle analyzes in terms of right/left and above/below), which it only has because it is the motion of a living being that has an orientation and distinguishable δυνάμεις related to right/left, above/below. This living being—the outermost sphere—has the δυνάμεις for rotation in the direction that it does, Aristotle appears to think, because that direction is the "best" one for it to rotate in: see *De cae.* II.5. I have no wish to try to defend Aristotle's argument for an orientation for the heavens, still less his doctrine of the superiority of one direction of rotation over the other; my point is that Aristotle's line of thought provides a clear sense in which the directional rotation of the *outermost sphere* is like animal motion rather than like the motions of the four elements, while at the same time allowing the close analogy between αἰθήρ and those ele-

[20] This is Guthrie's view (1939), though he bases it on the more general tension that he detects between assigning a natural motion to αἰθήρ and describing the heavenly sphere as alive: see next note.

ments.[21] If this interpretation is correct, then Aristotle would have to hold that, if αἰθήρ were left to itself, its nature would make it move in a circle, but that there would be no explanation of the particular direction in which it happened to rotate: it would be ὡς ἔτυχε καὶ ἀπὸ ταὐτομάτου (to echo 287b24–25).[22]

To sum up: if we wish to discount II.2 as a temporary aberration, we should conclude that heavenly motion in the De caelo is entirely due to the nature of the αἰθήρ of which the heavens are composed. The change of doctrine in Meta. Λ,[23] on this view, is as great as it could well be: the αἰθήρ's capacity for natural motion must be demoted to a merely "dormant" one, and the entire superstructure of the soul's involvement in the motion must be added. On the view of De caelo that I propose, the sphere's soul is already involved. The arguments for the unmoved mover presented in Phys. VIII and Meta. Λ still require the demotion of αἰθήρ's capacity for motion to a dormant one. But the story that I have just told about the soul's involvement in the direction of rotation could (though Meta. Λ is silent on this) be taken over as it stands, except that it would now be played one register up, as it were—at the level of the soul's ὄρεξις.

2. THE TRANSCENDENCE OF THE UNMOVED MOVER

And so to the unmoved mover, and the question of whether its introduction marks a sharp rejection of the De caelo's doctrine of heavenly self-motion. Kosman, as I have said, claims that there is no such rejection: the unmoved mover is not a new entity at all, but simply the soul of the outermost sphere.[24] Kosman offers little positive support for his thesis, beyond its general economy. I shall focus on just two objections, each of which gives us good reason to believe in the transcendence of the unmoved mover.

The first is a difficulty that goes to the heart of the claim that the Prime

---

[21] Guthrie fails to see either the possibility that the function of living spheres might be something other than the production of motion, or the possibility that the sphere's soul could be involved in its motion without destroying the parallelism between αἰθήρ and the other elements. Though he notes Aristotle's evident endorsement of this parallelism, he regards this as in tension with Aristotle's ascription of life to the heavenly spheres (Guthrie 1939, introduction, xxxii–xxxv); likewise he sees De cae. II.8's claim that the stars are alive as in tension with the αἰθήρ doctrine (xxxv–xxxvi).

[22] This might also make it easier to understand how the other heavenly spheres can move in different directions without constraining their own αἰθήρ against its nature.

[23] As I have already mentioned, Aristotle says nothing directly about these matters in Phys. VIII.

[24] A similar view of the unmoved mover has also been defended (in connection with Meta. Λ) by Sarah Broadie, in a paper entitled "What Does Aristotle's Prime Mover Do?" given at the Princeton Ancient Philosophy Colloquium in December 1990.

Mover is the immanent soul of the outermost sphere. This is the question of whether this soul is itself in motion. Aristotle's settled doctrine is that whenever the soul is the efficient cause of a bodily movement, it operates as an "unmoved mover," but nonetheless is in motion, "incidentally," in virtue of being the soul of a body that is moving.[25] Thus we should expect the soul of the outermost sphere to be moved incidentally (that is, to be moved round with its body), and Kosman agrees that it is so moved.[26] In both *Phys.* VIII and *Meta.* Λ.8, Aristotle insists that the primary unmoved mover is not moved even incidentally;[27] the obvious inference is that the unmoved mover is *not* the soul of the outermost sphere, but a separate entity.

Kosman tries to avoid this conclusion by arguing that, although the sphere's soul does move incidentally, there is also a sense in which it does not so move:

> The principle of the outermost sphere's motion does not exhibit the incidental motion that my soul might exhibit . . .; for there is, as we have seen, no larger περιέχον, no surrounding environment, in relation to which as a whole it might be said to move *from one place to another*. (See Kosman above, 146; italics original)

But in this sense, the *body* of the outermost sphere does not move either. It too, as a whole, does not move from one place to another. So on Kosman's interpretation, Aristotle's claim that the Prime Mover is unmoved both per se and incidentally is just a dishonest pun. In the sense of "move" in which it is a cause of motion (rotation), it does move incidentally; and in the sense in which it is not moved incidentally (change of place as a whole), it is not a cause of motion.

The problem could be avoided if Kosman adopted the view that the soul of the outermost sphere is not incidentally moved after all.[28] But this view

---

[25] *Phys.* VIII.6, 259b16–20; *De an.* I.3–4. It operates as an unmoved mover in the sense that the soul does not cause motion by *transmitting* a motion of its own. (I shall set aside here the question of how Aristotle feels able to claim both that the soul is unmoved qua cause of motion and [as he does in *De an.* III.10 and elsewhere] that desire is a movement.)

[26] "We need not imagine that as the sphere of the fixed stars makes its daily orbit about the earth, this principle [i.e., the sphere's soul] remains immobile, situated at Control Center somewhere in a cosmic Houston and directing from afar that first motion" (Kosman, in this volume, 146). Likewise he speaks of the "eternal and circular self-motion of the divine first mover" (ibid.).

[27] *Phys.* VIII.6, 258b13–16, 259b7–31. In the second passage, the claim arises out of a discussion of the intermittent self-motion of animals, and Kosman takes it to be restricted to intermittent incidental motion (141–42 above); but in the first passage the denial of incidental motion is wholly unrestricted, as it is at Λ.8, 1073a23–25.

[28] This interpretation was suggested by Steven Strange at the Pittsburgh Self-Motion Conference.

is hard to accept. Although Aristotle never explicitly says in *Phys.* VIII that the soul of the outermost sphere is moved incidentally, it is implied, as we have seen, by his general doctrine about souls' motion; indeed, it is difficult to see how one could maintain that something that stays perfectly still while the sphere rotates could be its (Aristotelian) form or soul—its aloofness from the sphere in this respect seems enough to mark it as a separate entity. We can add that in the *De caelo* Aristotle does ascribe motion to the soul of the sphere. The god whose "body" is the outermost sphere is said to be in ceaseless motion:[29] this must mean that the soul is moved around with the sphere, whether Aristotle is thinking of this god as the soul itself or as the composite of soul and sphere.

The second objection to Kosman's interpretation arises from the structure of Aristotle's general program for *Meta.* Λ. Aristotle announces at the start of *Meta.* Λ that he will investigate the principles and causes of substance (1069a18–19); he divides substances into perceptible—including both eternal and perishable—and unchangeable. *Meta.* Λ.1–5 deal with the two types of perceptible substance; at the start of chapter 6 Aristotle explicitly turns to the third class, unchangeable substance, and then presents an outline of the proof of the unmoved mover; the discussion of the contemplative activity and supreme goodness of this being occupies chapters 7, 9, and 10. But if we ask where in this program a discussion of the soul of the outermost sphere would belong, the answer is, not in chapters 6–10, but in chapters 1–5. Because Aristotle labels his subject in chapters 1–5 "perceptible substance," and because one might think that souls (and substantial forms generally) are imperceptible, one might infer that souls and forms would be dealt with in the second half of *Meta.* Λ. But of course it is clear that Λ.6–10 do not discuss souls or substantial forms in general; these chapters discuss one very special entity.[30] Souls and substantial forms are dealt with, insofar as they are at all, within the discussion of "perceptible substance" in Λ.1–5.[31] Since Λ.1–5 are supposed to cover eternal perceptible substances as well as perishable ones, the souls of the heavenly

---

[29] *De cae.* I.9, 279b1: καὶ ἄπαυστον δὴ κίνησιν κινεῖται εὐλόγως. A few lines earlier, at 279a32, Aristotle also describes the god as "entirely immutable" (πᾶν ἀμετάβλητον). Kosman seems to see this as anticipation of the *Physics* doctrine of the unmoved mover (144 above); but the context makes it clear that Aristotle simply means that the god is unchanging in every way *except* for its eternal rotation. Note that at 288b4–5 he actually says that the moving sphere "does not change" (τὸ κινούμενον οὐ μεταβάλλει). (On the provenance of this passage, see note 18 above.)

[30] Or 55 special entities, if we take Λ.8 into account.

[31] See Λ.3, 1070a9–13: "There are three types of substance [this is a new classification, not the original one set out in chap. 1]: the matter which is a this something †through appearing† (for what touches and does not have a natural unity is matter and what underlies); the thing's nature, which is a this something and a certain state-toward-which; moreover the third [substance] is the particular from these—e.g., Socrates or Kallias."

spheres must be included within their ambit. Had the climax of the study of substance been the soul of the outermost heavenly sphere, Aristotle could have organized *Meta.* Λ in a different way so as to reach this soul in chapters 6–10; but he did not.

3. THE UNMOVED MOVER AS A CAUSE OF MOTION

In what sense is the unmoved mover a cause of motion? Our starting-point is *Meta.* Λ.7, 1072a25–27: "There is something that produces motion without being moved, being eternal, and substance, and activity. That is how the objects of desire and of thought produce motion; they produce motion without being moved." As it stands, this reference to the objects of desire is ambiguous: Aristotle could be simply pointing out one way in which X can move Y while being unmoved, or he could be explaining how the prime unmoved mover actually moves things.[32] *Meta.* Λ.7, 1072b3–4, makes it clear that Aristotle means the latter: the unmoved mover moves things by being an object of desire.[33]

It is clear, therefore, that the unmoved mover in *Meta.* Λ acts as a final cause: it produces motion as the objects of desire do, and it is in virtue of being good that it is an ἀρχή (1072b10–11). But it is often held that being a final cause is incompatible with being an efficient cause (in Aristotle's sense) of the motion, and I do not think that this is true. To see this, we need to distinguish three different types of case involving a final cause.

   1. The final cause does not operate in association with a desire on the part of the subject, S, at all (as when we explain the movements of an animal's heart muscles in terms of its survival or well-being).
   2. S has a desire for the final cause, but the goodness of the final cause plays no role in explaining why S has that desire. One kind of example of this type involves objects of desire that do not exist (either at all or not yet): the generosity of Santa Claus does not explain why my daughter has a desire to meet him (it is my *stories* about Santa Claus that explain that).
   3. S has a desire for the final cause, and the goodness of the final cause *does*

---

[32] The general theory of objects of desire as unmoved movers is given at *De an.* III.10, 433a27–b17: "It is always the object of desire which produces movement, but this is either the good or the apparent good; and not every good but the practicable good. . . . That which produces movement is twofold: that which is unmoved, and that which produces movement and is moved. That which is unmoved is the practicable good, and that which produces movement and is moved is the faculty of desire."

[33] κινεῖ δὴ ὡς ἐρώμενον. Cf. Λ.8, 1074a17–31, and note that 1072a27–b3 would be a pointless digression if the unmoved mover did not produce motion by being an object of desire. *MA* 6 also states this view.

explain why *S* has it. This type of case occurs when, for example, the sweetness of the cake explains why I form a desire for it and so eat it.[34]

In (1) and (2), the final cause pretty clearly has no role as an efficient cause of the motion/action, a "whence the motion came." But it is equally clear that in case (3) it does have such a role: in (3) the object of the desire helps to explain how the motion came into being because it helps to explain how the desire came into being, and the desire is an efficient cause of the action. Note that type (3) cases are neither anomalous nor exceptional; on the contrary, this type represents the normal causal structure when intentional action is focused on an already existing object.[35] Note also that in this type of case, there is a sense in which the object of desire is a final cause primarily, and an efficient cause only in virtue of being a final one. This is because it can only act as an efficient cause in the way it does (that is, by being perceived to be good) if it also acts as a final cause; whereas it could in principle act as a final cause in the way it does (by being the object of a desire) without being the efficient cause of the desire.[36]

I shall briefly consider three objections to this account of type (3) cases. First, "*S*'s desire is the efficient cause of *S*'s action; so nothing else can be its efficient cause." But Aristotle recognizes that things have not only proximate but also more remote efficient causes.[37] In cases of intentional action, *S*'s desire to φ is the most important efficient cause of *S*'s φing, but many other things may be (more remote) efficient causes of the φing as well.

Second, "An efficient cause acts by expending energy; the Prime Mover does not do that, so it is not an efficient cause." But we can distinguish two sorts of Aristotelian efficient cause.[38] Some involve the transmission of energy or motion (and typically involve some interaction between agent

---

[34] There are also those cases in which the subject has the desire to φ because it promotes the animal's survival or well-being to have the desire. In these cases we have two final causes: the good of the animal and the object of its desire. As far as the latter is concerned, it will be a case of type (2) if φing is sufficiently distinct (intentionally) from "surviving or doing-well"; if not, it will be a case of type (3).

[35] I am assuming that in the normal case, *S*'s perception of the (real or imagined) goodness of the object brings about *S*'s desire. Cases in which a "blind" desire causes the object to seem good will be cases of type (2).

[36] In the case of the Prime Mover, of course, this asymmetry will hold only at a rather abstract level.

[37] Aristotle draws the distinction between proximate and more remote causes (of all four kinds) in *Meta.* H.4, and applies it specifically to efficient causes at Λ.5, 1071a14–17: "[The causes of a human being include] something else external, for example the father, and besides these the sun and the circle of the ecliptic, which are neither matter nor form nor privation nor the same in form, but which initiate change [i.e., are efficient causes]." Cf. Λ.4, 1070b27–35; Z.17, 1041a27–31; GC I.7, 324a30–34.

[38] As Aristotle himself does in the discussion of moved and unmoved movers in GC I.6–7.

and patient that involves some change to the agent)—let us call these "energetic" efficient causes.[39] Other efficient causes do not: let us call them "nonenergetic" causes. When souls act as unmoved movers they are efficient causes of this sort; so is the τέχνη of building or medicine.[40] In type (3) cases, the final cause is an efficient cause of the second, nonenergetic sort.

Third, "There is no trace of this doctrine in Aristotle." But *De an.* iii.10 seems to provide an example of it: "That which initiates motion (τὸ κινοῦν) is twofold: that which is unmoved and that which moves and is moved; and that which is unmoved is the achievable good" (433b14–16).[41] Of course, one *could* take this to show that κινοῦν has no specific connection with the operation of an efficient cause; but I think that it is much more natural to take the remark as meaning that there are two ways of being an efficient cause of motion: by being an unmoved cause (that is, by being a final cause that is also an efficient cause), or by transmitting motion. A yet clearer statement of the doctrine, this time in connection with the cosmic unmoved mover(s), can be found at *Phys.* ii.7, 198a24–29:

> [The formal, efficient, and final causes] often coincide. For the what it is and the for the sake of which are one, while the primary source of motion is the same in form as these; for human being generates human being, and, in general, so it is with everything that causes motion by being moved; and those which do not [cause motion in this way] fall outside the subject of natural science, for they cause motion not by having motion or a principle of motion in themselves, but by being unmoved.[42]

There is thus no reason to see being a final cause as incompatible with being (derivatively) a nonenergetic efficient cause; and there is good reason to suppose this combination to be realized in type (3) cases—and to suppose that Aristotle recognized this. To return to *Meta.* Λ, my claim is that the Prime Mover is both a final and an efficient cause in this way. Its production of motion is clearly of type (3): its perfection acts primarily as a final cause, the object of the heavenly sphere's desire; but it is also (in virtue of being a final cause) an efficient cause, since it helps to bring about the existence of that desire. This interpretation has a number of further advan-

---

[39] This use of "energy" may seem anachronistic; but in Aristotle's own physics, not all cases of "interactive" causation involve the transmission of motion, the case of heating being a good example.

[40] See *GC* i.7, 324a35–b4; *Meta.* Λ.4, 1070b28–34.

[41] τὸ δὲ κινοῦν διττόν, τὸ μὲν ἀκίνητον, τὸ δὲ κινοῦν καὶ κινούμενον, ἔστι δὲ τὸ μὲν ἀκίνητον τὸ πρακτὸν ἀγαθόν.

[42] I am grateful to Malcolm Schofield for drawing my attention to this passage. To it we may add Λ.6, 1071b12: see below.

tages. It brings *Meta.* Λ into line with the *Physics* passage just quoted. Also, at Λ.6, 1071b12, Aristotle applies the terms κινητικόν and ποιητικόν to the unmoved mover: on my interpretation we can take these terms in their standard sense—that is, as referring to efficient causation[43] —without undermining the central claim of *Meta.* Λ that the Prime Mover moves as an object of love. We can moreover lay to rest a vexed question about the relationship of the doctrines of *Phys.* VIII and *Meta.* Λ. The argument for the necessity of the unmoved mover in *Phys.* VIII is conducted entirely in terms of efficient causation; this has led some to regard it as advancing an efficient-cause conception of the unmoved mover in contrast to Λ's final-cause one. On my account of Λ, there is no need to see any change of view. The unmoved mover, the first principle of all things, is both the first efficient cause and the first final cause: "On such a principle depend the heavens and nature."[44]

APPENDIX: A FINAL PROBLEM

Two of Aristotle's arguments concerning the Prime Mover are baffling on any account of its mode of causation. The first can be found at *Phys.* VIII.10, 267b6–9, where Aristotle endeavors to show that the unmoved mover must be located at the circumference of the cosmos (ἐν κύκλῳ):

> So [the unmoved mover] must occupy either the center or the circumference, since these things are the principles. But the things nearest the mover move the quickest, and it is the motion of the circumference that is the quickest; therefore the mover [is] there.[45]

Note first that the circumference of the cosmos is not an Aristotelian *place*, strictly speaking.[46] This is no bar to its possessing what we might call a "location": the outermost sphere has a location but no place, for instance. But one might well wonder just what it is, in Aristotelian terms, that makes it true that the unmoved mover is in one location rather than another. Second, it is left unclear whether the unmoved mover occupies the whole of the circumference of the outermost sphere or just a point on the circumference. If the former, how is this compatible with its having no magnitude? Is it because it has no thickness? Yet even so, there would appear to be a

---

[43] Cf. my remarks on *De an.* III.10, 433b14–16 above.

[44] *Meta.* Λ.7, 1072b13–14.

[45] ἀνάγκη δὴ ἢ ἐν μέσῳ ἢ ἐν κύκλῳ εἶναι· αὗται γὰρ αἱ ἀρχαί. ἀλλὰ τάχιστα κινεῖται τὰ ἐγγύτατα τοῦ κινοῦντος. τοιαύτη δ' ἡ τοῦ κύκλου κίνησις· ἐκεῖ ἄρα τὸ κινοῦν.

[46] This is because for Aristotle, place is "the limit of the surrounding body" (*Phys.* IV.1–5), and nothing surrounds the circumference of the cosmos. And indeed, the unmoved mover cannot occupy an Aristotelian place for another reason, namely that it has no magnitude; the argument for its lack of magnitude will concern us later.

sense in which it is bigger than it would be if it were at the center of the earth. If, on the other hand, it occupies only a point, its precise location might seem arbitrary: why should it be at this point on the circumference rather than at that point? Perhaps Aristotle holds that the point on the circumference at the South Pole is the "best" point, and that the unmoved mover is there.[47]

But surely these questions are ridiculous, and stem from reading Aristotle's words too literally? In saying that the unmoved mover is at the outermost circumference of the the cosmos, isn't Aristotle trying to say that it has no spatial relation to the physical world at all? It would be nice to think so; but this idea is ruled out by the fact that Aristotle here introduces "being at the circumference" as the alternative to its being at the center. Moreover, the argument he gives for the unmoved mover's being at the circumference only makes sense if what is in question is the spatial relation of the unmoved mover to what it moves.[48] This constitutes one respect in which the argument at 267b6–9 is puzzling. But—more importantly for

[47] See De cae. II.2 and 5, and Guthrie's comments (1939, 136–37 and 162–65).

[48] I defend this claim below. H. S. Lang believes that the traditional understanding of the passage we are considering is erroneous: in her view, Aristotle's argument is not concerned with the location of the unmoved mover, but with that of the primary eternal continuous *motion* whose necessity Aristotle has earlier been anxious to establish. She understands the passage along the following lines: "So [the primary eternal motion] must occupy the center or the circumference. . . . But the things most *immediately related to* the mover move most quickly, and it is the motion of the circumference that is the quickest; therefore the mover [produces motion] there" (Lang 1981; see esp. 330–35). I have two main objections to this interpretation. First, it is true that the subject of εἶναι in the first sentence of the passage is left underdetermined by the sentences that precede it: given only what they say, the subject could be τὸ κινούμενον (i.e., the primary *moving object*), τὸ κινοῦν (i.e., the unmoved mover), or—less probably—the primary moving object's *motion*. But it is hard to read ἐκεῖ ἄρα τὸ κινοῦν as meaning anything other than "therefore the mover is there." It is, moreover, especially difficult to understand it in the way that Lang's interpretation requires. For Lang, "the things nearest the mover" (τὰ ἐγγύτατα τοῦ κινοῦντος) must mean "the things that are most directly related causally to the mover" (see below); hence Aristotle must be seen as having in mind the point that the unmoved mover moves *many* things—the outermost sphere directly, and the other spheres, the sublunary elements, etc., less directly. So the claim that ἐκεῖ ἄρα τὸ κινοῦν has to be read not simply as "the unmoved mover produces motion there [i.e., at the circumference]," but as "the unmoved mover produces motion in its most direct way there": this is a great deal for the reader to supply. These considerations resolve the question of the first sentence's subject in favor of the traditional reading. Second, Lang's interpretation requires that Aristotle here entertain the idea that the primary eternal motion might be at the *center* of the cosmos; but in Aristotle's cosmos, of course, the center is occupied and surrounded by unmoving earth. (A volume of earth around the center might, in principle, move slightly under the force of a large mass falling to the earth's surface [see De cae. II.14]: but this sort of motion plainly could not be a candidate for Aristotle's single, eternal, continuous motion.) Lang suggests that what Aristotle has in mind are the cyclical transformations of the elements into one another; but in the sense of "center" in which the center is a principle (ἀρχή) of the cosmic sphere, these transformations simply do not take place at the center of the cosmos.

our purposes—it is also puzzling because it apparently depends on the idea that the nearer the cause, the quicker the motion caused. This only seems plausible (though even then not compelling) in the case of "energetic" efficient causes—those which produce motion by transmitting motion or energy. An example of the type of case in which this idea looks most plausible is that of someone stirring a bucket of treacle with a stick: the treacle near the stick moves more, and more quickly, than the treacle further away.[49] The idea that a causal agent is more efficacious the closer it is to the patient is quite out of place both in the case of nonenergetic efficient causes and in the case of final causes. Its application to the unmoved mover is thus very hard to understand.

Joseph DeFilippo has suggested (in correspondence) that, even on what I have called the traditional interpretation of the passage,[50] τὰ ἐγγύτατα τοῦ κινοῦντος could be understood causally rather than spatially. On this reading, Aristotle's argument for the location of the unmoved mover does not rely on the idea that the *nearer* the cause is, the quicker is the motion caused; instead it would appeal to the idea that the motion that the cause *immediately* or *most directly* brings about will be quicker than any motion that it produces less directly (that is, via moved intermediaries). This principle is just as false as my "the nearer the quicker" principle, but someone who found it plausible would not have to have energetic efficient causation in mind. It is certainly true that ἐγγύτατος can have a causal meaning in Aristotle,[51] but I do not think that invoking it here will free Aristotle from the charge of confusion over the type of efficient causation that the unmoved mover exemplifies. On DeFilippo's account, Aristotle's argument would be: "The unmoved mover must be either at the center or at the circumference; its most direct effect must be at the circumference (since motion is quickest there); so the unmoved mover must be at the circumference." Although the ἐγγύτατα premise, so construed, no longer introduces the notion of energetic efficient causation, the inference from the location of the unmoved mover's effect to the location of the unmoved mover itself simply introduces that notion all over again. Someone might well think that an energetic efficient cause must be contiguous with what it most directly affects; but a final cause need not be anywhere near what it most directly affects as a final cause.

The second argument is designed to demonstrate that the unmoved mover has no magnitude and no parts and is indivisible; we can call it the "infinite δύναμις argument." In *Phys.* VIII.10, it runs as follows:

1. Nothing with finite magnitude can cause an infinite motion.

---

[49] This example was suggested to me by David Rees.
[50] See the discussion of Lang's interpretation in note 48 above.
[51] See *Meta.* H.4, 1044b1–3, and note 37 above.

2. Causing an infinite motion requires infinite δύναμις, but nothing with finite magnitude can have infinite δύναμις.

3. Premises (1) and (2) each independently show that:

4. The cause of an infinite motion cannot be a thing with finite magnitude.

5. Nothing possesses an infinite magnitude (proved elsewhere).

6. So, by (4) and (5), the cause of an infinite motion can have neither a finite nor an infinite magnitude.

7. So it must have no magnitude.

The argument also appears in *Meta.* Λ (7, 1073a5–11).[52]

But the arguments that Aristotle gives for both (1) and (2) in *Phys.* VIII.10 rely on the idea that the cause of the infinite motion is acting on the sphere(s) that it moves by expending—and so losing—energy. But the unmoved mover simply does not act in this way if it causes motion by inspiring the spheres. It does not require an infinite δύναμις of this sort to cause an infinite motion because it does not require *any* δύναμις of this sort to cause motion.[53]

Thus at two points we have found arguments that appear to treat the unmoved mover as an energetic efficient cause. Yet in *Meta.* Λ, the unmoved mover is clearly conceived as an "inspirational" mover[54] that does not operate like this, whether or not we also take it to be a nonenergetic efficient cause in the way that I have suggested.[55] The argument for the unmoved mover's location is bizarre for other reasons, as we have seen; so we might feel able to dismiss it as wholly aberrant. But the infinite δύναμις argument is not so easy to dismiss. Its presence in *Meta.* Λ, moreover,

---

[52] *Meta.* Λ does not use (1), but otherwise appears to rely on the same argument starting from (2). Nor does *Meta.* Λ explain why (2) is true—we still have to go back to the *Physics* version for that.

[53] In this case, too, DeFilippo has suggested to me that Aristotle can be saved. This is because Aristotle could provide an argument that nonenergetic finite causes could not cause motion for an infinite time either: the argument would be that even though such causes do not spend energy in acting as a cause of motion, they would nonetheless need a δύναμις for existing for an infinite time, and this could not be located in a finite magnitude. But although some Neoplatonists maintained for precisely this reason that the Prime Mover must be the cause of the *existence* of the outermost heavenly sphere as well as of its motion (see Sorabji 1988, 249–54), there is no trace of this idea in Aristotle. Indeed, as DeFilippo admits, Aristotle's view is that the heavenly spheres, which are finite in magnitude, have *in themselves* no potentiality for ceasing to exist (their matter is of a special kind that involves only potentiality for locomotion—"matter for whence and whither" [Λ.3, 1069b24–26]), and hence have a δύναμις, in whatever sense of the term is appropriate here, for eternal existence. (For discussion of some of the later history of this issue, see Sorabji 1988, chap. 15; and Judson 1987.)

[54] I.e., one whose goodness inspires the sphere to desire circular motion.

[55] It does need, to Aristotle's mind, to be eternally active, if it is to avoid the objection that he raises against the Platonic Forms in Λ.6. But being active in this sense is not the same as expending energy on the outermost heavenly sphere.

means that we cannot explain away the problem by supposing that when writing *Phys.* VIII, Aristotle's view was that the unmoved mover was an efficient cause of the energetic sort, and that the inspirational unmoved mover of *Meta.* Λ represents a change of view.[56]

Do these arguments constitute a difficulty for the interpretation of the unmoved mover's causal role that I have been advancing? Yes and no. They cannot be reconciled with my interpretation; but on the other hand, they do not seem to be reconcilable with *any* interpretation of the unmoved mover. This is because they require the unmoved mover to be a cause that expends its energy on the sphere, and that is, for Aristotle, a requirement that is simply incompatible with being an unmoved mover of any sort.

[56] Note *Phys.* VIII.10, 267b2–3: "For it is not necessary for [the unmoved mover] to change along with that which it moves, but will be able to cause motion always (for the causing of motion in this way *involves no work* [ἄπονον])." (In the *De caelo*, Aristotle had applied ἄπονον to the motion of the divine heavenly sphere [II.1, 284a14–16].)

Part II

THE ARISTOTELIAN TRADITION

CHAPTER 9

Self-Motion in Stoic Philosophy

DAVID E. HAHM

SELF-MOTION is an elusive subject in Stoic philosophy. This is not because self-motion was unimportant to the Stoics. On the contrary, self-motion was found everywhere in Stoicism, because the Stoics regarded the universe as a living creature, whose every motion and activity were due to an innate vital force.[1] Greek philosophers for centuries had believed self-motion to be preeminently manifested in the motion and activities of living beings, so it comes as no surprise to find that the Stoics attributed all motion ultimately to a self-moving vital force. But despite the prominent role played by self-motion in Stoic philosophy, the conception itself finds explicit mention in very few surviving sources; and those few that mention it raise more questions than they answer.[2]

The clearest and most comprehensive discussion occurs in a Stoic proof for the existence of god, reported by Sextus Empiricus (*Adv. math.* 9.75–76 [=LS 44C; SVF 2: 311):[3]

> The [material] substance of things that exist, they claim, since it is of itself without motion and shapeless, needs to be moved and shaped by some cause. For this reason, just as when we see a very beautiful bronze work, we want to know the artist (inasmuch as its matter is in itself immobile); so when we see the matter of the universe moving and possessing form and structure, we

I would like to thank Steven Strange and Brad Inwood for reading earlier versions of this chapter and for generously offering their criticism and advice. I would also like to thank the anonymous referees for many useful suggestions. Above all, I wish to express my appreciation to Mary Louise Gill for her patience, encouragement, and advice. Her incisive queries and challenges have done more than I can say to help me clarify my understanding and exposition. Finally, I would like to thank Chris Hahm for producing the figures and illustrations.

[1] SVF 1: 110–14; 2:633–34, 636 (cf. LS 53X); see Hahm 1977, 136–74.

[2] The term "self-moving" (αὐτοκίνητος) is rare. Origen uses it of fire and flowing springs of water in a text that we will be discussing (*De princ.* 3.1.2). Seneca uses the Latin equivalent (*se moveo*) of a wise man exercising his virtue (*Ep.* 109.2) and of air accelerating to the point of becoming fire, viz., lightning (*Nat. quaest.* 2.15). Slightly more frequent, but still uncommon, are a variety of expressions for "moving of itself," the most relevant of which will be discussed in the course of this chapter.

[3] This passage is not explicitly attributed to the Stoics, but its content and context suggest a Stoic source; see LS 2: 266.

might reasonably investigate the cause that moves it and gives it its variety of shapes. It is not plausible that this is anything else than a power that pervades it, just as soul pervades us. Now this power is either self-moving or moved by another. But if it is moved by another power, this second power will be incapable of being moved unless it is moved by still another power, which is strange. So there exists some power that in itself is self-moving (αὐτοκίνητος), and this power would be divine and eternal. For it will be in motion either from eternity or from some particular time. But it will not be in motion from some particular time; for there will be no cause of its moving from some particular time. Therefore, the power that moves matter and directs it in orderly fashion to generations and changes is eternal. So this power would be god.

In this argument, to avoid the logical pitfall of infinite regress, the Stoics trace all motion and change back to a single eternal self-mover, which they consequently postulate to be god.[4]

To anyone acquainted with the earlier history of Greek philosophy, the Stoic argument sounds vaguely familiar. One line of thought has a distinct Aristotelian ring, namely, the argument that there can be no infinite series of moved movers and that the eternal first mover must be god.[5] On the other hand, insofar as this first mover is emphatically a self-mover within the universe, pervading its matter and giving it all its qualities and motions, as soul does in a human being, the Stoics approach the position of Plato.[6] Yet a little reflection shows that these similarities to Plato and Aristotle tell us almost nothing about the Stoics' real relation to their philosophical predecessors on the subject of self-motion.[7] Though the rejection of an infinite series of movers reminds us of *Phys.* VIII.5 (esp. 256a4–b3), there is no hint in the Stoic argument of any recognition of the problems that Aristotle raised immediately thereafter (257a31–258b10; cf. 256b13–27), problems that led Aristotle himself to reject the primacy of a *self-moving* first mover in favor of an *unmoved* first mover.[8] Moreover, against the background of both Plato's and Aristotle's attempts to define the scope of self-motion in the universe and to clarify its relation to other kinds of

---

[4] Cf. Dragona-Monachou 1976, 128. Sextus's testimony that the first mover is a self-mover is confirmed as Stoic by Simplicius, who classifies the Stoics with the ancients in denying the existence of an unmoved mover and in regarding every mover as moved (*In phys.* 420.6–11 [=*SVF* 2: 339]).

[5] It is particularly reminiscent of Aristotle's argument in *Phys.* VIII.5, 256a14–21; cf. LS 1: 271; 2: 266–67.

[6] Plato regards soul as a source of motion in *Laws* X.894B–896B, 899B, and stresses that soul is a self-mover in *Phaedrus* 245C–246A and *Laws* X.895E–896A.

[7] On the controversial issue of Aristotelian influence on Stoic philosophy in general, see Sandbach 1985; and Hahm 1991.

[8] On Aristotle's own position, see the debate between Kosman and Judson in this volume.

motion, the brief Stoic argument for the existence of god seems an unsatisfactory oversimplification or an evasion of the philosophical issues involved in the concept itself. However important the argument reported by Sextus is as evidence for the Stoic commitment to the existence of a self-moving force and for their conception of god, it does not contribute much to the philosophical discussion of the nature of self-motion. We must look elsewhere if we hope to understand the Stoic conception of the nature and role of self-motion or of the Stoics' relation to their predecessors on this subject.

Additional evidence on the Stoics' conception of self-motion is meager, but a few tantalizing clues suggest that at least some Stoics went beyond simply postulating a vaguely defined divine self-mover to explain movement and change in the universe. In a number of texts of the second and third centuries A.D., an allusion to different kinds of self-motion or self-movers occurs in arguments brought in support of human responsibility. Among these are texts by Clement and Origen of Alexandria and a polemic by Alexander of Aphrodisias.[9] In two of these accounts, both by Origen, several different kinds of self-motion are distinguished and denoted by an uncommon set of technical terms that Simplicius attributes to the Stoics, namely, motion "out of itself" (ἐξ ἑαυτοῦ), motion "from itself" (ἀφ' ἑαυτοῦ), and motion "through itself" (δι' ἑαυτοῦ).[10] Simplicius's explicit attribution of this classification to the Stoics, combined with a number of undeniably Stoic elements in the arguments of Clement, Origen, and Alexander, make it highly probable that all these arguments involving the concept of self-motion ultimately emanated from the Stoa and hence may be useful for shedding further light on self-motion in Stoic philosophy.[11]

---

[9] The texts are Clement of Alexandria *Stromat.* 2.20 (173.17–25 Stählin [=*SVF* 2: 714]); Origen *De orat.* 6.1 (311.16–312.5 Koetschau [=*SVF* 2: 989]); *De princ.* 3.1.2–3 (196.3–197.11 Koetschau; 18.13–24.54 Crouzel-Simonetti [=*SVF* 2: 988]); and Alexander *De fato* 13 (181.15–182.8 Bruns; 26.15–27.18 Thillet [=*SVF* 2: 979]).

[10] Simplicius *In Cat.* 306.19–27 (= *SVF* 2: 499). I have consistently used the literal translations of these terms in spite of their stylistic infelicity, both to avoid biasing the question of their original meaning to the Stoics, which will emerge in the course of this chapter, and to call attention to the literal spatial sense, which I believe governed the additional semantic content assumed in the Stoic theory.

[11] The evidence for the Stoic origin of Clement and Origen is discussed by Inwood 1985, 21–26, 78–81 (see also Hahm 1992, 23–24 and nn. 3 and 4); for Alexander, see Sharples 1978, 253–58; 1983, 142–43. It should be noted that the arguments constitute several distinct applications of the concept of self-motion to a long-standing philosophical debate within the Stoa. Though over the course of their history of over half a millenium, the Stoics tended to anchor themselves to a number of key positions, they often developed new defenses for their positions and continued to modify their philosophical positions in response to external criticism and internal debates regarding unsettled issues. The precise origin of the several applications of self-motion is not explicitly attested. The conceptual affinities of one of the arguments (found in Origen *De orat.* 6.1) tend to link it to later authors rather than to the

1. THE EVIDENCE

The relevant texts display two different approaches to self-motion. In one we find a division of things that move, among which are several kinds of self-mover (Clement *Stromat.* 2.20; Origen *De princ.* 3.1.2–3; *De orat.* 6.1). In the other we encounter an enumeration or catalog of kinds of self-motion (Simplicius *In Cat.* 306.19–27; Origen *De orat.* 6.1).[12] These two different applications of the concept are not necessarily incompatible; in fact, Origen, who was sensitive to the philosophical nuances of the arguments that he uses, combines both applications on one occasion.[13] Nevertheless, the differences among the texts preclude any straightforward derivation of the Stoic belief from them. We can only use them for reconstructing the Stoic conception if we probe behind the Christian adaptation and the Peripatetic polemic to tease out the underlying Stoic presuppositions.

It is easiest to begin this endeavor with the series of accounts of the division of things that move. Origen's version, which is the most instructive, can best be comprehended in summary form (see Figure 1).[14] The function of this division is obviously to articulate the relationship between

---

Old Stoics, Zeno, Cleanthes, and Chrysippus (cf. Hahm 1992, for one example; see below, 185–200, for others). Such affinities might suggest a post-Chrysippean date at least for the catalog of self-motions found in Simplicius and Origen. Yet other conceptions found in or implied by these texts go back to Zeno and Chrysippus, suggesting an early and widespread currency for the general conception and analysis. The question of the historical origin of the various elaborations and applications of the theory is beyond the scope of this study. Here I shall concentrate on the philosophical conceptions shared by all the arguments or elaborated by the most specific of them.

[12] One aspect of this catalog has also found its way into Diogenes Laertius's doxography of Stoicism (7.148–49, 158); see below, 200–202.

[13] Origen *De orat.* 6.1; See Hahm 1992, for discussion of his combination of arguments.

[14] Origen spells it out completely in *De princ.* 3.1.2– 3 (196.3–197.11). In *De oratione*, a slightly later work, he conflates the first part of the division with a catalog of self-motions to reproduce a composite argument (for analysis of this composite argument, see Hahm 1992). In my reconstruction of Origen's division, I have enclosed in parentheses the adverbs "only" and "also" where they are implied by the pattern of Origen's division, but not explicitly expressed. I have added in their proper locations (enclosed in brackets) descriptions that Origen consolidated into his generic descriptions at the next higher level. For further discussion of this division, see Hahm 1992, 31–34. I have chosen to use Origen's version as the basis for discussing the Stoic division because it is parallelled in its pattern (asymmetrical dichotomy) by the Stoic Seneca (*Ep.* 58.14; cf. 8–11), who uses it as a division of corporeal things (*corpora*). Philo's symmetrically dichotomous division of things that exist (*Quis rerum divinarum heres* 137–39; cf. note 65 below) and its parallel, Clement of Alexandria's symmetrical division of things that move (*Stromat.* 2.20), are probably Stoic as well; but their symmetrical dichotomy does not exhibit the concomitance principle (see below, 207–8) as well as does the asymmetrical dichotomy of Origen. The relation of these other texts, which presuppose the same conceptions of self-motion, cannot be considered in this chapter.

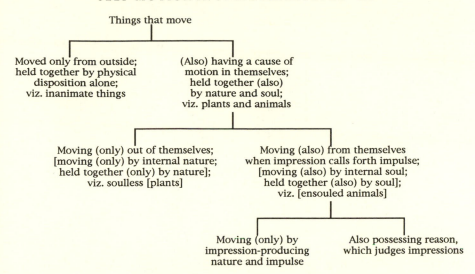

Figure 1. Division of Things That Move

the various components of the natural world. Origen's account divides the world along the lines of the well-known Stoic scale of nature, which comprised four classes of beings: (1) inanimate objects, (2) plants, (3) animals, and (4) human beings.[15] This division differentiates these classes of beings specifically on the basis of their kind of motion and the principle or source of that motion. It also presupposes that the kinds of motion and the principles of motion are not uniformly distributed, with one unique motion and principle characterizing each class. Rather, each class is properly differentiated by the *number* of different kinds of motion that it possesses. Thus Origen's division is an asymmetrical dichotomy, in which each successive division adds another source of motion and another kind of motion to those possessed by the prior subdivisions, making the *additional* kind of motion the differentiating characteristic of the class. Origen's division thereby assigns the four classes of things that move to an ordered series in which each member possesses the motion and source of motion of all prior members of the series in addition to its own proper motion and principle of motion.

The structure of motion in the universe, as articulated in Origen's division, is summarized in Table 1. This analysis gives us a foundation on which to begin reconstructing the underlying Stoic conception of self-motion. It shows, first of all, that motion was regarded as a distinguishing

---

[15] For the Stoic scale of nature, see below, 207–17 and note 57. For further discussion, see Rieth 1933, 120–33; Long 1982; and Inwood 1985, 23–27.

TABLE 1
The Structure of Motions

	Inanimate Objects	Plants	Animals	Human Beings
Source of Motion	External movers	External movers Nature	External movers Nature Soul	External movers Nature Soul Reason
Kind of Motion	Transportation	Transportation Growth	Transportation Growth Impression and impulse	Transportation Growth Impression and impulse Judging impressions

mark of the various classes of things in the scale of nature.[16] It also shows that members of at least some of these classes were believed to be moved by an internal mover and therefore were regarded as self-movers. Further, it distinguishes kinds of internally induced motion as characteristic of these self-movers, and so indicates that the Stoics viewed these internally induced motions (namely, growth, impression and impulse, and judgment) as specifically distinct kinds of self-motion. Finally, it stipulates that the three kinds of self-motion are distributed in an ordered pattern of concomitance among the self-moved members of the scale of nature, with each self-mover possessing one type of motion as its characteristic motion in addition to all the types possessed by prior members of the series.

Let us now look at the other Stoic application of the concept of self-motion, that is, the catalog of various kinds of self-motion. Here discrepancies between two versions of the catalog make recovery of the underlying Stoic theory more difficult. The discrepancies can be seen most easily by viewing the two catalogs in parallel columns.

Origen

Of things that move some have their mover outside, such as inanimate things held together by physical disposition alone and also things that are moved by nature and soul, at times when they are not being moved as such, but rather in the manner of things held together only by physical disposition . . . , such as wood that has lost its capacity to grow.

The second class of things that move . . . are the things that move by the agency of their internal nature or soul, which are also said *"to move out of them[selves]"* (ἐξ αὐτῶν κινεῖθαι) by those who are authorities on the terminology.

Simplicius

The Stoics differentiate as separate classes (διαφορὰς γενῶν λέγουσιν: (1) *to move out of oneself* (ἐξ ἑαυτοῦ κινεῖσθαι) as (ὡς) the knife has cutting out of [ἐκ = as a result of] its own particular constitution (κατασκευῆς), for (γὰρ) its action (ποίησις) is carried out in conformity with its shape and form;

(2) *to activate motion through oneself* (δι' ἑαυτοῦ ἐνεργεῖν τὴν κίνησιν), as (ὡς) natures and curative powers produce their action (ποίησιν), for (γὰρ) a seed, when sown, unfolds[17] its own formulas (λόγους), draws up the surround-

[16] Other Stoic accounts of the scale of nature associate each class with a distinct form of *pneuma* as a principle of existence (see below, 203–6). So stones are held together by physical disposition (ἕξις), plants by nature (φύσις), and animals by soul (ψυχή). This principle of existence is also assumed in Origen's division (cf. συνεχόμενα, συνέχεται, *De princ.* 3.1.2; *De orat.* 6.1), where for the classes regarded as self-moving it becomes a principle of motion as well.

[17] I read ἀναπλοῖ with Kalbfleisch (1907), rather than ἀναπληροῖ, as accepted by von Arnim, *SVF* 2: 499 (161.29).

<table>
<tr><td>Origen</td><td>Simplicius</td></tr>
</table>

Origen

Third is the motion in animals, which is named *"motion from it[self]"* (ἡ ἀπ' αὐτοῦ κίνησις);

and I believe that the motion of rational beings is [called] *"motion through them[selves]"* (δι' αὐτῶν . . . κίνησις, Origen *De orat.* 6.1 = *SVF* 2: 989).[18]

Simplicius

ing material, and transmits the form of its internal formulas (διαμορφοῖ τοὺς ἐν ἑαυτῷ λόγους);

and especially (3) *to act from oneself* (ἀφ' ἑαυτοῦ ποιεῖν), which is, generically, to act from one's own impulse (ἀπὸ ἰδίας ὁρμῆς ποιεῖν),

or else from rational impulse, which is called "acting" (πράττειν), or, even more specifically, to be active (ἐνεργεῖν) in accord with virtue" (Simplicius *In Cat.* 306.19–27 = *SVF* 2: 499).

The most obvious discrepancy between these two catalogs lies in their order of presentation. Origen gives the series as: (1) motion out of itself, (2) motion from itself, and (3) motion through itself.[19] Simplicius reverses the last two. Though order of presentation in itself is not significant, it takes on significance when the items represent an ordered series, as Origen indicates these terms do.[20] Moreover, though Simplicius's catalog makes no explicit claims about the order, as Origen's does, it illustrates and describes the three motions in a way that seems to imply correlation with the ordered series of the Stoic scale of nature. The first motion appears to be illustrated by an inanimate object (a knife), the second is described by the growth of a seed (which suggests that it applies to plants), and the third is interpreted as covering impulse, both in the generic sense and in the sense of rational impulse and virtuous action, thereby giving the appearance of embracing animals and rational human beings. Thus Simplicius's catalog would seem, at least at first glance, to reflect some correlation with the Stoic scale of nature, just as Origen's enumeration does, albeit less perspicuously.[21]

[18] I have followed the manuscript of this text in retaining the nonreflexive forms of the pronouns after the prepositions. Origen's choice of the nonreflexive form is based on Greek grammatical considerations and does not indicate a different conception from that of Simplicius. English style, however, demands the reflexive form, which I have accordingly used, but with the reflexive portion in parentheses. For full discussion, see Hahm 1992, 26 n. 8.

[19] This text of Origen is the one that combines a division of self-movers with a catalog of self-motions (see above, note 14). It is only the catalog that we are interested in here.

[20] Origen indicates an ordered series by the use of the ordinal numerals δεύτερα (second) . . . τρίτη (third). Simplicius does not number his series. The numbers in parentheses in the translation are my own additions to indicate that Simplicius regards the motions as a series of "different classes" (διαφορὰς γενῶν).

[21] So it is construed by Rieth (1933, 130–31) and Inwood (1985, 23–24).

TABLE 2
Comparison of Types of Self-Motion in the Catalogs of Origen and Simplicius

	Origen	*Simplicius*
Inanimate Objects	(no self-motion)	ἐξ ἑαυτοῦ
Plants	ἐξ ἑαυτῶν	δι' ἑαυτῶν
Animals	ἀφ' ἑαυτῶν	ἀφ' ἑαυτοῦ
Humans	δι' ἑαυτῶν	(same as animals)

If this is the case, there is an even more serious discrepancy than mere order of presentation; there is a discrepancy between the reference of the terms in the two versions (see Table 2). What makes the discrepancy between these two accounts particularly troublesome is the fact that there are no clear external grounds for preferring one account to the other.[22] Simplicius avers an authentically Stoic source, but he quotes the catalog out of context and as a hostile critic. Origen is a friendly reporter and sets the catalog in a philosophical context, but he makes no pretense of presenting an authentic Stoic point of view; instead he conflates it with the division of things that move and presents the composite as a Christian analysis.[23] Our only hope of extracting an underlying common Stoic conception is to assess each account independently for its value as a witness to the Stoic theory and then to attempt to integrate the best authenticated elements of each account. Let us begin with Origen's account because it is the easier account to assess.

Though Origen does not overtly tell us that his arguments for human

[22] Inwood (1985, 23–24) prefers Origen's version because Origen seems to know Stoicism well and much of Origen's account is confirmed by other sources. Inwood regards Simplicius's account as confused and suspects contamination with Peripatetic elements, introduced, he conjectures, by a Neoplatonic adapter of the Stoic doctrine. Rieth (1933, 127–31), on the other hand, accepts Simplicius's version with no reference at all to Origen. Rieth (120–24) takes the sources that link motion out of itself to nature (φύσις, e.g., Diogenes Laertius 7.148, on which see below, 200–202) as references to pneumatic motion, which moves into and out of itself and produces qualities and shape specifically by its motion out of itself (Nemesius *De nat. hom.* 2 [18.5–8 Morani; = *SVF* 2: 451]; cf. Alexander *De mixt.* 224.23–25 [=*SVF* 2: 442]). This he then assimilates to *hexis*, which holds inanimate things together and gives them their qualities (cf. Simplicius *In Cat.* 238.10–12 [=*SVF* 2: 393]). The problem with Rieth's approach, beside ignoring the conflicting scheme of Origen, is that it gives an unacceptable sense to Simplicius's example of motion out of itself (see below, note 43) and assigns no significance to the different prepositions used in naming the three kinds of self-motion. In fact, Rieth does not even comment on the expression "acting from oneself" (1933, 131–32), and he dismisses "activating motion through oneself" with only a reference to Diogenes Laertius 7.107 (= *SVF* 3: 493) and the observation that it extends to plants and animals (1933, 130–31).

[23] On the purpose and composition of Origen's account, see Hahm 1992, esp. 42–46.

responsibility are not his own, he frankly acknowledges that he has taken over from elsewhere the prepositional phrases used in his argument. In *De principiis* he says, "And of those that have the cause of moving within themselves, some, *they claim* (φασιν), move out of themselves and others from themselves" (*De princ.* 3.1.2 [196.3–4] = *SVF* 2: 988 [287.41– 288.1]). In *De oratione* he is even more explicit. Describing the second classification of things that move (a reference specifically to plants), he adds, "which are also said to move 'out of them[selves]' *by those who are authorities on terminology*" (παρὰ τοῖς κυριώτερον χρωμένοις τοῖς ὀνό- μασι; *De orat.* 6.1 [312.2–3] = *SVF* 2: 989 [289.2–3]). This deferral to authority for his terminology reveals that Origen is not following his own linguistic usage, but is conforming to the vocabulary of his source, a source that is alleged to be of more than average philosophical sophistication and linguistic precision. This gives us an excellent reason to trust the accuracy of Origen's report about the reference of the term "motion out of itself."[24] We can draw the same conclusion about the second term. Since in *De principiis* Origen attributes his information on moving from themselves to his source (φασιν), and in *De oratione* he implies as much by claiming that the motion of animals *is named* (ὀνομάζεται) "motion from itself," we have no reason to doubt that he has also derived this term from his source, which must be the same source from which he derived the term "motion out of itself."[25] When Origen in *De oratione* goes on to identify the motion of rational beings, however, though he gives this third self-motion another prepositional designation, "motion through themselves (δι' αὐτῶν)," he expresses obvious reservation regarding the validity of his nomenclature: "And *I believe* (οἶμαι) that the motion of rational beings is motion through themselves" (*De orat.* 6.1 [312.5] = *SVF* 2: 989 [289.4–5]).[26] Origen's mode of expression forces us to conclude that whereas we may depend on

---

[24] At the same time, his claim to follow the "more authoritative" (κυριώτερον) usage indicates that there were other usages known to him either from his own experience or from claims made by his "more authoritative" source. If so, the use of the term "motion out of itself" for the motion of plants, and perhaps the entire set of terms in Origen's catalog, may be that of a single, philosophically sophisticated source at variance with the usage of other philosophers, even other Stoics. The term ἐξ ἑαυτοῦ is common in Greek philosophical texts, but is not restricted to the growth of plants, as it is here. Origen's explicit attribution to a "more authoritative" source should serve as a warning that not all references to motion out of itself may be applicable to the theory he is presenting.

[25] The reference of this term is, in any case, not in doubt, since Simplicius agrees with Origen on its application to animal motion.

[26] We might notice that when he refers to this motion again a few lines later, he says: "It is to this that *we have given the name* (ὠνομάσαμεν) 'moving through it[self]'" (*De orat.* 6.1 [312.9–10] = *SVF* 2: 989 [289.8]). The contrast of the first-person active verb, ὠνομάσαμεν, with the third-person passive, ὀνομάζεται, used of "motion from itself," supports the impression that Origen felt reluctance to attribute to his source the use of the term "motion through itself" for the motion of rational animals.

what he tells us about motion *out of itself* and motion *from itself* in reconstructing the Stoic theory of his source, we cannot do the same for the
claims he makes about motion *through itself*.

When we approach Simplicius's report, we cannot detect any comparable distinction between attribution to his Stoic source and extrapolation
from or speculation about the Stoic conception; Simplicius attributes his
account as a whole with all its components to the Stoics without equivoca-
tion. Simplicius's account, however, shares a strikingly idiosyncratic presupposition with Origen's account, or, to put it more accurately, with the
account of Origen's source. This shared presupposition constitutes a different kind of clue to the philosophical position taken by their Stoic sources,
but one that is no less useful for our reconstruction of the underlying Stoic
theory.

The parallel in the presuppositions of the sources of Simplicius and
Origen is first and most easily noticed in a formal feature of the two
accounts. Simplicius's catalog consists of three, and only three, different
kinds of motion. Origen, in turn, counts motions with ordinal numerals up
to three and then stops counting; his last motion, the motion of rational
beings, he simply adds to the third without an ordinal numeral. That this is
not a coincidence becomes clear when we examine specifically how the
sources behind the two accounts treated the motion of rational beings.
Simplicius subdivides his third category into three species (*In Cat.* 306.24–
27). The series of introductory adverbs (κοινῶς μὲν . . . , ἕτερον δὲ . . . ,
τούτου δὲ ἔτι εἰδικώτερον, which might be translated "[1] generically
. . . , [2] also . . . , and [3] even more specifically than this") indicates that
their relationship is that of genus to species in a continuous series (see
Figure 2). In the Stoic classification reported by Simplicius, "acting from
oneself" obviously includes not only the motion of animals, but also the
action of rational beings and the virtuous actions of wise men; the motion
of rational beings is assigned no distinct prepositional term of its own.[27]
Origen's argument in *De oratione* makes the same assumption.[28] Origen
abandons ordinal numeration when he reaches the motion of rational
animals; and (as we just noted) he expresses reservation in assigning to the
motion of rational human beings a distinct prepositional designation.

[27] The three-level asymmetrical division of acting from oneself is parallelled by a three-level
asymmetrical division of animals in a (presumably Stoic) text quoted by Alexander *De fato*
205.24–29 (= *SVF* 2: 1002).

[28] It should be noted that the division of things that move, which is found in Clement
Stromat. 2.20 and in Origen's other text, *De princ.* 3.1.2–3, does not share this point of view.
In this application, the characteristic motion of rational beings is registered as reason (λόγος),
suggesting that reason is a distinct motion on a par with perception and growth, which are
registered by Origen as self-motions of a prepositionally denominable type (*De princ.* 3.1.3
[196.9–11] = *SVF* 2: 988 [288.7–10]).

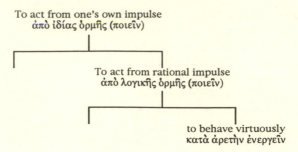

Figure 2. Division of Action from Impulse

These facts can most plausibly be explained by the assumption that Origen's source assigned the motion of rational creatures no unique prepositional denomination, but rather explained the difference between rational human beings and irrational animals on some basis other than a fourth kind of self-motion. If so, Origen's and Simplicius's sources must have shared the assumptions that there were only three distinct, prepositionally differentiable self-motions, and that rational motion was not one of them.

If there were, in fact, only three kinds of self-motion distinguished in the Stoic analysis reported by Simplicius and adapted by Origen, we can establish their relationship to the scale of nature with little difficulty and thereby arrive at a plausible basis for reconstructing the underlying Stoic theory. Simplicius and Origen agree that "motion from itself" is the characteristic motion of the third class in the series, that is, of animals. Origen assures us that those who are authorities in the use of these terms apply the term "motion out of itself" to the characteristic motion of the second class, plants. Given Origen's care in distinguishing between accepted, technical terminology and more dubious, unconfirmed nomenclature, we have no reason to doubt the validity of his claim that his Stoic source assigned "motion out of itself" to plants.[29] That leaves only "motion through itself" still *sub iudice*. Since Origen clearly registers doubt regarding the application of that term to the fourth and highest class, and since he begins his enumeration of self-motions only with the second class, telling us nothing about the first class except what he imported from an analysis structured in a completely different way (that is, as a division of things that move), we can plausibly conjecture that his authoritative source assigned "motion through itself" to the first class of the scale of nature, namely, to inanimate objects.[30]

[29] Confirmation comes also from Diogenes Laertius's Stoic doxography (7.148, 158), which uses "moving out of itself" as a component of definitions of nature (as the motive force of plants) and of seed; see below, 200–202.

[30] This conjecture is further confirmed by the evidence of Alexander of Aphrodisias, which

If Origen's source did, in fact, apply the term to inanimate objects, it is incumbent on us to explain why Origen transferred this term to the motion of rational beings; but this is easy. It is obvious that Origen created his argument in *De oratione* by conflating a list of three characteristic self-motions with a division of four things that move.[31] The division of things that move differentiated the four classes of the scale of nature on the basis of the number of motions and the proper principle of motion possessed by each. In that division, inanimate objects were regarded as moved only from outside, with no reference to any kind of self-motion. Hence Origen could not assign "motion through itself" to this class. On the other hand, the division of things that move included three different kinds of self-mover: plants, animals, and rational beings. Origen's reconciliation of this incongruity was accomplished by transferring "motion through itself" from inanimate objects, which in his composite version lacked self-motion, to rational beings, which in the Stoic enumeration of prepositionally differentiated motions had no separate name.

This conjecture that Origen's Stoic source originally assigned "motion through itself" to inanimate objects receives confirmation from Chrysippus's characterization of an element that can only be fire as "the one that moves *through itself* with most speed or vigor" (τό . . . δι' αὐτοῦ εὐκινητότατον; Stobaeus = *SVF* 2: 413 [137.1–2]).[32] Even though this characterization is quoted out of context and there is no reason to think that Chrysippus was contrasting fire's self-motion to any other kind of self-motion, it does show that the Stoic tradition at an early date acknowledged that inanimate things possess self-motion and that "moving through itself" was considered a valid description of an inanimate element's self-motion.

But coming to a plausible conclusion regarding the probable distribution of the prepositionally differentiated types of self-motion among the classes of the Stoic scale of nature in the original version of the Stoic catalog only creates more difficulties for interpreting Simplicius's report, since we are now confronted with the task of explaining what relevance the cutting of a knife has to motion out of itself, the characteristic motion of plants,

---

will be discussed below, 192–94. Rieth (1933, 130–31) attempts to relate it to plants on the basis of Diogenes Laertius 7.107 (= *SVF* 3: 493), which describes appropriate action (καθῆκον) as an ἐνέργημα and at the same time claims that appropriate action extends to plants and animals. This conjecture is unacceptable because ἐνέργημα by itself cannot plausibly be taken as a reference to self-motion, despite the fact that Simplicius uses ἐνεργεῖν to denote the activity involved in motion through itself.

[31] He had used the division in its original, unmodified form in an argument in his earlier work, *De princ.* 3.1.2–3 (= LS 53A; *SVF* 2: 988).

[32] The text offers this as one of several attributes of an element without indicating whether it is a specific element or every element; but since several of the other attributes can apply only to fire, there can be little doubt that this description was excerpted from a description of fire.

and likewise what relevance the growth of a seed has to motion through itself, the motion that we have just assigned as the proper motion of inanimate objects.

We may begin to resolve this difficulty by observing exactly what Simplicius's report does and does not do. It does not attempt simply to correlate the self-motions with members of the scale of nature, as Origen's accounts do. This observation is supported particularly by Simplicius's description of the third motion, "acting from oneself," which simply registers the motions characteristic of animals and human beings without any explicit reference to their *possessors*. In fact, for the third motion Simplicius makes no comment at all; he simply divides it into three subspecies. In so doing, he not only leaves the correlation with the scale of nature unstated, but also deviates from the practice he followed in describing the other two self-motions, both of which he illustrated with a lengthy ὡς clause, itself explained by a γάρ clause. His inconsistency in describing and illustrating the three Stoic self-motions makes it highly doubtful that he was attempting to tell his readers how the Stoics correlated these motions to the scale of nature. But then we must ask: What was he trying to accomplish with his descriptions?

Simplicius makes it clear that his real purpose in quoting the Stoic classification was to rebut erroneous conceptions of the Aristotelian categories of acting (ποιεῖν) and being acted upon (πάσχειν).[33] The first criticism that Simplicius brings against the Stoics is that they err in considering the three self-motions to be different classes (γένη). He himself claims that they are really three species of a single class (γένος), namely, action (ποιεῖν), differing only in their origins (ἀρχή [*In Cat.* 306.27–31]). The basis of Simplicius's rebuttal is that the Stoics *themselves* understood the three kinds of self-motion as species and so erred in calling them "classes" (γένη). Simplicius's purpose in recounting the Stoic self-motions, therefore, was to show that on the Stoics' own understanding, each of the three self-motions is (1) an action, and (2) differentiated from the others specifically by virtue of its origin.

If we examine what Simplicius reports about each of the motions, we see that in each case he includes a reference to the motion in question under the term ποιεῖν or ποίησις, and a statement regarding the origin or internal source from which the motion arises. For the third motion, the statement that it is an action occurs in the term itself, "*acting* from itself" (τὸ ἀφ᾽ ἑαυτοῦ ποιεῖν). Its origin or internal source can be found in the relative clause that subdivides the motion, namely, "which is generically to act (ποιεῖν) *from one's own impulse* (ἀπὸ ἰδίας ὁρμῆς) or else *from rational impulse* (ἀπὸ λογικῆς ὁρμῆς), etc." (*In Cat.* 306.24–27). Thus in the case

---

[33] Rieth (1933, 128–29) reviews Simplicius's major objections.

of the third self-motion, Simplicius fulfills his polemical goal merely by appending a list of the different subspecies of motion from itself without any further description. For the first two motions, however, the name of the motion (τὸ ἐξ αὐτῶν κινεῖσθαι, τὸ δι' ἑαυτοῦ ἐνεργεῖν τὴν κίνησιν) does not contain an explicit reference to action (ποιεῖν); Simplicius finds the reference to action and its internal origin only in a supplementary explanation of the motion. So for motion out of itself Simplicius finds the internal source specified in the illustrative ὡς clause (ἐκ τῆς οἰκείας . . . κατασκευῆς) and the reference to the motion as an action in the added explanation of the γάρ clause (ἡ ποίησις ἐπιτελεῖται). For motion through itself, the relevant information is reversed. The claim that it is an action occurs in the ὡς clause (τὴν ποίησιν ἀπεργάζονται), and the internal source is stipulated in the explanatory γάρ clause (ἀναπλοῖ τοὺς οἰκείους λόγους . . . καὶ διαμορφοῖ τοὺς ἐν αὐτῷ λόγους). Simplicius's verbal frugality is noteworthy; he does not include a single sentence or clause beyond what he needs to support his polemical objective.

If Simplicius's selection of material from his Stoic source was determined primarily by his polemical objective of demonstrating that the Stoics called every self-motion an action and derived each from a different origin or internal source, we can understand why he presented different amounts and kinds of information on each type of motion and why he selected the information that he did. Since his polemical strategy required no stipulation of the relationship between the types of self-motion and the scale of nature, nor any specification of the proper possessors of the respective self-motions, we should not strain his text in an attempt to make it yield such information. In fact, we have no right to expect a complete, coherent account of the Stoic position, or even any agreement in detail with our other accounts, in which the possessor of the motion is the chief concern. The value of Simplicius's polemical report consists chiefly in furnishing information supplementary to that of Origen, and hence potentially capable of clarifying and expanding our conception of the various kinds of self-motion that we have come to know from Origen's differently oriented account.

Before we attempt to exploit Simplicius's report for such supplementary illumination, we have to consider a potentially damaging objection to any use at all of the specific information found in his account. Simplicius's expressed polemical bias might raise the suspicion that Simplicius has totally reformulated the Stoic account to make it an easy target for his criticisms. If so, we can have little confidence either in the formulation or in the specific details that he reports. This objection, however, need not worry us. The formal style of Simplicius's account strongly suggests that Simplicius has not seriously distorted his source. A brief glance at his style will make this apparent.

Simplicius's rebuttal depends on the particular linguistic formulation in which the Stoic account is presented. His principal criticism that the Stoic motions are all species of action (ποιεῖν) is based on the occurrence of the word "to act" (ποιεῖν or ποίησις) in the description of each of the three types of self-motion. Similarly, his other two criticisms and his sole approbation are based on grammatical idiosyncrasies in the formulation of two of the Stoic self-motions.[34] Yet despite the importance of the precise formulation for his rebuttal, none of Simplicius's criticisms is made particularly obvious in the Stoic text as he cites it. If Simplicius had totally reformulated the Stoic self-motions in more generalized terms, using words like κινεῖν, κινεῖσθαι, ποιεῖν, πάσχειν, and ἐνεργεῖν (306.28–307.1).[35] This reformulation suggests that Simplicius himself felt that the confusions and contradictions he hoped to impute to the Stoics were not apparent enough in the description that he attributed to them. If that description was already a paraphrase, Simplicius apparently thought that it was still so close to the original Stoic formulation that it could only be refuted in a more vulnerable paraphrase.

phrase, Simplicius apparently thought that it was still so close to the original Stoic formulation that it could only be refuted in a more vulnerable paraphrase.

Second, though Simplicius's account of each motion contains evidence conveniently supportive of his various criticisms, it does not present this evidence in an obviously uniform way. In fact, it is easy to miss it. Take, for example, the evidence that the Stoics regarded each self-motion as an action differing from the others only in its origin. The evidence that the

[34] His charge that the Stoics make the active "to cause motion" (κινεῖν) a species of the middle-passive "to be in movement" or "to be moved" (κινεῖσθαι [306.33–307.1]) must be his own generalization from the ostensibly Stoic illustration of the first self-motion, "to move" (middle voice: κινεῖσθαι) out of oneself with its example of "cutting" (active voice: τέμνειν [306.19–20]). The charge that their definition (ὅρος) of actualization (ἐνέργεια) is confused because it is expressed in terms of actualization (ἐνέργεια), i.e., in terms of itself (306.31–32), must refer to the second self-motion "to actualize (ἐνέργειν) the motion through itself" (306.21–22); cf. Rieth 1933, 129. Simplicius apparently takes the ὡς clause to stipulate a species of the genus (γένος): ἐνεργεῖν. His criticism must be that the verb in what he takes to be the species (ἀπεγάζονται [306.22]) is synonymous with ἐνεργεῖν. The one feature of the Stoic account of which he approves is making "to be active" (ποιεῖν) and "to be passive" (πάσχειν) separate γένη (306.32–33). This must refer to the fact that the first Stoic self-motion is expressed by the passive form, κινεῖσθαι, whereas the second is expressed by the phrase ἐνεργεῖν τὴν κίνησιν, an expression that Simplicius himself elsewhere contrasts to the passive experiencing of motion and regards as virtually equivalent to the active verb, κινεῖν (In De an. 36.16–37.2; see below, note 41).

[35] His practice may be seen as translating his description of the three Stoic self-motions into Peripatetic terminology. The terms κατασκευή, σχῆμα and εἶδος in his account of the Stoic self-motions, though sometimes taken as evidence of Peripatetic paraphrase (e.g., by Inwood 1985, 24), are well attested as Stoic; see below, 197–99, and notes 46, 47, and 49.

motion in question is an action (ποίησις, ποιεῖν) occurs once in the final γάρ clause (306.21), once in the initial ὡς clause (306.22), and once in the term for the motion itself, which is repeated in the relative clause in which that motion is further subdivided (306.25). The evidence for the difference in origin is contained once in a prepositional phrase in the initial ὡς clause (ἐκ τῆς . . . κατασκευῆς [306.20]), once in verbs with objects in the γάρ clause (ἀναπλοῖ τοὺς . . . λόγους, διαμορφοῖ τοὺς . . . λόγους [306.23–24]), and once in a prepositional phrase in the relative clause subdividing the motion (ἀπὸ . . . ὁρμῆς [306.25–26]). This lack of uniformity in documenting his polemical point weighs in favor of a close paraphrase or abridgment, rather than a Neoplatonic or Peripatetic reformulation of the original Stoic text.

Finally, in spite of Simplicius's verbal frugality and his apparent desire to make every clause bear polemical weight, he still includes some information extraneous to his polemical purposes. Here we might mention the use of a knife to illustrate motion out of itself and the added clarification of how an artificial object like a knife can be thought to move "out of its own constitution"; the piling up of several different examples of motion through itself (natures, curative powers, and a seed); and the gratuitous division of acting from oneself into three subdivisions with the even more gratuitous parenthetical note that the verb πράττειν is a synonym for one of them, namely, "acting from rational impulse." Simplicius's reformulation of the alleged Stoic misconceptions in terms more congenial to his refutation, combined with the variation in format and quantity of content, is sufficient to prove that Simplicius's account is not a hostile reformulation, but an abridgment, which must have come (directly or indirectly) from a more extensive Stoic account. As such, we can feel secure in using it as a source of information on the Stoic theory.

If we can trust Simplicius's report, at least for the restricted purpose for which he cited it (that is, as a source of information on the three types of self-motion and the internal origin of each), and if we are not deterred from using his account on the unwarranted assumption that it contains an incorrect reference to the possessors of the several self-motions, we can begin to exploit it to refine and enhance our conception of the Stoic distinction among the three kinds of self-motion. We are still hampered, however, by the brevity of Simplicius's reports. The polemical conciseness that furnishes us little more than is necessary to ground the intended criticisms makes it difficult to discern the original basis for the tripartite distinction. The only way we can gain further insight into the nature of this distinction is by going to other sources for clarification.

Simplicius's description of motion through itself, which refers obscurely to natures, curative powers, and the growth of seeds (306.22–24), may be illuminated by another text that brings together self-movers, natures, and motion that comes about "through" something. In *De fato*, Alexander of Aphrodisias recounts an argument for human responsibility that has justifiably been traced back to a Stoic source (*De fato* 13.181.15–182.4 = LS 62G 3–22; *SVF* 2: 979):[36]

> Since [1] the natures (φύσεις) of things that are and come to be are different and various, as, for example, the [natures] of animate and inanimate things are not the same, nor, in turn are the natures of all animate things the same (for the specific differences in the things that exist reveal the differences in their natures), and since [2] things that come to be by [the agency of] each [thing that exists] come to be in accord with its [namely, the agent's] own specific nature, those by [the agency of] stone in accord with [the nature of] stone, those by [the agency of] fire in accord with [the nature of] fire and those by [the agency of] a living being in accord with [the nature of] a living being, they conclude (φασιν) that none of the things that come to be by the agency of each [thing] in accord with its own specific nature can be otherwise, but each of them comes to be necessarily (κατ—αναγκασμένως), not by the necessity of force (ἐκ βίας), but by the necessity that is due to the fact that anything whose nature it is to move in a given way under a given set of circumstances (circumstances that cannot be otherwise) cannot move in any other way than in that particular way.[37] So, for example, if stone is released from a height, it is unable not to move down, as long as nothing prevents it. For, since it has weight in itself and this is responsible for such motion in accord with [its] nature, whenever the external causes that contribute to the production (συν—τελοῦντα) of the natural motion for stone are present, stone of necessity moves as is its nature to move [namely, falling down]. So then, if the causes of its [the stone's] motion are present at that time of necessity (since it is not only unable not to move when they are present, but it moves of necessity), such motion comes to be by the agency of fate (ὑπὸ τῆς εἱμαρμένης) *through* [the nature of] stone (διὰ τοῦ λιθοῦ).

The Stoic argument reported here by Alexander is based on an assumed fact of nature, namely, that different kinds of things have different essential natures, and that a thing's specific character determines the particular kind of motion the thing will exhibit.[38] Though these essential natures cannot

---

[36] Though Alexander reports the argument anonymously (cf. φασίν, 181.15, 22, 182.5; λέγουσιν, 182.13; λέγοντες, 182.18), its attribution to a Stoic source has never been seriously doubted. The evidence for attribution to the Stoics is discussed by Sharples 1978, 253–58; 1983, 142–43; and Inwood 1985, 88–91.

[37] I have followed the traditional punctuation and interpretation of the end of this sentence. For another version of punctuation and interpretation, though still yielding approximately the same sense, see the text and translation of Thillet 1984, 26–27.

[38] Alexander's argument is difficult to follow, to a large degree because of the tortuous Greek style in which it is expressed. The interpretation is discussed in more detail by Long (1970, 260–62; 1971a); and Sharples (1978, 253–58; 1983, 142–46). Some of the diffi-

be perceived directly, the Stoics assume they can be recognized by examining the observable differences in behavior of the various kinds of things. The argument continues with the claim that things that happen by the agency of each different kind of thing happen in accord with the agent's own specific nature (φύσις). Moreover, nothing that happens by the agency of anything in accord with its own specific nature can happen differently, but every such event occurs necessarily (καταναγκασμένως), not because the agent is under any compulsion by force (ἐκ βίας), but because anything whose nature it is to move in a certain way under a given set of circumstances cannot under those circumstances move in any other way. Therefore (the argument concludes), such motion in accord with nature happens of necessity when the circumstances are right for it. Hence it can be said to happen by the agency of (ὑπὸ) fate *through* (διὰ) *the moving object.*

According to Alexander, the Stoics illustrated this theory with two kinds of things: inanimate materials like stone and fire, and animate creatures. Stone always moves in accord with its own nature. If it is released from a height, it always moves down, provided that nothing prevents it. It cannot fail to do so, because it possesses heaviness within itself as its nature; and this is the cause of motion in accord with its nature whenever external circumstances allow. Fire, on the other hand, possesses a nature that causes it to heat. So fire presumably always necessarily heats, just as stone necessarily moves down.[39] From this the Stoics conclude that, when the circumstances are such as to allow the natural motion of stone or fire to occur, that natural motion must be regarded as "of necessity" (ἐξ ἀνάγκης) and hence "by the agency of fate through [the nature of] stone" (διὰ τοῦ λίθου) or "through [the nature of] fire." Alexander goes on to say that the Stoics apply the same analysis to living creatures, which also possess a motion in

---

culties arise because the argument seems to be slightly similar to an argument attributed to Chrysippus in Cicero *De fato* 42–43 (= LS 62C 5–10). This has encouraged interpreters to attempt to assimilate the two arguments, a strategy that, in my view, further obscures the logic of the argument in Alexander. (On the difference between the two arguments see below, note 67, and the comments by Sharples [1978, 253–56; 1983, 142–43]). It should be noted that these essential "natures" (φύσεις) refer to all natural materials and entities. This is a different use of the Greek word φύσις from the one we encountered in Origen, where "nature" (φύσις) referred to the capacity for growth and reproduction found in plants and higher living beings.

[39] It should be noted that the essential natural motion of fire here is not a spatial motion, as it is in the case of earth, but rather the motion of heating. This may be deduced from Alexander *De fato* 13.182.17 (= LS 62G 6; *SVF* 2: 979), where the internal cause of fire's motion is specified as heat (θερμότητα) in contrast to the heaviness (βαρύτητα) of earth (cf. also *De fato* 13.182.10, 19 [=LS 62G 2, 4]). Alexander himself acknowledges this (*De fato* 14.183.11–15; 15.184.17), *pace* Inwood (1985, 284 n. 220; cf. 263 n. 35). Nemesius *De nat. hom.* 35 (= *SVF* 2: 991), quoting a similar Stoic argument, also claims that the natural motion of fire is burning (106.8–9 [Morani]), though earlier he had said its fated motion was to move up (105.9).

accord with their specific nature, namely, movement by impulse (καθ’ ὁρμῆς κίνησιν). They finally conclude that every animal moving qua animal by impulse moves in accord with necessity and hence its motion occurs by fate through the nature of an animal (διὰ ζῴου [182.4–8]).

Though this argument does not actually use the prepositional characterization to differentiate the various kinds of self-motion and never explicitly mentions the term "motion through itself," it entails a conception of "happening through something" that illuminates the meaning and reference of Simplicius's statement on the subject. At the heart of the Stoic argument recorded by Alexander is the assumption of a causal connection between a thing's essential nature and its motions or activities. It denotes this relationship by means of the prepositional phrase "through the thing." Thus it presupposes that the phrase "through x" means "by virtue of and in correspondence with x's essential nature." Any motion that corresponds to the essential nature of a material substance or thing may be described as occurring *through* the thing in question. When stone falls or fire heats or when an animal acts by impulse, the particular activity of the subject is due to its essential nature as stone, or as fire, or as animal, respectively. So its motion may be described as occurring *through* stone or fire or animal. If one were to generalize this conception, one would have to say that self-movers effect their motions *through themselves*, because their movements are caused by their respective natures and correspond to those natures in respect to their particular forms or configurations.[40]

Alexander's report is of particular interest for understanding the Stoic analysis of self-motion for two reasons: It gives us a sense in which to interpret the prepositional phrase "through itself"; and it affirms that, given this meaning, the phrase applies not to one level of the scale of nature alone, but to any and all levels. Alexander's argument, in fact, goes out of its way to underline the universal applicability of the relationship denoted by the preposition "through" (διά). His examples are taken from both the inanimate and the animate levels of the scale of nature and so confirm that the Stoics extended the concept of self-motion to inanimate motion, such as the falling of heavy bodies and the heating caused by fire. Thus Alexander's report gives us a way in which to understand the reference to natures and curative powers (αἱ φύσεις καὶ αἱ ἰατρικαὶ δυνάμεις) in Simplicius's report. The natures are the essential natures that in Alexander's argument initiate and determine the specific character of natural motions. The "curative powers" may be construed as an example of such natures. The essential natures of the various ingredients in medicinal preparations are responsible for the particular curative effect of that medication.

[40] I.e., whether an inanimate object will fall down or heat something depends on whether its nature includes heaviness or heat.

If the Stoics cited by Simplicius understood motion through itself in this universal sense as any motion that comes about as a result of and in conformity with the essential nature of any natural material or thing, we can understand how it may be illustrated by the particular examples cited; but we now have to wonder how such motion can be differentiated from any other kind of self-motion. Simplicius's list of self-motions was cited expressly as a Stoic classification of different kinds (γένη) of self-motion. If the self-motion of animals is a "motion through itself," as Alexander's report claims, what warrant has Simplicius's catalog for assigning the motion of animals and human beings the status of an independent kind of motion, distinguishable in some way from motion "through itself"?

To answer this question, we have to look again at what Simplicius really claims is "through itself." Simplicius's report uses a different expression to denote the motion for each of the three kinds of self-motion. The expression used for motion through itself is "activating the motion (ἐνεργεῖν τὴν κίνησιν) through itself" (306.21–22). Though stylistic variation on the part of either Simplicius or his Stoic source cannot be ruled out a priori, it seems improbable that a catalog designed to make a subtle distinction among three kinds of motion would put literary variety ahead of philosophical precision in the choice of vocabulary. If we press Simplicius's expression used to denote motion through itself, we cannot fail to notice that it picks out the process whereby the motion is initiated or causally effected. The term implies that it is specifically the *activation* of the motion that comes about through the thing itself, regardless of whether the full scope of the motion can properly be said to occur "through itself."[41] The subsequent illustration in the ὡς clause, then, need not be a list of things that *move* (κινεῖσθαι) through themselves, but rather a list of things that *activate* (ἐνεργεῖν) motion through themselves. This explains why the illustration in the ὡς clause can be given, not in terms of natural objects or items that possess the motion in question as their proper motion, but rather in terms of the essential natures that cause the motion and determine its specific character. The Stoics are, in effect, claiming that "activating the motion through itself" is the way in which (ὡς) the *natures* of self-movers produce their corresponding motions in those self-movers. They are further claiming that among these *natures* are the powers inherent in medicinal preparations.[42]

[41] The transitive usage of ἐνεργεῖν is post-Aristotelian (cf. LSJ, s.v. ἐνεργέω, II). Simplicius himself regularly uses the expression ἐνεργεῖν τὴν κίνησιν to denote the active causation of motion (e.g., In Cael. 596.19; In Phys. 817.26; In De an. 36.19–37.2, 39.38–39), which he contrasts to the passive experiencing of motion (In De an. 36.19–37.2).

[42] Galen provides an illuminating parallel in his conception of the action of drugs, e.g., 6.70.1–4; 6.468.2–7; 11.706.13–16; 12.245.7–246.9; 15.40.3–5 (Kühn); and De propriis placitis. 7.21–8.4 (Helmreich 1894). Galen holds that drugs (φάρμακα) effect health by "acting" (ἐνεργεῖν), using as his standard verb for the action of drugs the same verb that

If the ὡς clause offers what is, in fact, an illustration of the sense in which a self-motion may be described as "arising through itself," the following γάϱ clause may be read as a specific instance in which one "nature" brings about its corresponding motion. The nature of the plant, embodied in the internal formulas of the seed, brings about the growth of the plant by activating an "unfolding" (ἀναπλοῖ) process in which the seed draws up matter from outside and imposes the internal "formulas" of the plant on this matter. The activation of motion through itself in a plant is the same as it is in an inanimate material, such as a medication, except that the definition of the motion programmed into the plant's nature includes "growing" (φύειν), the characteristic motion of plants.

If this is how Simplicius's explanation of "activating motion through itself" is to be construed, we can plausibly reconcile it with Origen's claim that "growing" (φύειν) was called "moving out of itself" by those who use the prepositional terminology in its strict sense. The resolution of the apparent discrepancy lies in the distinction between "moving" (κινεῖσθαι) and "activating the motion" (ἐνεϱγεῖν τὴν κίνησιν). Origen tells us that growth (φύειν) is by definition "*moving* out of itself" (κινεῖσθαι ἐξ ἑαυτοῦ). Simplicius's account tells us that growth (φύειν) is a motion (κίνησιν) that a plant *activates* (ἐνεϱγεῖν) through itself. In other words, Simplicius's account does not claim to tell us what growth is, but only how it is initiated or executed. Strictly speaking, then, motion *through* itself must refer to the internal process whereby an object actualizes its fullest natural potential for motion or action, whether that object is an inanimate material substance (like stone, fire, or medicine), a plant, an animal, or a rational being. What differentiates the self-motion of a plant from that of an inanimate object is not that one possesses one kind of self-motion and the other a different kind, but rather that inanimate objects possess *only* the capacity of "activating motion through itself," whereas plants, in the process of being set into the motion that corresponds to their essential nature, embark on a second kind of self-motion, the motion of growth. In the classification of the catalog, this motion is called "motion out of itself." Thus we can say that *through* itself a seed activates motion *out of* itself. As the *only* self-motion possessed by inanimate self-movers, it is the proper motion of the lowest class of the scale of nature; but as the internal process that activates or actualizes other motions, it is also involved in the execution of the higher motions that are characteristic of all other members of the

---

Simplicius cited as the Stoic term for motion through itself (ἐνεϱγεῖν τὴν κίνησιν). Galen also maintains that drugs perform this activity *through* (διά) the powers of heating, cooling, etc. (15.40.3–5 [Kühn]). This implies that Galen could agree with the Stoics quoted by Simplicius that the powers that cause healing activate their healing effects *through* themselves.

scale of nature. On this interpretation, there is no inconsistency between the accounts of Origen and Simplicius; Simplicius has merely reported on a different aspect of the Stoic theory.

Once we begin to see Simplicius's account as a set of excerpts derived from a Stoic attempt to codify distinctions both in the nature of each of the three kinds of self-motion and in the relationship of each motion to its internal source, we can give Simplicius's description of moving *out of itself* a satisfactory interpretation, one that will further illuminate the Stoic conception of self-motion. In the description of motion *through itself*, the ὡς clause clarified the conception of activating motion *through itself* by citing examples of the "self" (namely, the internal nature) *through* which the motion was activated. In the description of motion *out of itself*, we can also interpret the ὡς clause as citing an example of a "self" *out of* which a moving (κινεῖσθαι) emerges (306.20). The movement in this case is cutting (τέμνειν), which is the movement of a knife; and the "self" out of which the cutting comes is the knife's particular construction (κατασκευῆς).[43] The only interpretive problem is that cutting is not a self-motion of the knife, since a knife will not cut unless the cutting is effected by an external mover, such as a human being.[44] This problem disappears, however, as soon as we see Simplicius's descriptions as clarifications of the nature of the motions involved and their relationship to their internal source. Then we need not necessarily look for specification of self-movers or self-motion, and the cutting of the knife need not be construed as an *instance* of self-motion.[45] Instead it may be viewed as an *analogy*, introduced to clarify the nature of motion out of itself and its difference from the other self-motions.

What this analogy illustrates may be inferred from comparison of the description of motion *out of itself* with the parallel description of motion *through itself*. Simplicius, we have noted, quoted the two syntactically parallel descriptions because he believed that he had found in each the Stoic specification of the internal source of the self-motion, accompanied by a reference to that motion under the term "action" (ποίησις, ποιεῖν). When we look carefully at his two descriptions, we find that the parallels

[43] Rieth (1933, 130) implausibly interprets the knife's motion out of itself as the tonic motion of its constitutive *pneuma*, which gives the knife its particular features by means of tonic motion "out of itself" (see above, note 22); but Rieth buys this interpretation at the cost of having to ignore the obvious sense of Simplicius's text, which is that a knife's motion out of itself is cutting.

[44] One could argue that a knife does, in fact, possess self-motion insofar as it is made of a heavy substance and will fall if dropped from a height, just as stone does; but the self-moved falling of a knife qua heavy, earthy substance must be distinguished from the externally moved cutting of a knife qua knife. It is this cutting that is used to illustrate "moving out of itself."

[45] That we need not expect to find the possessors of the respective self-motions mentioned in the descriptions was argued above, 189–91.

between them go even farther. Both illustrate the self-motion in question with an activity that is properly attributable only to the class of things of the next higher rank in the scale of nature than the proper possessor of the motion in question. In the description of activating motion *through* itself (presumably the proper motion of inanimate things), we find an allusion to the growth of a plant, which is by definition a motion *out of* itself. In the explanation of motion *out of* itself, we find "cutting," an active, transitive verb, which may be subsumed under the generic term "acting" (ποιεῖν). "Acting" (ποιεῖν), according to Simplicius's account, is the term that the Stoics used to denote motion *from* itself, the motion characteristic of animals and human beings. Moreover, both descriptions trace the cause of this next higher motion back to the innate nature of the object. The growth of the seed is traced back to the internal formulas (λόγους), which presumably constitute the nature (φύσις) of the plant. The cutting of the knife is traced back to its constitution (κατασκευῆς), which comprises its shape and form (τὸ σχῆμα καὶ τὸ εἶδος). Finally, both explanations consider the preposition found in the name of the motion to be useful for describing the origin of the motion. A plant's growth "transmits the form (διαμορφοῖ) of its internal formulas." The knife "has cutting from its own constitution" (ἐκ τῆς οἰκείας . . . κατασκευῆς).

These parallels strongly suggest that Simplicius derived the analogy of the knife from an account that was functionally equivalent to the account from which he derived the analysis of the growth of a plant from a seed. The growth of a plant from a seed is by definition a motion *out of itself*. Its role in the Stoic account of motion *through itself* was to show how motion *through itself* in the case of a plant initiates and actualizes growth and how the motion *through itself* can be logically differentiated from the motion *out of itself* (growth) that results from it. If the Stoics carried this analytical pattern forward to the next level, they would have had to explain how growth, or motion *out of itself*, in the case of animals produces motion by impulse and how the motion *out of itself* can be logically differentiated from the motion *from itself* (acting by impulse) that results from it. Extrapolating from the analytical pattern used in the case of motion through itself, we can interpret the analogy of the knife as a device to clarify the relationship between animal action (ποιεῖν) and the process of growth, which creates the organs by which animals receive impressions and move in their execution of animal action.

The analogy of the knife is taken from the world of human craftsmanship and is obviously keyed into the exposition of motion out of itself by the concept of κατασκευή. Κατασκευή was a common Stoic term for the inner nature of a thing, the nature that causes and determines its behavior. As such it served as a virtual synonym for φύσις, in the sense in which we

found that term used by Alexander's Stoic opponents.[46] The chief difference between φύσις and κατασκευή is that φύσις carries implications of a
biological process, whereas κατασκευή resonates with overtones of the
artificial world of human craftsmanship.[47] By using an analogy of an artificial object, like a knife, Simplicius's Stoic source directed attention toward
the artificial overtones inherent in the word κατασκευή. This had a particular advantage in that the word κατασκευή denotes either the process of
construction or the result of that process, namely, the particular form or
shape with which an artificial thing is endowed in its manufacture.[48] The
Stoic assertion that a knife has cutting from its own particular construction
conveys two things: a knife derives its ability to cut from its particular
shape and form, since (as Simplicius's account goes on to point out) its
activity is carried out in accord with its shape and form; and a knife derives
its ability to cut from its particular process of manufacture, which originally imposed the requisite shape upon the material from which the knife
was constructed. The analogy is especially suited to illustrate a state of
affairs in which imposing a particular shape and form (τὸ σχῆμα καὶ τὸ
εἶδος) upon indeterminate matter is a necessary precondition for its particular kind of motion or activity.[49] As such, it makes an ideal analogy to the
relationship between motion out of itself (vegetative growth) and action
from itself (animal action through impression and impulse).

Animal action requires sense organs to receive impressions, a central
psychic organ (τὸ ἡγεμονικόν) to collect, store, and process the impressions, and a complex arrangement of limbs, muscles, ligaments, and nerves

[46] For its widespread use by Epictetus, see the index of Schenkl 1916. The term is generally
preferred to φύσις by Epictetus, though on one occasion φύσις and κατασκευή are linked as
virtual synonyms (Diss. 1.6.15). There are also several instructive parallel formulations of the
same idea, but with different terminologies. Epictetus makes the same arguments as some
made by the Stoics whom Alexander quotes; but where Alexander's source uses φύσις,
Epictetus uses κατασκευή; compare Diss. 1.6.16 and 3.6.10 with De fato 13.181.15–20 and
26–28 (= SVF 2: 979 [285.4–8, 16–19]). See also its use in Diogenes Laertius 7.107 (= SVF
3: 493).

[47] E.g., Epictetus used the verb κατασκευάζω for creating a piece of sculpture (Diss.
2.24.7; cf. 2.19.26), building a house (3.21.4), or craftsmanship in general (1.6.7). The Stoic
doxography in Stobaeus uses it to denote the artificial refinement (as distinct from natural
emergence) of traits of character (SVF 3: 366).

[48] Cf. LSJ s.v. κατασκευή I and II.

[49] Several Stoic texts, including the Stoic argument for god as self-mover (quoted above
from Sextus Adv. math. 9.75–76 [=SVF 2: 311]), cite imposition of shape (σχηματίζειν) and
form (εἰδοποιεῖν, μορφοῦν) as the effects of god or pneuma on matter (cf. also Seneca Ep.
65.2 [=SVF 2: 303] and Alexander De mixt. 225.1–3 [=SVF 2: 310]). Both Seneca and the
argument quoted from Sextus identify this action with the origination of motion. Specifically,
σχῆμα seems to denote spatial configuration (cf. SVF 2: 383, 456), whereas εἶδος must
include all the physical characteristics that define a thing as an individual or species (cf. Seneca
Ep. 65.2; Diogenes Laertius 7.61 [=SVF 3: Diogenes of Babylon 25]).

to carry out impulses to locomotion and various kinds of action.[50] These organs or tools are formed by the process of fetal development, a process of vegetative growth that, as we have seen from Simplicius's account of it, entails the imposition of form upon matter drawn in from outside. The analogy of the knife draws attention to the causal role played by the articulation of the specialized structures involved in animal action and supports the claim that animal action (action from itself) is the final product of growth (motion out of itself). Motion out of itself may thus be seen to play a role in the structure of self-motions analogous to that played by motion through itself; it is causally involved in the motions above it in the scale of nature. Whereas motion through itself gives matter the essential form that makes everything in the scale of nature what it is, motion out of itself produces the physical structures necessary for the implementation of the higher motions and actions.

Confirmation of this interpretation comes from an unimpeachable source, Diogenes Laertius's doxography of the Stoics. In a series of Stoic definitions of nature (φύσις), we find one based on the prepositional classification of self-motions: "Nature is a physical disposition (ἕξις) that moves out of itself in accord with seminal formulas, bringing to maturity and sustaining things out of itself on their appointed schedules and creating things of the same kind as those from which they have sprung" (Diogenes Laertius 7.148 (= LS 43A; *SVF* 2: 1132). The fact that nature is here defined as a particular species of physical disposition (ἕξις) shows that the nature in question is the constitutive and motive principle of the second level of the scale of the nature, the level of plants.[51] What differentiates this principle of being and motion from physical disposition, the constitutive and motive principle of inanimate materials and objects, is that it "moves out of itself." In other words, nature is a physical disposition that is programmed by genetic formulas to "move out of itself" in the motion of organic growth. Though this Stoic definition operates with terms for genus and species (φύσις, ἕξις) that we found only in Origen's division and there

---

[50] For the Stoic conception of the animal soul and the Stoic theory of action, see Long 1982, 45–49; and LS 1.313–23; cf. Inwood 1985, 37–101.

[51] We have previously seen physical disposition (ἕξις) as the constitutive principle specifically of inanimate objects (Origen *De princ.* 3.1.2 [196.4–6] [=LS 53A; *SVF* 2: 988]; *De orat.* 6.1 [311.16–21] [=*SVF* 2: 989]), and as such as coordinate with and distinct from nature (φύσις). Here ἕξις is the genus of φύσις and therefore is of wider scope than φύσις. Physical disposition (ἕξις), construed as constitutive principle in the generic sense, will be equivalent to φύσις in the broad sense in which it is used in the reports of Alexander and Simplicius, viz., the constitutive and motive principle of all things, including inanimate things. This suggests that the Stoic terminology was not rigidly fixed. The generic concept could be expressed by either φύσις or ἕξις, with the other denoting a species of it; but in their usage as species, ἕξις is applied to the constitutive principle of the lowest level of the scale of nature (inanimate objects) and φύσις is applied to the second level (plants).

denoting the internal *source* of (self-)motion, the relationship stipulated between them is equivalent to the relationship we have discovered between the prepositionally differentiated self-motions of Simplicius's catalog. In Diogenes' definition, (inanimate) physical disposition (ἕξις) moving out of itself in accord with its particular genetic formula constitutes nature (φύσις). This definition is logically equivalent to the proposition presupposed by Simplicius's account, namely, that in the case of a seed, motion through itself is programmed by the particular formulas of the seed to initiate the motion of growth, which constitutes movement out of itself.

The subsequent description of the motion of nature in Diogenes' definition constitutes an instructive parallel to Simplicius's description of the motion involved in the growth of an organism from seed. Simplicius's description of growth, cited as an example of motion through itself, picks out the process by which a seed springs to life on the basis of its preprogrammed formulas and begins to incorporate and enliven inanimate matter from outside (*In Cat.* 306.23–24). The definition in Diogenes amplifies *moving out of itself* with a description of the function of biological life: "Development to maturity (ἀποτελοῦσα), maintenance or sustinence (συνέχουσα), and creation of things of the same sort as those from which they have sprung (τοιαῦτα δρῶσα ἀφ' οἵων ἀπεκρίθη)."[52] The fact that the causes and mechanisms of growth are cited to exemplify motion through itself, whereas the functions of life are cited to specify the nature of motion out of itself, confirms our supposition that the Stoics saw the difference between these two self-motions as a difference between activating a process and the process itself.

But the most important confirmation of the Stoic theory to be derived from Diogenes' evidence comes, not from the definition itself, but from the sentence that follows it: "And it [namely, nature] aims at (στοχάζεσθαι)

[52] These terms are typically misunderstood by those who take φύσις here in the generic sense as the constitutive principle of the universe as a whole. If, however, nature here is understood as the motive force of the second level of the scale of nature (biological growth and reproduction), the functions here described can easily be recognized as maturation (ἀποτελοῦσα), nutritive sustenance (συνέχουσα), and reproduction (τοιαῦτα δρῶσα ἀφ' οἵων ἀπεκρίθη). The latter expression is confirmed as a reference to reproduction by the definition of seed found in Diogenes Laertius 7.158 (= SVF 2: 741): "Seed is that which is capable of generating things of the same sort as that from which it also has sprung" (γεννᾶν τοιαῦτα ἀφ' οἵου καὶ αὐτὸ ἀπεκρίθη). Ps.-Galen *Definitiones medicae* 94 (19.370.14–16 [Kühn] [=SVF 2: 742]) also cites a (presumably Stoic) definition of seed that mirrors the definition of nature quoted by Diogenes: "Seed is warm *pneuma* in moisture moving out of itself (ἐξ ἑαυτοῦ κινούμενον) and capable of generating a thing of the same sort as that from which it has also sprung" (τοιοῦτον γεννᾶν οἷον ἀφ' οὗ καὶ ἀφείθη [text quoted in standardized spelling from SVF]; cf. also *Definitiones medicae* 95 [19.371.7–12, 15–17 (Kühn)] [=SVF 2: 1133 in part]). Note that δρῶσα in Diogenes Laertius 7.148 may be taken as synonymous to ποιοῦσα; cf. Galen (SVF 2: 411), who uses δρᾶν as the opposite of πάσχειν in a report of Stoic doctrine.

both benefit and pleasure, as is clear from human craftsmanship" (Diogenes Laertius 7.149 [=LS 43A; *SVF* 2: 1132]). Here we see the aim of the moving principle that governs motion out of itself. That aim is both benefit and pleasure (τοῦ συμφέροντος . . . καὶ ἡδονῆς). The traditional Stoic view rejected pleasure as the end (τέλος) of life and regarded it as, at best, a by-product (ἐπιγέννημα) of the process by which nature constitutes an organism and only an occasional concomitant of a properly fashioned constitution (Diogenes Laertius 7.85–86 [=LS 57A 3; *SVF* 3: 178]).[53] But if nature here refers specifically to the moving force of biological growth, which includes nutrition and reproduction, two of the areas in which pleasure was popularly sought, we can see this statement of the aim of nature as a statement of the function of nutrition and reproduction at the level of biological life.[54] The claim, therefore, that nature (as motive power of biological life) aims at pleasure and utility must be a claim that the functions of life specified in the definition (maturation, sustenance, and reproduction) have as their aim pleasure and utility.[55] What is relevant to our investigation, however, is the fact that this claim is justified by analogy to human craftsmanship (ὡς δῆλον ἐκ τῆς τοῦ ἀνθρώπου δημιουργίας). It indicates that this particular account of biological life, in which life is viewed from the perspective of the prepositionally differentiated self-motions, may have explained the aim and benefits of growth and reproduction by use of an analogy taken from human craftsmanship. If so, it is consistent with the interpretation we have given to Simplicius's explanation of motion out of itself, which is best interpreted as using the analogy of the construction (κατασκευή) of a knife, the product of human craftsmanship, to illustrate the way in which motion out of itself serves a teleological function and one that benefits both itself and an organism of the third level of the scale of nature. In this way, Diogenes' definition and description of nature can be seen to parallel the conception of motion out of itself found in Simplicius, thereby confirming our interpretation of the latter as an explanation of biological growth and reproduction.

We shall have to return to the philosophical significance of this line of thought for the Stoic analysis of self-motion; but for now it is sufficient to

[53] The inclusion of pleasure as an aim of nature has troubled interpreters who have attempted to construe this statement and its preceding definition as referring to nature in the generic sense; see, e.g., Rieth 1933, 124, and LS 2: 264–65.

[54] That it was not a universal concomitant may be deduced from the parenthetical remark, εἰ ἄρα ἔστιν. It might be noted that pleasure was regarded as the natural object of one of the irrational capacities of the soul in Posidonius's nontraditional Stoic theory of action; cf. frags. 158, 160, 161 with the commentary of Edelstein and Kidd 1972–88, esp. 2: 574–75.

[55] As such it does not conflict with the Stoic contention that pleasure is not the τέλος of life; for it does not apply to life as a whole (which includes rational life), but only to certain nonrational aspects of life.

show that Simplicius's account not only is compatible with the other accounts embodying the Stoic analysis of self-motion, but also adds crucial
information not found in other sources.[56] Thus even if the catalog of self-
motions distinguished by prepositional phrases was an unusual and not
widely used Stoic attempt to refine the conception of self-motion, it shows
without doubt that self-motion was important enough to Stoic philosophy
to merit careful analysis and systematic discussion in some circles.

2. THE THEORETICAL BASIS

We are now in a position to synthesize the conceptions and assumptions
that we have extracted from the abridged account of Simplicius, the two
arguments adapted by Origen, and the argument summarized for rebuttal
by Alexander of Aphrodisias. If we fill out these assumptions with what we
know of Stoic doctrine from other sources, we can obtain a relatively
complete picture of the most highly articulated version of the Stoic theory
of self-motion.

We may begin by observing that the Stoics distinguished several essentially different forms of self-motion (see Table 3). To each class in the scale
of nature the Stoics assigned a different internal source of motion, one or
more different characteristic or proper self-motions, and, in three of the
four cases, a different prepositional description of the nature of the self-
motion.

This classification is predicated on a causal analysis of self-motion. Each
type of self-motion is traced back to a specific internal source, which can be
considered the efficient cause of the self-motion. If we pursue the causal
chain further back, we find that this internal source consists of a material
substance, called *pneuma*, which is capable of existing in different physical
states (πῶς ἔχοντα). These physical states account for differences among
the various internal sources of motion. So the physical disposition (ἕξις) of
a material body, the nature (φύσις) of a plant, the soul (ψυχή) of an animal

---

[56] There is still the enigma why Simplicius reversed the seemingly more natural order of (1)
motion through itself and (2) motion out of itself. If he was only concerned to show that the
Stoics differentiated three kinds, he would, of course, have had no particular reason to
preserve the original Stoic order. Yet he had no particular reason to change that order either,
so we should have expected him simply to have followed the order of his source. But as long as
we do not know the philosophical context from which Simplicius (or his intermediate source)
extracted the Stoic distinction of three types of self-motion, we cannot know on what principle
they were originally ordered by the Stoics, or even whether they were ordered at all. One can,
for example, imagine that the latter two self-motions occurred in a digression designed to
bring out the particular nature of motion out of itself by contrasting the other two kinds of
self-motion. Without any secure knowledge of the order of the original Stoic source, it is
pointless to speculate on reasons for reordering.

TABLE 3
Classifications of Self-Motions

Class of Moved Object	Internal Source of Motion	Characteristic (proper) Movements	Theoretical Type of Self-Motion
Inanimate objects ἄψυχα	Natural disposition ἕξις	Natural motions, such as falling, heating, etc. φέρεσθαι κάτω θερμαίνειν	Through itself δι' ἑαυτοῦ
Plants φυτά	Nature φύσις	Growth αὔξησις	Out of itself ἐξ ἑαυτοῦ
Living creatures ζῷα	Soul ψυχή	Sense-impression and impulse φαντασία καί ὁρμή	From itself ἀφ ἑαυτοῦ
Rational creatures λογικά ζῷα	Reason, understanding λόγος λογική δύναμις παρακολούθησις	Judging impressions, understanding the use of impressions (δια)κρίνεω τάς φαντασίας, παρακολουθεῖν	

or human being, and the reason (λόγος) of a human being, each consists of the same physical material, *pneuma*, but in a different physical state. This *pneuma* is responsible for all the properties and functions of the bodies in which it resides.[57]

For inanimate objects or substances, the *pneuma*, existing in a physical state (ἕξις), holds the substance together, gives it its physical properties, such as hardness, density, and color, and supplies it as well with the capacity to move or cause change. The particular motion that the *pneuma* produces in inanimate things depends on the nature of the object or material substance that the *pneuma* has constituted. One example is the intransitive motion displayed by stone, namely, "moving down" (φέρεσθαι κάτω), a motion that occurs if and only if the stone is dropped from a height and nothing prevents it from falling. The physical state of the *pneuma* of stone constitutes stone's particular nature, which includes weight (βαρύτης). Presumably stone's *pneuma* in this particular state causes stone to move in accord with that state; and as a consequence the resulting motion takes the form of falling or settling down through permeable substances (like air or water) toward the center of the cosmos, until it comes to rest on the main mass of stone and earth.[58] Other examples of inanimate motion are transitive or active processes, such as the cooling produced by water and the heating produced by fire.[59] Thus inanimate self-motions include both change of place and change of state, like heating and cooling.[60] Of these

[57] See LS 1: 313–23. Frags. LS 53A–B, G–K are especially instructive. See also LS 47N and *SVF* 2: 1051; 2: 715, 716. For full discussion see Long 1982.

[58] Alexander *De fato* 181.26–27 (= LS 62G 2) says "moving down" (φέρεσθαι κάτω); cf. Nemesius *De nat. hom.* 35 [105.8–9 Morani]. Other texts talk of earth settling down in water (ὑφίστασθαι, e.g., *SVF* 2: 579). This probably refers to the same natural motion. The dynamics of gravitation in Stoic theory is a puzzling and controversial subject. The conflicting evidence is analyzed with different conclusions by, e.g., Hahm 1977, 107–26; Algra 1988; and Wolff 1988.

[59] Cf. Alexander of Aphrodisias *De fato* 13.181.19, 182.8 (= LS 62G 2, 6; *SVF* 2: 979 [285.9–10; 286.1]) and Nemesius *De nat. hom.* 35 (105.6–106.10 [=*SVF* 2: 991, not in LS]), where it is attributed to the Stoic Philopator. Sharples 1978, 253 n. 109, lists all the references in Alexander *De fato* to the heating capacity of fire; but we should note that the account of Nemesius also says that the nature of fire is to move up (τὸ ἀνωφερές [LS 53O [=*SVF* 2: 991]). Unless Nemesius has inaccurately represented the Stoics, we have to consider the possibility that the Stoics assigned more than one natural motion to the elements. Nemesius contains another peculiarity. He attributes to the Stoics the belief that the natural capacity of water is to cool. This is hard to reconcile with the well-attested Stoic view that the primary property of water is fluidity (ὑγρόν [Diogenes Laertius 1.136] [=*SVF* 2: 580]), whereas air is primarily cold (*SVF* 2: 429, 430 [=LS 47T in part]). Strictly speaking, we must say that the cooling power of the water is due to the coldness of the *pneuma* (composed of cold air and hot fire) that permeates everything and gives everything its sensible properties.

[60] Among the physical changes we should probably include the effects of medicinal preparations causing the cure of diseases (see above, 191–94). In this process, heating and cooling, no doubt, play a role for the Stoics, as they do for Galen (see above, note 42).

motions some, like falling, primarily affect the inanimate object itself, whereas others, like heating and cooling, also affect things with which the object comes into contact.

The second kind of self-motion is the motion characteristic of plants, which the Stoics claimed are constituted by nature (φύσις). Their self-motion consists in the process of growth (αὔξησις) and reproduction. Diogenes Laertius's doxography gives us a good description of this process: "Nature is a physical state that moves out of itself in accord with its seminal formulas (κατὰ σπερματικοὺς λόγους), bringing to maturity and sustaining organisms out of itself and reproducing others of the same kind as those from which they sprang" (Diogenes Laertius 7.148 [=LS 43A 2; *SVF* 2: 1132]). The same process, but seen in terms of its internal mechanism, is described for us by Simplicius: "A seed when sown unfolds its own formulas (λόγους), draws up the surrounding material, and transmits to it the form of its internal formulas" (τοὺς ἐν ἑαυτῷ λόγους).[61] The formulas (λόγοι) of the seed, or "seminal formulas" (σπερματικοὶ λόγοι), seem to be formulas or codes programmed into the natural *pneuma* (φυσικὸν πνεῦμα) to control growth through appropriate incorporation and manipulation of matter from outside. In the process of growth (αὔξησις), the plant both increases in size and changes shape. Epictetus describes the progressive nature of the change in the specific case of grain. First the root grows, then the first node (γόνυ) emerges, then the second and the third nodes, and finally the fruit "forces out its nature" (ἐκβιάσεται τὴν φύσιν [*Diss.* 4.8.40; cf. 4.8.36]). The culmination of the entire process is the production of seed or fruit, which ensures the continuation of the process and provides food for higher members of the scale of nature (*Diss.* 2.6.11–12; 3.24.91–92).

The third kind of self-motion, "motion from itself" (ἀφ' ἑαυτοῦ), is characteristic of things held together by soul (ψυχή). It manifests itself in the motions of sensation and of movement arising from impulse. These are the characteristic motions of animals and human beings. On the Stoic theory, animals and human beings have the capacity to receive impressions (φαντασίαι) from outside through the sense organs. These impressions leave an imprint on the soul in the form of a qualitative alteration of the *pneuma*. Upon its reception by the psychic *pneuma*, an impression stimulates an impulse to action (ὁρμή) and the living creature begins to move.[62] For the irrational animals this is the full extent of their motion, but for human beings there is more.

The fourth and final motion is the motion that is characteristic of only a fraction of living creatures, namely those endowed with the power of rea-

---

[61] *In Cat.* 306.23–24. On the text, see above, note 17.
[62] For fuller discussion, see LS 1: 236–41, 313–33.

son. This power gives human beings the capacity to judge or discriminate among (κρίνειν, διακρίνειν) impressions and to make decisions (κρίνειν). Animals are by nature moved to yield automatically or in a quasimechanical fashion to impressions. Human beings have the added capacity of evaluating the impressions that impinge on their senses and of choosing to which ones they will assent. Rational creatures, therefore, do not have to be carried along by their impressions, but may interrupt the process leading to action by rejecting undesirable or inappropriate stimuli. The characteristic motions of the third and fourth classes thus are generically similar, with the result that the behaviors of human beings and of animals have much in common; but there is also a profound difference in that rational creatures have a power to control their actions in a way that irrational animals cannot.[63]

These four types of self-motion are not distributed uniformly in the scale of nature, one to each class, but rather in a hierarchically ordered pattern so that each class possesses in addition to its own characteristic motion all the motions of the classes below it in the scale (see Figure 3).[64] Inanimate objects possess only one or more physical motions. Plants also possess the motion of vegetative growth and reproduction. Animals are capable of physical motions, vegetative growth and reproduction, and the power of sensation and impulse leading to locomotion. Human beings possess all four capacities for motion. As physical, material objects, human beings move with the inanimate movements of physical substances, as when they warm up a cold object held in their hands or when they fall off a horse or a cliff. As living beings, they develop from the seed of their parents, grow to maturity and reproduce themselves, and eventually decline and die. As animals endowed with soul, they perceive the world through their senses, move around from place to place, and act in their environment by impulse. Finally, as rational creatures, they can understand the divine order of the universe, decide which impressions they will approve, and so govern their actions in conformity with the moral order of the universe.

This ordered pattern of distribution of the four types of self-motion among the four classes of the scale of nature was regarded by the Stoics as a reflection of the hierarchically ordered ontological structure of reality. We can catch a glimpse of this structure in the Stoic prepositional description of self-motions, motion *through* itself, motion *out of* itself, and motion *from* itself. None of the extant texts makes explicit the significance of this particular choice of terms, but one correlation immediately suggests itself. The three prepositions, taken literally, stand in an ordered series of spatial

---

[63] For a full discussion of human action, see Inwood 1985, 42–101; cf. the references cited in note 50 above.

[64] For further discussion, see Long 1982; Inwood 1985, 21–22, 24–27.

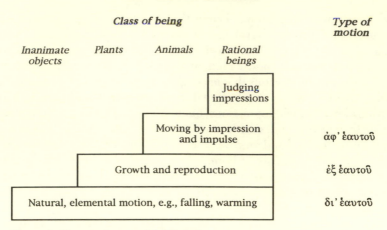

Figure 3. Concomitance of Self-Motions

relationships (see Figure 4). "Movement through," construed spatially, should refer to internal movement that does not pass beyond the boundary of the object. "Movement out of" would imply movement that does not remain within its original boundaries, but passes from within to a region beyond the original perimeter. "Movement away from" connotes departure from a position. Origen's division of things that move similarly implies that the first three classes stand in an ordered series with respect to their spatial movements. According to Origen's division, objects in the first class (inanimate things) are by themselves spatially unmoved. Those in the second (plants) move by increase in size, but remain fixed in their original position as long as they are growing. Those in the third (animals) move about from place to place.[65] For two of these motions, the prepositional denominations are singularly apt. When a plant grows, its roots and leaves sprout from within the seed and extend to the region originally outside the seed. The spatial configuration of such a change is precisely described by the term "motion *out of* itself." In fact, any kind of increase in size (αὔξ-ησις) can be construed as moving *out of* itself (ἐξ ἑαυτοῦ) in that it consists of an expansion of a thing's own surface boundary. Likewise, animal motion is appropriately described by its prepositional denomination. When an animal moves, unlike a plant, it departs from its initial position and moves *away from* (ἀπό) its initial position.

[65] The earliest division to articulate the differences among the four members of the Stoic scale of nature (Philo *Quis rerum divinarum heres* 137–39) differentiates the four classes as (1) those remaining in the same place, held together by a bond of physical disposition (ἕξις); (2) those that move not by changing places (οὐ μεταβατικῶς), but by growing in size (αὐξ-ητικῶς); (3) irrational ensouled creatures; and (4) rational ensouled creatures. Philo does not identify the motion of the last two classes, the ensouled creatures (animals and human beings); but the denial of change of position to plants implies that ensouled creatures are in his division endowed with the capacity to move by change of position (μεταβατικῶς).

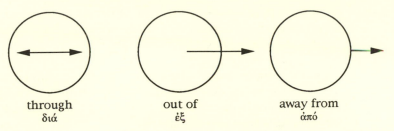

| through | out of | away from |
| δια | ἐξ | ἀπό |

Figure 4. Spatial Denotation of Greek Prepositions

For the remaining member of Origen's series, the first member, we cannot claim a comparable correspondence. In Origen's division, inanimate things are said to be moved *only* from without, and therefore by implication are devoid of any self-motion. The catalog of self-motions, in contrast, without denying the capacity for externally induced motions, assigns to inanimate materials and objects a variety of self-motions arising on their own, such as falling, heating, cooling, and curing.[66] This discrepancy raises a question about the uniformity of the Stoic tradition regarding the nature of the changes and movements of material substances and objects; but we cannot enter into that question here.[67] Regardless of whether the

[66] Origen was well aware of the discrepancy between his division and the set of prepositionally differentiated self-motions. It was presumably to eliminate this discrepancy that he chose to apply "motion through itself" to rational animals, rather than to the first member of the series, where the catalog of self-motions appears to have originally positioned it; see above, 184–85.

[67] The discrepancy appears most blatant when one compares the accounts of Origen and Alexander. Both use stone or stones as an example of movement by an inanimate object. Alexander says that stone necessarily falls down if nothing prevents it, and that this falling motion is in accord with its own nature (κατὰ φύσιν, *De fato* 13.181.15–30). Origen says stones have their mover outside and are moved only from outside (*De princ.* 3.1.2 [196.4–6]; *De orat.* 6.1 [311.16–21]). In this, stones are different from things that have their cause of motion within themselves, among which he includes plants that are moved by the nature (φύσις) within them, *De princ.* 3.1.2 [196.8–9]; *De orat.* 6.1 [312.1–2; cf. 311.16–18]). We cannot here analyze the consistency of these and other Stoic views of inanimate motion (e.g., Chrysippus *apud* Cicero *De fato* 42–43 [=*SVF* 2: 974]; and Aulus Gellius *Noct. Att.* 7.2 [=*SVF* 2: 1000]; for discussion of Chrysippus's argument, see Meyer, 76, and McGuire, 305–29, in this volume); but we can at least point out that the two versions are not as far apart as they seem at first glance. The discrepancy in the attribution or denial of φύσις to inanimate things is easily recognized as a simple, semantic difference. Alexander uses φύσις in the generic sense to denote the constitutive principle of every natural object or material. Origen divides this generic constitutive principle into four subtypes and restricts φύσις to the constitutive principle only of plants (φυτά), whose proper motion is to grow (φύειν). For the constitutive nature of inanimate objects, he used ἕξις. The discrepancy in attributing or denying internally induced self-motion to stone and other inanimate substances is mitigated by the fact that the authors are not talking about the same kind of motion. Origen refers to horizontal, spatial motion. Alexander and the catalog of self-motions look at gravitational fall and the nonspatial motions of heating and cooling. Both would have agreed that inanimate objects are not capable of self-induced, horizontal spatial motion; the only question is

two ways of differentiating self-movers and self-motions are consistent, in both differentiation schemata the Stoics recognized an ordered pattern of increasing spatial motion as one proceeds up the scale of natural motions.[68]

There is, moreover, another more interesting and philosophically significant distinction implicit in the prepositionally differentiated series of self-motions. This distinction inheres not only in the prepositional phrases, but also in the verbal designations of the respective motions. Whereas Origen designates each of the three self-motions with the same verb, the intransitive middle κινεῖσθαι (or the noun κίνησις), Simplicius uses three different verbs: activating the motion (ἐνεργεῖν τὴν κίνησιν) through itself; moving (κινεῖσθαι) out of itself; and acting (ποιεῖν) from itself. This variation presupposes an ordered series of motions. "To *activate* (ἐνεργεῖν) the motion" refers, not to the motion itself, but to the causal initiation of the motion; "to move" (κινεῖσθαι: intransitive) denotes the motion itself; and "to act" (ποιεῖν), a transitive verb, signifies the production of an effect or some change or motion in another.[69] These verbs pick out features of motion that stand in an ordered series of expanding effect. The first picks out an element internal to the motion, that is, its initiation; the second picks out an intransitive motion of a thing in its environment; and the third picks out a transitive motion, which possesses the capacity for causing change or motion in another.

The Stoic understanding of the specific activities that fall under these three species of motion exhibits the same ordered structure. This is clearest for the latter two types. The motion of plants, motion out of itself, comprises two components: growth or increase in size (αὔξησις), and production of seed. Each involves some spatial motion. In growth, the periphery of the plant expands, and in the production of seed, the seed physically moves out of the mature plant.[70] But this second component of the motion of plants, the intransitive movement of the seed out of the parent plant, has another effect that extends still further beyond the plant: it serves to supply food or nutrient matter for higher members of the scale of nature.[71] The

---

whether Origen consciously denied that the fall of a stone and heating by fire are self-induced, or whether he unwittingly overgeneralized on the basis of horizontal spatial motion.

[68] This holds true at least for the first three members of the series. In the quadripartite division of the scale of nature, the highest level (rational creatures) may possess the same degree of spatial movement as the level below (irrational animals).

[69] On the meaning of ἐνεργεῖν τὴν κίνησιν, see above, 195–96 and note 41.

[70] Epictetus uses the words "carry out" (ἐξενέγκῃ) and "force out" (ἐκβιάσεται) for the process of bearing fruit (*Diss.* 4.8.36, 40).

[71] Epictetus considers the drying up of a plant and its fruit, not as a curse, but as the purpose of its existence and as a change that is part of an ordered economy of the world (*Diss.* 2.6.11; 3.24.91–92). His choice of examples (grain, figs, and grapes) shows that he is thinking of the teleological role of plants as food.

specific motion of plants, therefore, has an influence on the world beyond the plant by virtue of the fact that it makes nutrient matter available to other beings.

The motion of animals, motion from itself, like that of plants, comprises several components: sensation, impulse, and locomotion. This process entails spatial movement; and just as the spatial movement of animals surpasses the spatial movement of plants by carrying the animal from place to place, so the environmental impact of animals surpasses that of plants. Whereas plants provide the *passive* matter for others, animals also provide the *active* cause of motion in others.[72] This is implicit in the verb "to act" (ποιεῖν) and is made explicit in Epictetus's description of the dual function of animals: to provide food in the form of meat and cheese, and to provide agricultural labor.[73] It also underlies Origen's division of things that move. His first division (things that are moved only from without, like rocks, sawed wood, the carcasses of animals, and harvested plants) are moved only when they are "carried by someone" (*De princ.* 3.1.2 [196.3–5]; *De orat.* 6.1 [311.16–24]). This "carrying" can only refer to motion produced by animals (either rational or irrational). Thus the Stoic analysis explicitly invokes the dual capacity of animals to move themselves spatially and to be an active cause of movement in others, thereby registering the motion of animals as superior to the motion of plants in its effect on the rest of the universe.

In the light of this distinction between plant and animal motion (namely, as sources of passive matter and active movement respectively for the world outside), we might expect the Stoics who used the prepositional terminology to have regarded the proper activities of inanimate materials or things as affecting only their possessor, and then only from within by means of some internal causal activity (ἐνεργεῖν). Direct evidence on how proponents of the prepositional distinction might have conceived of motions like falling and heating is lacking; so we cannot be sure that they ever pushed the distinction to this point. We can only speculate on how they might have done so on the basis of accepted Stoic conceptions.

The examples mentioned in the Stoic discussions of inanimate self-motion consist of two types: passive motions, like the falling of a stone, and active motions, like heating, cooling, and curing disease. The passive inanimate motions, like the falling of a stone, present no problem. However we imagine the innate *pneuma* to cause such motion, it can easily be construed as triggering and directing the motion of falling from within.[74] The active

---

[72] It is significant that the references to motion from itself incorporate both intransitive and transitive verbs: κινεῖσθαι, κινεῖται (Origen *De princ.* 3.1.2 [196.12–197.1] = LS 53A 4 = SVF 2: 988 [287.42–288.1]); ποιεῖν (Simplicius *In Cat.* 306.25).

[73] Epictetus *Diss.* 1.6.18: "[God] constitutes one animal to be eaten, another to serve in farming and another to produce cheese."

[74] See note 58 above.

self-motions, which include heating, cooling, and curing, seem to present a problem in that, as transitive motions, they act upon objects other than their possessors.[75] Nevertheless, if we consider them in terms of the principles of Stoic physics, we can see a way in which they, too, might be regarded as acting only within their possessors. On a Stoic interpretation, the active motions, like heating and cooling, are functions, not of the object as a whole, but of the *pneuma*, which permeates (διοικεῖν) everything in total mixture (ὅλον δι' ὅλου) and gives it its qualities. This *pneuma* consists of a total mixture of fire and air. Hence the ability of an object to heat is ultimately a function of the fire in its *pneuma*. Moreover, in Stoic physics, the way in which fire is mixed with air in the *pneuma*, and also with earth and water in other inanimate materials and objects, is a peculiar kind of mixture that the Stoics called "total mixture" (κρᾶσις δι' ὅλου).[76] According-ing to this paradoxical Stoic conception, material substances can mix in such a way that each becomes coextensive with the other, so that there is no region in which one of the constituents subsists in unmixed purity. The process of heating is one in which fire, or *pneuma* with its admixture of fire, flows into an object that is to be heated and there mixes totally with the *pneuma* already in the object, so that the fire and the object occupy the same space. On such an understanding of "heating," fire always brings about heating from within the object that it heats. Similarly, cooling can be explained as the effect of the presence of the cold air in the *pneuma*, in this case mixed with a proportionately smaller amount of fire.[77] Thus as long as one remains within the assumptions of Stoic physics, the Stoic examples of active inanimate motion through itself can be construed as activating or transmitting no motion without transmitting the primary possessor of the motion as well, and they can therefore be regarded as causing their effects from within the region occupied by their possessors. Whether the Stoics who adopted the prepositional terminology ever took this line of defense to explain heating and cooling is not known, but it does illustrate a way in which the spatial connotations of the prepositional terminology could have

---

[75] Curing can be viewed as a special case of heating and cooling applied to the human body; cf., e.g., Galen's similar position cited in note 41 above.

[76] On this concept, see Todd 1976, 30–65; LS 1: 290–97; and Lewis 1988.

[77] Nemesius *De nat. hom.* 35 (105.6–7 [Morani] [=*SVF* 2: 991]), however, attributes cooling to water, not to the air of the *pneuma*. Since water is by its proper nature wet (i.e., fluid), it must derive its power to cool from the *pneuma* in it. But in that case it is hard to see how the *water* could be said to cool through itself. Unlike the cold air in it, the water could not permeate the recipient of the cooling and cool it from within. I do not know how to account for this. It could be either an inaccurate representation of the Stoic view, or a generalization of the theory in which the literal "moving only from within" has been slackened slightly. We should also remember that in Simplicius's first example of an instantiation of inanimate motion, the motion through itself was attributed not to material things per se, but to their active natures or powers (φύσεις, δυνάμεις).

been reconciled with the behavior of the self-movers to which they were presumably applied.

At any rate, the three prepositionally differentiated self-motions that characterize members of the first three levels of the scale of nature can, for the most part, be viewed as standing in an ordered series with respect to their causal effects: (1) internal change of form or state, (2) external transmission of passive matter, and (3) external transmission of active movement. When (1) inanimate substances activate motion through themselves, they generally change the properties of an object or substance *from within*, affecting only the *form or state* of the thing in which they reside. When (2) plants move out of themselves, they ultimately produce foliage or seeds that affect others *external to themselves* by supplying *passive matter* to serve as food for others. When (3) animals or humans act, they become *active movers* setting in motion other things *external to themselves*.

Furthermore, if we consider how these self-motions are generated, we notice that, just as they differ in their effects on the outside world, so they also differ in their dependence on it. The inanimate motions (motions through themselves), which actualize a form in their possessors, neither affect the environment external to their possessors, nor require anything from outside to become active. The other two motions, in contrast, cannot occur without external assistance. The proper motion of plants, which produces nutrient matter for animals and humans, does not create that matter out of nothing. A plant, we have learned, "draws up the matter that surrounds it" (Simplicius *In Cat.* 306.23–24) and transforms it into its own body and into fruit, both of which subsequently become nutrient "matter" for animals or people.[78] Thus a plant requires nutrient matter from outside in order to perform its own function of producing nutrient matter for others. "Motion out of itself," therefore, plays a vital role in the causal network of the universe by transforming inanimate matter into vegetable matter for the nourishment of higher members of the scale of nature. In the course of this process, passive matter enters into (εἰς) the plant and subsequently passes out of (ἐξ) it again.

The motion of animals likewise requires external assistance. Animal motion can occur only if it is triggered by an impression from outside. In fact, animal motion, when distinguished from the motion of plants, is

---

[78] Epictetus is chiefly interested in the role of fruit (especially grain) as food for animals and humans (see above, note 71); but Origen speaks of "the fodder of (formerly live) plants" (τὰ φορητὰ τῶν πεφυτευμένων, *De orat.* 6.1 [311.22]; = *SVF* 2: 989 [288.42]) as an example of something carried by someone. Though in *De princ.* 3.1.2 (196.5; = *SVF* 2: 988 [287.35]) he had used φορητά ("portables") generically of wood, stones, and all inanimate things, he adds τῶν πεφυτευμένων in *De orat.* and makes it parallel to τὰ τῶν ζῴων σώματα ("the carcasses of animals"), thereby indicating that he is thinking of plants as fodder (a well-established meaning of φορητά; cf. LSJ s.v. φορητός) and the carcasses of animals as meat.

frequently described as a dual motion, impression (φαντασία) and impulse (ὁρμή).[79] Origen in his division tells us that "ensouled creatures move from themselves when impression calls forth impulse" (De princ. 3.1.2 [196.13–197.1]). An impression is an alteration in the pneuma of the soul that occurs when something perceptible strikes against (προσβάλλω, προσπίπτω) the psychic pneuma of a sense organ. Philo puts it most succinctly: "An impression is produced by the approach (πρόσοδον) of a thing outside striking the mind through sensations" (Legum allegoriae 1.30 [=LS 53P 2; SVF 2: 844). In this process, nothing material enters the body; the operative event is a blow by a material object outside the body against (πρὸς) the material substance of the soul.[80] This motion or action "from itself," like motion "out of itself," requires some external assistance and so plays a role in the causal network of the universe. But whereas in the motion of plants (motion out of itself) passive matter entered into the plant and then passed out to become matter for something else, animal action is triggered by an active cause and is, in turn, capable of setting other things into motion. Thus whereas motion out of itself plays a role in the causal chain that keeps the universe and its inhabitants supplied with passive matter, motion from itself plays a role in the causal chain that transmits action and active motion in the universe.

The three kinds of self-motion, therefore, articulate a differentiation of causal interaction in the universe; and it is not hard to see that the paths along which the three self-motions perform their causal functions are appropriately described by their respective prepositional designations (see Figure 5). We may never know how closely the Stoics who used the prepositional distinction actually tied their analysis of the natural world to the prepositional terminology, nor even how widely the prepositional terminology was used for differentiating the three kinds of self-motion.[81] Nevertheless, the prepositional differentiation must be recognized as a manifestly useful tool to analyze the causal structure and function of the various self-motions; as such, it may give some indication of how the Stoics saw the role of each in the causal network of the universe.

The prepositional differentiation of the kinds of self-motion also serves

[79] E.g., Clement Stromat. 2.20 (= SVF 2: 714); Philo Legum allegoriae 1.30 (= SVF 2: 844; LS 53P); Alexander De fato 34.205 (= SVF 2: 1002); and Hierocles (LS 53B 4: αἰσθήσει τε καὶ ὁρμῇ).

[80] Cf. προσβάλλω, πρόσβλητα (Hierocles LS 53B 5, 6); τὴν τοῦ ἐκτὸς πρόσοδον of the outside (Philo LS 53P 2); πρὸς τῷ ὁρωμένῳ (Diogenes Laertius 7.157 [=LS 53N; = SVF 2: 867; cf. 866]). For "hearing," the verb προσπίπτω is used (Diogenes Laertius 7.158 [=SVF 2: 872]).

[81] The fact that the full range of the terminology appears in only two late sources (Origen and Simplicius) and that most Stoic texts do not use it, or at least not uniformly (e.g., Alexander), suggests that it was not standard.

Motion through Itself
(Inanimate Substances)

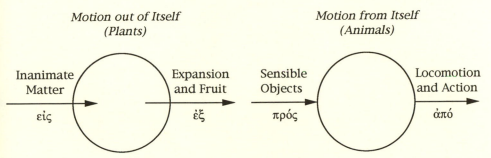

Motion out of Itself   *Motion from Itself*
(Plants)   *(Animals)*

Figure 5. Paths of Causal Interaction in Self-Motions

another purpose: it articulates the relationships between the various self-motions. Here we have more explicit testimony on the role of the prepositional concept. According to a statement preserved in the account of Simplicius, the Stoics claimed that the activation of motion *through* itself, by unfolding a seed's guiding formulas, draws in matter from outside and imposes the specified form on this additional matter. As a result, the thing in question begins to grow, that is, to move with the second type of self-motion, motion *out of* itself (Simplicius *In Cat.* 306.21–24). Another statement preserved by Simplicius reflects the assumption that such motion *out of* itself, by producing articulated physical structures, when led to do so by the unfolding formulas, produces the particular organic structures needed for the third type of self-motion, motion *from* itself (ibid., 306.19–21).[82] Thus in the case of animals (and human beings), there is a continuous process of self-motion that at certain critical moments brings into existence another motion in the hierarchically ordered set of self-motions, and does so in such a way that each successive self-motion becomes the agent of the subsequent one.

We can illustrate this conception visually with a three-dimensional

[82] See above, 198–99.

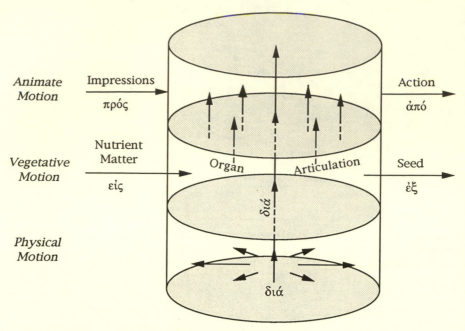

Figure 6. Dynamic Structure of Self-Motion

model (see Figure 6). On this model, the internal motion through itself (via genetic formulas) continues up *through* the development of the vegetative organism into the animate organism, providing the controlling or governing causal formulas for the initial development and the ongoing function of each successive motion. The second motion, motion out of itself, once activated by the internal process of unfolding genetic formulas, instantiates the self-motion that takes in matter and converts it into informed organic material; but it does not, as happens in the case of plants, emit all its vegetative matter again in reproduction or as nutrient for animals. Instead, it articulates organic structures that, when fully developed, persist to serve as physical and psychological organs for the third self-motion.

This analysis takes into account only the range of motions with which the three lowest members of the scale of nature are endowed. We have yet to consider the self-motion of the highest member of the scale of nature, rational human beings. Their characteristic motion is ambiguously described in the texts we have been examining. From one point of view, since human beings are the fourth and highest member of the scale of nature, their activity of judging impressions may be regarded simply as the fourth and highest kind of self-motion, derived from a unique internal source, reason (λόγος). This point of view is embodied in the division of things that move and was followed consistently by Origen. But from the point of view of its causal relations to the outside world, human action is no different from that of animals. Its external input (impression) and its output (action by impulse) are the same as for animals. Since the prepositional classification uses causal relation to the outside world as its basis for differentiating self-motions, it construes rational action as a species of animal action, differentiated from animal action only by an internal factor, namely, the internal causal mechanism whereby assent is given to impressions to initiate action. Whereas animals respond to impressions in an automatic, quasimechanical way, rational beings are capable of evaluating impressions and managing their responses to conform to the divine moral order of the universe. This capacity is presumably programmed into their genetic nature and therefore develops, like the other self-motions, from motion through itself in the course of the unfolding of the genetic formulas. Thus even from the perspective of the prepositionally differentiated self-motions, the development of reason may be regarded as the fourth and highest stage in the developmental process of a human being; but its presence does not alter the way its possessors interact with the causal network of the universe. Thus whether the judgment of reason is regarded as a distinct kind of self-motion or as an improved form of animal motion depends on whether one defines the self-motions in terms of their functional characteristics and internal principle or in terms of their causal interactions with the outside world. It is an important difference in perspective, but it does not affect our understanding of the underlying Stoic conception of self-motion.

Summing up our review of the assumptions underlying the division of self-movers and the prepositional classification of self-motions, we may say that the Stoic analysis of self-motion appears to have served two functions: to differentiate the various types of self-motion on the basis of their functional characteristics and causal interactions with the outside world, and to map causal interrelationships among them. The analysis of self-motion thus shows itself to be an integral component of the Stoic attempt to give a causal explanation of the entire realm of natural phenomena from the behavior of inanimate physical materials and objects through the biological sphere to the complex behavior of human beings.

3. AN APPLICATION

To test the reconstruction that we have distilled from the handful of texts that explicitly address the subject of self-motion, we can look at the application of this analysis to the most complex and comprehensive embodiment of self-motion, the process leading to the development of a rational human being. Since a rational human being is endowed with all four types of self-motion, it passes through four stages of development en route to complete formation as a rational human being. The process begins with conception.[83] The Stoics construed conception exclusively as a product of physical motions. The reproductive process begins when the male seed is ejected into a woman's womb. The seed consists of *pneuma* mixed with moisture. This *pneuma* is a fragment of the soul of the male parent. The vocabulary of the release of the seed is instructive. The man ejaculates (μεθίησιν) and releases (ἀφέθη) the seed into the woman's womb. The seed performs no action of its own; it is moved only passively from without. In fact, one of the expressions, "to be released" (ἀφέθη), is the same expression Alexander used in his example of a stone that falls from a height (*De fato* 13.181.26). The human seed upon its release, other sources tell us, "falls into" (ἐμπέσῃ) or "falls down" (καταπεσόν) into a place in the womb (LS 53B 1; SVF 2: 750, cf. 745). Here the seed does display self-motion, its very first self-motion—the inanimate motion of "falling." At the end of its "fall" into the womb, the male seed strikes the female seed, which is lying passively in the womb, consisting like its male counterpart of *pneuma* in moisture.[84]

At this juncture, the *pneuma* of the male is "grasped" (συλληφθὲν) by the *pneuma* of the female, and becomes "grown together" with it (συμφυὲς γενόμενον) and "hidden" (κρυφθέν [LS 52B 1; SVF 1: 128]). This segment of the process is presented as another passive experience for the male seed, but the female seed now begins to take action. Its motion, like the first motion of the male seed, proves to be entirely inanimate. Hierocles and Eusebius describe its action as "grasping" and "hiding" the male seed. This must refer to the mechanical movement of the fluid, flowing around the thing that falls into it. Eusebius also uses the term "becoming grown together" (συμφυὲς γενόμενον [SVF 1: 128]), which might give the impression of biological growth; but the Stoics almost certainly did not so construe it. In the parallel versions of Theodoretus and Diogenes Laertius,

[83] The early Stoic theory of conception is described in detail by Eusebius (*Praeparatio evangelica* 15.20.1 [=SVF 1: 128]) and by Hierocles, a Stoic of the second century A.D., whose work survives on papyrus fragments. Hierocles, first edited by von Arnim (1906), now appears in a new edition in *Corpus dei papiri filosofici graeci et latini* (1992). The relevant passage is also edited and translated in LS 53B. Cf. the doxographic reference newly reconstructed and attributed to Diogenes of Babylon by Tieleman (1991).

[84] The conception of the female seed as *pneuma* in moisture is not stated in so many words, but is upheld by Eusebius's description of the next stage, in which the male seed is "grasped" by the *pneuma* of the female, receiving water and growing from the female *pneuma* (= SVF 1: 128). The statement attributed to Zeno's student, Sphaerus (SVF 1: 129; 626), that female seed is watery, sparse, and nongenerative (ἄγονον), cannot mean that it lacks *pneuma*; it must be the Stoic explanation for the fact that females cannot conceive without male seed. Presumably, it takes the *pneuma* of two seeds to constitute sufficient vital heat and motion to trigger conception.

the relation between the two seeds is called "mixing" (κέρασμα, μῖγμα, συγκίρνασθαι, σύμμιγμα [*SVF* 1: 128]), suggesting nothing more than the inanimate process of physical mixture. Thus on the Stoic theory, conception begins with an entirely inanimate and passive process: the male seminal fluid "falls" into the female seminal fluid and the two fluids mix.

In this mixed condition, a change occurs in the moist mixed seed. Eusebius describes it as "being moved and rekindled." Hierocles says it no longer "remains at rest" (ἠρεμεῖ), but is "set into motion again" (ἀνακινηθὲν [LS 53B 1]). The effect is a sudden and dramatic change in the activity level of the seed. From this point on, Eusebius says, "it begins to grow (φύει), . . . continuously taking up moisture and increasing in size out of itself (προσλαμβάνον ἀεὶ τὸ ὑγρὸν καὶ αὐξανόμενον ἐξ αὑτοῦ [*SVF* 1: 128]).[85] Hierocles describes the new behavior with the words, "It begins its own activities (ἄρχεται τῶν ἰδίων ἔργων) and, drawing in matter (ἐπισπώμενον τὴν ὕλην) from the body that carries the fetus, it fashions the embryo in accord with inescapable patterns" (LS 53B 1). This new development has all the marks of vegetative growth, including the prepositional designation, "motion out of itself."[86] Obviously the change that occurred when the two seeds mixed was the onset of the second level of self-motion.

That makes Hierocles an ideal text from which to extract the Stoic conception of the relationship between the physical motions of inanimate substances and the vital motion of vegetative growth. That development is crucial because it constitutes the transition from the inanimate physical motions of falling and mixing to the vital motion of vegetative growth. To understand it we have to pay careful attention to the vocabulary. Both accounts say the mixing of the two seeds is accompanied by or followed by a "motion" (κινούμενον, ἀνακινηθὲν). Hierocles elaborates by contrasting this motion to the state of rest that preceded it: "Simultaneously with being grasped by the womb . . . , it no longer rests, as it did up until that moment (οὐκέτι ἠρεμεῖ καθάπερ τέως); but its motion is reactivated and it begins its own activities" (LS 53B 1).

What Hierocles means when he says "it no longer rests, as it did up until that moment; . . . but its motion is reactivated" is not immediately clear. Since he has just told us the seed "fell down" (καταπεσὸν) into the womb,

---

[85] *Praeparatio evangelica* 15.20.1 (= *SVF* 1: 128). I follow Diels (1879, 470) in deleting εἰς before τὸ ὑγρὸν.

[86] It is called "growing" (φύει), the verb from which the words for plants (φυτά) and their internal principle of motion (φύσις) were derived. It is also called "growth in size" (αὐξανόμενον), the term we found for the specific self-motion of plants. It incorporates the concomitant physical process alluded to in Simplicius's catalog of self-motions (taking up nutrient matter), and most significantly, both accounts specifically call the process a form of self-motion. Hierocles says it "begins its own activity," and Eusebius gives it the technically correct prepositional designation ("increasing *out of* itself ").

one might think Hierocles thinks the seed comes to rest for a time in the womb before it is "grasped" (συλληφθὲν) and "set into motion again (ἀνακινηθέν). That would require us to take motion in a generic sense and to construe Hierocles as making the trivial claim that one kind of motion (inanimate "falling") ceases, and then after a lapse of time a "grasp" occurs that initiates a different kind of motion, vegetative growth. This is unlikely to be what Hierocles had in mind. According to a report by Simplicius, the Stoics claimed that rest (ἠρεμεῖν) was a property of animals and denied that stone can be said to rest (ἠρεμεῖ [In Cat. 436.10; = SVF 2: 500]). If Hierocles is following this Stoic usage, "rest" (ἠρεμεῖν) cannot describe the cessation of the inanimate spatial motion that occurred during the "fall" of the seed into the womb; it has to refer to some state that can be regarded as the cessation of a motion that is specific to an animal. Similarly, the subsequent verb of motion (compounded with ἀνα-) implies that the seed had at some previous time possessed the motion upon which it is now embarking, that is, the motion of vegetative growth.

Another point that Hierocles makes suggests the same conclusion. Hierocles expressly stipulates that he is talking about seed that falls "at the right time" (ἔν τε καιρῷ τῷ προσήκοντι) and a womb that is "in a good, healthy condition" (ἐρρωμένου). He has no interest in telling us what happens to seed that falls at the wrong time or into a womb that is weak. If he is describing an ideal case of conception, there is no reason to think that Hierocles imagines any incidental lapse in time between the end of the "falling" and the beginning of the "grasping." Thus when he explicitly states that "as soon as the seed is grasped (ἅμα . . . συλληφθὲν), it ceases to rest," the period of rest must include the time during which the seed was "falling down."

The "motion" that is reactivated after a period of "rest" can be deduced from the account of Eusebius. Eusebius, too, says that the seed is moved (κινούμενον); but he adds an explanatory synonym, the word "rekindled" (ἀναρριπιζόμενον [SVF 1: 128]). This verb suggests that the change in question can also be described as "rekindling" and, compounded with ἀνα-, implies that the new state is a restoration of a prior state of "kindling." Moreover, Eusebius's account specifies the agent that causes this rekindling, namely, "the other *pneuma*, part of the soul of the female." This information is enough to allow us to reconstruct the Stoic understanding of the process of conception.

The soul consists of warm *pneuma* (πνεῦμα ἔνθερμον [SVF 1: 135; 2: 773; 3: 305]). In fact, *pneuma* is a mixture of fire and air (SVF 2: 310, 447, 786). In the production of semen, a very small portion of the male's soul leaves his body in the seminal fluid. In that process it cools down so much that the vital heat is almost extinguished. The same thing happens to the *pneuma* of the female in the womb.[87] The cooling deprives the seed of each parent of all vital motion and leaves that seed with only the motions characteristic of the physical materials of which it is composed. The male seed, being predominantly water, is heavy and accordingly falls into the womb. The seed of the female, also predominantly water, offers no resistance to the relatively smaller amount of male seed that falls into it and so envelops it, and the two fluids mix together. But the two portions of seed are not water alone; they also contain *pneuma*. Although this *pneuma* is in a cooled state, it does contain some heat.[88] When the two portions combine in total mixture, they apparently constitute in aggregate a critical degree of heat sufficient to "rekindle" the seed and reactivate the natural motion of the *pneuma*. The precise nature of the physical process here is obscure, but there seems little question that the Stoics regarded the combination of the two portions of *pneuma* as responsible for what they called "rekindling" (ἀναρριζόμενον) the seed or "restoring the motion" (ἀνακινηθέν) of the seed, and that they believed this restoration of the heat or motion initiated the motion of vegetative growth. If this is how the Stoics viewed the process of conception, we can conclude that the internal cause that triggers the process of vegetative growth is itself an inanimate motion, namely, heating. This entails that "motion out of itself" is initially generated by two concurrent, but logically distinct, "motions through themselves": the passive motions of "being grasped" or "mixed," and the active process of heating, which occurs spontaneously when a substance becomes mixed with another substance endowed with heat.[89]

From this point on, as long as the embryo is in the womb, it grows like a plant; but another radical change occurs when the baby leaves the womb and begins to breathe the air of the atmosphere for the first time. The effect, as in the case of conception, is sudden and dramatic: the immobile plant-like embryo becomes an animal endowed with sensation and impulse.[90] The description of the process leading to this change is again revealing of the Stoic explanatory theory. Hierocles prefaces it by pointing out that

[87] See above, note 84.

[88] *Pneuma* is by definition a mixture of fire and air and hence cannot exist without some heat.

[89] The fact that animal conception may be a reciprocal process, in which the heat of each seed warms the other, does not affect the principle that it is a spontaneous, inanimate process. The further question of how the Stoics imagined that two bodies of the same temperature could heat each other (or, what seems to amount to the same thing, how two bodies with the same degree of motion could each augment the motion of the other simultaneously) is an issue of Stoic physics that is beyond the scope of this paper.

[90] Philo *Legum allegoriae* 2.23 (= *SVF* 2: 458) reflects the Stoic view when he characterizes soul (ψυχή) as "nature with the addition of impression and impulse" (φύσις προσειληφεῖα φαντασίαν καὶ ὁρμήν).

throughout gestation, as the embryo was increasing in size, its pneumatic principle was changing gradually in its physical constitution from a denser (παχύτερόν πως) to a finer state (ἀπολεπτύνεται [LS 53B 2]). During birth itself, the embryo can take no action to move spatially on its own. Like the seed prior to conception, the embryo "falls" out of the womb (ἔκπεσον) into the environment (ἐμπεσοῦσα τῷ περιέχοντι [LS 53B 3]). This is consistent with its status as a plant; the only spatial movement to which it is susceptible is either externally caused or, as in the case of birth, the natural movement of its material constituents, that is, falling down. But as soon as it enters the environment, its *pneuma* changes from nature (φύσις) to soul (ψυχή).

Hierocles uses the same Greek word (μεταβάλλω) both for the conversion of the *pneuma* of the seed into vegetative nature (φύσις) and for the conversion of vegetative nature into "soul" (ψυχή [LS 53B 2–3]); but he intimates that physically the change consisted in a further "thinning" of the *pneuma*. Throughout the process of gestation, he maintains that the nature of the embryo was being prepared for birth by becoming thinner (LS 53B 2). He compares the actual plunge into the atmosphere to the "tempering" that occurs when iron is plunged into water and to the striking out of spark (ἐκπυροῦται) from stones on the occasion of a blow (LS 53B 3). The sparking of the stone, which he describes as "the *pneuma* in the stones [being] kindled" (τὸ ἐν τοῖς λίθοις πνεῦμα . . . ἐκπυροῦται), is reminiscent of Eusebius's description of conception as "rekindling" the *pneuma* of the seed and suggests that the transformation of natural *pneuma* into psychic *pneuma* was regarded as the same kind of physical change as that of seminal *pneuma* into natural *pneuma*. Hierocles' stipulation that the natural *pneuma* was prepared for this change by prior "thinning" and Plutarch's report that Chrysippus considered soul to be rarer and finer *pneuma* than nature (*De Stoicorum repugnatiis* 1052e–f [=SVF 2: 806]) shows that this physical change was a further degree of thinning. The only difference between the two transformations is that the transformation into natural *pneuma* was effected by the inanimate motion of mixing and "heating," whereas the transformation into psychic *pneuma* was effected by the vegetative motion of drawing in a nutrient, namely, air. Thus it is a motion *out of itself* that, by drawing in a material substance from outside, triggers the third form of self-motion, motion *from itself*.

The same process occurs at the last level, the development of reason, which reaches its completion when a person comes to the age of 7 or 14.[91] Reason (λόγος), the Stoics held, developed from the reception and accumulation of impressions (φαντασίαι).[92] Thus the fourth type of self-

[91] SVF 1: 149; 2: 83; cf. 3: 477. The sources disagree on the specific age.

[92] For a brief introduction to this subject, see LS 1: 236–40, and for bibliography, see ibid., 2: 499–500.

motion is brought into existence by the exercise of the third kind of self-motion, namely, sensation (αἴσθησις) and impression (φαντασία). In every case, then, each kind of self-motion is triggered by the exercise of the motion immediately below it in the ontological order.

The Stoic analysis of the development of the rational human being endowed with all four kinds of self-motion shows clearly how the Stoic analysis of self-motion was applied to give a causal explanation of the development of each type. This account shows much more clearly than do the divisions of self-movers and the classifications of self-motions how the Stoics viewed the relationship among the four types. Each type serves as a causal factor for the generation of the next higher motion, but it is not the only causal factor. Since self-motions are functions of the *pneuma*, the generation of a new type requires a change in the physical state of the *pneuma*. This is accomplished by a causal factor supplied by the external environment, other "seed," nutrient matter, or impressions. Yet not every seed, nutrient matter, or impression will produce the requisite alteration of the *pneuma*. The other seed has to have sufficient heat or motion; the nutrient matter has to be the fine variety known as "air"; and the impressions apparently have to come in the form of successions of impressions of a similar kind (LS 39E). If and when the external causal factor is correct, the critical alteration of the *pneuma* will occur. But access to the appropriate external cause for the next transformation is obtained only through the operation of the prior self-motion. It is the cooperation of the internal self-motion and the external cause that brings about the quantum shift to a new physical state and a new self-motion in the *pneuma* or in a region of the *pneuma*.[93]

There is one other causal factor involved in the change, and that is the set of preprogrammed formulas of the *pneuma*, the so-called seminal formulas (σπερματικοὶ λόγοι). Hierocles tells us the *pneuma* "moves in a regular methodical course (ὁδῷ κεινούμενον) from beginning to end (τέλος [LS 53B 2]) and shapes the embryo in accord with inescapable patterns (κατά τινας ἀπαραβάτους τάξεις) until it arrives at its goal" (τέλος [LS 53B 1]). In defining the end and the course to that end, the formulas programmed into the *pneuma* supply an additional causal factor governing the development of the self-motions. In defining the goal (τέλος), the governing formulas determine at what point the transformations of the *pneuma* will come to an end, that is, whether vegetative growth will produce a plant, undergo a transformation to soul and produce an animal, or continue on

---

[93] In conception, the entire *pneuma* of the seed changes to "natural *pneuma*." In the later changes, presumably only a portion of *pneuma* changes. So only the *pneuma* in the *hegemonikon* and the other seven parts of the soul changes into psychic *pneuma*. Subsequently only the *pneuma* in the *hegemonikon* changes into rational *pneuma*; cf. Long 1982; and LS 1: 320.

to produce a rational human being. It also defines what form the final product will take, and this definition includes both the generic form of its motion(s) (namely, whether it is growth and reproduction alone, growth and reproduction with sensation and impulse, or all three higher forms of self-motion), and the specific instantiation of that motion (namely, whether growth produces grass or an oak tree, a cat or a dog, or a human being).

We undertook this review of self-motion in Stoic philosophy to see what the Stoics did with the concept after Aristotle had subjected it to intense philosophical scrutiny. The ravages of time have swept away most Stoic philosophical literature, leaving us with very little evidence on the subject. Nevertheless, what can be teased out of the few references that have survived indicates that the subject must have received a thorough and perspicacious treatment, at least in some circles in the Stoa.

If what we have seen is a reliable reflection of the Stoa's approach to the subject, we have to conclude that the Stoa paid little or no heed to the issues that exercised Aristotle. For instance, the Stoics showed no attempt to confront the logical puzzles inherent in the concept of a thing moving itself; they seem to have blithely accepted a self-moving vital force as completely unproblematic. Nor were the Stoics concerned to sort out precisely which things in nature are self-moved or to justify applying the term "self-motion" to one kind of motion, but not to another. Their approach was simply to regard as a self-mover anything that has a principle or cause of motion within. So, having postulated that all form and movement in the universe can in one way or another be traced back to an internal self-moving force, they seem to have regarded all natural motion as self-motion, even the motion of the elements and of inanimate things.[94] The fact that Aristotle had denied self-motion to the elements and inanimate objects was either ignored by them or unknown to them.[95]

The issue with which the Stoics were really concerned was the causal basis of motion in the universe and the relationship between internal sources of motion in natural objects and external sources of motion. In taking up this issue, the Stoics made use of a distinction that was fundamental to Aristotle's analysis of self-movers, the distinction between internal and external causes.[96] But the Stoics shifted the focus of philosophical

---

[94] Origen takes it for granted that one can apply the term "self-moving" (αὐτοκινητόν) to anything that has an internal cause of motion, including fire and flowing springs of water (*De princ.* 3.1.2 [196.8–11]).

[95] In view of the current uncertainty about how much the Stoics knew about Aristotle (see above, note 7), it seems best not to speculate further on the Stoics' relation to Aristotle on this issue.

[96] See the chapters by Furley, Gill, and Meyer in this volume.

concern from the individual problems, like those of elemental and celestial motion, growth, perception, and thought, to their integrated interaction. The primary objective of the Stoics in their analysis of self-motion seems to have been to understand the complex causal structure of motion in the universe. In this pursuit, understanding the precise role of the divine self-moving force, resident in and acting through the vital *pneuma*, became a primary consideration. The evidence that we have, fragmentary as it is, suggests that the concept of self-motion became a vital tool with which to dissect the tangled causal network that produces motions of all kinds in the universe. The Stoic strategy was to analyze the motion of self-movers as an internal interaction among separate causal factors, some internal and some external. By distinguishing different types of self-motion, involving different patterns of interaction among different causal factors, the Stoics developed an analytical tool capable of sorting out the causal factors affecting every variety of self-mover in the universe, including the complex interaction of causal factors that controls human life and behavior. They went on to apply this analysis to an enormous range of scientific and philosophical problems, from gravitation and embryology to epistemology, moral responsibility, and divine providence. By incorporating the analysis of self-movers and self-motion into a comprehensive, systematic theory of causality, designed to explain the dynamics of the universe and everything in it, the Stoics gave the analysis of self-movers a new role in the history of philosophy after Aristotle.

CHAPTER 10

Duns Scotus on the Reality of Self-Change

PETER KING

DUNS SCOTUS radically departs from his medieval predecessors on the subject of self-change. Prior to Scotus, the consensus on Aristotelian doctrine that formed the core of traditional High Scholasticism held the following theses: (1) self-change is impossible in the physical world; (2) self-change, if possible at all, only applies where nonphysical causes such as free will are involved; and (3) all apparent cases of self-change in the physical world are in fact cases of interaction between an agent and a patient that are really distinct.[1] This "common position" (as Scotus calls it)

I would like to thank Sarah Broadie, Alan Code, Mary Louise Gill, Anna Greco, Timothy Noone, and Calvin Normore for information, comments, and advice.

References to Scotus's *Quodlibetal Questions* are taken from Alluntis 1968; all other references to Scotus's works are to the Vatican Edition (abbreviated "Vat.") wherever possible, to the Wadding-Vivès text (abbreviated 'WV') otherwise. I have had the benefit of consulting Alan B. Wolter's unpublished translation of *QSM* IX, but all translations are my own. Citations of Aristotle's text are taken from the Oxford Classical Texts series. Translations of Aristotle are taken from Scotus's Latin text or from the relevant edition of *AL*, rather than from the Greek original, since the Latin is not always in conformity with the Greek.

Effler 1962 is a study of Scotus's views on self-motion. The historical information he provides has to be used with caution. With regard to philosophical content, I fundamentally disagree with almost all of Effler's analysis, to the extent that I understand it.

[1] Aquinas and Bonaventure are representative of the thinkers of their generation. Aquinas, in several places throughout his works (*Commentary on Aristotle's "Physics"* 8.4, *lectio* 7; *Commentary on the "Sentences"* I d.8 q.3 art.1; *Summa contra gentiles* 1.13; *Summa theologiae* Ia q.2 art.3; *Quaestiones disputatae de veritate* q.22 art.3; *Compendium theologiae* chap. 3), notoriously denied the possibility of self-change in defending the principle that everything that is in motion is moved by another. Bonaventure accepts a restricted version of the same principle, holding that self-change is only possible in the case of nonphysical causes; in his *Commentary on the "Sentences"* I d.37 art.2 q.2 n.4, he writes: "As for the objection that everything that is in motion is moved by another, it should be stated that it is true in the case of natural motion, where nothing moves itself because nothing reflects upon itself due to being bound up with matter, but it is not true in the case of the will, which is an 'instrument moving itself,' and the power that is in a spiritual substance is able to reflect on its substance— and so the mover is the same as what is moved." (The description of the will as an *instrumentum se ipsum movens* is taken from Anselm, *De concordia* chap. 11 [Schmitt 1946, 283– 84].) Aquinas and Bonaventure agree on (1) and (3); Bonaventure explicitly disavows (2), whereas Aquinas's position on (2) is unclear.

In the generation immediately prior to Scotus, the debate was sharpened by a running

was taken to be the correct interpretation of Aristotle's discussion of self-change in *Phys.* VII–VIII, supported by three independent arguments as well as Aristotle's texts.

Scotus rejects the common position. He argues that self-change is a widespread feature of the physical world, where the agent and the patient involved in self-change are really the same—and, furthermore, that this is the view put forward by Aristotle.

Scotus's articulation and defense of his view is subtle and sophisticated. He discusses particular cases of self-change throughout his writings, but he treats the general possibility of self-change in *QSM* IX q.14.[2] I shall concen-

---

controversy between Henry of Ghent and Godfrey of Fontaines over (2). Henry of Ghent argued in his *Quodlibeta* IX q.5 (Macken 1981) that there were six levels of motion, each corresponding to a different degree of separation between mover and what is moved, and at the first two levels—that of the divine and the created will, respectively—the term "motion" is used improperly, not corresponding to any real distinction but only an "intentional distinction"; in the remaining levels, self-motion is impossible other than as the interaction of really distinct parts. Godfrey of Fontaines then argued against Henry's position in his *Quodlibeta* VI q.7 (de Wulf and Hoffmans 1914), maintaining self-change to be simply impossible and concluding that the will is essentially passive. Henry replied at length in his *Quodlibeta* X q.9 (Macken 1983), defending the thesis that the will is essentially active, emphasizing the difference between the self-determination of the will and merely natural motion. Godfrey offered a counterreply in his *Quodlibeta* VIII q.2 (Hoffmans 1921), insisting that the principle that nothing changes itself is a universal metaphysical principle without exception, and hence must apply to the will as well as to the natural world.

Scotus's own discussion of self-change clearly reflects this recent controversy. If either, Scotus sides with Henry, but Scotus finds the agreement between Henry and Godfrey on (1) and (3) at least as problematic as their debate over (2). The substantive agreement between them is the basis of the "common position" as Scotus recognizes it.

[2] Scotus's major discussions of particular cases of self-change, apart from *QSM* IX q.14, are as follows. Local motion, and in particular the movement of light and heavy bodies, is taken up in *Ord.* II d.2 p.2 q.6 (Vat. 7.350–74). Quantitative self-change in augmentation/diminution is taken up in *Rep. Par.* IV d.44 q.1 (WV 24.530a–540b), and in condensation/rarefaction in *Op. Ox.* IV d.12 q.4 (WV 17.614b–631b). Qualitative self-change in the activity of seeds and semen is taken up in *Op. Ox.* II d.18 q.unica (WV 13.84a–96b) and III d.4 q.unica (WV 14.182a–200b). The self-change involved in appetitive potencies, i.e., the will, is discussed extensively in *QSM* IX q.15 and *Op. Ox.* II d.25 q.unica (WV 13.196b–224b). The self-change involved in cognitive potencies, i.e., the intellect, is discussed in *Ord.* I d.3 p.3 q.2 nn.486–94 (Vat. 3.289–93); II d.3 p.2 q.1 (Vat. 7.517–34); *Op. Ox.* II d.25 q.unica (WV 13.196b–224b), and in the *Questions on Aristotle's "De anima"* q.13 (WV 3.544b–546b). (This last work is considered by some to be spurious.)

The dating of Scotus's work is a major undertaking, but it seems to be a well-founded conclusion that at least *QSM* IX is a late and fully mature work. This is the opinion held by the editors at the Franciscan Institute who are preparing the critical edition of *QSM* for the Vatican Commission. Two pieces of evidence among many: (1) in *QSM* IX qq.3–4 n.5 (WV 7.546a) Scotus refers to his *Tractatus de primo principio*, which has been established to be a late work; (2) in *QSM* IX q.14 n.17 (WV 7.595b) Scotus refers the reader "elsewhere" for a fuller discussion of how heavy bodies are moved downward primarily, and the only such discussion is found in *Ord.* II d.2 p.2 q.6 nn.481–84 (Vat. 7.371–73), which is known to be a late work.

trate on this discussion, giving particular attention to the movement of heavy bodies downward—thought by most medieval philosophers to be the least defensible case of self-change in the physical world, since it involves inanimate objects.

I shall proceed as follows: section 1 takes up the medieval analysis of change, introducing some of Scotus's terminology and distinctions; section 2 presents three arguments against self-change—the Modal Argument, the Primacy Argument, and the Continuity Argument—as well as textual evidence from Aristotle in support of the common position of Scotus's predecessors; section 3 looks at Scotus's "General Argument" for the possibility of self-change; section 4 concerns Scotus's response to the Modal Argument; section 5 explores Scotus's response to the Primacy Argument; section 6 discusses Scotus's response to the Continuity Argument; and section 7 regards Scotus's interpretation of Aristotle.

1. SCOTUS'S ANALYSIS OF CHANGE

Taken most generally, "change" (*mutatio*) refers to any case in which nonbeing is prior to being.[3] In this sense, God's act of creation *ex nihilo* counts as a change, despite the lack of any preexistent persisting substratum. For most purposes, however, a stricter sense of "change" was thought to be more useful, captured in the view that change involves "a movement toward form."[4] Three principles are involved:

1. The *subject* of the change, which is the persisting substratum.
2. A *form* φ.
3. The initial *privation* of φ in the subject, analyzed as follows:
   a. The subject is not φ.
   b. The subject is in potency to φ.

The *terminus a quo* of a change consists in the subject being merely in potency to φ; the *terminus ad quem*, the subject being actually informed by φ. Each terminus is one of the opposite poles of a change. This is the level at which Scotus typically discusses change, and the sense in which he argues for the existence of self-change.[5]

---

[3] Any kind of relation of priority/posteriority will serve here, not merely a temporal relation. This is part of the motivation for Scotus's doctrine of nontemporal "instants of nature."

[4] Scotus discusses this sense of "change" in *Op. Ox.* IV d.11 q.1 art.3 n.5 (WV 17.322a-324b), when he takes up the question of whether transubstantiation is possible; he argues there that transubstantiation does not qualify as a case of change, due to the absence of a persisting substratum. The same point is made in a similar discussion in *QQ* §§10.65–70 (Alluntis 1968, 396–99).

[5] Aristotle's remark in *Phys.* VI.5, 235b6–7, that "change is that by which something is otherwise than it was previously," was understood to be the nominal definition of "change" in this sense.

Because change essentially involves the actualization of a potency, another factor must be added to the analysis:

4. The *cause* of the potency's actualization.[6]

The abstract relation involved in (4) is called "causation" (*causatio*), and the activity corresponding to it is called "causing" (*causare*). The result of causal activity is what is caused (*causatum*), in this case called the "effect." In a case of causation, a cause causes its effect; causation is understood as a relation among things: the father causes his son, and so the father is identified as the cause of his son, the son as the effect. Hence the explanation of a particular change will cite some thing responsible for the change as its cause, where the change is the effect of causal activity.

Scotus often prefers to couch his discussion of change at a slightly more abstract level, speaking of *principles* instead of *causes*. Principles stand to causes as genus to species: causes are only one kind of principle (*Meta*. Δ.1, 1013a17). Roughly, insofar as principles are taken as metaphysical constituents of beings and not as rules or laws (for example, the Principle of Noncontradiction), a principle is the source of some feature or property possessed by a thing. Form and matter are principles of a material substance in this sense. Potency and act may also be construed as principles. Scotus therefore replaces (4) with the following factor required for an explanation of change:

4*. The *principle* of the potency's actualization.

Distinctions parallel to those drawn in the case of causation apply to principles as well, for which Scotus coins an artificial vocabulary.[7] The abstract relation involved in (4*) is called "principiation" (*principiatio*), and the activity corresponding to it is called "principiating" (*principiare*). The result of principiative activity is called the "principiatum" (parallel to the effect in a case of causation). Yet unlike a causal effect, the result of principiative activity need not be some thing that is distinct: the principiatum may be the principiating itself, as in the case of potencies generally called "operations" (potencies whose acts are internal to and perfective of the agent: see QQ §13.47–63). Thus causal explanation is only one variety of principiative explanation; like causal explanation, a principiative explanation of a particular change will cite some thing as the principle responsible for the change, where the change is the result (principiatum) of principiative activity. This level of generality is central to Scotus's analysis of change and his defense of the possibility of self-change, as we shall see.

---

[6] The Greek term τὸ αἴτιον and the Latin term *causa* are each ambiguous between "reason" and "cause." I shall follow the common medieval practice and speak only of causes.

[7] The distinctions that follow deliberately simplify Scotus's discussion in QSM IX qq.3–4 n.3 (WV 7.544a–b). They will be cleaned up at the end of section 4 below.

The actualization of a potency, as described, is a case of change: the existence of the form in the subject depends on principles that are logically, if not temporally, prior.[8] Because the dependence in question need not be temporal, Scotus recognizes the continuous causation or actualization of an attribute (*passio*) in its primary subject as a kind of change as well; such attributes are said to be "coeval" with their subjects. Finally, substantial generation counts as a case of change, one in which the persisting substratum is identified as the matter belonging to the substance, and the form in question is a substantial form.[9]

There are also changes that qualify as cases of motion, namely, whenever the persisting substratum is a substance, and the form in question belongs to one of the categories Quantity, Quality, or Place.[10] The remarks that follow apply generally to self-*changers*, in the sense outlined above, and thereby to the more particular case of self-*movers*.

2. THE CASE AGAINST SELF-CHANGE

The common position of Scotus's predecessors holds that explanations of particular changes never offer the same thing as both the subject and the cause of the change. The impossibility of self-change was thought to be demonstrated by three arguments inspired by, but independent of, Aristotle's texts: the Modal Argument, the Primacy Argument, and the Continuity Argument. In addition, Aristotle's discussion in *Phys.* VII–VIII was interpreted to rule out all cases of putative self-change.

The Modal Argument

The most widely accepted argument for the impossibility of self-change is based on an application of the Law of Noncontradiction to the theory of

---

[8] This fits well with Aristotle's remark that "motion or change" (*motio vel mutatio*) is "the actualization of a potential to the extent that it is potential" in *Phys.* III.1, 201a11–12, where the clause "to the extent that it is potential" was taken to refer to all the states of the subject that are intermediate between each terminus of the change. Scotus, as most medieval philosophers, accepted this remark as the real definition of change, applicable to the more restricted cases of change that also qualify as motions (see below), which themselves were more precisely defined in *Phys.* III.1, 201a28–29, as "the actualization of the mobile insofar as it is mobile." Note that (1)–(3) serve to spell out what it is for a subject to be in potency to a given form.

[9] For Scotus, prime matter has *esse* of itself, and hence may persist throughout a change; this is compatible with the substantial form creating an essential unity with the matter. See *Op. Ox.* II d.12 q.1 and q.2.

[10] Scotus's terminology most likely derives from *Phys.* v.1, 225a34–b3, where Aristotle asserts that changes in quality, quantity, and place are κινήσεις (*motiones*, "motions") in the strict sense, whereas the term μεταβολή (*mutatio*, "change") applies to all these and to substantial generation and corruption as well.

modality, together with the definition of change and two causal axioms. Scotus presents the Modal Argument in *QSM* IX q.14 n.2 (WV 7.583a):

> [The Modal Argument] is taken from *Phys.* III.2 [202a10–13]. . . . The mover moves insofar as it is in act, and the mobile is moved insofar as it is in potency, as is evident from the definition of motion given in [*Phys.* III.1, 201a11–12].[11] However, it is impossible that the same thing be at once in potency and in act with respect to the same and according to the same. Therefore, [nothing can be moved by itself].

The Modal Argument may be reformulated at a more general level as follows:

> [A1] The *subject* of a change must be in potency to φ.
>
>   (definition of change)
>
> [A2] Causes must "contain" their effects.   (Causal Axiom 1)
>
> [A3] Hence the *cause* of a change must be in act with respect to φ.
>
>   ([A2], definition of change)
>
> [A4] Proximate causes must be spatiotemporally concurrent with their immediate effects.   (Causal Axiom 2)
>
> [A5] It is impossible for one and the same thing to be at once in potency and act with respect to the same and according to the same.
>
>   (application of the Law of Noncontradiction to potency and act)

> *Therefore*: Anything that changes must be changed by another.

Scotus accepts the two causal axioms used in the Modal Argument. The justification for [A2] is derived from the principle *nemo dat qui non habet*, itself derived from the metaphysical first principle *ex nihilo nihil fit*: if the effect did not preexist in the cause, then its existence is something completely new, not indebted to what preceded it, and thereby incapable of explanation—which is impossible. Now the agent that induces a form in a recipient subject has some causal power to do so, and causal powers are themselves rooted in forms. Hence an agent exercises its causality by possessing some form in virtue of which it is able to induce a form in a recipient subject. If the induced form is of the same species as the form that informs the agent causally responsible for the effect, the causality involved is said to be *univocal*—otherwise, the causality is said to be *equivocal*, as when the architect has in her imagination the form of the house she is going to build (the form of the house is "contained" or "preexists" in the imagination). No matter which kind of causality is involved, [A2] must hold in all cases.

  The justification for [A4] depends upon "cause" and "effect" being relative terms, much as "master" and "slave" are. The requirements of proximity and immediacy serve to rule out any kind of separation between

---

[11] See notes 4 and 8 above.

the cause and the effect: if there were some spatial or temporal separation, there would have to be some means whereby the causal power of the agent could be transmitted across the intervening spatial or temporal medium—but then this means itself, or the intervening medium, would be identified as the proximate cause of the effect.[12] (This argument rules out action at a distance: see *Phys.* vii.2, 243a3–4.) The link between the proximate cause and its immediate effect is a real relation of causation, where each terminus of the relation must be copresent with the other. Just as a master is not in fact a master unless he is the master of some slave, so too a proximate cause is not in fact a proximate cause unless there is some immediate effect it produces. Thus [A4] must hold in all cases.[13]

The causal axioms, then, are unexceptionable; the definition of change is not open to question; the Law of Noncontradiction is indisputable. Hence the Modal Argument was taken to prove that, for any given change, there must always be an independent agent that is the cause of the change. This conclusion was reinforced by its close similarity to another fundamental causal principle, namely that nothing is the cause of itself, which would apparently be violated by the existence of self-change. Therefore, putative cases of self-change, such as the downward motion of a stone, must be explained by citing some extrinsic causal factor responsible for the change in question.

The Primacy Argument

Scotus states the Primacy Argument against self-motion in *QSM* ix q.14 n.2 (WV 7.583a):[14]

---

[12] In *QSM* ix q.14 n.4 (WV 7.585a), Scotus mentions an objection to self-change based on this point, namely that "the agent should be in close proximity to the patient, and thereby distinct in position [from the patient], so that the same thing cannot be related to itself." His response in n.5 is that identity satisfies [A4] even better than close proximity does (WV 7.585b).

[13] The spatiotemporal concurrence of cause and effect was also taken to be grounded on Aristotle. See *Phys.* ii.3, 195b17–20, and *Meta.* Δ.2, 1014a21–23, which Scotus cites in *Ord.* ii d.2 p.2 q.6 n.453 (Vat. 7.358) as follows: "The efficient cause in act, and what is caused in act, simultaneously exist and do not exist (*simul sunt et non sunt*)." Scotus also adds another argument: "The point is also clear—even if there were no authoritative passage [from Aristotle]—for an obvious reason: what does not exist, when it does not exist, does not produce something for *esse*." There is a looser way of talking, in which the object that is identified as the effect can persist without the object that is the cause—the son may outlive the father, the slave the master—but, strictly speaking, these locutions are improper. The son ceases to be a son when the father dies, though the thing that was the son continues to exist, and likewise for the slave.

[14] Scotus sketches the same argument, even more briefly, in *Ord.* ii d.2 p.2 q.6 n.442 (Vat. 7.350–51). The medieval Latin text of the *Physics* was continuous, not divided as Ross proposes in his edition of the text (with the *textus alter* of bk. vii).

[The Primacy Argument] is taken from Aristotle, *Phys.* vii.1 [241b34–242a17]. Nothing is moved by itself primarily, since then it would not come to rest at the rest of another [thing], because [it would not come to rest] at the rest of a part. For everything mobile has a part, and, that [part] being at rest, it is clear that the whole is not moved primarily. [Therefore, nothing can be moved by itself.]

This argument is "taken" from Aristotle only in a loose sense. Scotus derives the qualification "primarily" from its single occurrence at *Phys.* vii.1, 242a43, where Aristotle remarks that something is not moved per se and primarily (ὥστε οὐ καθ᾽ αὑτὸ κινηθήσεται καὶ πρῶτον), and Scotus's later discussion of the argument, considered in section 5 below, turns on its precise sense. The remainder of the Primacy Argument is derived from a combination of 241b34–242a3 and 242a45–49, producing a composite argument against self-motion based on Aristotle's text that may be reformulated, with several implicit steps spelled out, as follows:

[B1] Anything that is moved by itself primarily is unaffected by the fact that another thing[15] is at rest (τῷ ἄλλο ἠρεμεῖν = *ad quietem alterius*). (definition of "primarily")

[B2] Everything capable of motion is divisible (διαιρετόν), that is, it must have parts, and so be a whole. (hypothesis)

[B3] Any part of a whole that is capable of motion being at rest, the whole is not moved primarily.
  (definition of "primarily" and "motion")

[B4] Wholes are not predicated of their parts.
  (definition of "whole" and "part")

[B5] A part is "another thing" than its whole, that is, parts differ from their wholes. (by [B4])

[B6] Anything that is moved by itself primarily is unaffected by the fact that a part of it is at rest. (by [B1], [B2], and [B5])

[B7] Even if some part of a whole that is capable of motion were at rest, the whole could be moved by itself primarily. (by [B6])

[B8] Even if some part of a whole that is capable of motion were at rest, the whole could be moved primarily. (by [B7])

[B9] If some part of a whole that is capable of motion were at rest, then the whole both *could* be moved primarily and *could not* be moved primarily. (by [B3] and [B8])

Therefore: No whole is moved by itself primarily.

The Primacy Argument, however, permits something to be moved by itself "nonprimarily"—either accidentally or incidentally—in that the quan-

---

[15] For example, a proper part of something counts as "another thing," a fact that will be important in Scotus's interpretation of the Primacy Argument in section 5 below.

titative whole that is in motion is said to be changed "by itself" because one part of the whole acts upon another part. Thus at least some putative cases of self-motion can be analyzed as cases wherein distinct physical parts of a given whole interact.[16] In *QSM* IX q.14 n.11 (WV 7.590a), Scotus points out that defenders of the common position use this strategy to explain what occurs when an animal walks or jumps:

> The motion is composed of pushing and pulling, in such a way that the posterior part [of the animal] pushes the anterior [part of the animal], and this push brings the posterior [part] along after itself, and that [part], having been brought along, pushes again, and thus [motion] comes about continuously—in the case of ordinary walking about as well as in the case of jumping. This is manifest to sense-experience in the (unexpected!) case of the inchworm.

Hence the demand for an extrinsic causal factor to explain a putative case of self-change may be moderated to the demand that really distinct interacting parts of the subject be specified, and this permits a nonprimary kind of self-change to obtain in the world.

The Continuity Argument

Scotus states the Continuity Argument in *QSM* IX q.14 n.1 (WV 7.582b):

> Again, [the common position] is argued for by means of [the Continuity Argument] that is suggested in *De an.* II.5 [417a3–9]. For [if something could change itself], then it would always act in such a way if it is a natural agent, because that action would not depend on anything external [to the agent]. And in virtue of this [fact], the same thing is [both] the agent and the patient (*passum*). [But] it is clear that the consequent, [namely, "the agent would always act in such a way"], is false. [Therefore, nothing can change itself.]

The consequent is false because there are examples of noncontinuous change. Whereas continuous activity—unless interfered with—seems a plausible characteristic to ascribe to, say, the movement of heavy bodies downward, or to hot water cooling itself off, it does not apply to animal locomotion: cats walk, but they also change direction, and indeed stop walking; frogs jump, but not always. Yet if self-change is admitted, one and the same thing—the frog—is the cause of both its jumping and its resting. This possibility raises two problems about the nature of physical explanation.

First, an appeal to one and the same thing as the cause of incompatible

---

[16] Scotus explicitly links the conclusion "anything that moves itself is divided into two [constituents], of which one is primarily the mover and the other primarily what is moved" with *Phys.* VIII.5, 257b12–13: see *Ord.* II d.2 p.2 q.6 n.442 (Vat. 7.350). This latter discussion, he holds, depends on the Primacy Argument for its force.

conditions seems to be explanatorily vacuous, tantamount to saying that something changed from one condition to another either for no reason at all or just because it did so. But if this is the case, then the same problem applies to simple cases of apparently continuous self-change: the stone moves downward because it is in the nature of stones to move downward—and this seems to be no explanation at all, but, like Molière's doctor, "explains" the fact that a certain herb produces sleep by saying that it has a *virtus dormitiva*. Hence self-change explanations fail to be genuine explanations.

Second, there seems to be no difference between the case of the frog's change from jumping to resting and the case in which the water in a pot placed on a stove changes from tepid to boiling. If self-change explanations are permitted, why do we not say that the water changes itself from tepid to boiling, rather than claiming that it is the causal activity of the stove's heat that causes the change? Self-change threatens to undermine particular causal accounts of natural phenomena by the possibility that there need be no causal links between objects in order for changes to take place—the world could be an indeterministic muddle, with no cases of real change in it (apparent cases of change being explained rather by self-change on the part of the putative patient).[17] Thus there is no principled way to distinguish genuine from merely apparent cases of transeunt causality, if self-change is admitted.

ARISTOTLE ON SELF-CHANGE

In addition to the three arguments presented above, self-change was taken to be directly ruled out by Aristotle's texts in a variety of ways. Scotus

---

[17] This seems to be the intent of the second objection to Scotus's fourth general conclusion, reported in *QSM* IX q.14 n.14 (WV 7.593a): "Nature has proportioned the active and the passive in the universe to be not always the same [thing] with respect to itself, but to be different with respect to the other [of the pair], as there seems to be a greater connection among things [in this way]. And so in every case [a greater connection] will be granted [to obtain] with respect to possible perfection in whatever [situation] in which there is some agent, but [the agent] is different from that [which is able to be the patient—reading *passibili* for *possibili*]. Confirmation: why did nature not give to everything a principle that is active with respect to every perfection possible for it, so that the connection among things based upon mutual action and being acted upon would thereby be taken away?" The initial claim "to be not always the same [thing] with respect to itself, but to be different with respect to the other [of the pair]" seems to mean that it is not always the case that one and the same thing is both active with respect to itself and passive with respect to itself, but a thing that is active differs as regards what is passive with respect to its activity and that a thing that is passive differs as regards what is active with respect to its passivity. Briefly: nature has arranged things so that at least in some cases matching agent-patient roles devolve upon really different things, which produces genuine unity by a reciprocal causal "connection among things."

mentions two remarks that seem to cut against the possibility of self-change in general in *QSM* IX q.14 n.1 (WV 7.582b). First, natural unity is incompatible with self-change:

> In the text of *Meta.* Θ.1 [1046a28–29], the Philosopher says: "Nothing is acted upon by itself, insofar as it is naturally unified,[18] for it is one thing and not another." Hence it can be asked whether something can be moved by itself. . . . On the basis of Aristotle's text, [it is clear that nothing can change itself].

Second, since the potency for change is an active potency, it cannot operate on itself (by definition):

> Likewise, in [*Meta.* Θ.1, 1046a19–28], it appears that a proof derived from the definition of [active] potency is suggested.[19] For [active potency] is the principle of transforming *another*. [Therefore, nothing can change itself.]

Moreover, if we consider only the particular kind of self-change that is involved in the downward motion of heavy bodies, our test case, Aristotle seems to rule out self-motion in the *Physics*, as Scotus recognizes in an objection reported in *Ord.* II d.2 p.2 q.6 n.445 (Vat. 7.352–53):[20]

> [The claim that heavy bodies are self-movers] is false and against the Philosopher's intent in *Phys.* VIII.4 [255a3–18], it seems, where he seems to produce four arguments specifically against this—[namely] (i) due to the fact that the heavy [body] is not an animal; (ii) due to the fact that it cannot bring itself to a halt; (iii) because it cannot move itself with diverse motions; (iv) because it is continuous (i.e., of the same disposition in the part and in the whole) and as such cannot move itself—and [furthermore], in resolving the question, [Aristotle] says that "natural things only have a principle of being acted upon in respect of motion, and not of doing [anything]" ([*Phys.* VIII.4, 255b29–31]).

These four arguments also have a role to play in the larger argument of the *Physics*: the rejection of self-motion for "natural things" is part of the argument for the principle that everything in motion is moved by another, which plays a central role in Aristotle's regress argument for the existence of the Prime Mover.

Given the argumentative and textual support for the common position,

---

[18] "Naturally unified": *simul natum*, which translates συμπέφυκεν (literally, "growing together"). See *Meta.* Z.16, 1040b15.

[19] The "definition" of active potency is given in *Meta.* Θ.1, 1046a9–11, which Scotus cites as "the principle of transforming another insofar as it is another": *principium transmutandi aliud inquantum aliud*. There are some complicated textual questions with regard to this passage and Scotus's response to it. See the discussion at the beginning of section 7 below.

[20] Scotus refers to the same arguments in *QSM* IX q.14 n.3 (WV 7.583b). The recognition of four distinct arguments in Aristotle's text is not original to Scotus; see, for example, Aquinas's *Commentary on Aristotle's "Physics"* 8.4, *lectio* 7, §§6–8.

Scotus's predecessors concluded that self-change, at least in the case of natural phenomena, was impossible and explanatorily vacuous, diametrically opposed to the received view of the way the world works. Hence, prior to Scotus, most philosophical discussions focused on two issues. First, it was debated whether the arguments that rule out self-change in the physical world also rule it out in the case of nonphysical (or "spiritual") causes such as the will, a point on which there was no consensus.[21] Second, physical investigation sought to identify the really distinct agent and patient in natural phenomena, such as the downward motion of heavy bodies, without having recourse to self-change. Scotus's defense of the reality of self-change as a widespread feature of the physical world was a startling break with tradition.

3. SCOTUS'S GENERAL ARGUMENT FOR SELF-CHANGE

Scotus's procedure is first to argue that self-change is possible in general, thereafter to consider the reality of self-change in particular cases, and finally to refute the argumentative and textual support for the common position. His "General Argument" for self-change is presented in *QSM* IX q.14 n.4 (WV 7.584b–585a):

> Anything active looks to a *kind* of passive thing, not to *this* passive thing, as its primary object. For example, what in general is able to heat, as well as any given thing that is able to heat, looks to what is able to be heated in general as its primary object, not to this or that [thing that is able to be heated]. Contrariwise, what is passive, e.g., what is able to be heated—and this as either [what is able to be heated] in general or any given thing that is able to be heated—likewise looks to what is able to heat as its primary object, not to this or that [thing that is able to heat], but [to what is able to heat] in general. It follows from these points that whatever is contained under the primary object of anything is a per se object of the same [thing]: whatever is able to heat looks to whatever is able to be heated as its per se object, and, conversely, whatever is able to be heated [looks to] whatever is able to heat [as its per se object]. But it

---

[21] If all change is due to an agent that is really distinct from what is in change, it seems to follow that the will is not the originator of its own acts. But then how can a person be held morally responsible for these selfsame acts? This seems to be the problem Scotus has in mind when he writes in *QSM* IX q.14 n.13 (WV 7.592b): "Nor do those [philosophers] holding [the will] to be purely passive, [moving] by the object itself [alone], seem to be able to preserve genuine or full freedom in man, but merely, it seems, the necessity of proceeding in such a way as heat also does in heating, or only being able to be otherwise by chance." The characterization of the will as "purely passive" is clearly a reference to Godfrey of Fontaines (see note 1 above). Also, see Calvin Normore's contribution to this volume for a discussion of free will and self-change in the Middle Ages.

is possible that (i) something be active regarding *A* in the same way in which something else is active regarding *A*, and (ii) the same [thing] be passive regarding *A* just as something else is passive regarding *A*. Therefore, that thing in the *ratio* "active" has itself as object in the *ratio* "passive" just as much as [it has] something else [that is passive as its object].

Scotus's General Argument, stripped to its essentials, may be reformulated as follows:

[1] The primary object of a potency for φ, whether active or passive, must be common.

[2] Whatever is contained under the primary object of a potency must be a per se object of the same potency.

[3] It is possible for one and the same thing to have an active potency for φ and a passive potency for φ.

Therefore: It is possible for one and the same thing to be the passive per se object of its own active causal potency.

The argument is called "general" because it only establishes the *possibility* of self-change, not its reality. The intent of the General Argument should be clear: potencies are directed toward kinds of individual, and there is no reason why an individual with a given potency should not fall under the general kind toward which the potency is directed, and so possibly be the recipient of its own causal activity. In order to appreciate how the General Argument rigorously proves its conclusion, we have to take a closer look at four technical notions: (1) the distinction between active and passive potencies; (2) the per se object of a potency; (3) a *ratio*; and (4) the primary object of a potency.

The distinction between active and passive potencies is roughly equivalent to the modern distinction between *abilities* and *capacities*, respectively: an ability or active potency enables its possessor to do something, whereas a capacity or passive potency enables its possessor to be the recipient of some action. (The locution "potency for φ" is deliberately ambiguous between an active or a passive potency.) All potencies, whether active or passive, are defined by their corresponding actualizations—what the potency is a potency *for*. An active potency, when actualized, operates on a patient; a passive potency, when actualized, is operated on by an agent.

Whatever most strictly counts as the patient (in the case of an active potency) or the agent (in the case of a passive potency) is the "per se object" of the potency.[22] For example, when Jones sees a black sheep, his passive potency of vision is actualized by the particular blackness of the sheep's

---

[22] The notion of a "per se object" of a potency is derived from Aristotle's discussion in *De an.* II of the "objects" of the various senses, which are themselves potencies of the sensitive soul.

wool, strictly speaking, which is therefore the per se object of his vision; the sheep itself is "seen" only accidentally or incidentally. Hence the per se object of a potency is something particular, either a particular substance or a particular accident in the world.[23]

A *ratio* is a generalization of the strict notion of "definition": a *ratio*, like a definition, picks out the feature or set of features that make something to be what it is.[24] All definitions are *rationes*, but not conversely: there are things that lack strict Aristotelian definitions, yet have an "intelligible content," a set of features that make them what they are—accidental unities, the four causes, potencies, and the like—and these have *rationes*. A potency cannot have a strict Aristotelian definition, but it does have a *ratio*, and the *ratio* of a given potency spells out that in virtue of which it is the potency it is (for example, the potency for φ rather than the potency for ψ).

By combining notions (2) and (3) above, we can ask what the *ratio* of the per se object of a given potency is—the feature or set of features in virtue of which the per se object of a given potency *is* the per se object of that potency—and so work toward a definition of the "primary object" of a potency. Whereas a per se object is always something particular, such as the blackness of the sheep's wool, the *ratio* is a feature that may be common to many particular objects. By definition, the *ratio* according to which the blackness of the sheep's wool actualizes Jones's passive potency of vision is the feature in virtue of which the blackness of the sheep's wool actualizes Jones's vision. In this example, it is the *ratio* "black" (since Jones can see all black things) or, trivially, the *ratio* "visible" (since Jones can see all visible things). The *ratio* of the per se object of a given potency must be intimately related to the *ratio* of the potency itself—that which makes the potency what it is. To specify adequately the *ratio* of the per se object of a potency, however, is not a matter of simply reading it off the *ratio* of the potency: to say that Jones's vision is actualized by anything visible is true but trivial,

---

[23] Scotus holds that there are particular accidents, that is, individuals in categories other than Substance. Accidents are not individuated by their bearers, however, because an accident need not inhere in anything (as witnessed in the Eucharist): it is by nature able to inhere in a substance, and in the ordinary course of events actually does so inhere, but it is capable of independent being. An absolute accident, for Scotus, is individuated by a haecceity, by its very "thisness"; a nonabsolute accident by the particulars it involves.

[24] The term *ratio* translates λόγος, and shares many of its characteristics and ambiguities. Just as definitions have scope, so too do *rationes*: we may speak of "the definition of man" or "the definition *man*," and equally of "the *ratio* of the active" or "the *ratio* 'active.'" The features picked out by a *ratio*, like the features picked out by a definition, are those in virtue of which something is what it is, and hence are the features that make it intelligible. A *ratio* therefore has some resemblance to an abstraction-operator: the *ratio* "black" picks out the property of blackness, for example, and the *ratio* "man" picks out rationality and animality. Concrete objects possess the features by which they fall under a *ratio*—the sheep falls under the *ratio* "black," because blackness inheres in the sheep, in virtue of which the sheep is black.

since "visible" is a relational term that means "able to actualize the faculty of vision."[25] Nor is it a matter of simply reading it off the per se object: to say that Jones sees the blackness of the sheep's wool in virtue of the *ratio* "black" is equally true and equally trivial, since it does not point to any more general feature.[26] Rather, an adequate assignment of the *ratio* of the per se object of a given potency specifies the most common nonrelational feature in virtue of which something is a per se object of the potency. Specifying this feature depends on the *ratio* of the potency itself. Such an adequate assignment is what Scotus calls the "primary object" of a given potency, as he says in *Ord.* 1 d.3 p.1 q.3 n.187 (Vat. 3.112–13):[27]

> The [feature] that is adequate to the potency, on the basis of the *ratio* of the potency, is assigned as the "primary object" of the potency.

For example, the *ratio* "color" specifies the most common nonrelational feature in virtue of which anything can be the per se object of the passive

[25] In *Ord.* 1 d.3 p.1 q.3 n.183 (Vat. 3.111), just before the definition of "primary object" cited below in the text, Scotus rules out any relational specification of the *ratio* of the per se object of a potency, as follows: "I state that the '*ratio* of the object' is that according to which the object is capable of moving the potency [to act], as the *ratio* of the active, or of acting, is said to be that form according to which the agent acts. Furthermore, the *ratio* of the object cannot be a relationship to a potency. The Philosopher also speaks in this way in *De an.* II.7 ([418a26–30]), where he assigns the primary object of vision. He says: 'That of which it is the sight, e.g., [the sight] of the object, is the visible,' [and again (*De an.* II.6, 418a10–17)]: '[Yet] not *per se primo modo* but rather *secundo modo*, such that it is put into the *ratio* of the visible.' But if the formal *ratio* of the object of a potency were a relationship to such a potency, then the primary object of vision would be the visible *per se primo modo*, since visibility itself would be the formal *ratio* of the object. And then it would be easy to assign primary objects, since the primary object of any potency would be correlative to such a potency, e.g., vision 'the visible,' hearing 'the hearable.' And the Philosopher does not assign primary objects of potencies in this way, but rather [assigns] some absolute [things], e.g., vision color, hearing sound, and the like." An "absolute thing" is a nonrelational item, either a substance or a quantity or a quality. Scotus in fact uses the relational specification of the primary object of a potency in his presentation of the General Argument, but it is clear that it is only by way of example. One thing is predicable of another *per se primo modo* when the predicate is contained in the definition of the subject, and *per se secundo modo* when the subject is contained in the definition of the predicate.

[26] In a later annotation to *Ord.* 1 d.3 p.1 qq.1–2 n.24 (Vat. 3.17), Scotus remarks: "The per se object [of a potency] is clear from the acts of the potency; the primary object, however, is derived from many per se objects, because [the primary object] is adequate." Scotus clearly has the commonness of the *ratio* in mind here when he says "adequate."

[27] Scotus takes the notion of "primacy" at work here from *Po. An.* I.4, 73b32–74a3, where Aristotle writes: "An attribute belongs to a subject universally when it can be shown to belong to anything whatsoever belonging to that subject and to belong to that subject primarily (πρώτου). . . . The universal is that which can be shown in anything whatsoever and primarily." In *Ord.* 1 d.3 p.1 qq.1–2 n.49 (Vat. 3.49), Scotus explicitly states that "primarily" in this passage expresses priority "in the order of adequacy," which he also terms "the order of precise causality"—a sense he will use extensively in his discussion of the Primacy Argument (see section 5).

potency of vision, and is therefore the primary object of vision—a fact that can be established on the basis of the *ratio* of vision.

The rigorous force of the General Argument should now be apparent. The notions of "per se object" and "primary object" can be applied to both active and passive potencies, and specifically to active causal powers and passive potencies to receive causal activities. The premises [1] and [2] hold by definition: the primary object of any potency whatsoever must be common, since a *ratio* is able to apply to many particulars, whether it actually does so or not; the features specified by the *ratio* are predicable *in quid* of these particulars, and hence they are per se objects of the potency.[28] For example, it seems plausible that all bodies can be heated, and that at least some bodies actually heat others (such as a brick recently removed from an oven). Hence *body* is, or at least falls under, the primary object of both the active causal power for heating and the passive potency to be heated. Thus a hot brick can exercise its active causal powers by heating up some body, which will be its per se object. But that is compatible with the hot brick itself having the passive potency to be made even hotter—say, by putting it back in the oven—and thus to be the per se object of the active causal power of the oven to heat things up, including bricks. Hence it is possible for one and the same thing to be both active, as regards the induction of a form in an object, and passive, as regards being receptive of the same form in itself, as [3] says. One and the same thing can fall under both the *ratio* "active" and the *ratio* "passive." Thus it is at least *possible* that one and the same thing be the recipient of the form that it induces in another.[29]

Now the example of the hot brick obscures an important point—not least because bricks do not heat themselves up! The reason they do not do so is that the induction of the form *heat* in a recipient subject takes place through the possession of the same kind of form in the hot brick—that is, the causality in question here is univocal. More exactly, causation is univo-

[28] To be predicable *in quid* is to be predicable of something as a way of spelling out *what* the subject is—a form of essential and substantial predication. Scotus asserts that [1] and [2] are clear "on the basis of the primary relation that holds among the common [terms]," i.e., are true by definition, in *QSM* ix q.14 n.4 (WV 7.585a). He states a version of [2] with respect to cognitive potencies in *Ord.* i d.3 p.1 q.3 n.118 (Vat. 3.73): "Whatever is known per se by a cognitive potency is either its primary object or is contained under its primary object." It should be noted, however, that Scotus's views are more complex than I have made them out to be in this discussion. In *Ord.* i d.3 p.1 q.3 n.127 (Vat. 3.79–80) and in *QQ* §5.26 (Alluntis 1968, 179), Scotus distinguishes two kinds of "adequacy" for the primary object of a potency: (1) according to commonness, such that the primary object can be predicated of the per se object of the potency; (2) according to virtuality, such that the primary object has the power to produce all the acts of the potency in question. In (1), the "object" may be a common *ratio* rather than a particular object, as color is the primary object of vision; in (2), it may be either common or particular.

[29] This argument is adapted from Scotus's proof of the minor premise of the General Argument in *QSM* ix q.14 n.4 (WV 7.585a–b).

cal when the induced form is specifically the same as a form contained in the cause, and equivocal otherwise.[30] Self-change is only possible in cases of equivocal causality, as Scotus argues in *Ord.* 1 d.3 p.3 q.2 n.514 (Vat. 3.303–4):[31]

When it is argued that the "possible" [as in the conclusion of the General Argument] cannot have any causality, since nothing acts upon itself—
I reply that the proposition ["Nothing acts upon itself"] is only true as regards a *univocal* agent, and that the proof of [this proposition], [namely] that then the same thing would be in both act and potency, goes through only when the agent acts univocally, i.e., [the agent] induces in the patient a form of the same *ratio* as that [form] through which [the agent] acts. For if something were to act upon itself in this manner, then it would have at once a form of the same *ratio* as that toward which it is moved, and when it is moved to that [form] it would also lack it [by the definition of "change"]; therefore it would at once have it and not have it—at least, this follows for two forms of the same species, or for the same [form]. However, in *equivocal* agents (i.e., in those agents that do not act by means of forms of the same *ratio* as that toward which they act) the proposition that nothing moves itself has no necessity, nor does its proof, [namely] that something would be in potency and in act in respect of the same, establish anything: for in this case the agent is not formally in act in the way in which the patient is formally in potency.

In order for there to be a case of change, much less self-change, the subject must initially be deprived of the form, as stated in (3a) in section 1 above; hence univocal self-change is impossible. Equivocal self-change, however, is another matter.[32]

---

[30] If the induced form is numerically the same as the form contained in the cause, it is a fortiori specifically the same, and hence the causation is univocal. (See note 31.) Scotus is only concerned with specific sameness, since he holds that the objects of potencies are all specific in nature. It should be noted, though, that Scotus leaves the sense in which the form is "contained" in the cause deliberately vague: a form may be contained in the cause by informing the cause (either as a substantial or an accidental form), by being present in the imagination (as with an artificer), or, in general, by being able to be produced by another form that is more "perfect" or "eminent." This allows [A2] to be satisfied in the case of equivocal causation. See the discussion in section 4 of virtual containment.

[31] Scotus initially asserts that the requirement of equivocal causality is clear on the basis of the General Argument, in *QSM* IX q.14 n.6 (WV 7.586a), but then goes on to prove it as his Second Particular Conclusion in n.7 (WV 7.586b). His proof—that if the causality were univocal then there would be two distinct individuals of the same species in a single subject—is based upon his rejection of this point in *QSM* V q.7 (WV 7.232a–246a). In this discussion, however, Scotus argues that this is *naturally* impossible because it cannot come about through change, a point he makes more clearly in the passage cited from the *Ordinatio*. God could make two individuals of the same species in a single subject, but only through creation and not through change.

[32] Scotus offers a confirmation of the General Argument explicitly based on equivocal

Therefore, self-change is in general possible when the following two conditions are satisfied, as Scotus writes in his First General Conclusion in *QSM* IX q.14 n.5 (WV 7.586a):

> And so it should be held as a rule that, in every case, something is only able to act upon itself when those two [conditions] occur together—namely (i) that it possesses a form that is a principle of acting equivocally, and, along with this [condition], (ii) that it is receptive of the terminus of such an action.

What kinds of self-change are possible? Scotus rules out cases of substantial generation: nothing can be the cause of its substantial form.[33] It is possible, however, for growth and locomotion to be the result of self-change: neither quantity nor place is an "active" form, that is, a form possessing active causal powers, and hence these forms can only be induced by equivocal causality. Alteration (qualitative change) may also be a case of self-change: some qualities are "nonactive," and other active qualities may be produced by equivocal causes.[34]

---

causality, in which the possibility of self-change is analogous to the possibility of two objects each inducing the same form in the other, in *QSM* IX q.14 n.5 (WV 7.586a): "If *A* per se were a form that is active with respect to *B*, and *A* were to exist in *C*, nobody denies that it is active with respect to *B* coming to exist in *D*. And, conversely, if *A* were to exist in *D*, it would be a principle that is active with respect to *B* in *C*. Therefore, if *A* exists in *C* and in *D*, then *C* as well as *D* would be in potency to *B*, and both *C* and *D* will mutually act upon one another according to *A*, mutually producing *B* in one another. Yet [this first case] ([namely] that the same thing in the same respect is [both] active and passive according to the same) appears to be unacceptable to the extent that [the second case] ([namely] that the same thing [is both active and passive] with respect to itself) [is unacceptable]. (For it is similar to other [situations]: just as nothing is the cause of itself, so too a circle among causes, so that the same thing in the same respect is both the cause and what is caused, is not possible.) Therefore, if the first case is possible, then the second case [is possible] as well." Mutual equivocal causality of the sort described here is conceptually on a par with self-change: if an object *C* has a form *A* that equivocally causes the form *B* in a recipient subject, then it is possible for *C* to be the subject in which *B* is induced. The loop through a second object, *D*, is unnecessary. There seems to be a problem, says Scotus, only because the case at first glance seems to be similar to a different situation, one that is prohibited by the principle that nothing causes itself (as noted in discussing the conclusion of the Modal Argument in section 2 above).

[33] It is clear that nothing can be the cause of the substantial form that it possesses, for that would be an instance of univocal causality. But why could an object not be the cause of having a new substantial form, one "higher" in the hierarchy of substantial forms? Scotus's reason, which may resonate all the way to Descartes, is presented in *QSM* IX q.14 n.7 (WV 7.586b): "No [substantial form] can newly advene so that it makes a composite that is one per se, unless that [form] is more perfect than any given beingness (*entitas*) preceding it. However, the more imperfect is not a principle that is active with respect to the more perfect." Scotus does not consider the case of substantial corruption—something causing itself to have a "lower" substantial form—since the explanation of corruption does not parallel that of generation: corruption is essentially a passive process undergone by the subject.

[34] Scotus's claims about quantities, qualities, and places are put forward in *QSM* IX q.14 n.6 (WV 7.586b). The notion of an "active" quality is taken from Aristotle, *GC* II.2, 329b19–22.

4. SCOTUS'S RESPONSE TO THE MODAL ARGUMENT

According to Scotus, then, self-change is possible when one and the same thing both has a form φ that grounds the active causal potency to cause equivocally another form φ, and also is in passive potency to receive φ. The conclusion of the General Argument directly contradicts the conclusion of the Modal Argument. Where is the flaw in the Modal Argument?

Scotus holds that [A5], the application of the Law of Noncontradiction to potency and act, is the culprit: for Scotus, "potency" and "act" carry several senses, not all of which are incompatible with each other. Further-more, the sense in which [A5] fails is paralleled by a failure of [A3] for the equivocal causality required for self-change. In general, then, the Modal Argument goes astray by conflating various distinct ways in which some-thing can be in potency and in act; the sense in which [A3] and [A5] hold do not exclude the possibility of self-change. A brief sketch of Scotus's account of modality, presented at length in *QSM* IX qq.1–4, will provide the theo-retical background relevant to Scotus's response to the Modal Argument.

Scotus holds that the central distinction in the analysis of modality is between a modality as a *mode of being* (which we may call "modal" modality) and a modality as a *principle* (which we may call "principiative" modality), as he states in *QSM* IX qq.1–2 n.2 (WV 7.530b):

> It is necessary to draw a distinction with regard to potency: in one way, "potency" expresses a certain mode of being; in another way, ["potency"] specifically brings in the *ratio* of a principle.

The two kinds of modality may be intertranslatable, but they are nonethe-less distinct.[35] Thus the pure modal contexts,

$$x \text{ is in potency to } \phi,$$
$$x \text{ is in act as to } \phi,$$

are therefore ambiguous, depending on the kind of modality they are taken to involve.[36] We shall consider each kind of modality in turn.

---

[35] Scotus comments on their intertranslatability immediately after his statement of the distinction, in *QSM* IX qq.1–2 (WV 7.530b): "Now it is doubtful on which of these the name ['potency'] was initially imposed and thereafter transferred to the other.

"Yet if ['potency'] was initially imposed in order to signify a certain mode of being, [then], since this is suitable to such a being only through some principle belonging to it by means of which it can exist, the name 'potency' can appropriately be transferred to the principle, as [transferred] to that by which the possible can exist—[taking] 'by which' [in 'that by which the possible can exist'] not formally, but rather causally.

"Likewise, if ['potency'] was initially imposed on the principle by means of which a thing can exist, it can be transferred in order to signify generally a mode of being (*modus essendi*) similar to that which the *principiatum* has in the principle."

Strictly speaking, the two kinds of modality are distinct, but they are connected in the manner that Scotus describes such that the same term can apply to both with equal propriety.

[36] Ascriptions of potency are inherently *relational*, as Scotus argues in *QSM* IX qq.1–2 n.4

Modal Modality

Scotus discusses modality as a mode of being in *QSM* IX qq.1–2. A "mode of being" is a *way* in which something can be said to be, either as a "potential being" or as an "actual being." If the pure contexts above are interpreted as referring to modal modality, they could naturally be reformulated as the following:

x is a potential φ,

x is an actual φ,

and from this reformulation it is but a short step to:

φ*x* is a potential being,

φ*x* is an actual being.

Scotus holds that there are two distinct conditions that have to be satisfied in order for φ*x* to be a potential being in the sense relevant to metaphysics:[37]

(WV 7.532a–b): "For some [things] to be opposed 'relatively' can be understood in two ways: either (a) mutually, namely that each has a relationship *per se* to the other, or (b) nonmutually. . . .

"Now act and potency are *not* opposed [mutually]. The reason for this is that, because such [mutually related] things are simultaneous in nature and definition, it would then follow that act would not be prior in *ratio* to potency; neither would the *ratio* of potency be taken from act rather than conversely, which is contrary to Aristotle (*Meta.* Θ.8).

"[Act and potency] *are* opposed [nonmutually]. The reason for this is that, in considering the significate of the name 'potency,' it is clear that 'it expresses an order to act,' and the order is essentially a respect to act. Therefore, insofar as [potency] is the kind of thing that has a respect essentially to something else, it is not opposed to that 'something else' except relatively. But the converse [of this claim] is not the case, since the ratio of act is absolute, as has been proved from the Philosopher's intent ([*Meta.* Θ.8]). Furthermore, there is a clear example of how there can per se be a relation to something absolute according to the Philosopher in *Meta.* Δ.15 [1021a29–32]: knowledge is essentially referred to the knowable, but not conversely; therefore, the knowable is absolute, insofar as there is a relation of knowledge to it. Indeed, *being referred to* is not the same as *being the terminus of a relation*." Such "nonmutual relations" fall under Aristotle's third class of relatives (*Meta.* Δ.15). For a clear and sensible discussion of Scotus's theory of relations, see Henninger 1989, chap. 5.

[37] Scotus formulates these two conditions in *QSM* IX qq.1–2 n.5 (WV 7.533a): "Metaphysical potency taken precisely, namely as it abstracts from all natural potency, is founded precisely in an essence that is called a possible being (*possibilis esse*), and the order of that essence to *esse* is as though to a terminus. . . . Furthermore, each of the two, [namely (i) the essence that is a possible being, and (ii) the *esse* of this essence], can be denominated by this potency, which exists 'between' them: [it denominates] (i) as though it were the subject, and (ii) as though it were the terminus." Scotus deliberately refuses to discuss the ontological status of the merely possible being that is the foundation of the relation of modal potency, in *QSM* IX qq.1–2 n.6 (WV 7.534a–b): "But there is a great difficulty concerning the foundation of [modal potency]—[namely] what sort of ontological status (*entitas*) does [the founda-

[MP1]   The essence of ϕx is possible, that is, there is no incompatibility among the features that constitute ϕx.

[MP2]   The essence of ϕx is logically and strictly prior to the existence (*esse*) of ϕx.

An ascription of modal potency is in fact a disguised relational claim: it is to assert that there is a nonactual possible being defined in terms of its actuality, what we might think of as a merely possible being. The sense of "possible" that enters into [MP1] is a matter of metaphysical consistency, grounded on the *ratio* of each constituent of ϕx.[38] The "strict logical priority" in [MP2] involves two claims: the *ratio* of the possible being is derived from its existence, and the possible being does not exist.[39] Therefore, it is clear that modal potency, defined by [MP1] and [MP2], "does not obtain along with act as regards the same [subject]," as Scotus says in *QSM* ix qq.1–2 n.3 (WV 7.532a): everything (taken widely) is either a potential being or an actual being, but not both.

---

tion] have before it exists?—and [this difficulty] ought not to be investigated here, for [the answer] would perhaps seem more diffuse and prolix than the principal [question]." He does assert, however, that "the metaphysical potency in the possible essence is postulated to be some ontological status of a sort that is not in a chimaera."

[38] Scotus distinguishes such "metaphysical consistency" from mere logical possibility ("logical potency"). The latter is fundamentally a semantic notion, as Scotus asserts in *QSM* ix qq.1–2 n.3 (WV 7.531b): "[Logical] potency is a certain mode of composition: it is produced by the intellect [and] caused from the disposition (*habitudo*) of the terms of that composition (namely, that [the terms] are not incompatible). Although some real potency in the thing commonly corresponds to [logical potency], nevertheless this does not pertain per se to the ratio of [logical] potency." Logical possibility is to be distinguished from genuine metaphysical consistency, which is not a property of terms but of real things (or features of things), as Scotus goes on to point out (WV 7.531b–532a): "In one way, ['metaphysical potency'] is opposed to 'impossible'—not as it expresses a mode of composition (as in the case of [logical potency]), but rather as it expresses the disposition of something incomplex, in the way in which, according to Aristotle (*Meta. Δ.29* [1024b26–27]), some *ratio* is called false in itself because it includes a contradiction. The possible converts with being as a whole in this fashion, for the reason that nothing is a being whose *ratio* includes a contradiction." The text of Aristotle to which Scotus refers is λόγος δὲ ψευδὴς ὁ τῶν μὴ ὄντων ᾗ ψευδής, rendered into Latin by William of Moerbeke as *ratio vero falsa est quae non entium inquantum falsa*. Scotus interprets *non entium* as referring to the "contradictory things" described immediately before (1024b25–26). Scotus denies that mere logical possibility entails a corresponding metaphysical modal potency in *QSM* ix qq.1–2 n.6 (WV 7.534a); semantic consistency may not reflect genuine metaphysical consistency. Therefore, all beings (in this sense) are metaphysically consistent, and those that are nonactual but are ordered to act are potential beings.

[39] Scotus's notion of a "potential being" can be given a close parallel in modern possible-worlds accounts of modal semantics: to say that ϕx is a potential being is to assert that ϕx exists in some possible world *and* to assert that the possible world in question is not the actual world—a relational claim. Scotus's analysis of modal potency in terms of metaphysical consistency is exactly on a par with modern accounts that presuppose the existence of possible worlds to offer a semantics for modality.

Scotus takes modal potency to be central to physics, because he holds that the definition of "motion or change" in *Phys.* iii.1, 201a11–12, as "the actualization of a potential to the extent that it is potential" should be understood in terms of modal potency and modal act. Two distinctions regarding modal potency are relevant to his analysis: the distinction between *objective* and *subjective* modal potencies, and the distinction of subjective modal potency into *simultaneous* and *successive*. Roughly, something is in objective modal potency if the whole of it is merely possible, whereas it is in subjective modal potency if the subject already exists, although the terminus (usually some form) does not.[40] For example, the nonexistent twin brother of Socrates is in objective modal potency, whereas Socrates himself is in subjective modal potency to becoming white. Since all cases of change involve a persisting substratum, the definition of change involves only subjective modal potency. Subjective modal potency can be either *simultaneous* or *successive*, depending on whether the subjective modal act that is incompatible with the subjective modal potency is also incompatible with further subjective modal potency (by "using up" the potency): if so, the subjective modal potency is simultaneous, and if not, it is successive.[41] The distinction roughly corresponds to that between poten-

---

[40] Scotus offers technical definitions of objective and subjective modal potency in *QSM* ix qq.1–2 n.8 (WV 7.536a–b): "Now since every formal act is *esse*, by extending *esse*, then, some *esse* can belong to something either simply or in a respect—whether [the *esse*] is proper or whether it is not proper but rather as though extrinsic. But this [modal] potency will be twofold with respect to the [following] primary division:

a. some [modal potency] is for proper *esse* and simply belongs to that which is in potency;
b. other [modal potency] is for extrinsic *esse*, as though in a respect belonging to that which is in potency to that *esse*.

"Now (a) is characteristic of any given substantial or accidental essence as regards its first *esse*, and is founded in that essence of which it is the proper *esse*. Indeed, just as the essence of an accident or whiteness is in potency to its proper *esse*, so too the essence of a soul that is to be created is in potency to its *esse*. Now (a) is most properly a differentia of being, and (a) can be called 'objective potency' to the extent that the whole is in potency to existence, and not in act, as its subject as well as its terminus. . . .

"Now (b) is not characteristic of any given being, since it belongs to only that which, apart from its proper *esse*, is naturally apt to receive another *esse* than [its proper *esse*]; and thus, when it does not have that [other *esse*], it is in potency to it. For example: a body that is not white is in potency that it be so—not simply [that it *be*], but rather that it be *white*, which is its *esse* in a respect and as extrinsic. And (b) can be called 'subjective [potency]' in this way."

[41] Scotus's technical definitions of these notions in *QSM* ix qq.1–2 n.9 (WV 7.537a) cite his earlier definition of them for the case of objective potency in n.8 (WV 7.536b–537a): "According to the diversity of essences, potency is for the act to be received, in diverse ways: sometimes as a whole simultaneously, as the essences of permanent [things] are naturally apt to receive *esse*; at other times successively, such that the potency for a further act always obtains along with the act terminating the potency, as in the case of successive [things], such that in that case the act opposed to the potency never succeeds it simultaneously." Scotus then

cies whose actuality spans a continuous range and those whose actuality is a fixed endpoint. For example, a brick has the subjective modal potency to be hot, and even while this potency is being actualized—while the brick is heating up another ten degrees, say—the brick retains the "further" potency to be heated to a higher temperature; this subjective potency is therefore successive. On the other hand, the brick's subjective modal potency to be exactly 91 degrees is a potency that exists at all temperatures less than or greater than 91 degrees, and does *not* exist when the brick is exactly 91 degrees; this subjective modal potency is therefore simultaneous. Scotus holds that Aristotle's definition of motion or change involves two distinct subjective modal potencies, one simultaneous and directed toward the terminus, the other successive and directed toward the process of change, as he explains in *QSM* ix qq.1–2 n.11 (WV 7.539a–b):

> Subjective [modal potency] is that which is put into the definition of motion; the [subjective modal potency] is not for the motion, but rather for its terminus.
>
> The reason for this is that the [modal] potency for the motion exists before the motion, and thus it is eliminated when the mobile begins to be moved— namely, as [the modal potency] is naturally apt to be eliminated: not as a whole all at once, but rather successively. Motion is an act with respect to this [modal] potency.
>
> But along with this act there obtains the [modal] potency for the terminus, which either (a) was not present before the motion, or (b) was present before [the motion]—which I believe to a greater extent as regards that metaphysical subjective potency—but it is not reduced to act immediately by a natural agent, unless that [modal potency] for motion were previously reduced [to act].

A case of change thus involves the potency to *be* φ and the potency to *become* φ. If a brick changes from 75 degrees to 91 degrees, it must have the potency to be 91 degrees and also the potency to become 91 degrees. The process of changing—the change itself—is the actuality of the brick's becoming 91 degrees, which ends when the brick reaches 91 degrees. On the one hand, the subjective modal potency for the change is successive: the clause "to the extent that it is potential" in Aristotle's definition refers to this subjective modal potency. On the other hand, the subjective modal potency for the terminus of the change is not successive but rather simultaneous: it remains an unactualized potency throughout the process of

---

remarks that subjective modal potency is divided into simultaneous and successive because "just as any essence that informs something is reduced to its proper *esse* simultaneously or nonsimultaneously, so too what has been informed is reduced to the same *esse* as though it were [something] participated in."

change and is incompatible with the final modal actuality of the terminus. Thus Aristotle's definition may be reformulated as follows:

> Change is the modal act of a successive subjective modal potency for the change, insofar as this modal act exists along with a simultaneous subjective modal potency for the terminus.

Both modal potencies involved in change may exist prior to the change, and both will be destroyed when the change reaches its terminus.

Yet in spite of the prominent role of modal modality in the definition of motion, the Modal Argument, if taken as referring to modal modality, fails: [A5] holds but [A3] does not. The Law of Noncontradiction holds when reformulated in terms of modal potency and modal act:

> [A5*] It is impossible for one and the same thing to be at once in modal potency and modal act in the same respect.

Nothing is both *merely* possible and also actual, as we might summarize [A5*]. But the corresponding reformulation of [A3] does *not* hold when the causality is equivocal:

> [A3*] The cause of a change must be in modal act with respect to the form it induces.

In such a case, the subject is informed by a form φ that causally induces the form ψ in its recipient, and the subject contains ψ in modal potency. Hence the subject is in modal act with respect to φ and the recipient is in modal potency with respect to ψ, and these are not ruled out by [A5*], even when the recipient and the subject are one and the same. To argue that the subject would also be in modal act as regards the equivocal effect it induces would be to commit a fallacy of the consequent, as Scotus says in *QSM* IX q.14 n.18 (WV 7.596a–b):

> If "potency" is taken as opposed to act (as the discussion in *QSM* IX qq.1–2 considered it), [then] the same thing is never together in [modal] potency and in [modal] act in the same [respect]. For when water is actually hot, at that time it is not actually cold, but only potentially [cold]. And there is a fallacy of the consequent when one argues [as follows]:
>
> > If [water] is able to move itself to coldness, it is therefore in [modal] act in the way in which what is able to be moved is in [modal] potency,
>
> understanding ["in act"] as regards formal [modal] act, for [the corresponding argument],
>
> > The Sun is able to change matter through putrefaction into the form of a worm; therefore, the Sun is a worm in [modal] act,
>
> does not follow.

The agent of an equivocal change is not in formal modal act as regards its induced effect, but only in formal modal act with regard to the principle from which its equivocal causal power stems. Now [A2] requires that the equivocal cause "contain" its effect in some fashion. Given that a univocal cause is sufficient to produce its univocal effect, where the induced form also informs the cause, a "more excellent" or "eminent" form is that much more sufficient: the eminent form that informs the cause can be said to contain *virtually* the induced form it produces equivocally, and so to be in "virtual act" as regards the induced form, but not in formal act as regards the induced form.[42] This is the answer Scotus briefly sketches in *QSM* ix q.14 n.18 (WV 7.596a–b), immediately following the passage cited above:

> Indeed, if sometimes an active perfection[43] is sufficient to produce an effect of the same *ratio* as that which is in the effect, how much more sufficient is the

[42] To say that *x* "virtually contains" φ, or that *x* is in "virtual act" as regards φ, is to say no more than that *x* has the causal power to produce equivocally φ—that *x* has a certain causal power (*virtus*). I propose we understand Scotus's use of "virtual" in these cases as a place-holder: there *is* no general answer to the question how *x* contains φ. In the case of a builder building the house, for example, the builder virtually contains the house by having the form of the house in her imagination, and this phenomenon—"having a form in the imagination"— is open to philosophical and scientific investigation. The determination of causal powers is not a matter to be settled a priori by the metaphysician.

There is a striking anticipation of Scotus's vocabulary, though not of his doctrine, in a text with which Scotus was assuredly well acquainted: in response to the question whether a subject could be the adequate *per se* cause of its own accidents, Henry of Ghent replies (*Quodlibeta* x q.9 221.14–24): "It should be stated that the question at hand is generally about the efficient cause of an accident, but specifically about the accident that is the very act of willing: how it could be caused by the will itself, which is its subject. And there is a reason for doubt in this case, since the subject is the material cause with respect to its accident. Thus, although it is in act as regards substantial form, nevertheless insofar as it exists in itself it is only in potency to accidental form—and hence it necessarily acts by means of something existing in act in the way in which that [subject] is in potency, by means of which it is reduced from potency to act.

"However, I state that [it acts] by means of something existing in act as such, at least in virtual [act] even if not in form, just as the Sun, which is hot in potency, produces heat in virtual act, even if it is not formally hot."

The Sun cannot itself be hot, since *being hot* is a property of corruptible bodies. Scotus uses the very same example in *QSM* ix q.14 n.22 (WV 7.600a) while answering an objection about formal potency and virtual act: "I reply generally on the basis of the definition (*ratio*) of virtual [act] and formal act . . . *being hot* is formally incompatible with the Sun, since it is a quality that is proper to a corruptible body, and consequently the Sun is not a subject that has a capacity for it. (Neither does fire have a capacity for whiteness, which is a quality proper to mixed [bodies].) But it is not the case on that account that the Sun does not have the capacity for heat, since [the Sun] is virtually hot. Indeed, it is clear that Saturn, which is held to be virtually cold, does not have the capacity for heat formally any more than the Sun does." Scotus also discusses this example in *Ord.* i d.3 p.3 q.2 nn.519–520 (Vat. 3.308–9) and *Op. Ox.* ii d.25 q. unica n.14 (WV 13.208b–209a). It seems likely that Scotus adopted Henry's terminology while modifying his theory.

[43] A "perfection" is, roughly, a feature such that it is better to have it than not to have it.

more excellent? And so any given equivocal agent is in [modal] act with respect to its effect, not formally having a similar [modal] act (for then it would not be an *equivocal* agent), but virtually having [a similar modal act], namely because it formally has a more eminent [modal act].

Hence [the question might be raised]: according to what is [the agent] in [modal] act and according to what is it in [modal] potency?

I answer: it is in [modal] potency according to the terminus of the motion, [and] it is in [modal] act according to the active principle that is equivocal with respect to the terminus [of the motion].

Now talk of causal "powers" and "active principles" is a part of the second kind of modality Scotus recognizes, namely principiative modality.

Principiative Modality

Scotus discusses modality as a principle extensively in *QSM* IX qq.3–4. Now a "principle" is a metaphysical constituent of something, one from which something results as its principiatum (as described in section 1 above). Hence principiative modality is a real feature of something, on the order of an ability or capacity on the one hand, and the exercise of the ability or capacity on the other hand. If the pure modal contexts "x is in potency to ϕ" and "x is in act as to ϕ" are interpreted as referring to principiative modality, they could naturally be reformulated as the following:

x has the potency to ϕ,
x has an act as to ϕ,

and from this reformulation it is but a short step to:

x has the principle to ϕ,
x actualizes its principle to ϕ.

Unlike modal modality, which contrasts nonactual beings with actual beings, ascriptions of principiative modality always refer to some feature that a being possesses.

As noted in section 3 above, a principiative potency is rather like the possession of an ability or a capacity. This analogy is fruitful, and it will help to bear it in mind in what follows. The most important feature of principiative potencies is that they are divided into *active* and *passive*—

Forms are perfections when their possession "perfects" the agent, and this is settled objectively by the nature of the agent in question. Here Scotus means no more than that an agent may have an active causal power or an active principle consonant with its nature.

roughly equivalent to the distinction between abilities and capacities: they are real constituents of things, by means of which their possessors can perform or undergo some activity. Since potency is ordered to act, it might be thought that the distinction between active principiative potency and passive principiative potency is all that need be said: once we distinguish between an ability or capacity and the result of its exercise—between the principle, its principiating, and the principiatum—there is no more work to be done; principiative potencies, like any ability or capacity, are clearly related to and defined by the results of their corresponding exercise.

Scotus thinks, however, that there is a fundamental distinction to be drawn at this point. For principles are not only related to their principiata as their actualizations, but they may also be related to other principles as their actualizations—roughly, active principles and passive principles are made for each other. Scotus presents this distinction in *QSM* IX qq.3–4 n.5 (WV 7.546a):

> It should be known that a principle does not have only a relation to its principiatum, and *such* a principle to *such* a principiatum (e.g., the efficient [cause] to its effect [and] the matter to the materiate), but also one principle has a respect to another principle, since, whether the [principles] are extrinsic or intrinsic, the one and the other never mutually cause [anything] unless they are united and concur among themselves in some way, for no one [cause] is sufficient to cause that which essentially depends on many causes. (How the four causes concur in causing the same [thing], and how they are essentially ordered in causing, is clear from the Ninth Thesis of [my] *Tractatus de primo principio* c.ii.) Those two relations are of completely different *rationes*, and both can be founded in the same absolute [subject]—rather, they are necessarily founded [in the same absolute subject].

Scotus explicitly refers to this presentation of the distinction in discussing self-change, so it is important to be clear about what the distinction amounts to.[44] In *Meta. Δ.*15, Aristotle offers two examples of active potencies that illustrate Scotus's distinction. The first example is the relation between "what is able to heat" and "what becomes hot" (1021a16–17); the second example is the relation between the craftsman and what he produces, or the relation between the father and the son (1021a22–24).

---

[44] When Scotus turns to the interpretation of the Modal Argument as involving principiative modalites, in *QSM* IX q.14 n.18 (WV 7.596b), he begins by drawing this distinction: "However, if 'potency' is taken so that it expresses a relation to a principle (in the way in which [the topic] has been discussed in *QSM* IX qq.3–4), [then] it expresses either a relation of the principle: (a) to the principiatum, (b) to another principle, as was initially distinguished in *QSM* IX qq.3–4." This immediately follows Scotus's discussion of modal modalities, cited above.

These examples are very different from each other, as Scotus remarks in *QSM* IX qq.3–4 n.5 (WV 7.546a–b):

> [As for Aristotle's first example]: It is plain that "what is able to produce heat" is not said with reference to what becomes hot in the way in which a principle [is said] with reference to its principiatum, but rather as, for example, an active principle with reference to a passive [principle], from which there follows one principiatum, with reference to which both [principles] are said.
>
> [As for Aristotle's second example]: But "father" is not said with reference to his son in this way; neither is what is going to make [said] with reference to what is to be made as with reference to a principle, but rather as with reference to its principiatum. . . .
>
> In this [discussion], too, there is a clear example of how Aristotle says that (a) a passive principle has a passive potency in respect of another principle, not in respect of the principiatum, but (b) [the passive principle] has potency in respect of the principiatum as well, insofar as the principiatum can come to be from it.

The craftsman is *immediately* related to his product, as is the father to his son. But what is able to heat is at best *mediately* related to something hot; the active potency to heat something is, strictly speaking, directed at its object's passive potency to be heated, and it is only their joint action that produces the result—the hot object—as their mutual principiatum. Hence the actualization of a principle may be directed toward another principle, and both principles together produce the principiatum. Active and passive principles are, literally, made for one another.

There is a special case to add to these two ways in which principles are related to their actualizations, namely, the relation between a passive principle (matter) and a form, which together make up a composite substance. The substantial form of a composite substance is not any sort of potency, but instead is an act, and thereby an intrinsic principle of the composite. Hence the form is not a principiative potency (since it is not a potency at all), yet it does combine with a passive principiative potency, namely matter, to produce a genuine unity. Scotus mentions this case in passing in *QSM* IX qq.3–4 n.6 (WV 7.546b):

> A passive principle also has a respect to a form, along with which (as along with an intrinsic principle) it principiates the principiatum. And [Aristotle] says of this that [something] that is one [results] from matter and form because the latter is act and the former potency (*Meta.* H.6 [1045a22–23]).

A substantial form, as an active principle, need not have an intrinsic relation to matter; there are immaterial forms, forms that do not require matter for their existence. Hence the analyses of passive potency and active potency are not symmetric.

Scotus concludes that ascriptions of principiative potency are distinguished first into active and passive principiative potencies, and then into the various ways each can be actualized. He presents the "physical" definitions of each in *QSM* ix qq.3–4 n.7 (WV 7.547b):[45]

Understand that "passive [principiative potency]" is triply equivocal, namely as it expresses a relation:

[PP1]   to the principiatum passively,

[PP2]   to an active principle—not insofar as it is the active [principle] of an act, but insofar as it is the actual active [principle] of the actuable (since an active principle is referred [to][46] a passive [principle] in the converse way),

[PP3]   to an actual principle that along with itself constitutes the composite by producing along with [the passive principle] something that is one.

Likewise, understand that "active [principiative potency]" is doubly equivocal, namely [as it expresses a relation]:

[AP1]   to an actual principiatum,

[AP2]   to another actuable principle.

It is perhaps not necessary to postulate a third [relation], namely, [a relation] to the form.[47]

---

[45] In *QSM* ix qq.3–4 n.8 (WV 7.548a–b), Scotus says that abstract "metaphysical" definitions can be obtained from the "physical" definitions in the following manner: "[Namely] by leaving out what restricts [the definition] to naturalness and by putting in more generally what is pertinent for the metaphysician. Active potency is:

[AP1*] the principle of doing what can be done;

[AP2*] [the principle] of actuating an actuable [principle].

Passive potency is:

[PP1*] the principle in virtue of which something can be changed;

[PP2*] the principle of being passively actuated by an active act;

[PP3*] the principle that is actuable either as able to be informed by an act, or by an actual principle."

Note that these "metaphysical" definitions omit any reference to the characteristics of their subjects, unlike the "physical" definitions.

[46] Reading *ad* for *et*.

[47] Matter, as a passive principiative potency, has a special relation to substantial form: it is organized into something per se one by it. There is no active principiative potency, however, that stands in a similar "special" relation to substantial form. Substantial forms need not be potential before being actual. The substantial form is itself an actuality, and although it may be the actuality of the matter, it need not be.

Passive principiative potency may be related to its principiatum in the way in which the capacity for undergoing something is related to that which it undergoes ([PP1]); it may be related to an active principle that actualizes it—not as the active principle is related to its principiatum, as in [AP1], but rather as the active principle is a real principle whose actualization is to actuate a passive principle ("the actuable"), as in [AP2]—in the way in which the capacity to be heated is linked with the ability to heat something ([PP2]); it may be related to a form, as matter and form together produce the composite as a unity ([PP3]). Active principiative potency may be related to the principiatum it actually produces, as the father to his son ([AP1]); it may be related to a passive ("actuable") principle, the converse of [PP2], as the ability to heat something is related to the capacity to be heated ([AP2]). Thus [AP1] and [PP1] are each ways in which a principiative potency is immediately related to a principiatum, whereas [AP2] and [PP2] are correlatives, each mediately related through the other to their mutual principiatum.

To return to the case of self-change: [A5], the application of the Law of Noncontradiction to potency and act, has to be carefully distinguished according to the several kinds of potency and act that can obtain. We have seen above that [A5*], construing the modalities as modal modalities, is true but irrelevant to the case of self-change. What about the following interpretation of [A5]:

> [A5**] Nothing has both a principiative potency and a principiative act
>   that are related to the same object,

where the modalities are construed as principiative modalities?

There is not a simple answer, because principiative modalities are far more complex than modal modalities: [A5**] is sometimes valid, sometimes not. Scotus considers five cases. First, if [AP1] is combined with the claim that the principiatum is the "act" of the active principiative potency, then [A5**] will be interpreted as follows:

> [a] Nothing both (1) has an active principiative potency that is related to
>   its actual principiatum, and (2) is that very principiatum.

It should be clear that [a] holds necessarily, because it describes a situation in which one and the same thing actively principiates *itself*—which is ruled out by the general principle that nothing can be its own cause. Furthermore, if [PP1] is substituted for [AP1] in this schema, [A5**] will be interpreted as follows:

> [b] Nothing both (1) has a passive principiative potency that is related to
>   its actual principiatum, and (2) is that very principiatum.

It should also be clear that [b] holds necessarily, because it describes a situation in which one and the same thing passively principiates itself, that is, is defined solely by its capacity to receive itself as an act, which is impossible. Therefore, it is impossible for one and the same thing to be both the (active or passive) subject and the recipient of the principiatum. This is in fact what Scotus says in *QSM* IX q.14 n.18 (WV 7.596b):

> If ["potency" expresses a relation] to its principiatum, [then], if the [principiatum] were called an "act," I grant that nothing essentially the same is potency and act, since no essence that is one properly principiates itself effectively (*nulla una essentia seipsam principiat proprie effective*), nor [does it do so] in the case of any kind of principle whatsoever.

It remains to be seen whether the impossibility of self-causation rules out self-change—whether there is some interpretation of [A5**] that does not hold.

Scotus immediately offers such an interpretation, albeit somewhat strained. Assume that a concrete thing (*suppositum*) can have within itself two distinct natures.[48] If [AP1] is combined with the claim that the production of its principiatum, although received by the other nature of the *suppositum*, allows us to call the active principiative potency itself an "act," then [A5**] will be interpreted as follows:

> [c] Nothing is composed out of two natures such that both (1) one nature has an active principiative potency that actually principiates a principiatum, so that the active principiative potency is itself an act, and (2) the other nature is receptive of that very principiatum.

Scotus denies that [c] holds in *QSM* IX q.14 nn.18–19 (WV 7.596b–597a):

> Nevertheless, the same *suppositum* can have two natures in itself, of which the one [nature] is the active principle and the other [nature] the principiatum, and so it is in potency—i.e., it is potent by means of the active principle—and [the active principle] is in act (or it is an "act") due to its principiatum. But in this way, "act" has not typically been taken generally for what has acted.

But [c] is not relevant to self-change, because it is improper to use "act" to refer to the actualization of the active principiative potency itself. Strictly speaking, the active principiative potency is such that its actualization is the act that is received in another nature; the active potency is "what has acted," not an "act" itself.

Scotus then turns to another case in which [A5**] fails to hold. If [PP3] is combined with the claim that the form of something, which is an actual principle of the composite, is an "act," then [A5**] will be interpreted as follows:

> [d] Nothing has both (1) a passive principiative potency (such as matter) that, along with an actual principle (namely, the form), produces

[48] The term *suppositum* is a technical theological term used to describe the concrete object that was Christ, which possessed both a human nature and a divine nature.

along with it something that is one; (2) an actual principle, namely, a form, which is the act of the passive principiative potency (namely, matter).

It is clear that [d] does not hold, since the combination of matter and form does produce a unity—indeed, one that makes their concrete combination fall under a category. And this is exactly what Scotus says in *QSM* ix q.14 n.19 (WV 7.597a):

> If, however, "potency" expresses the relation of a principle to act as to another intrinsic principle, then to accept that both are not in any one *suppositum* is to accept that no *suppositum* is in this way categorial, and thus [to accept] that no *suppositum* will be composed out of a potential principle and a principle that is called an act—which is false.

Yet [d] is irrelevant to self-change, whether it holds or does not hold, since it describes the fundamental composition of matter and form, which does not involve any change at all.

The final case Scotus takes up secures the possibility of self-change. Consider what happens if [PP2] is combined with [AP2]—a case in which active and passive principles are conjoined mutually to principiate their joint principiatum. In this case, [A5**] will be interpreted as follows:

> [e] Nothing has both (1) an active principiative potency related to a passive principiative potency it actualizes, resulting in a joint principiatum, and (2) an act with respect to the principiatum.

Yet [e] simply begs the question. Consider how Scotus describes the case in *QSM* ix q.14 n.19 (WV 7.597a):

> Yet if in the end "potency" expresses the relation of a passive principle to an active principle that is said to be in act (i.e., active) but is *not* called an "act," then to accept that nothing that is the same is both in potency and in act is only to express in different words the fact that nothing that is the same is both active and passive—and this is not an a priori proof, but rather begs the question by taking the same point in different words [in order to]⁴⁹ prove itself.

We can recast Scotus's charge that [e] begs the question in the form of an argument, one that turns on the nature of equivocal causality and principiative modality:

> [EC1] Suppose that x has an active principiative potency in virtue of being informed by some form ϕ.　　　　　　　(hypothesis)
>
> [EC2] Then we can say that x is active with respect to ϕ, since x is informed by ϕ.　　　　　　　(by [EC1])

---

⁴⁹ Reading *ad* for *ab*.

[EC3] Suppose also that x has a passive principiative potency for some form ψ. (hypothesis)

[EC4] Then we can say that x is in potency to ψ by means of its passive principiative potency. (by [EC3])

[EC5] Hence x is passive with respect to ψ. (by [EC4])

[EC6] Suppose that the actualization of x's active principiative potency is to actualize x's passive principiative potency, so as jointly to produce a form ψ that informs x. (hypothesis)

[EC7] Then x is active with respect to ψ by means of its active principiative potency.[50] (by [EC6])

[EC8] The active principiative potency is not an "act" of ψ. (by [EC6])

Therefore: x is active and passive with regard to ψ.
(by [EC5] and [EC7])

An example will clarify the argument. A brick is informed by the form *heaviness* ([EC1]). Hence it is active with respect to *heaviness*, or, in plain English, the brick is actually heavy ([EC2]). Now, it is a fact that a brick has the passive principiative potency *being moved downward* ([EC3]): bricks can be moved downward, after all. Hence the brick is in potency to downward motion ([EC4]), and it is passive as regards downward motion ([EC5]). Now suppose that the form *heaviness* produces an active principiative potency in the brick ([EC1]). What might this active principiative potency be for? It seems clear that the heaviness of a body is closely linked to its moving downward. In keeping with [EC6], then, suppose that the active principiative potency engendered in the brick by *heaviness* serves to actualize the brick's passive principiative potency *being moved downward* so that the pair of principiative potencies jointly produce the principiated form *moving downward* in the brick. Hence the brick is active with respect to moving downward in virtue of its active principiative potency ([EC7]), even if it is not *actually* moving downward ([EC8]). Therefore, the brick is passively able to be moved downward, and is active with respect to moving downward—it is a self-mover. No wonder Scotus finds the insistence on [e] question-begging: [EC1]–[EC8] describe a consistent case, given the assumption of equivocal causality and the interpretation of the modalities as principiative.[51]

---

[50] Scotus is ambiguous on the "by means of" clause in [EC7]: is x active with respect to ψ solely in virtue of the equivocal causality of its active principiative potency, or is x active with respect to ψ in virtue of the interdefined active and passive principiative potencies that jointly principiate ψ? I am inclined to the latter interpretation, but Scotus's argument holds no matter which interpretation is adopted. Note that [EC7] is the correct interpretation of [A3] regarding principiative modalities.

[51] The conclusion drawn here is stronger than Scotus's statement of it, namely that "nothing that is the same is both active and passive." Yet this statement has force only if it is

Scotus often summarizes his conclusion by saying that formal potency and virtual act are compatible as regards the same form, but this summary, too often mistaken for an explanation, does not reveal the subtle analysis of modality and causality at work behind the scenes.

In the critical case, then, the Modal Argument fails: [A3] and [A5] fail to hold. Hence the common position against self-change is deprived of its central argument, and Scotus can maintain the conclusion of his General Argument that self-motion is at least possible, having now given a complete description in [EC1]–[EC7] of the conditions that must be met for a genuine case of self-change to occur.

Denomination

Scotus's account of the modality of self-change allows one and the same thing to become ψ only in virtue of that thing possessing two distinct principles, one of which acts on the other, that jointly produce ψ. Since these principles are real features of a single thing, Scotus's claim that there is literally one and the same *thing* involved in a case of self-change has some force. Yet a defender of the common position might well maintain that, strictly speaking, the agent and the patient are distinct: what primarily becomes ψ is the passive principiative potency, not the whole subject, although the whole subject is ψ in virtue of the actualization of its passive principiative potency.

Scotus's response to this objection is to be found in his account of denomination—how terms derived from abstract relations, such as "cause" and "principle," are correctly applied to things.[52] In *QSM* IX qq.3–4 n.3 (WV 7.544a–b), Scotus writes:

> It should be known that sometimes several denominative [terms] are said on the basis of the same abstract [term]—namely, denominative [terms] that are naturally apt to denominate diverse [things]—and what is designated by the abstract [term] has a relationship (*habitudo*) to these diverse [things]. (One could multiply examples [of this], if prolixity were not to prevent it!) Thus on the basis of the relation called "principiation," designated in the abstract, one denominates in diverse ways:
>
> 1. what principiates,
> 2. that by which it principiates,

---

interpreted as "active and passive *in the same respect*," which is how I have formulated his conclusion.

Note that the case of downward motion will be examined, with a good deal more precision, in connection with the Primacy Argument; here it serves merely as a convenient example.

[52] The discussion that follows amplifies and corrects the terminology introduced in section 1 above.

because that by which [something principiates] is immediate, and what [principiates] is mediate. In accordance with this, two denominative [terms] can be made appropriate to them, namely so that:[53]

1*. what [principiates] is called the "principiator,"
2*. that by which [it principiates] is called the "principle.". . .

Thus it is clear that "principle" essentially brings in the relation of principiation, and it does this in the concrete—namely, as it is naturally apt to concern its immediate foundation, which is *that by which*, but not its remote [foundation] or subject (which is not *that by which*).[54]

Similar distinctions could be drawn for causation: what causes is called the "causer," and that by which it causes is, strictly speaking, the "cause." The common use of "cause" for both of these is inaccurate. But it is precisely this inaccuracy that gives the objection stated above its force. What brings about the change is *not* the principle, though it is often harmless to speak loosely in this way, but rather the principiator. The principle is that by means of which a principiator principiates the principiatum. Likewise, that which causes is the causer, not the cause, which is that by which a causer causes the effect. Therefore, strictly speaking, the agent and the patient in a case of self-change are *not* distinct: the principiator (or causer) is one and the same thing as the principiatum (or effect).

Scotus's solution is more than a verbal trick. It rejects the objection as ill-formed and based on a confusion between two levels: the level of primary substances, in all the richness of their properties and principles, and the level of principles themselves. But principiation and causation only occur at the former level, not at the latter. To be sure, primary substances exercise their principiative and causal powers *by means of* their principles and causes, but the principles and causes themselves are only means, not agents.

The objection, though ill-formed, appears to make sense because it is easily confused with a second question: whether the principles or causes involved in a case of self-change are really distinct, that is, whether it is possible for something to have some but not all of the principiative modalities requisite for a case of self-change.

Scotus grants that principiative modalities are real features of things, distinct by their *rationes*, but beyond that he has little to say.[55] The reason

---

[53] I have reversed the order of Scotus's sentence here so as to conform to (1) and (2) above.

[54] When Scotus writes "Its immediate foundation . . . its remote [foundation] or subject," he is referring to the immediate or remote foundation of the relation *principiation*.

[55] It is important, however, that the principiative modalities be *real* features of things that are distinct by their *rationes*. For self-change, such principles are clearly distinct as active and as passive. Scotus further insists that this is not merely a distinction of reason when he discusses Henry of Ghent's "intentional distinction" between the agent and the patient, mentioned in note 1, in *QSM* IX q.14 n.17 (WV 7.595b): "According to those [philosophers

for his reticence is simple. If x has an active principiative potency to induce ψ in a recipient subject, a power rooted in a form ϕ, then it is clear that if x lacks the corresponding passive principiative potency for ψ, it cannot change itself. There is no general answer, I take it, to the second question; it depends on the nature of the subject in question. For example, Scotus claims that the active and passive principiative potencies required for the self-actualization of the will cannot be lacking to the will, since these potencies constitute the very foundation of the will's nature as a self-determining faculty of choice.[56] On the other hand, an animal's power of locomotion is due to the relevant potencies being "localized" in distinct constituent parts of the animal: the soul has the active principiative potency to move the body, and the body has the passive principiative potency to be moved, the combination of which results in locomotion. Insofar as souls can be separated from bodies, so can the relevant principles. Therefore, the answer to this second question will depend on the way in which the principiative modalities are realized in their subject, and this has nothing to do with their capacity to bring about self-change when they are jointly present.

5. SCOTUS'S RESPONSE TO THE PRIMACY ARGUMENT

In his discussion of the Primacy Argument, Scotus makes extensive use of three distinctions, addressing the Primacy Argument at a higher level of generality than that at which Aristotle presents it. The first distinction is between a *homogeneous whole* and a *heterogeneous whole*. A whole is homogeneous when the same *ratio* applies to the whole and to each of the things that fall under it, namely, its parts (in an extended sense).[57] For

---

who accept Henry of Ghent's reply], there is no intentional difference in the thing, except in potency. Now [an intentional difference] is complete and in act only by means of the intellect. However, if some difference is required in something for moving itself, since [*moving itself*] is a real effect, that difference must be real [and not merely intentional], because a real effect does not depend upon an act of reason." Scotus discusses Henry's position at length, but this argument is enough to show that there is not merely a distinction of reason between the agent and patient in a case of self-change. Rather, there is a distinction of principles as real features of things.

56 Scotus makes this assertion in *Op. Ox.* II d.25 q.unica n.13 (WV 13.208b), speaking of the will: "It is absurd that the most noble form, of which sort is the intellective soul, not have active potencies for its own accidental perfection and receptive [potencies] for the same. And since active and passive potencies cannot be granted in such forms, which are not distinct in subject since they are not organic potencies, then they are not distinguished in subject, and so they will be there unitively, without a distinction by reason of [their] subject, yet not without a formal distinction." This is the only passage I am acquainted with in which Scotus asserts a formal distinction (see note 78 below) among the principles involved. He seems not to be interested in the question.

57 Scotus does not restrict himself to the consideration of quantitative wholes, which

example, each part of fire is itself fire. Wholes that fail to be homogeneous are heterogeneous.

The second distinction is between a *homogeneous attribute* and a *heterogeneous attribute*. An attribute is homogeneous if it is "of the same *ratio* for the whole amount and for a partial amount" of its subject, as Scotus says in *Ord.* II d.2 p.2 q.6 n.485 (Vat. 7.374).[58] Any part of something yellow is itself yellow, in the same way and to the same extent that the whole is yellow. On the other hand, an attribute is heterogeneous if it is not homogeneous, such that it applies to its subject in virtue of one part of its *ratio* applying to one part of the subject, another to another, and so on (for example, the attribute "left-handed bald man").

The third distinction is between two kinds of primacy. Scotus takes Aristotle to define one kind of primacy in *Po. An.* I.4, 73b32–74a3 (call this "primarily$_1$"), and another kind of primacy in *Phys.* V.1, 224a21–30 (call this "primarily$_2$"), each described below.[59] Scotus holds that Aristotle's argument, strictly speaking, only shows that there is a contradiction if a homogeneous attribute φ, such as *locally moving*, is predicable of a whole *x* with *both* kinds of primacy.[60] In order to see why this should be so, and to follow Scotus's revision of the Primacy Argument at the higher level of generality at which he formulates it, let us consider each kind of primacy in some detail.

---

strictly are the only wholes to have parts, but includes any relation of greater and lesser generality as a whole–part relation. Hence class-inclusion qualifies as such a relation, as does the relationship between superordination and subordination that characterizes genus and species—the paradigmatic case of a universal whole–part relation in contradistinction to a quantitative whole–part relation. In Scotus's extended usage, whatever is less general counts as a "part" of what is more general. The isosceles triangle is a part of the triangle in this sense, and likewise the hand of Socrates is a part of Socrates; a species is a part of its genus, and a subclass of its class. Aristotle's move in [B2] from divisibility to quantitative wholes was too swift, in Scotus's eyes: all that Aristotle is entitled to conclude is that in cases of putative self-motion, some distinction between parts and wholes is appropriate, not that the wholes must be quantitative.

58 Repunctuating the text of the Vatican edition to read: "*inquantum illa passio accipitur ut homogenea (hoc est eiusdem rationis toti quanto et parti quanti)—quia*," according to the sense of the passage.

59 Scotus describes both kinds of primacy in *QSM* IX q.14 n.16 (WV 7.594b); he also describes them in *Ord.* II d.2 p.2 q.6 nn.475–76 (Vat. 7.369–70), where "primarily$_1$" is called "the primacy of precise causality" and "primarily$_2$" is called "the primacy according to the whole." See note 27 above for *Po. An.* I.4, 73b32–74a3, and note 69 below for Scotus's description of Aristotle's distinction in *Phys.* V.1, 224a21–30.

60 In *QSM* IX q.14 n.16 (WV 7.594b), Scotus asserts that Aristotle is investigating whether a homogeneous attribute can be present in a whole primarily$_1$ and, "along with this," that it be present primarily$_2$ as well. He gives the same analysis of the Primacy Argument in *Ord.* II d.2 p.2 q.6 n.477 (Vat. 7.370): "Hence I say, then, that Aristotle's argument in *Phys.* VII.1 [241b33–242a16] correctly proves that no body is moved by itself primarily with this double primacy at once." Scotus's revision of the Primacy Argument will show that a stronger conclusion is available, namely that no homogeneous attribute is present in a heterogeneous whole primarily$_1$.

The First Kind of Primacy

Now "primarily" is an adverbial modifier that characterizes the way a predicate is said of a subject, or, in the material mode, the way some attribute is present in a subject. With regard to the first kind of primacy, the proposition

$$x \text{ is } \phi \text{ primarily}_1$$

is true when x is the "commensurate subject" of ϕ—the most general subject such that any given case is characterized by ϕ. Aristotle's example of an attribute that is present in its subject primarily$_1$ is the attribute "internal angles equal to 180 degrees" applied to the subject "triangle." This attribute does not characterize all plane figures, or even all rectilinear plane figures, though it does characterize some of them (namely, the triangles). Furthermore, whereas this attribute does apply to any given isosceles triangle, there is a more general subject to which it applies, namely, the triangle. Hence the elimination rule for primarily$_1$,

[E1] Anything that is ϕ primarily$_1$ is ϕ,

holds by definition. Thus, for instance, anything that is locally moved primarily$_1$ is thereby locally moved. Now given that x is ϕ primarily$_1$, it is possible for a part y of x—that is, something less general than x—to be ϕ as well. What is impossible is for y to be ϕ primarily$_1$: the isosceles triangle has internal angles equal to 180 degrees, but it cannot have internal angles equal to 180 degrees primarily$_1$. Therefore, the proper reformulation of [B1] (see p. 234 above) at a higher level of abstraction is:[61]

[B1*] Anything that is ϕ primarily$_1$ is ϕ even if another thing is not ϕ.

What makes a thing "another" is that the initial subject is not predicated of it. Yet this last condition does not obtain in the case of homogeneous wholes, since a homogeneous whole (the "initial subject" of an attribute) *is* predicable of its part. Every part of water is water. By definition, the homogeneous whole and its part have the same *ratio*, and so a part of a homogeneous whole is not "another thing" aside from the whole. Hence the claims about wholes and parts in [B4] and [B5] have to be restated more accurately as follows:[62]

---

[61] The replacement of [B1] by [B1*] is the intent of Scotus's first remark after distinguishing the two kinds of primacy. As he says in *QSM* ix q.14 n.16 (WV 7.594b): "Such a predicate is never removed from that in which it is present primarily for the reason that its opposite is present in something that does not receive the predication of that initial subject," where "such a predicate" refers to a predicate picking out a homogeneous attribute.

[62] The revisions [B4*] and [B5*] seem to be what Scotus has in mind as he continues in *QSM* ix q.14 n.16 (WV 7.594b): "But a quantitative part does not [in general] receive the predication of a quantitative whole, although the same whole *is* predicated as a universal of

[B4*] Heterogeneous wholes are not predicable of their parts.

[B5*] A part of a heterogeneous whole differs from that whole.

Since [B4*] and [B5*] apply only to heterogeneous wholes, a reformulation of [B2], the supposition that everything capable of motion must be a whole, is available along the same lines:

[B2*] Assume that φ is predicable of something that is a heterogeneous whole.

Thus Aristotle's Primacy Argument, as well as Scotus's Revised Primacy Argument, is addressed to heterogeous wholes rather than homogeneous wholes. This logical shortcoming leaves open the possibility that homogeneous wholes may be self-changers, a possibility about which the Primacy Argument (in its several versions) has nothing to say. Scotus will exploit this shortcoming in due course, as we shall see.

The Primacy Argument stands in need of clarification even when restricted to heterogeneous wholes. In order to combine [B1*] with [B5*], we have to take into account the character of the attribute with respect to heterogeneous wholes and their parts. Now in order for an attribute to belong to a heterogeneous whole primarily₁, the attribute must be homogeneous, according to the following argument.[63] If a whole is φ primarily₁, then an attribute φ does not belong to it in virtue of any less general feature that it possesses, by the definition of "primarily₁." Belonging to a subject only in virtue of strictly belonging to a part of the subject *is* a "less general" feature of a whole, provided that the part is not the same as its whole—that is, that the whole is heterogeneous. (The part is not less general than the whole, but belonging to the whole only in virtue of a part is less general than belonging to the whole in virtue of the whole.) What about the attribute? If the attribute is also heterogeneous, it could apply to part of a heterogeneous whole in one way and to the entire heterogeneous whole in

---

each [part] in the case of homogeneous [wholes]." Only homogeneous wholes are truly predicable of their parts.

[63] The argument that follows is based on Scotus's remarks in *Ord.* II d.2 p.2 q.6 n.478 (Vat. 7.370–71): "If a whole is moved by itself primarily [= primarily₁], then this predicate 'being moved' is not removed from the [whole] for the reason that it is removed from something that is not it, nor is it dissociated from the [whole] for the reason that it is removed from something that is something belonging to it. . . . Therefore, *being moved* is not removed from a whole to which it is present 'primarily' by means of this primacy [= primarily₁], even if it be removed from a part of [the whole] (and the part is not the [whole] itself). Hence if the whole is moved 'primarily' by this primacy [= primarily₁], it does not rest at the rest of a part." Scotus is careful to say that *being moved* is predicable of its subject primarily₁ even if "*it*"—the predicate *being moved*—is denied of a part. For a homogeneous attribute φ, the fact that a heterogeneous whole is φ primarily₁ entails that no part of the heterogeneous whole is φ, as the argument in the text shows. This is not to be confused with the claim that no part of the heterogeneous whole is φ primarily₁, which is true by definition but does not advance his argument.

another way. Yet since the part differs from its heterogeneous whole, the attribute cannot apply to merely a part—a less general feature—and still be predicable of the heterogeneous whole primarily$_1$. Hence the attribute cannot be heterogeneous, and so must be homogeneous. Therefore, the homogeneous attribute ϕ cannot apply to any part of a heterogeneous whole that is ϕ primarily$_1$. This argument permits [B7] to be reformulated as follows:[64]

> [B7*] Any part of a heterogeneous whole that is ϕ primarily$_1$ is not ϕ, for any homogeneous attribute ϕ.

Thus heterogeneous wholes that are the commensurate subjects of a given homogeneous attribute cannot have parts that the attribute characterizes.

For example, it seems as though an animal's body is the commensurate subject of the homogeneous attribute *being overweight*. (Flowers are not overweight; neither are mountains or molehills.) Furthermore, an animal's body is a heterogeneous whole that may include arms, legs, tail, stomach, chest, and so on. The homogeneous attribute *being overweight* does not apply to any single part of an animal's body, though: we do not say that someone has an overweight arm or an overweight finger; *being overweight* is a feature that characterizes the whole that is the animal's body, and nothing more general (such as inanimate bodies). Scotus's point is that the relations illustrated in this example obtain in virtue of the formal characteristics of the whole, the attribute, and the whole's possession of the attribute. If they are respectively heterogeneous, homogeneous, and primarily$_1$, then the attribute will never characterize any proper part of the whole.

The preceding remarks all depend on taking the sense of "primarily" in [B1] as primarily$_1$. There is an alternative to this interpretation: Scotus admits another kind of primacy, to which we now turn.

---

[64] Scotus himself proceeds to derive [B7*] from [B1*], [B2*], and [B5*], for the particular case of the homogeneous attribute *locally moved*, in his next remark in *QSM* IX q.14 n.16 (WV 7.594b): "Therefore, a [heterogeneous] whole that is moved primarily, taking 'primarily' in the [first] way, does not rest at the rest of a part—i.e., [the whole] does not lack what is predicated as inhering primarily because a part, which is not that whole, does lack [what is predicated as inhering primarily]." The use of [B2*] in the derivation is implicit, to guarantee that the subject discussed in [B1*] and [B2*] can be characterized by a homogeneous attribute.

Note that from [B7*] the result follows a fortiori that such a heterogeneous whole is unaffected by the fact that a part fails to possess the homogeneous attribute in question—it being impossible for any part to do so, by [B7*]—and hence we can offer the following as the correct reformulation of [B6]:

> [B6*] Any heterogeneous whole that is ϕ primarily$_1$ is ϕ even if a part of it is not ϕ, for any homogeneous attribute ϕ.

However, [B6*] plays no logical role in Scotus's Revised Primacy Argument, its work being done by the stronger claim [B7*].

The Second Kind of Primacy

When Scotus introduces the second kind of primacy in *QSM* IX q.14 n.16 (WV 7.594b), he deliberately *contrasts* it with the case in which φ is predicated of *S* only in virtue of applying to a proper (integral) part of *S*, for example, when Socrates is said to be healthy because the part of him that was diseased is now recovered.[65] To put the point suggestively, we may say that the proposition

$$S \text{ is } \phi \text{ primarily}_2$$

holds only when φ applies to *S* as a whole. Hence the elimination rule for primarily$_2$,

[E2] Anything that is φ primarily$_2$ is φ,

holds by definition; for example, anything that is locally moved primarily$_2$ is thereby locally moved. Now if some part of a whole that is φ primarily$_2$ were itself not φ, the homogeneous attribute φ would apply to the whole only in virtue of the *remainder* of the whole being φ.[66] But the remainder of a whole is itself a proper part of the whole, and hence the attribute φ would apply to the whole only in virtue of applying to some proper part of it. By the definition of primarily$_2$, then, the whole is not φ primarily$_2$, which contradicts the initial assumption that the whole is φ primarily$_2$. Hence if some part of a whole is not φ, the whole is not φ primarily$_2$.[67]

---

[65] Scotus also describes "primarily$_2$," in *Ord.* II d.2 p.2 q.6 n.475 (Vat. 7.369–70), called there the "primacy according to the whole": "In one way, ['primarily' is taken] insofar as it expresses the same thing as what is 'according to the whole,' and it is opposed to what is 'according to the part.' Aristotle takes ['primarily'] in this way in *Phys.* v.1 [224a21–29], where he distinguishes that something is moved according to an accident or according to a whole, and something according to a part. Aristotle also takes 'being moved primarily' in this way in *Phys.* VI.6 [236b19–23], where he says that 'whatever is moved at some time, primarily, is moved at any [part] of that time.' (He frequently [takes 'primarily' in this way] elsewhere [as well].)" The main contrast, for our purposes, is between an attribute that applies to a subject merely in virtue of a part, and applying in virtue of the whole.

[66] The assumption that the attribute is homogeneous rules out the possibility of heterogeneous "emergent" properties that are only applicable at the level of the whole. If health were a heterogeneous property, such as the proper balance of all the parts of an animal's body taken together, then any part would by definition fail to be healthy, but the animal would nevertheless be healthy as a whole—the animal would be healthy primarily$_2$ despite the fact that no part of it is healthy (strictly speaking).

[67] Scotus offers a version of this argument in *Ord.* II d.2 p.2 q.6 n.477 (Vat. 7.370), under the further assumption that the whole is homogeneous: "For if [a body] were moved by itself primarily, i.e., according to itself as a whole, then the motion would be in any given part of it. The consequence holds by the fact that that which is a whole, insofar as it is moving, is homogeneous, and *being moved* is a homogeneous attribute. Now a homogeneous attribute is not present in a whole 'primarily' with the primacy ['according to the whole'] unless it is present in any given part of [the whole]. Therefore, it follows that if a whole is moved

The conclusion drawn at the end of the preceding paragraph specifies a logical condition that any whole must satisfy for a homogeneous attribute. In particular, it does not assert the existence of a causal connection: the part's not being ϕ is not the *cause* of the whole's not being ϕ primarily$_2$, but rather is a *sufficient condition* for the whole's not being ϕ primarily$_2$. The condition of the part is not an efficient, material, formal, or final cause of the condition of the whole. Causal connections are not to be assimilated to logical conditions. Scotus argues that once this further distinction is drawn, there is only one possible way to read [B1] and [B3], as he says in *QSM* IX q.14 n.16 (WV 7.594b–595a):

> But every whole *does* rest [at the rest of another], because it is divisible—and so (a) "another" [in the phrase "at the rest of another"] is taken in Aristotle for that which does *not* receive the predication of the motion primarily, [namely, the part], and (b) the "at" [in the phrase] is held consecutively, not causally. Now if the phrase were formulated by means of an absolute [grammatical construction],[68] "that part being at rest," it should [still] be analyzed by "if" and not by "because," for although [B1] would be true with "because," nevertheless [B3] is false [with "because"].

The phrase "at the rest of another" occurs in [B1]. The grammatical reformulation of [B1] Scotus mentions here, so as to have a distributed middle term to connect [B1] and [B3], should be interpreted consecutively rather than causally, whereas [B1] may hold consecutively or causally, [B3] does not hold when taken causally, as noted above. By implication, then, a consecutive reading should preserve the truth of [B1] and [B3], so as to produce a valid argument.[69] Hence the correct reformulation of [B3] is:

> [B3*] If any part of a whole is not ϕ, then that whole is not ϕ primarily$_2$, for any homogeneous attribute ϕ.

Substitution on [B3*] readily yields another premise for the Revised Primacy Argument:

> [B10] If any part of a whole that is ϕ primarily$_1$ is not ϕ, then that whole is not ϕ primarily$_2$, for any homogeneous attribute ϕ.

where [B10] illustrates a link between the two kinds of primacy.

'primarily' in this way, that if a part is at rest, the whole is at rest." According to the argument given in the text, the requirement that the whole be homogeneous can be dispensed with; Scotus only mentions it here since he is concerned with the particular case of the local motion of a homogeneous body. All that he needs in order to establish the "consequence" to which he refers is that the attribute be homogeneous.

68 Literally: "But if the claim were formulated by means of an ablative absolute." I have given the corresponding nominative absolute (the only absolute construction English possesses).

69 Scotus asserts that [B1] can be read either consecutively or causally, for the simple reason that it makes a negative assertion: a causal connection or logical condition fails to hold. The statement of [B1*] given above is consecutive rather than causal.

The Connection Theorem

There is another, more fundamental link between the two kinds of primacy. According to [E1], anything that is φ primarily$_1$ is φ. If φ is a homogeneous attribute, then, as in the argument for [B7*], it cannot apply to its subject in virtue of applying to any less general feature of its subject. On the one hand, if the whole in question is heterogeneous, then φ does not apply to its subject only in virtue of applying to something that *merely* belongs to its subject, as a part belongs to a heterogeneous whole. On the other hand, if the whole in question is homogeneous, the part is of the same *ratio* as the whole, and so the part is not "another thing"; thus each part of the homogeneous whole must be φ as well.[70] Hence the homogeneous attribute φ applies to a whole "as a whole," that is, the whole is φ primarily$_2$. Therefore, we can state the following Connection Theorem:[71]

> [B13] Any whole that is φ primarily$_1$ is φ primarily$_2$, for any homogeneous attribute φ.

With this, Scotus's modifications to and clarifications of the Primacy Argument are complete.

The Revised Primacy Argument

Scotus does not explicitly state the Revised Primacy Argument in *QSM* IX q.14, but he offers a lucid and compact summary of it in *Ord.* II d.2 p.2 q.6 n.485 (Vat. 7.373–74):

> Hence Aristotle's argument precisely proves that a whole is not moved by itself primarily: i.e., that *being moved*, which is a homogeneous attribute, is not

[70] Note that [B7*] only asserts that a *heterogeneous* whole is φ primarily$_1$ only if no part is φ, whereas [B3*] asserts that *any* whole is φ primarily$_2$ only if each part is φ. Each part of a homogeneous whole that is φ primarily$_1$ must itself be φ. Clearly no nonatomic heterogeneous whole can have an attribute φ both primarily$_1$ and primarily$_2$, as Scotus goes on to point out.

[71] There is a clear use of the Connection Theorem, under slightly stronger assumptions—Scotus here is concerned with heavy bodies that are homogeneous wholes—in *Ord.* II d.2 p.2 q.6 n.482 (Vat. 7.372): "Hence this whole homogeneous heavy [body] is not moved by itself primarily, such that *being moved*, as it is common to itself and to any given part of it, is present to it primarily according to this primacy [= primacy$_1$], since then it would not be removed from the whole even if it were removed from the part.

"However, this [claim]—[namely 'it would not be removed from the whole even if it were removed from the part']—is false according to the other primacy [= primacy$_2$], necessarily concurrent with this one [= primacy$_1$] (*propter aliam primitatem necessario concurrentem cum ista*) if it is postulated in a homogeneous subject in respect of a homogeneous attribute." Scotus rejects the conclusion drawn in the first paragraph because primacy$_1$ must be accompanied by primacy$_2$: the "necessary concurrence" of primacy$_2$ with primacy$_1$ in the case of a homogeneous attribute, described at the end of this passage, is a version of the Connection Theorem. The conclusion Scotus draws from this whole argument, namely that homogeneous bodies are locally moved primarily$_2$ but not primarily$_1$, is due to the Revised Primacy Argument presented below.

present in a homogeneous whole "primarily" (i.e., according to precise causality [= primarily$_1$]) insofar as that attribute is taken as homogeneous (i.e., as of the same *ratio* for the whole amount and for a partial amount)—since then it would not be removed from the whole if it were removed from the part, which is false according to the primacy of totality [= primacy$_2$], which is here deduced from the *ratio* of precise causality [= primarily$_1$].

The argument runs as follows. Assume that a homogeneous attribute is present in a homogeneous whole primarily$_1$; by definition, the attribute can fail to apply to some part of the whole and nevertheless still characterize the whole. Yet if the attribute is present in the whole primarily$_1$, it must therefore also be present in the whole primarily$_2$. But a homogeneous attribute that is present in a homogeneous whole primarily$_2$ must apply to each part of the whole in order to characterize the whole. This result conflicts with the previous claim, derived from the attribute being present primarily$_1$, that the attribute may fail to apply to a part and nevertheless apply to the whole. Since the argument is completely general, it shows that no homogeneous attribute is present in a homogeneous whole primarily$_1$.

Scotus's argument turns on showing that it is contradictory for a homogeneous whole to have a homogeneous attribute with a double primacy, and he establishes the contradiction by inferring from the hypothesis that the whole has the attribute primarily$_1$ that it must thereby have the attribute primarily$_2$. But this inferential move is just the Connection Theorem: the whole that is moved primarily$_1$ must also be moved primarily$_2$, and this result is "deduced from the *ratio*" of primacy$_1$, that is, it is true by the definition of primacy$_1$.

The Revised Primacy Argument can be stated in its full generality as follows:[72]

[B1*] Anything that is φ primarily$_1$ is φ even if another thing is not φ.
(definition of "primarily$_1$")

[B2*] Assume that φ is predicable of something that is a heterogeneous whole. (hypothesis)

[B3*] If any part of a whole is not φ, then that whole is not φ primarily$_2$, for any homogeneous attribute φ. (definition of "primarily$_2$")

[B4*] Heterogeneous wholes are not predicable of their parts.
(definition of "heterogeneous whole")

[B5*] A part of a heterogeneous whole differs from that whole.
(by [B4*])

---

[72] The premises are not numbered consecutively: [B1*]–[B7*] are Scotus's revisions of [B1]–[B7] respectively, where [B6] (and the revision [B6*]) are no longer needed for the proof; [B8]–[B9] are dropped from the original Primacy Argument as given in section 2; [B10]–[B15] are new premises added to the Revised Primacy Argument.

[B7*] Any part of a heterogeneous whole that is φ primarily$_1$ is not φ, for any homogeneous attribute φ. (by [B1*], [B2*], [B5*])

[B10] If any part of a whole that is φ primarily$_1$ is not φ, then that whole is not φ primarily$_2$, for any homogeneous attribute φ. (by [B3*])

[B11] Any heterogeneous whole that is φ primarily$_1$ is not φ primarily$_2$, for any homogeneous attribute φ. (by [B7*] and [B10])

[B12] There is no heterogeneous whole that is φ primarily$_1$ and φ primarily$_2$, for any homogeneous attribute φ. (by [B11])

[B13] Any whole that is φ primarily$_1$ is φ primarily$_2$, for any homogeneous attribute φ. (Connection Theorem)

[B14] Any heterogeneous whole that is φ primarily$_1$ is φ primarily$_2$, for any homogeneous attribute φ. (by [B13])

[B15] Any heterogeneous whole that is φ primarily$_1$ is both φ primarily$_2$ and not φ primarily$_2$, for any homogeneous attribute φ. (by [B11] and [B14])

Therefore: There is no heterogeneous whole that is φ primarily$_1$, for any homogeneous attribute φ.

Scotus identifies the intermediate result [B12] as Aristotle's conclusion.

Despite the forbidding formal appearance of the argument, Scotus's point can be made directly. According to the Connection Theorem, any whole that is φ primarily$_1$ is also φ primarily$_2$, for any homogeneous attribute φ. But in the case of a heterogeneous whole x, being φ primarily$_1$ entails that (1) no part of x is φ; (2) x is φ primarily$_2$; and (3) according to (2), each part of x is φ. Clearly (1)–(3) are incompatible—and the incompatibility stems from the initial assumption that x was φ primarily$_1$, as Scotus concludes.

There are only four possibilities for any heterogeneous whole x:

1. x is φ neither primarily$_1$ nor primarily$_2$.
2. x is φ primarily$_1$ but not primarily$_2$.
3. x is φ primarily$_2$ but not primarily$_1$.
4. x is φ both primarily$_1$ and primarily$_2$.

Now (1) is a nonstarter, since there is no reason to say that something is a self-mover if it is locally moved neither primarily$_1$ nor primarily$_2$. Scotus takes Aristotle's argument to be directed toward and to rule out (4). The Revised Primacy Argument, however, leads to a stronger conclusion: (2) is also excluded. This leaves open (3), however, and hence the Revised Primacy Argument excludes only a restricted range of cases with regard to heterogeneous wholes—to say nothing of homogeneous wholes, which are not even addressed by the Revised Primacy Argument.[73]

---

[73] The limited scope of the conclusion of the Revised Primacy Argument should not be

Scotus recognizes the limitations of the final conclusion of the Revised Primacy Argument. As he remarks in *QSM* IX q.14 n.16 (WV 7.594b–595a), "It is futile to cite Aristotle here in order to prove this conclusion—that nothing moves itself—generally," since there are many cases to which the Revised Primacy Argument does not apply. For example, as Scotus continues, it is possible that some whole is φ primarily$_2$, for some homogeneous attribute φ, and yet is *not* φ primarily$_1$—for example, the homogeneous whole *fire* is hot primarily$_2$ but not primarily$_1$:[74]

> For if fire is the effective cause of its proper heat, [then] even though the whole makes itself hot as a whole, and so the same thing changes or moves itself or acts upon itself primarily (taking "primarily" as it is taken in *Phys.* v.1 [224a27–29] [= primarily$_2$]), nevertheless that fire does not make itself hot primarily (taking "primarily" according to the [first] signification [= primarily$_1$]).
>
> What is surprising [in this result]? For that particular amount of fire, from whatever it may come to be, is not hot primarily ([taking "primarily"] in the [first] way [= primarily$_1$]).

Scotus makes a similar point for the downward motion of heavy bodies in *Ord.* II d.2 p.2 q.6 nn.479–80 (Vat. 7.371):

> Nevertheless, by means of precisely one primacy [= primacy$_2$], some whole can be moved by itself primarily. Now in the case at hand, I say that a heavy [body] *is* moved by itself primarily [= primarily$_2$], since it both moves and is

---

overstated, for it does rule out a variety of cases. For example, a heterogeneous mixture of elements does not move downward primarily$_1$. This conclusion should be supported by intuition: the *mixture* cannot be the commensurate subject of the downward motion; rather, each element in the mixture has its own proper direction (perhaps even downward), and the mixture itself moves only derivatively.

[74] If my reconstruction of Scotus's argument is correct, Scotus stumbles badly after presenting the example of fire. For he immediately goes on in *QSM* IX q.14 n.16 (WV 7.595a) to say: "Indeed, a contradiction follows, namely that [the fire] is not hot if a part of it is not hot, and that [the fire] is hot if a part of it is not hot. The first follows from [taking] the primacy in the second way [= primacy$_2$], the second follows from [taking] the primacy in the first way [= primacy$_1$]." But no contradiction follows: fire is a homogeneous whole, not a heterogeneous one. The claim that the fire "is hot if a part of it is not hot" does *not* follow "from [taking] the primacy in the first way": [B2*] is invalidated, and hence neither [B4*] nor [B5*] holds, making it impossible to derive the key premise [B7*] from [B1*]. A homogeneous whole is predicable of its part, and hence there is no way to apply "another thing" in [B1*] to the part.

There is some indication that Scotus is aware of the problem: in *QSM* IX q.14 n.17 (WV 7.595a–b) he raises the question of what is hot primarily$_1$, if anything, and he replies that a universal whole (rather than an integral whole) that is homogeneous with regard to its parts is the commensurate subject of such an attribute. The problem in the text cited above would therefore be that a "*particular* amount of fire" is under discussion, not the universal *fire* in general.

moved in accordance with any part whatsoever, and to any part whatsoever—though not "primarily" in the first way [= primarily$_1$], but insofar as it is in the whole [= primarily$_2$]—both *moving* and *being moved* are suitable.

The soundness of the Revised Primacy Argument does not exclude the possibility of self-change, although it does exclude self-change (as a homogeneous attribute) being present in a heterogeneous whole primarily$_1$.

The Downward Motion of Heavy Bodies

Yet the last case mentioned above—the downward motion of heavy bodies—raises a difficulty: isn't it true that downward motion stems from the very nature of heavy bodies as heavy? Shouldn't the attribute *moving downward naturally* be applicable to heavy bodies as its commensurate subject, such that heavy bodies move downward naturally primarily$_1$? Despite the real limitations of the Revised Primacy Argument, it seems after all to exclude such a case. This is a serious challenge to Scotus's account, as he recognizes.[75]

Scotus begins his response to this challenge by distinguishing the level of generality at which such assertions are made. At the level at which one speaks of attributes stemming from the nature of something, the singular is not in question, as Scotus asserts in *QSM* ix q.14 n.17 (WV 7.595a–b):

> It has heretofore been customary of no proper attribute (*passio*) that something singular be assigned as its primary subject, but rather [something] universal, which abstracts from every amount, and is equally preserved in this whole homogeneous amount and in [any] part belonging to it. And it is true that [a proper attribute] is never removed from that universal if something of which that universal is not predicated (due to some other circumstance) were not hot [as in the case of fire].

Generally speaking, then, an attribute takes a *kind* of thing as its primary subject, and the attribute applies at this level even if the universal fails to apply to a part of anything falling under it, "due to some other circumstance."

Yet Scotus's reply is incomplete at best. If an attribute applies to a kind, a corresponding individual attribute should apply to an individual that falls under that kind. Scotus offers a more nuanced response, one that disre-

---

[75] This challenge is presented as an objection in *QSM* ix q.14 n.17 (WV 7.595a) and in *Ord.* ii d.2 p.2 q.6 n.481 (Vat. 7.371). The objection applies to the account given in note 73 above: granted that a mixture is heavy, why should the heterogeneity or homogeneity of its elements make a difference regarding its attributes? After all, isn't the commensurate subject of *moving downward naturally* the heavy body, not the heavy simple body?

gards the heterogeneity or homogeneity of the whole at issue, in *Ord.* II d.2 p.2 q.6 n.481 (Vat. 7.372):

> I say that we can speak of either:
>
> 1. *being moved* in general [as it is suitable to the heavy body in general];
> 2. this *being moved* as it is suitable to this whole heavy [body];
> 3. a part of this *being moved* as it is suitable to a part of this heavy [body].
>
> I state that just as the whole heavy [body] and part of the heavy [body] are homogeneous in *heaviness*, so too the total *being moved* (which is an attribute of the total whole) and the partial *being moved* (which is an attribute of the part) are "being moved" of the same *ratio*—and just as *being moved downward naturally* in general is present primarily by a primacy of precise causality [= primacy$_1$] to the heavy [body] in general, so too *this* total *being moved* is present to *this* total heavy body by a like primacy [= primacy$_1$], and this partial *being moved* (which is part of this *being moved* belonging to the total) is present to a part of this heavy [body] by a like primacy [= primacy$_1$].

The attribute *being moved downward naturally* is applicable primarily$_1$ to a heavy body in general, which entails that "*this* total *being moved* is present to *this* total heavy body by a like primacy." Yet Scotus's claim does not contradict the conclusion of the Revised Primacy Argument, despite its appearance of so doing, because a "total" attribute is not homogeneous but rather heterogeneous.

The description of an attribute may be ambiguous: "being moved downward naturally" certainly can be taken as a homogeneous attribute. In that case, it does not apply primarily$_1$ to an individual heavy body.[76] However, Scotus asserts, we should interpret it as a heterogeneous attribute, one that is cumulative: the "total" attribute *being moved downward naturally* is literally composed of the individual motions of each of the heavy body's parts. Scotus's description of "total motion" as a cumulative heterogeneous attribute is given in *Ord.* II d.2 p.2 q.6 n.484 (Vat. 7.373):

> I state that this total heavy [body], insofar as it is homogeneous, is [composed] out of similar parts (and these parts are prior in some way to that whole), such that were they destroyed in the *ratio* of parts, the whole does not remain. Thus I maintain that it is not unacceptable that their own attributes and partial motions be present to them (and in a certain way [are present] before the total motion is suitable to the whole itself), since the total motion is also composed out of the partial motions of the parts, just as the whole heavy [body] is [composed] out of the parts of the heavy [body].

---

[76] Scotus recognizes that the attribute *being moved downward naturally* cannot apply to an individual heavy body as a homogeneous attribute, and he says so immediately after the cited passage—the text of his statement is given in note 65 above.

Since "the total motion is also composed out of the motions of the parts," the total motion is a heterogeneous attribute rather than a homogeneous attribute, as required by the Connection Theorem. Furthermore, the heavy body itself is homogeneous, and so [B5*] does not hold.[77] Hence the Revised Primacy Argument does not rule out this case.

The Primacy of Self-Change

Scotus's discussion of the Primacy Argument shows that there can be cases of primary self-change, where this is compatible with the admission that there may be really distinct parts of a subject that interact so as to produce the self-change. Nevertheless, the resulting change—the coming-to-be of φ in the subject—is primarily present in the subject. Scotus mentions one such case in response to Aristotle's remark in the *Physics* that self-motion always breaks down into a mover and a moved, in *Ord.* II d.2 p.2 q.6 n.474 (Vat. 7.369):[78]

> I state first, as regards that authoritative passage in *Phys.* VIII.5 [257b12–13], that obviously anything moving *by cognition* is divided into two [constitu-

[77] Scotus explicitly mentions [B5*] as an objection to his account at the beginning of *Ord.* II d.2 p.2 q.6 n.484 (Vat. 7.373). Immediately after his description of "total motion" as a cumulative heterogeneous attribute, he explains why [B5*] does not hold: "And then I deny the assumed proposition:

> What is suitable to something primarily (i.e., according to precise causality [= primarily$_1$]), is not removed from it because something that is not that predicate is removed from something that is not that subject.

Indeed, this proposition is universally false where the subject has a prior subject and the attribute a prior attribute; for then, upon the removal of the prior attribute from the prior subject, it would follow that the posterior attribute is removed from the posterior subject." The "assumed proposition" simply is the relevant version of [B5*]. I have altered the punctuation of the Vatican edition, based on the objection given at the beginning of n.484, to read as follows: *Et tunc nego hanc propositionem assumptam "quod convenit alicui primo (id est secundum causalitatem praecisam), non removetur ab eo quia aliquid quod non est ipsum praedicatum removetur ab aliquo quod not est ipsum subiectum." Haec enim propositio.*

[78] Scotus is concerned to show that there need not be a "real distinction" between the mover and the moved—that is, that the mover and the moved need not be distinct things (*res*). The common view held that a real distinction involved separability: two items are really distinct if and only if one could exist without the other (at least by God's absolute power). The real distinction is at the opposite end of the spectrum from a "distinction of reason," where there are two distinct concepts of one and the same real thing. Now Scotus introduced an intermediate less-than-real distinction called the "formal distinction." Roughly, two items are formally distinct if and only if they are really the same (i.e., neither can be separated from the other), but the definition of one does not include the other, e.g., intellect and will. Items that are formally distinct have some ontological foundation for their distinctness; the difference between them is not a purely conceptual matter—but the precise content of the ontological

ents], of which one is primarily the mover and the other primarily what is moved. The reason is as follows: the motive potency of such a mover is an organic potency, such that it not only requires a distinction between body and soul as between the mover and the moved, but perhaps [also] requires in the body itself (in which there is the organic power) a moving part of the body that is distinct from the moved part. However, [the distinction into two constituents] is not necessarily the case for something moving itself nonorganically, since the whole is uniform with respect to first act, and the whole is in potency with respect to second act.

The motion of inorganic bodies, such as a stone's natural downward motion, is not due to the interaction of physically distinct constituents: the principiative modalities that are responsible for its motion are not located in different parts of the stone. The motion of organic bodies may be due to principles that are located in physically different parts of the body, as in the case of jumping mentioned above (p. 235), which explains how non-uniform and discontinuous motion is possible in the case of animals. Nevertheless, whether the body is inorganic or organic, its motion is present to it "primarily" (in one of the two available ways).

The fact that a real distinction may hold between the location of the principiative modalities responsible for self-change is irrelevant to whether the change is present primarily. The question is whether the attribute that comes to be in the subject is present in it as a commensurate subject or is present only in virtue of a part of the subject—and this question has nothing to do with the source of the attribute (internal or external to the subject). The ascription of primacy to the presence of an attribute in a subject does not depend on whether the attribute is present through the subject's own activity or through the activity of an external agent. Therefore, the Revised Primacy Argument not only fails to rule out the possibility of self-change, but also shows that the conclusion drawn on the basis of the Primacy Argument—that self-change is only accidental or incidental, due to the interaction of really distinct factors—has no force. Self-change is due to real features of things, but these features may or may not be really distinct, and the fact that self-change is due to real features keeps it from being merely incidental or accidental.

---

foundation has proven to be quite difficult to spell out. In any event, Scotus holds that principles are real features of things ("real" in the sense that they are not artifacts of how we think about them), but that they need not be really distinct: principles may be only formally distinct from one another. Whether a real distinction holds is a matter for case-by-case investigation. If principles are located in physically distinct parts of a body, then it is likely that they are separable (by simply removing the parts in question), and hence that a real distinction obtains. The converse, however, does not hold. A real distinction between principles need not entail physically distinct locations for each principle. See note 56 above.

6. SCOTUS'S RESPONSE TO THE CONTINUITY ARGUMENT

The first difficulty with explanation posed by the Continuity Argument, that ascriptions of self-change are explanatorily vacuous, has already been effectively countered by Scotus: an ascription of self-change depends on a nuanced view about the possession of principiative modalities. Most of Scotus's energies are therefore directed at the second difficulty, explaining conditions under which such ascriptions are legitimate.

First, Scotus grants a limited version of the conclusion of the Continuity Argument: inanimate natural beings capable of self-change *do* always act. (Animal movement and the exercise of free will are separate cases; see the discussion in section 7.) Inanimate natural beings can also be interfered with, however, as Scotus asserts in *QSM* IX q.14 n.10 (WV 7.589a):

> First of all, it could be said in general that a natural cause, although termi-nated of itself at its effect, can nevertheless be interfered with. However, when the interference is removed, [a natural cause] immediately acts for the produc-tion of the effect—just as it would have acted from the beginning if there had not been interference. Thus wherever the two conditions (described above [in the First General Conclusion]) that are necessary for something to act upon itself are fulfilled, then, if one supposes interference from the beginning due to something external, after the interference is removed [the natural cause] will immediately act upon itself.

Thus stones will fall unless prevented, hot water cools itself off, and so on. In order to keep this reply from being vacuous, Scotus is careful to describe how a natural agent can be interfered with, in *QSM* IX q.14 n.25 (WV 7.603a–b):

> As for the [Continuity Argument], I reply that the agent [does not act in the following six cases]:
>
> 1. [The agent] does not act when the terminus is given.
> 2. [The agent does not act] when [the terminus] is not given but the agent can be interfered with by a stronger contrary power so that it does not act.
> 3. If [the agent] is not the entire active cause, but there is another [factor that must act] along with it, [then] if that other [factor] is not present, [the agent] does not act.
> 4. [The agent] will not act if it does not have that in which or on which it acts.
> 5. [The agent] will not act if another action is naturally presupposed by it and that [action] does not take place.
> 6. [The agent may not act] if [the agent] is free, capable of itself of not acting.

By means of any one of (1)–(6), it can be explained for any given motive [agent] why it does not always move itself.

These six ways in which self-change may be prevented form a sort of checklist for the natural philosopher, and provide a list of legitimate grounds on which to claim that an inanimate being changes itself even though it is not occurrently doing so.

Given the restrictive conditions, why should anyone ever postulate self-change? Scotus argues that self-change is a way in which the world is "more perfect," in *QSM* IX q.14 n.14 (WV 7.592b–593a):

> Finally, it is stated in general that something ought not to be denied to any nature that, when postulated, would be characteristic of perfection in such a nature—unless it be shown on some other grounds that such a perfection is not present in that [nature]. For nature always does what is better when it would have been possible [to do so] and did not lack the necessary [means]. Generally, creatures are produced in being lacking some perfection that they are suited to attain. For instance, living [creatures] generally [are produced] in an incomplete quantity,[79] without even operations belonging to the soul; some other [things are produced] without proper qualities; yet others without a proper place. If [in these things][80] a principle that is active with respect to such perfection that they are suited [to attain] were granted [to exist], they would simply be more perfect, since [they would be] less dependent upon extrinsic [forces]. Therefore, whenever it is not apparent that such a nature does not have a principle that is active with respect to such a perfection (or rather [whenever] it especially seems that [the nature] has [such a principle]), this point should simply be conceded, since this dignifies nature.

Thus self-change is to be postulated whenever possible, if it is not prevented in any of the six ways Scotus has mentioned. Scotus's use of the "dignity of nature" may sound unconvincing to modern ears, but we can take it as a kind of regulative ideal for physical explanation: assume things actually possess causal powers unless there are good grounds for identifying an external principle that is solely responsible for bringing about a change.[81]

[79] "In an incomplete quantity": that is, not fully grown.

[80] Reading *eis* for *eius*.

[81] The modern regulative ideal of physical explanation inverts this proposition: assume an external causal explanation unless forced to grant self-change. Nevertheless, cashing out Scotus's adamant insistence on self-change explanations as a regulative ideal does serve to show how his views are not merely quaint or antiquated, for it presses the question *why* we should choose one regulative ideal rather than another. If the answer is simply instrumental—that one serves to generate and sustain more fruitful physical theories of the world—then that, I take it, is precisely why we are modern and not medieval physicists today. Scotus's views may have been superseded, but that does not make it silly for him to hold them, and the justification of our view should be, appropriately enough, a historical account of the adoption

The final worry raised by the Continuity Argument is that Scotus's world will not constitute a unity, that there will be physical phenomena in it that are not explained by external causes. Scotus has two replies to this worry. First, as noted in the preceding paragraphs, instances of self-change may not be causally linked to other physical events, but will nonetheless fall under the heading of a general physical principle, namely, that natural beings acquire and actualize all the perfections of which they are capable, unless prevented. Second, Scotus holds that there is no better alternative. To prohibit self-change would be to require that all causation is univocal. But how, Scotus asks, does univocal causality produce a connection among things in the world any more than equivocal causality does? Thus he writes in *QSM* ix q.14 n.15 (WV 7.593b):

> [I state] that a univocal action *never* produces a connection among the active and passive [elements] in the universe. Nor does the Philosopher seem to assume such a [univocal] agent and its effect, essentially ordered as regards a third such [effect]. Rather, there is a more essential connection due to equivocal agents and [their] effects. . . . Causes that are essentially ordered as regards a third effect have a different order in causing, according to what has been said in *QSM* ii qq.4–6 [n.16] ([WV 7.128b–129a]). And perhaps that [order] is the essential connection belonging to the universe, whether the ultimate cause be univocal or equivocal with its effect. And the connection is thus preserved by postulating in the same [thing] the *ratio* of an ultimate cause as regards its effect, just as [the connection is preserved] by postulating [the *ratio* of an ultimate cause as regards its effect] in another [thing].

Equivocal causes and their effects unite two distinct kinds of form, unlike univocal causes, and so can be taken to produce a genuine interconnection and unification of disparate elements in the world. Furthermore, cases of self-change are paradigmatically cases in which two principiative potencies concur to produce jointly their principiatum, which itself is a way of unifying distinct things, namely as partial co-causes (or co-principles). Yet if co-causality or co-principiation is the means by which disparate elements are united, this explanation of unification is essentially indifferent to whether the causes or principles are univocal or equivocal. Hence there is no reason to see Scotus's account as endangering the unity of the world.

Therefore, the worries raised by the Continuity Argument have all been put to rest, and the self-change explanation vindicated as a permissible kind of physical explanation. Self-change can therefore be regarded as a real feature of the world, and insistence upon it as a pervasive feature of physical explanation.

---

of progressively more fruitful theories that justify the modern regulative ideal of physical explanation.

7. SCOTUS'S INTERPRETATION OF ARISTOTLE

Scotus is not content merely to hold that self-change is a real feature of the world: he maintains that this is Aristotle's position as well as his own. To prove that this is so, Scotus takes up and carefully analyzes texts from Aristotle that seem to support the common position rather than his own (cited in section 2 above). The results are instructive.

Scotus's Response to Meta. Θ.1, 1046a28–29 and 1046a9–11

Scotus treats the first pair of passages from Aristotle together, offering a unified response to both. His discussion conceals a wealth of textual difficulties that suggest a striking conclusion: the existence of another, otherwise unknown, Latin translation of Aristotle's *Metaphysics*. Let us consider his solution and then turn to the textual difficulties.

Scotus presents his unified solution in *QSM* ix q.14 n.25 (WV 7.603a) as follows:

> As for the citation of Aristotle here ([*Meta.* Θ.1, 1046a28–29]) . . . Aristotle added "insofar as it is naturally unified" because he wished not to say "nothing moves itself" absolutely, but rather [only] with the restriction "*insofar as.*" And "naturally unified" is taken [here] for "the same [thing]," as is clear from his proof: "for it is one thing and not another." Thus in the definition of active potency ([in *Meta.* Θ.1, 1046a9–11]), [Aristotle] did not put "transforming another" absolutely, but correctly added "insofar as it is another."

This is an elegant solution: when Aristotle asserts that nothing acts upon itself insofar as it is naturally unified, Scotus suggests that this is to be read (on the basis of Aristotle's further remarks) as "nothing acts upon itself insofar as it is the same thing." But that, Scotus holds, is compatible with something acting upon itself insofar as it is another, and indeed explains why Aristotle offered a disjunctive definition of active potency as the principle of transforming another *or* transforming itself insofar as it is another.[82] Thus nothing acts upon itself insofar as it is the same thing, but only insofar

---

[82] Scotus also discusses Aristotle's definition of active potency in *QSM* ix qq.3–4, and he makes the same point there in n.12 (WV 7.551b): "As for the third [argument], it should be stated that [Aristotle] put 'another *or* insofar as it is another' into the definition of active potency ([*Meta.* Θ.1, 1046a9–11]). And [Aristotle] hints at why he does this in *Meta.* Δ.12 [1019a17–18], where he immediately appends [the remark]: 'The medical art may exist as a potential being (*potestas ens*) in what is healed, but not insofar as it is what is healed.'" The passage to which Aristotle's remark is appended states that active potency is the principle of moving or transforming "what is different *or* [itself] insofar as it is different" (1019a16). This passage also has textual difficulties: see the discussion above.

as it is another. When taken together, these passages have an effect opposite to that intended by the defenders of the common position—they support Scotus's contention that self-change is possible.

Scotus's response, however elegant it may be, depends on the fact that Aristotle's definition of active potency is disjunctive. There is no known channel of transmission whereby Scotus could have come by this information, however. There is no question that he has it; his extensive discussion in *QSM* IX qq.3–4, and especially the principal arguments for q.4, make it clear that Scotus's text of the definition read as follows:[83]

> *principium transmutandi aliud aut inquantum aliud.*

This reading holds for 1046a9–11 (and 1046b4), and a parallel reading for the definition of passive potency at 1046a13–14. Scotus also reads *Meta.* Δ.12, 1020a2 and 1020a6, in the same way. Yet in each case, Aristotle's text reads

> [AR1] ἀρχὴ μεταβολῆς ἐν ἄλλῳ <ἢ> ἧ ἄλλο,

where ἢ is omitted in some manuscripts.[84] As far as can be determined, Scotus read the parallel passages in *Meta.* Δ.12, 1019a15, 1019a20, and 1019a35 in a parallel way:

> *principium motionis vel transmutationis in diverso aut inquantum diversum.*

And here Aristotle's text reads

> [AR2] ἀρχὴ κινήσεως ἢ μεταβολῆς ἡ ἐν ἑτέρῳ <ἢ> ἧ ἕτερον,

where ἢ again is omitted in some manuscripts.[85] There are two textual problems: how Scotus knew about the disputed ἢ in each of the eight passages; and how Scotus knew that the gerund phrase *transmutandi aliud* was an appropriate replacement for μεταβολῆς ἐν ἄλλῳ in the first five passages—for neither is reflected in any known channel of transmission.[86]

---

[83] The citation of 1046a9–11 as the "initial text" for q.4 in *QSM* IX qq.3–4 n.1 has been filled in by the editors, not derived directly from Scotus's text. See WV 7.542a–543a for the principal arguments that Aristotle does *not* define "active potency" correctly in this passage, where Scotus takes each term in the definition and bases an argument on it: there the text is said to read *principium transmutandi aliud inquantum aliud*, to which his rejoinder, reported in the preceding note, is that it correctly reads *principium transmutandi aliud aut inquantum aliud*.

[84] Using the Ross-Jaeger standard sigla for manuscripts of the *Metaphysics*, the situation is as follows: A^b omits ἢ in all five passages; J omits ἧ at 1046a9–11 and ἢ at 1020a2 and 1020a6; E^1 omits ἧ at 1020a2. Ross and Jaeger mistakenly hold that J is a tenth-century manuscript, whereas it is in fact a ninth-century manuscript. The later manuscript E, however, is a witness to an earlier tradition. Both E and J belong to the same family of manuscripts; A^b belongs to a different family.

[85] Here A^b omits ἢ in all three passages.

[86] I have found only one possible, rather peculiar, anticipation of Scotus's reading. When

There are five known medieval translations of Aristotle's *Metaphysics*. Two are irrelevant: the partial twelfth-century translation from the Greek made by James of Venice (the *vetustissima*) and the anonymous thirteenth-century revision of James's translation (the *vetus*) do not cover the whole of the *Metaphysics*. *Meta.* Δ and *Meta.* Θ are covered in the three remaining translations, however: the anonymous twelfth-century translation from the Greek (the *media*); Michael Scot's translation (the *nova*) from the Arabic along with Averroes's "great commentary," dating from 1220–35; and William of Moerbeke's translation from the Greek, made prior to 1272. Once available, Moerbeke's translation apparently became the most widely used.[87]

All three translations, in each of the eight passages mentioned above, regularly omit ἤ.[88] They render [AR1] as follows:

principium transmutationis in alio inquantum aliud   (Moerbeke = *media*)

principium transmutationis in alio prout aliud est   (*nova*)[89]

Albert the Great offers his literal commentary on 1019a15, he glosses Aristotle's definition of active potency in his *Metaphysics* v.7 tract.2 as follows (capitalized words are Aristotle's text as translated into Latin): *Ergo TOTALITER sive universaliter PRINCIPIUM MUTATIONIS VEL MOTUS in movente DICTUR POTESTAS mutandi DIVERSUM re vel re idem, sed tamen movet et mutat INQUANTUM DIVERSUM EST* (Geyer 1960, vol. 16, pt. 1, 251.18–22). This is peculiar for two reasons. First, Albert denies that anything can act upon itself in his *Commentary on the "Sentences"* I d.3 art.12. Second, there is no evidence that Scotus was familiar with Albert's writings in general, much less the details of his commentary on the *Physics*. I suspect Albert's remark is simply anomalous.

[87] William of Moerbeke's translation survives in 217 manuscripts, the *nova* in 126 (most likely due to Averroes's fame as *the* Commentator), and the *media* in 24. See Kretzmann et al. 1982, 77.

[88] This in itself is a peculiar fact: only Aᵇ omits the disputed reading in each case, but none of the medieval Latin translations is believed to have been based on Aᵇ. I cannot speak to the Arabic source of the *nova*, and the possible Greek manuscripts used for translation into Arabic. The *media*, however, according to Vuilleman-Diem's statistical studies (in *AL*), was based directly on a close relative of E, which preserves the disputed readings.

William of Moerbeke apparently brought J back from Constantinople; in any event, it is certain that he used it. (Even some marginal annotations in J seem to be in the same hand as Moerbeke's autograph of his translation of Archimedes.) In addition to J, Moerbeke used a copy of the *media*, and often follows it slavishly. Moerbeke's treatment of these passages could therefore be explained by his following the *media* in disputed readings. But why does the *media* omit these readings, since they are all present in E? There is no obvious answer.

[89] Scotus would have been familiar with the *nova* along with Averroes's commentary; Averroes (1562, fol. 227B) paraphrases this passage several times, and explicitly argues against self-change: "[Active potency] is the principle of transformation into another in that it is another, not in itself, since it is clear that nothing acts upon itself" (*principium transmutationis in aliud secundum est aliud, non in se, cum sit manifestum quod nihil agit in se*). A similar argument to the same effect is found in Averroes's commentary on the *Physics*.

and [AR2] as follows:

> *principium motionis vel transmutationis in diverso inquantum diversum*
> (Moerbeke = *media*)

> *principium motionis vel transmutationis in altero prout alterum est*   (*nova*)

(with appropriate changes depending on context). There is no disjunction present in any of the three translations, despite Scotus's explicit assertion that Aristotle's definition is disjunctive. This rules out the possibility that Scotus derived his readings from borrowings among various translations. Furthermore, though it would be possible to read *transmutationis in alio* (or *in diverso* or *in altero*) as having the force of a gerund, Scotus is just as explicit that Aristotle's text is itself formulated with a gerund.

One hypothesis to explain these peculiarities is that Scotus knew Greek. But there is no good reason to think so; knowledge of Greek was a sufficiently rare commodity in his day to be remarkable, and none of his other discussions turns on a disputed point in Greek. Therefore, all we are entitled to conclude is that there were at least some systematic corrections to the Latin translations of Aristotle's text made by a person familiar with Greek, and that these corrections have come down to us only in the derivative form in which we find them employed by thinkers such as Scotus in their analyses of Aristotle.

Since nothing else in Scotus seems to turn on any knowledge of Greek, it seems unlikely that Scotus learned about the textual difficulties in these passages from a colleague versed in Greek: if such a person were available to Scotus, he surely would have made extensive use of his knowledge. Furthermore, the corrected readings occur systematically in several passages. Scotus might have asked someone versed in Greek about the correct reading of the passage that appeared problematic. But then he would only have a corrected version of that passage, and not all of them, as is the case.

If we rule out these possibilities, we are left with the hypothesis that these corrections were a part of the written tradition that has since been lost. They may have been circulated precisely *as* corrections: a medieval errata-sheet. Yet such correction sheets often acquired titles and lives of their own—for example, the treatises that "correct" the works of Thomas Aquinas, and are often referred to by name.

If these corrections did not circulate separately, the conclusion seems inevitable that they were incorporated into Aristotle's text. There are two possibilities, the second, I believe, more likely than the first. First, the corrections may have been made by someone familiar with Greek while copying of one of the standard translations (probably the *media*). If so, Scotus may well not have known that his translation was systematically different from others' translations, which would in part explain why he does not remark on the textual differences he found. Yet it seems hard to believe that someone versed in Greek would be given a menial copyist's task. Second, the corrections could have been part of an original translation of the *Metaphysics* that has since been lost to us. Scotus, like most medieval philosophers, cited Aristotle from memory for the most part and did not discriminate among the various translations with which he was familiar; his citation here may be due to an unknown translation—perhaps a corrected compilation from previous translations. In any case, it seems to me we are entitled to conclude that Scotus's discussion is evidence for the existence of a hitherto unknown Latin translation of the text of Aristotle's *Metaphysics*, one that has since been lost to us.[90]

Scotus's Response to Phys. VIII.4, 255b29–31

Aristotle's remark in *Phys*. VIII.4, 255b29–31, that "natural things only have a principle of being acted upon in respect of motion, and not of doing [anything]," was adduced in support of the thesis that self-change is impossible, intended to verify the conclusion of the four arguments given in *Phys*. VIII.4, 255a3–18. Scotus responds that the naturalness of x's motion is strictly due to x's possession of a passive principle receptive of the motion. He argues for this response in *Ord*. II d.2 p.2 q.6 n.466 (Vat. 7.364):

> Nevertheless, on account of the Philosopher's remark ([*Phys*. VIII.4, 255b29–31]), I add further that this motion is not "natural in itself" in virtue of the fact that it has an active principle in itself, but only in virtue of the fact that what is able to move has an intrinsic passive principle naturally inclining it to motion. This is clear by the definition of "nature" in *Phys*. II.1 [192b20–23]:
>
>> [Nature] is a principle of motion of that in which it is *per se* and not *per accidens*.

[90] One piece of evidence for the second rather than the first possibility is that this reading of *Meta*. Θ.1, 1046a9–11, is not unique to Scotus. We can find the same reading in Jean Buridan's *Questions on Aristotle's "Metaphysics."* Buridan begins book IX with the question "whether it is possible for the same [thing] to act on itself or to be acted on by itself"; one of his principal arguments reads: "The opposite is argued for by Aristotle in *Meta*. Δ and Θ, where he defines 'active potency,' saying: 'active potency is the principle of transforming another or [itself] insofar as it is another'" (Buridan 1518, fol. 56r). That is, *potentia activa est principium transmutandi alterum aut inquantum alterum*. It is unlikely that Buridan derived this reading from Scotus: there is no evidence that Buridan was familiar with Scotus's writings.

The editors at the Franciscan Institute, currently engaged in producing the critical edition of *QSM*, hold that the text of the *Metaphysics* that Scotus used is a pastiche, since his readings seem to be derived from the *media* in some places, Moerbeke in others, and so on. My view is that his text must have been more than a mere pastiche; its author must have examined the Greek text itself, at least to some extent, for the reasons given above.

Indeed, nothing is a principle of naturally moving (*principium naturaliter movendi*) for something except insofar as it is per se in that which is moved. However, it is not per se and primarily in something that is moved except insofar as it is passive. Hence it is not something by nature (or a natural principle belonging to something) except because there is a passive principle in what is moved. This point is also clear because something is moved naturally for the reason that it is moved as it is naturally apt for it to be moved.

Scotus, I believe, has in mind Aristotle's contrast between "natural" and "violent" motion drawn in *Phys.* VIII.4, 255b31–256a4: it is natural for a stone to move downward, not to be moved upward (as when thrown). But the "violence" of a stone's motion upward cannot be due to its being thrown; a stone can just as easily be thrown downward, in which case the motion is natural. Rather, the upward motion of a stone is contrary to its nature because it is contrary to its passive principiative potency for being moved downward. Therefore, judgments about the "naturalness" of a given subject's motion are true or false only as regards the subject's passive principles, and thus are simply *independent* of whatever active principles the subject may possess.

Scotus applies his general claim, sketched above, to the motion of heavy and light bodies in *Ord.* II d.2 p.2 q.6 n.467 (Vat. 7.365):

So it is in the case at hand, such that although here (as in many other cases) the active principle is the principle of moving, nevertheless [something] is not naturally moved on account of that active principle of moving, but rather due to a passive principle on account of which it is moved in this way. After [Aristotle] said that "the act of a light [body] is *being someplace upward*" [*Phys.* VIII.4, 255b12–13]), this is what he says next ([*Phys.* VIII.4, 255b14–15]):

And nevertheless the question is raised: why are [light and heavy bodies] moved into their places?

He replies ([*Phys.* VIII.4, 255b15–16]):

The reason is because they are naturally apt to be there.

[Aristotle] *explicitly* says "into their places" (i.e., they are naturally moved into those places) "because they are naturally apt to be there" (i.e., they have a natural inclination to that place). And this is the way slightly later he adds that "[natural things] only have a principle of being acted upon [in respect of motion] and not of doing [anything]" ([*Phys.* VIII.4, 255b29–31]), namely, in respect of motion insofar as [the motion] is natural.

Scotus interprets Aristotle in this passage as implicitly using the distinction between a subject's passive principiative potencies for movement and whatever its active principiative potencies may be:

Thus in the resolution of this doubtful point about the motion of heavy [bodies], [Aristotle] speaks there—as though between the lines—of a natural principle of this motion and of its effective principle (which is only passive).

The discussion of heavy and light bodies here makes sense, according to Scotus, only if Aristotle is drawing a distinction between active and passive principles implicitly (*quasi interscalariter*). Again, a careful examination of Aristotle's text reveals that a passage that apparently supported the common position does not undermine Scotus's own position.

Scotus's Response to Phys. VIII.4, 255a3–18

What of Aristotle's four arguments about heavy and light bodies, cited in section 2 above? First, Scotus separates the fourth argument from the first three arguments. There is a sense, Scotus holds, in which Aristotle's fourth argument establishes its conclusion, but it is not a sense that threatens the thesis that heavy and light bodies move themselves. Scotus writes in *Ord.* II d.2 p.2 q.6 n.469 (Vat. 7.366):

> Also, [Aristotle's] fourth argument, regarding a continuous [body], does not conclude precisely insofar as [a continuous body] is a particular amount.[91] But with regard to a continuous [body] (i.e., what is of the same disposition in every part), [Aristotle] proves that a heavy [body] does not move itself effectively, since there is not one part in act that can make another [part] in act according to the same quality, as he says in *De sensu* 6 [447a3–4]. I grant that in this way a part of a heavy [body], existing in act, does not cause motion in another part. But the whole heavy [body] *is* in act according to first act, and it causes itself in second act.

Aristotle is correct that a continuous homogeneous body is not in motion due to the interaction of its physically distinct parts: a part does not cause motion in another part. Yet this is compatible with the claim that the entire homogeneous body is a self-mover. On the one hand, it has distinct active principiative potencies[92] and passive principiative potencies, which make it a potential self-mover—the possession of these potencies makes the continuous homogeneous body to be in first act. On the other hand, the

---

[91] "Insofar as [a continuous body] is a particular amount": *inquantum quantum*. That is, as Scotus goes on to say, Aristotle is concerned here not merely with continuous bodies but rather with continuous homogeneous bodies.

[92] Scotus directly asserts that homogeneous bodies have such active principiative potencies. Scotus explains the apparent testimony of *Phys.* VIII.4, 255b30–31, to the contrary by pointing out that Aristotle was there trying to establish his position that motion is natural only in virtue of the passive principiative potencies a thing has, regardless of its active principiative potencies (if any). See 284–85 above.

exercise of these potencies such that it is an actual self-mover is due to itself alone, in the absence of any obstruction—and hence it is a self-mover in second act. The way in which such bodies move themselves primarily has been discussed in section 5 above.

Aristotle's first three arguments in *Phys.* VIII.4, 255a3–18, Scotus maintains, all amount to the same thing and are therefore irrelevant to the motion of light and heavy bodies, as he states in *Ord.* II d.2 p.2 q.6 n.468 (Vat. 7.365–66):

> The first three [arguments] (which have one force) show that the heavy [body] does not move itself as an agent moves itself by means of cognition.[93] Indeed, an animal could not move itself stopping short of its ultimate intended terminus—nor too could it turn itself aside or stop itself—unless it were to act by means of cognition. And from this point the Philosopher's thesis is adequately established, [namely,] that [light and heavy bodies] are not primary movers. For a primary mover moves by means of cognition, since "it is characteristic of wisdom to direct" [*Meta.* A.2, 982a17–18], as shown above in *Ord.* I d.2 nn.76–78 [Vat. 2.175–76] and *Ord.* I d.3 nn.261–268 [Vat. 3.160–64].

Heavy bodies are obviously not animals; the ability to cease one's motion or to move in contrary ways itself depends on cognition—that is, these abilities are proper to animals, and thus have no bearing on the self-motion of heavy bodies. Scotus is correct that the ability to move to the left, the ability to move to the right, and the ability to stop are active principiative potencies that go beyond the mere active principiative potency for movement in a single direction. The latter potency, as found in stones, is continuously actualized unless prevented, as established in section 6 above. Animal movement, on the other hand, is clearly discontinuous and can be directed in many ways. Hence there must be a principle or cause that actualizes the further active principiative potency to move, say, to the left. This cause must be the sensitive or intellective soul, since what it is to be an animal *is* to have within oneself the power of sensation and movement. If rocks could move up or down at will, they, too, would be animals. Hence Scotus is correct to point to the possession of a sensitive or intellective soul as the "source" of discontinuous and contrary motion.[94] Only beings endowed with cognition are primary movers.

---

[93] Scotus does not use "cognition" to mean "intellectual activity," but rather to refer to the activities of the sensitive soul as well as the intellective soul. Thus a frog jumps "by means of cognition."

[94] Scotus discusses animal movement extensively: in addition to his remarks in *QSM* IX q.14, see the texts mentioned in note 1. The difference between animals and humans in this regard is that in human beings, the will is itself a self-mover, whereas animals do not have a will. Without considering the details, it is clear that Scotus's account permits animals to be

Now Scotus recognizes that Aristotle's four arguments have a further role to play in the regress argument for the existence of a Prime Mover. Scotus replies to the objection that Aristotle's regress argument would not succeed if heavy and light bodies are self-movers in *Ord.* ii d.2 p.2 q.6 n.470 (Vat. 7.367):

> I state that [Aristotle] adequately establishes [his thesis] on the basis of the distinction of [first and second] potencies. Indeed, [light and heavy bodies] do not reduce themselves from second potency to act, unless they had been previously reduced from first potency to first act (or at least could be reduced to first act). I say this for the elements as wholes. These wholes, according to [Aristotle], are ungenerable and incorruptible.[95] Nevertheless, since these [wholes] are of the same *ratio* as their parts, it is not incompatible for them to be reduced from first potency to first act, just as their parts are reduced [from first potency to first act]. Hence it follows that although light and heavy [bodies] move themselves from second potency to second act, nevertheless what is capable of motion [either] is or is moved from first potency to first act by something else extrinsic [to it].

Scotus takes Aristotle's proof of the existence of a Prime Mover to be a regress argument, but the regression is *not* based on a series of actual motions (or at least need not be based on actual motions). Instead, the regression is based on the possession of the very potency to be moved. Why do stones, say, have principiative potencies to move and to be moved? Where does the active principiative potency for a stone's self-motion originate? Presumably, a heterogeneous body owes its active principiative potency for motion in a given direction to its composition, to the mixture of the four basic elements and the predominance of one over the others, which "moves" a heterogeneous body from first potency to first act. This "mixture" itself, characteristic of sublunary bodies, is due to the movement of the Sun in the plane of the ecliptic (*GC* ii.10, 336a31–b15). But what causes the passive principiative potency of the Sun to be moved in the plane of the ecliptic? And so on. There is a genuine regress, but it is not a

---

self-movers while allowing for external causal influences. These external causes do not cause the animal's movement directly, but rather affect its sensitive soul, which itself initiates the motion. This last claim is nevertheless compatible with the view that animals indeed move themselves, since the *proximate* cause of an animal's movement is its own active principiative potency, triggered by its sensitive soul: see the passage cited in note 95.

[95] Aristotle never says this, but it is taken as a direct conclusion from his remarks that the heavens are ungenerable and incorruptible and that the elements are integral parts of the heavens: see, for example, *De cae.* ii.1, 283b26–284a2, and *Phys.* iv.5, 212b18–22. Contrary to the modern reading of texts such as *GC* ii.4, on the standard medieval reading of Aristotle the four elements were taken to be sempiternal, and only composites and mixtures made from the elements come into being and pass away.

regression based on actual motion. Hence Aristotle's argument for the existence of a Prime Mover can proceed even in a world of self-movers.

Scotus is quite explicit about this last conclusion. He rejects the proposition that "everything that is in motion is moved by another." But a weaker proposition is sufficient for Aristotle's argument, namely, "Everything that is moved is moved by another," which does not entail the first proposition (*Ord.* II d.2 p.2 q.6 n.470 [Vat. 7.367]):

> Indeed, it is not necessary that if everything that is moved is moved by another that in every motion [what is in motion] be moved by another—and the first [proposition] is sufficient for the Philosopher, since by means of this [proposition] one arrives at something "other than all these" that neither in one motion nor in any given motion will be able to be moved by another, but is completely an immovable mover.

Aristotle's argument holds so long as there are things naturally capable of movement. Hence the admission of self-movers is compatible with the remainder of the argument in *Phys.* VIII.[96]

Scotus's analysis and defense of self-change is powerful and sophisticated, showing that he was worthy of his honorific title as *Doctor subtilis*. His defense of self-change, in the technical apparatus he uses as well in his

[96] Scotus offers another way of saving Aristotle's conclusion in *Ord.* II d.2 p.2 q.6 n.471 (Vat. 7.368): "Likewise, it can also be said that—in that motion—even if [light and heavy bodies] were moved by themselves effectively, nevertheless they are not moved as by primary movers, from which they also do not move by means of cognition. It follows that they presuppose something moving in this way by means of cognition. And thus, although they move themselves effectively, nevertheless they do not [move themselves] in this way unless they are moved by another, although they are not [moved by another] as by a proximate cause." It is not clear, however, that this alternative will work: why should the movement of heavy and light bodies presuppose the existence of beings endowed with sensitive or intellective souls? Why assume that there *are* "primary movers" in the sense required here? If we grant that there are, then this alternative does provide a basis for Aristotle's argument, but there is no reason to grant it.

It should be mentioned that Scotus is interested in defending Aristotle's argument only up to a certain point. In the first reconstruction, given in the text above, the existence of a world including things capable of being moved (even if only by themselves) is presupposed; on the alternative reconstruction described here, the existence of primary movers is presupposed. Scotus himself thinks that there is not much to choose between these presuppositions, since both color Aristotle's conclusion with a kind of contingency—a feature that applies to all "physical" proofs. Since the existence of a Prime Mover (or of a God) is, strictly speaking, a *metaphysical* question, however, Scotus thinks that it requires a metaphysical proof. He describes such a proof in many places, the most complete version of which is found in his late work *Tractatus de primo principio*, where the existence of God is proved by metaphysically necessary propositions. The structure of the proof is by regression based on natures.

textual exegesis, is thoroughly Aristotelian—at least in the sense that it is inspired by Aristotle—and he presents it as the proper account of Aristotle's own views. Duns Scotus has always been known as a great theologian; perhaps the time has finally come when we can also see him as a great physicist (albeit one with a pronounced theoretical bent) and a great interpreter of Aristotle.

CHAPTER 11

Ockham, Self-Motion, and the Will

CALVIN G. NORMORE

MEDIEVAL DISCUSSION of the problem of self-motion has two starting-points. One is a problem in physics, the problem of how to reconcile Aristotle's account of *natural* things in book II of his *Physics* with his apparent endorsement in book VII of the principle that "all that is moved is moved by another." The other starting-point is in the theory of the soul, and particularly in the theory of the will that, whether present in Augustine or not, was read into his work by later authors and developed during the twelfth century into an account of the will as a distinct part (or faculty) of the soul. There were various understandings of the theory of the will, but at least some of them endorsed Anselm's claim that the will was an (or even *the*) instrument that moved itself. It is with this second strand in the medieval picture that this paper is primarily concerned. The paper is inspired by a simple (not to say simpleminded) thesis. It is that the early Middle Ages inherited from Platonism a conception of the *soul* as a self-moving power, which was slowly altered into a conception of the *will* as a self-moving power. In the thirteenth century this conception met, and was for a time submerged by, Aristotle's psychology and his employment in it of the principle that all that is moved is moved by another; but it emerged again in a sharp and clear way in the aftermath of the condemnations of 1277. It was then understood by some of both its defenders and its opponents as incompatible with Aristotle's picture, but eventually, notably in the work of John Duns Scotus, a reconciliation was achieved that by Ockham's time was widely taken for granted and that paved the way for the early modern division between a completely determined nature and a realm of free spirits. To establish the whole of this thesis is well beyond the scope of a single paper and will not be attempted here. Instead I shall focus on Ockham's treatment of the will as a self-mover and on some of the background to that treatment. I shall sketch rather briefly some of the connec-

This paper began life as a commentary on an earlier version of Peter King's article in this volume. I would like to thank him for considerable help, Stephen Menn and Allan Silverman for discussion, and the editors for superhuman patience. The final revision of the paper was prepared in the warm and supportive ambience of Madame Lorraine Parent's home in Ville de Québec. Merci beaucoup, Madame.

tions between Ockham's views on the self-motion of the will and his view about the place in physics of what I shall call OQM, the principle that all that is moved is moved by another.

The physical and psychological starting-points for the medieval discussion are not unrelated. In *Phys.* II, Aristotle describes a nature as "a principle of movement or of rest in a thing." One very natural way to understand this would be that a nature, at least in some cases, is an active principle of motion in the thing whose nature it is. But it is also plausible to suppose that a thing is not really distinct from its nature and thus that a natural thing is (at least in some cases) an active principle of motion and rest in itself. This seems especially plausible when one applies the Aristotelian theory of nature to human beings as we were understood in medieval Christian theology. So understood, we are beings who will by our natures. If, then, a human being's will is the cause of its own willing, some natures must be active principles of change.

On the other hand, the principle that *Omne quod movetur ab alio movetur* (OQM) plays a central role in Aristotle's proof in *Phys.* VIII of the existence of an unmoved mover. This proof and variations on it (like Aquinas's "First Way") had considerable prestige among medieval theologians. To abandon the principle would seem to put the proof, and so the whole enterprise of proving the existence of God from God's effects in the world, in jeopardy. But if wills can move themselves, then it does indeed seem that the principle will have to be restricted, if not abandoned.

The basic arguments on both sides of OQM are rather straightforward. In support of the principle, there is the consideration advanced by the author of the *Centiloquium*. This author also makes the theological significance of the principle quite clear.

> Therefore Aristotle in VIII of the *Physics* deduces that the first mover is unmovable by such a means as "Everything that is moved is moved by another and there is not a regress to infinity in moving causes, therefore one [of them] is the first unmovable mover." The first part of the antecedent, namely "everything that is moved is moved by another," is evident from this: that it would otherwise follow that something would be able to move itself *primo and per se* (primarily and through itself) and then the same thing would be in act and in potency in respect of the same.[1]

---

[1] *Centiloquium* in Guillelmi de Ockham, *Opera Philosophica et Theologica* (Franciscan Institute, St. Bonaventure's University, St. Bonaventure, N.Y., 1964–85) (OP 7: 374.24–30). The volumes in the Opera Philosophica part of the series will be referred to as *OP* followed by a volume number, and those in the Opera Theologica by *OT* similarly followed.

The identity of the author of the *Centiloquium* is a matter of controversy. Perhaps the best candidate is Hester Gelber's suggestion of the English Dominican Arnoldus Strelley, but compare the discussion in the preface to the edition above.

It is precisely this question of how something can be both in active potency and in passive potency at the same time and in the same respect that requires explanation by anyone who wishes to restrict OQM.

The considerations on the other side seem at least as weighty. If everything that is moved is moved by another, then the will must be moved to act by something else. But, as the familiar arguments for determinism in our own day suggest, if the will is moved by another to act, then, if such movement is sufficient to cause the will's act, the will is not able to refrain from acting in that way under those circumstances. If some acts of will are sins, this would seem to imply that no sinner could have done otherwise and to threaten seriously Christian conceptions of moral responsibility.

Nor is that all. Human beings (and, perhaps, angels) are *rational* by nature. A rational nature possesses a rational power and, according to Aristotle, a rational power is a power for opposites.[2] This seemed to require that nothing outside the human being explain why a human exercised its power for opposites in one way rather than in the contrary way. Moreover, it came to seem to require that the human being could exercise this power in contrary ways even when the human was in precisely the same state so far as cognition, appetition, and physical disposition went. That a part of the human, its will, moved itself, came to seem the only explanation for this.

1. THE ORIGINS OF OCKHAM'S POSITION

The idea that the soul is an active power is central to Plato's conception of it. It seems, for example, that it is simply taken for granted in his proof for the immortality of the soul in the *Phaedrus*.[3] It is also a deep feature of late Platonism, whose adepts seem in addition to accept the view that the nobler the soul, the less subject it is to being affected by anything outside itself, and the less subject to necessity of any kind.[4] One classic passage in which this feature emerges is *Timaeus* 41C–42D. Even Proclus, who opposes Plotinus's view that the human soul is of the same dignity and substance as the divine soul, writes in his commentary on this passage that "the souls, in virtue of the highest life that is in them, are superior to Fate."[5] More important for the Latin Middle Ages (because it was in Latin and survived in the West) is Calcidius's discussion in his commentary on the

---

[2] Cf. Aristotle, *Meta.* Θ.5

[3] Cf. Bett 1986, esp. 15–16.

[4] I owe the thought that medieval discussions of the activity of the will might be rooted in the Platonic tradition to conversation with Stephen Menn and Allan Silverman.

[5] Cf. Proclus *In Platonis Timaeum commentarii* (Festugière 1966–68), 266.16–17

Timaeus. Calcidius defines the soul as "a substance lacking a body moving itself rationally."[6]

Calcidius's commentary was widely known throughout the early Middle Ages and was reinforced by echoes in Boethius's *Consolation of Philosophy*; yet it was to Augustine that later medieval writers turned to find authority for the view that the soul, and more specifically the will, can move itself. In *De libero arbitrio*, Augustine insists that nothing can coerce the activity of the will, and this theme is taken up and expanded by Anselm of Canterbury in his *De libertate arbitrii*. Anselm is perhaps the first author explicitly and unequivocally to propose the "two-wills doctrine" of human choice. On this picture, a human being has two "wills" (*voluntates*) or, less misleadingly, two motivating drives (*affectiones*). One of these moves us directly toward our own happiness; the other is a drive to do what is right (*honestum*) (which seems to be to do whatever God wants us to do because God wants us to do it). In the case of Satan before the Fall and in our own cases, it sometimes seems to us that what would make us happy and what is *honestum* are distinct and even incompatible. In such a situation we choose to act on one *voluntas* and not on the other. The result is that, although there is a causal story about why we act on the *voluntas* we do, there is no causal explanation of why we act on that *voluntas* rather than on the other. We so act, as Anselm insists, because the will is the will.[7]

Anselm's discussion had tremendous influence and was widely used and quoted throughout the Middle Ages. Thanks in part to his influence, when the theologians of Latin Christendom encountered Aristotle's *Physics* and *De anima*, they were inclined to assume that Aristotle thought the will a self-mover in the sense of being an efficient cause of its own motion. The problem they faced was largely that of explaining the relation between the will and the intellect, and, in particular, of determining whether the will moved the intellect to offer up an object for choice or whether the intellect moved the will by offering up an object as most suitable for choice. This debate flourished in the middle of the thirteenth century, with Thomas Aquinas emphasizing the role of the intellect in providing the will with its object and Franciscan thinkers emphasizing both the independence of the will and its own role in influencing the intellect.

But the shaping of Ockham's account begins, it seems, with Peter John Olivi. As Bonnie Kent has argued[8], Bonaventure and his immediate disciples, though certainly unwilling to accept Aquinas's formulation of the relationship between intellect and will, nonetheless hesitated to break with

---

[6] *Est igitur anima iuxta Platonem substantia carens corpore semet ipsam movens rationabilis*; Calcidius *In Timaeo* 263 (Waszink 1962, 241.8–10).

[7] The development of the "two-wills doctrine" in Anselm and Scotus is discussed in Boler 1993 and Normore forthcoming.

[8] In Kent 1984.

the Aristotelian idea that the will was to some extent a passive power and that it was moved by the intellect. Olivi has no such hesitation. He writes:

> Therefore the first thing in which Catholics differ from certain pagans and Saracens, namely that free acts are totally produced by the will or that free choice, or the will insofar as it is free, is totally an active power, should necessarily be maintained both according to the Catholic faith and according to right reason. For as is evident from the preceding question it is necessary that free choice may have the *ratio* of a first mover so that it is able to push and move and pull back itself and other powers and active virtues subject to it— and this not only when nothing is pushing it to the contrary, but also when there is something inclining to the contrary. Hence it is able to act against the inclination of its habits; otherwise the virtuous would not be able to fall away from virtue to vice nor on the contrary [the vice-ridden turn to virtue]. . . . Therefore the very essence of our liberty both according to faith and right reason calls us to hold evidently that the will, insofar as it is free, is totally active.[9]

Kent has emphasized that Olivi's rejection of the view that the will is moved by another is part of an overall rejection of Aristotelian psychology. Olivi harkens back explicitly to Augustine. He follows Augustine in denying that any spirit can be affected by any material object and in claiming that our knowledge of material things comes from God's movement (illumination) of our intellect. By rejecting the doctrine of abstraction, he rejects the view that the exercise of a power need be either efficiently or formally caused by its object. He is thus in a position to reject not only the view that the intellect moves the will to act, but also the view that the object of desire so moves it. This he does, arguing that the object of volition is not in any way an efficient cause of the volition. Nonetheless, as Kent has stressed, Olivi does not deny the object of volition *any* role in the volition; it remains as what Olivi calls a *causa terminativa*—which he locates in the genus of final cause.[10] Thus on Olivi's picture, the will is a totally active

---

[9] *Primum igitur in quo catholici a quibusdam paganis et Saracensis dissentiunt, quod scilicet actus liberi sint totaliter producti a voluntate seu quod liberum arbitrium vel voluntas, in quantum est libera, sit totaliter potentia activa, est necessario tenendum tam secundum fidem catholicam quam secundum rationem rectam. Sicut enim ex praecedenti questione patet, necesse est quod possit se et alias potentias et virtutes activas sibi subiectas impellere et movere et retrahere, et hoc non solum, quando nullum est impellens ad contrarium, sed etiam quando est ibi aliquis inclinans ad contrarium. Unde et potest agere contra inclinationem suorum habituum aliter virtuosus non posset declinare a virtutibus ad vitia nec e contrario. . . . Ipsa igitur essentia nostrae libertatis quam secundum fidem et rationem rectam oportet nos ponere clamat evidenter quod voluntas, in quantum est libera, est totaliter activa;* Olivi, *Sent.* II q.58. *responsio* (Jensen 1922–27, 2: 410–11).

[10] Compare Kent 1984, 192–93. Olivi's discussion (which Kent reports) is in Olivi, *Sent.* II q.72 *responsio* (Jensen 1922–27, 3: 36–37).

power that moves toward some object as a terminating cause, but is not efficiently moved toward that object by anything outside itself. It is thus a self-mover in the strong Anselmian sense.

A position rather similar to Olivi's in its stress on the active power of the will is one adopted by Henry of Ghent during his long and rather complex career as Master of Theology in the University of Paris. As Stephen Dumont has shown, Henry's position on the nature of the will and the relation between will and intellect underwent considerable development, and he is in fact responsible for many of the innovations (like instants of nature) that have been ascribed to Scotus.[11] But on some central points he seems to have remained firm. In his *Quodlibet* x q.9 dating from Christmas 1286, a full decade after he helped draw up the list of propositions condemned by Étienne Tempier, Henry argues that OQM must be restricted to corporeal agents because spiritual agents and, in particular, the will have the power to reduce themselves from potency to act. This power is not unlimited—for example, nothing could cause some intrinsic part of itself. But, Henry insists, a spiritual substance can cause its own accidents.

As Peter King points out,[12] Duns Scotus seems to have been the first thinker to insist that OQM had to be restricted not only to corporeal substances but even further. As King stresses, Scotus argues that in a wide variety of cases a corporeal thing can move itself in virtue of there being in it some less-than-real distinction between two *principles*, one of which serves as the agent and the other as the patient of the change. This is genuine self-motion, because what is really the same thing moves itself, but it is connected to the tradition that, strictly speaking, nothing can move itself by including a distinction (though not a real distinction) between the thing as mover and the thing as moved.

On the subject of the will itself, Scotus seems to have begun with a position very like that of Peter Olivi, but after he returned to Oxford from Paris, he seems to have moderated this position to grant the intellect a greater role in the determination of the will than Olivi would have allowed. In his Paris lectures Scotus insisted, as Olivi had, that the object of the will was in no way an efficient cause but rather was a cause *sine qua non*. For example, he writes: "An object of apprehension is required for there to be a volition, however it is not required except as a cause *sine qua non*."[13]

---

[11] Dumont's researches have been reported both in seminars he gave at the Pontifical Institute of Medieval Studies, University of Toronto between 1989 and 1991 and in papers read to the Society for Medieval and Renaissance Studies, December 1990, and the Canadian Philosophical Association, June 1991.

[12] See King's paper in this volume.

[13] *Utrum aliquid aliud a voluntate causet effective actum volendi in voluntate* ("Whether something other than the will may cause efficiently the act of willing in the will"); Alnwick, *Additiones magnae secundi libri*, app. 2, in Balic 1927, 212.

According to the *Additiones magnae* with which William Alnwick annotated his *Commentary on the Sentences*, however, Scotus, after returning to
Oxford, rejected this view in favor of the view that the object of volition is
one partial active cause of the volition and the will is another partial active
cause.[14] Thus, if Alnwick is right, in the work with which Ockham would
probably have been most familiar Scotus was prepared to allow that the
will was moved by another *partially* with respect to its volition.

2. OCKHAM'S VIEW

Ockham is the heir to both Olivi and Duns Scotus. From the former he
receives his picture of the freedom of the will and much of the associated
metaphysical framework. From the latter he receives the view that Aristotle
did not accept an unqualified form of OQM and that what he did accept
can be reconciled with right reason and the faith. Ockham has no analogue
of Scotus's discussion in his *Questions on Metaphysics*, book Θ; rather, his
views are scattered throughout his work. I will discuss them under three
heads: (1) the freedom of the will, (2) the *omne quod movetur* principle
itself, and (3) the consequences of the previous discussions for the proofs of
the existence of God.

Ockham on the Freedom of the Will

Ockham takes up the discussion of the freedom of the will in *Quod*. 1 q.16.
There he first defines the freedom of the will.

> I call "freedom" the power by which I am able indifferently and contingently
> to hold (*ponere*) different things so that I am able to cause and not to cause the
> same effect, there being no difference existing anywhere outside that power.[15]

Obviously, to be free in this strong sense, the will has to be an active power,
and Ockham does claim that it is. Indeed, on his account it is active in a

[14] *Ideo et aliter dixit Oxonie ad questionem, quod volitio est per se a voluntate, ut a causa
activa, et ab obiecto intellecto ut ab alia causa partiali, ita quod totalis causa volitionis
includit intellectum in actu primo et secundo, voluntatem in actu primo, et obiectum* ("Therefore at Oxford he replied differently to the question saying that the act of volition is of itself
from the will as from an active cause and from the object understood as from another partial
cause so that the total cause of the volition includes the intellect in both first and second act,
the will in first act, and the object"); Alnwick (Balic 1927, 282). I owe the reference to Kent
1984, 257.

[15] *Voco libertatem potestatem qua possum indifferenter et contingenter diversa ponere, ita
quod possum eumdem effectum causare et non causare, nulla diversitate existente alibi extra
illam potentiam; Quod*. 1 q.16 (OT 9: 87).

very strong sense, for it is able to be in a given state for a period of time, and then to alter that state without any influence whatsoever from anything else. In response to the objection that no agent existing for a period of time in essential potency to an act can alter itself in this way, Ockham writes:

> I answer that the assumption is true in natural agents whether they are corporeal or spiritual, but there is an obvious counterexample in free agents of the sort the will is, because the object can be cognized and present to the will and all the other requisites to the act of willing can endure through a time and yet afterwards [the will] is able to elicit (*elicere*) its act without any outside action, and this because of its freedom.[16]

He concludes the discussion by claiming baldly:

> To the principal [objection] I say that the same thing is able to be active and passive with respect to the same thing, nor is this unreasonable (*repugnat*).[17]

This is a direct rejection of the position explicitly endorsed in the previous generation by Thomas Aquinas's follower, Godfrey of Fontaines, and commonly attributed in Ockham's day to Aquinas himself.[18] Ockham's position gives the will a very special place. Alone among kinds of agent both corporeal and spiritual, the will is able to move from potency to act without a "triggering" cause. This feature of the structure of the will is crucial to Ockham's account of the will's freedom. Scotus was able to save the letter, if not the spirit, of Aristotle's defense of OQM by distinguishing within a single thing parts that were formally but not really distinct. A single real thing can move itself in virtue of one of these formally distinct parts moving another. Because the parts are formally *distinct*, a shadow of the intuitions behind OQM is preserved; because the parts are *merely* formally distinct, self-motion is countenanced. Scotus complemented this account of OQM with an account of the freedom of the will that employs a device closely related to the formal distinction, the notion of an instant of nature.

Scotus wants to account for the freedom of even a will that exists for only a single moment of time. Such a will obviously cannot change state. How then could it be that such a will in a given state (for example, hating God) is in that state only contingently? To be hating God contingently, Scotus

---

[16] *Respondeo assumptum est verum in agente naturali sive sit corporale sive spirituale, sed in agente libero cuiusmodi est voluntas est instantia manifesta; quia obiectum potest esse cognitum et praesens voluntati, et omnia alia requisita ad actum volendi possunt manere per tempus, et tamen post potest elicere actum suum sine omni actione extrinseca; et hoc totum est propter libertatem suam*; Quod. 1 q.16 (*OT* 9: 89).

[17] *Ad principale dico quod idem potest esse activum et passivum respectu eiusdem, nec ista repugnant*; Quod. 1 q.16 (*OT* 9: 89).

[18] For a discussion of Godfrey's views and for bibliography relevant to the discussion in Aquinas, see Wippel 1981.

suggests, the will would have to possess the power not to hate God at and for the very time at which it is hating God. But this would seem to imply that the will is in act and in potency with respect to the very same object (hating God) at the same time!

Scotus's solution is to distinguish within the single moment of time at which the will in question exists, two *moments of nature*, ordered as prior and posterior.[19] In the prior instant of nature, the will possesses the power to hate God or not. In the posterior instant of nature, the will reduces this power to act by hating God. Since both moments of nature are at the same moment of time, the will is at that moment of time both in potency and in act with respect to the same thing.

This subtle solution befits the Subtle Doctor, but it is unavailable to Ockham, who insists that both formal distinctions and instants of nature have no place in philosophy. He must take a different tack. His solution to the problem of how the will existing at a single time can be free is precisely to employ the feature of the will alluded to above—its capacity to change its act without any "triggering" cause at all. Thus, while the will existing for a single moment necessarily hates God at the moment it does hate God, it has at that moment a power whose nature can be stated only subjunctively: were the will to exist at a subsequent time, it could will differently at that time without being moved in any way from outside. It is in this power, Ockham thinks, that freedom consists.[20]

Ockham's Attitude to OQM in General

Because Ockham both gives a very special place to the will and rejects the machinery of formal distinctions that Scotus uses to account for the self-motion of even ordinary corporeal things like heavy bodies, one might well wonder what he makes of OQM in physics.[21]

The first thing to note is that Ockham does not believe that Aristotle held OQM in an unrestricted form. In his *Expositio in libros Physicorum Aristotelis* (which he explicitly claims to be an exposition *ad mentem Aristotelis* rather than a report of his own views) he claims, following Averroes, that the ground of Aristotle's defense of OQM is his belief in the self-evidence of the conditional that "if something moved per se is at rest if

---

[19] As Stephen Dumont has recently shown, this argument and this employment of the device of instants of nature are not original with Scotus but are borrowed by him from Henry of Ghent's discussion of the will in his *Quodlibet* x.

[20] For further discussion of this point, cf. Ockham's *Tractatus De praedestinatione* 9.3 (*OP* 2: 536).

[21] For Ockham's attack on the use of formal distinctions in philosophy, cf. his *Ord.* d.2 q.6 (*OT* 2: 162 ff.).

something else is at rest, then it is moved by something else."[22] But Ockham explicitly says that he believes that in this conditional, "moved per se" is taken in such a way as to exclude both (1) being moved (*moveri*) merely in the loose sense of being changed without a process (*mutari*), and (2) a thing's being moved in the proper sense but by something that is not properly something *else*—that is, by a part of itself. The will is moved in sense (1), and about it Ockham writes:

> It should be noted here in the first place that the Philosopher does not simply intend to deny that something is moved by itself—at least if to be moved is extended to include sudden change. For our will changes itself because it causes volition in itself. For since no exterior act is praiseworthy or blameworthy unless it is in our power, according to the Philosopher in the Third Book of the *Ethics*, it is necessary also that no act of liking or hating is praiseworthy or blameworthy unless it is in our power. But it is manifest that an act of loving someone is sometimes praiseworthy and sometimes blameworthy. Therefore such an act is in our power. But if it were caused by something else naturally and sufficiently it would not be in our power. It follows therefore that such an act is in some way brought about by the will. And thus the will itself causes such an act and so moves itself, taking "to move" loosely in this way.[23]

The second case is that of many natural bodies. For example, Ockham follows Scotus in insisting that Aristotle does not deny that a heavy body can move itself downward or that hot water can cool itself.[24] He also argues that nutrition provides a case in which the soul moves the whole, and hence a thing is moved by itself.[25] Ockham's confidence that Aristotle does not mean OQM to rule out such cases stems from his view that they are cases in which a whole is moved by a proper part of itself, taken together with his view that Aristotle did not intend to apply OQM to cases

---

[22] *Si aliquid motum per se quiescat si aliud quiescit, movetur ab alio*; *Exp. Phys.* 7 ch.1 para.4 (*OP* 5: 605.5–6).

[23] *Notandum est hic primo quod non intendit Philosophus simpliciter negare aliquid moveri a se, saltem extendendo moveri ad subito mutari. Voluntas enim nostra mutat se ex hoc quod in se ipsa causat volitionem. Cum enim nullus actus exterior sit laudabilis vel vituperabilis nisi quia est in nostra potestate, secundum Philosophum* III Ethicorum, *oportet etiam quod nullus actus diligendi vel odiendi sit laudabilis vel vituperabilis nisi quia est in nostra potestate. Sed manifestum est quod actus diligendi alium aliquando est laudibilis aliquando vituperabilis. Ergo talis actus est in nostra potestate. Sed si causaretur ab aliquo alio naturaliter et sufficienter, non esset in nostra potestate. Relinquitur ergo quod talis actus est aliquo modo effective a voluntate. Et ita voluntas in se ipsa causat talem actum, et ita movet se, sic large accipiendo movere; Exp. Phys.* 7 ch.1 (*OP* 5: 398.87–399.99).

[24] For example, cf. *Exp. Phys.* 7 ch.1 para.4 (*OP* 7: 605): *Nec etiam probat quin aqua potest frigefacere se quia nata est frigefieri per partem* ("Nor does he even prove anything against [the claim that] water is able to cool itself—since it is suited to be cooled through a part [of itself]").

[25] *Exp. Phys.* 7 ch.2 (*OP* 5: 608.40–55).

in which a part moves a whole. When a part moves a whole, the whole is moved by something but not, properly speaking, by something *else* (*alio*).

Although he neither accepts OQM himself nor believes that Aristotle accepted any very inclusive interpretation of it, Ockham nonetheless believes that it is indeed true that everything that is moved *locally* is moved by another either mediately or immediately.[26] This is significant because Ockham accepts only two kinds of change: one in which some real thing—either a substance or a quality—is created or destroyed, and another in which the parts of a thing are moved locally. Having granted that everything locally moved is, at some stage in the causal story of the motion, moved by something else, Ockham is forced to deny the spirit, if not the letter, of OQM only in a range of cases in which a real quality is created or destroyed.

It seems, then, that although Ockham did think that a corporeal body could move itself in the sense that a part of it could move the whole or move another part, he distinguished between the case of alteration, where there is the possibility that the substance itself might produce its own accidents without any extrinsic cause, and the case of local motion, where he claims that in every causal sequence of such motions there must be at least one step in which the motion of a corporeal body comes from outside that body. It is this last that makes acute the question of Ockham's attitude toward the Aristotelian arguments for a first mover of all moved things.

Ockham on the Argument for a Prime Mover

The relationship of his views about the will and about OQM to the arguments for a Prime Mover is one of which Ockham is acutely aware. For example, in considering the relationship of the freedom of the will to OQM in *Sent.* IV q.16, he advances the very strong position that

[26] *Per idem ad alias auctoritates potest dici quod in istis inferioribus naturaliter motis et non voluntarie, necesse est dicere quod omne motum localiter, movetur ab alio mediate vel immediate. Immo etiam de motis voluntarie est hoc concedendum, quia primum movens in talibus est voluntas quae non est primum motum localiter. Et ideo universaliter concedo quod omne motum localiter in istis inferioribus movetur an alio mediate vel immediate, hoc est, nihil movetur localiter nisi aliquid aliud moveat ipsum, vel moveat aliud ad cuius motum sequitur motus illius* ("By the same [argument] it can be said [in response] to the other authorities that in those things here below that are moved naturally and not voluntarily, it is necessary to say that everything moved locally is moved by another either mediately or immediately. Indeed this is even to be granted of those things moved voluntarily because in them the first mover is the will which is not the first thing moved locally. And thus I concede universally that everything here below moved locally is moved by another either mediately or immediately. That is, nothing is moved locally unless something else moves it or moves another thing from whose motion the motion of that [first] thing follows"); *Exp. Phys.* 7 ch.2 (*OP* 5: 608.56–63).

the intellect judging this to be the ultimate end, the will is able to reject (*nolle*) that end.[27]

He goes on to consider the objection that

then the will would move itself, contrary to the Philosopher in *Physics* VII where he says and proves that all that is moved is moved by another. Besides, it would then never be possible to prove that we come to an immobile mover.[28]

In his reply to this objection, Ockham points out that Aristotle assumes two principles that Ockham suggests, but does not say, he himself would not accept. These are (1) that what has no parts and cannot be divided cannot be moved, and (2) that everything that is moved is able to be moved by a more noble thing. Given these principles, Ockham seems to think that Aristotle's argument that there is an unmoved mover would go through. But Ockham does not accept the principles, and he concludes that the argument is a failure.

This is what we should expect on other grounds. In *Quod.* II q.1, Ockham argues that it cannot be established by reason that God rather than the celestial bodies are the causes of every sublunary effect.[29] He goes on to argue that it cannot be demonstrated that there is one Prime Mover rather than many efficient causes, each of which is the beginning of a causal chain and none of which is dependent on any other.[30] Indeed, he goes on explicitly to suggest that for all we can prove,

---

[27] *Secundo dico quod intellectu iudicante hoc esse finem ultimum, potest voluntas nolle illum finem. Quod probatur, quia potentia libera quae est receptiva duorum actuum contrariorum, qua ratione potest in unum et in reliquum. Sed voluntas tamquam potentia libera est receptiva nolle et velle respectu cuiuscumque obiecti, igitur si potest in velle* ("In the second place I say that [while] the intellect [is] judging this to be the ultimate end, the will is able to reject that end. This can be proved thus: a power is free that is receptive of two contrary acts by which reason it is able to [actualize] one or the other. But the will as a free power is receptive of rejecting and or accepting with respect to some object. Therefore it is able to will [the one way or the other]"); Ockham, *Sent.* IV q.16 (*OT* 7: 354).

[28] *Tertium est quia tunc voluntas moveret se, contra Philosophum, VII Physicorum ubi dicit et probat quod omne quod movetur, ab alio movetur—praeterea, tunc numquam posset probari quod est devenire ad movens immobile*; Ockham, *Sent.* IV q.16 (*OT* 7: 354–55).

[29] *Dico primo quod non potest probari naturali ratione quod Deus est causa immediata efficiente omnium . . . quia non potest probari sufficienter quin aliae causae, puta corpora celestia, sint sufficientes respectu multorum effectuum et per consequens frustra poneretur Deus causa immediata illorum* ("I say first that it cannot be proved by natural reason that God is the immediate efficient cause of all things . . . because it cannot be proved sufficiently that it is not the case that other causes, namely the celestial bodies, are sufficient with respect to many effects and consequently it would be in vain to suppose God to be the immediate cause of them"); Ockham, *Quod.* II q.1 (*OT* 9: 107.11–16).

[30] *Ad primum dico quod non potest probari sufficienter quin sint multa efficientia quorum nullum est causabile nec effectibile nec dependens quocumque modo ab alio inter illa prima* ("To the first objection I say that it cannot be proved sufficiently that there are not many efficient causes of which none can be cause of, nor brought about by, nor dependent in any way on, another that is first among them"); Ockham, *Quod.* II q.1 (*OT* 9: 109.61–63).

the universe of causes is caused, not by some one thing but by many, because one caused thing is caused by one first efficient cause and another by another and so on.[31]

We have seen Ockham argue that in every chain of locally moved movers we come eventually to something outside the thing originally moved. A locally moved thing can be moved by a part, and that part by another, and so on, but Ockham follows Averroes in suggesting that the chain must eventually lead outside the original moved body.

Ockham has suggested that, for all we can prove, the chain of efficient causes of natural things might lead back to the celestial bodies. But the celestial bodies are bodies and are moved locally. Hence they, insofar as they are bodies moved locally, must have a source of motion outside themselves. These movers, Ockham believes, are the celestial intelligences, which impart motion to the heavens. Thus, though he does not think that we can establish the existence of God by reasoning that relies on the restricted form of OQM that he accepts, Ockham does think that his restricted form of OQM will establish that the local motion in the world is due eventually to spiritual rather than corporeal sources.

During the late Middle Ages, many of the central features of Aristotle's world view came under increasing scrutiny. Aristotle's theory of change was, of course, one of them. I have tried to show here how Ockham, building upon a conception (originally owed to Plato) of the will as a self-moving cause and upon an interpretation of Aristotle as holding only a restricted form of OQM, developed a picture that allowed self-movement in certain cases of alteration but did not allow a chain of local movements to be entirely generated from within the moved body. Local movement, for Ockham, is ultimately produced by changes of another kind. It is not surprising, then, that as changes other than local movements become confined to the spiritual world, the picture of nature as active upon which Aristotle and Scotus had both insisted would, among those influenced by Ockham's physics, be replaced by a picture of corporeal objects as in themselves inert.

[31] *Dico quod universitas causatorum causatur, non ab aliquo uno, sed a multis, quia unum causatum causatur ab uno efficiente primo et aliud ab alio. et sic deinceps; nec potest contrarium probari sufficienter* ("I say that the universe of causes is caused, not by some one thing, but by many, because one caused thing is caused by one first efficient cause and another by another and so on; nor can the contrary be sufficiently established"); Ockham, *Quod.* II q.1 (*OT 9*: 111.94–98).

CHAPTER 12

Natural Motion and Its Causes:
Newton on the "Vis Insita" of Bodies

J. E. McGuire

IT IS a curious fact that puzzles me. Why should Newton hold that each and every bit of matter (large and small) is naturally endowed with a *vis insita*—an innate or inherent force? Recall the manner in which he enunciates his First Law: "Every body persists (*perseverare*) in its state of resting or of moving uniformly straight forward, except in so far as it is constrained to change that state by forces impressed."[1] As it stands, the law affirms three things. First, motion is simply a *state*, and when the body's motion is zero its *state* is rest. In other words, motion and rest are not contraries, but rather two equivalent ways in which every body is according to its basic nature. Second, strictly conceived, if something is in a state, it does not concurrently undergo change. And so the law seems to imply that if motion and rest are states, they express a primitive fact about the *nature* of any body that requires no further explanation. Third, what does explain a change in a given body is the manner in which something external acts upon it to change its state. Otherwise that body will continue naturally in a state either of resting or of moving *continually* along a right line.

In short, there are only two possible ways in which bodies are able *to be* naturally: either moving or resting, and both are states. On the face of it, it seems pointless to suppose that every body is also endowed with a *vis insita*. If motion and rest are natural states of things, what more needs explaining? Surely the fact that something does what it does according to its nature blocks any need for further explanation of what that something is and of what it does. It is only if and when a body is affected contrary to its nature that a change ensues that demands an account. But in this case the change is the result of the action of an external force or cause: the fact that a body persists in a state according to its nature—once it is in that state— would appear not to require further reference to an inherent force (*vis insita*) intrinsic to that nature. That it does what it does, in virtue of what it is, is a primitive fact about its nature.

I dedicate this essay to the memory of Charles B. Schmitt, student of Aristotelica, and champion of the classical tradition.

[1] Newton 1687, 12.

This is the conception of Newtonian natural motion that has descended to us from Newton's own time. Although it can be derived from the text of the *Principia*, it is not an account that Newton himself ever fully conceives of. The reason is this: In Definition III of the Eight Definitions preceding the enunciation of the three Laws of Motion, Newton discusses at length the phrase *vis insita materiae* or "inherent force of matter." Admittedly, the definition is not a model of logical clarity, containing as it does irksome conceptual tensions—so much so that generations of perplexed scholars (my former self included) have been inclined to explain away, or to ignore, this troublesome phrase. In this study I intend, once again, to take up this issue. Specifically, I want to ask: Why should Newton discuss the notion of the *vis insita* of matter, when he has at his explicit disposal (for explanatory purposes) his own technical conception of inertial mass? That is, why speak of *vis insita* if you are able (as Newton is) to invoke mass to explain how a body both maintains and resists changes in its state? The answer lies, I think, in the way in which Newton conceives of the individual *natures* of bodily things, and in the changes and nonchanges that are consistent with the having of such natures. In particular, I want to argue that natural motion is still a type of change for Newton, one that requires explanation, even though he speaks of motion as a state. In other words, to say that something is in the inertial state is not for Newton the simple invocation of a nonexplainable fact; rather, it is a reference to a state of affairs itself to be explained. Quite simply, natural motion is a change. And Newton (or so I shall argue) still assumes that all change must be explained in terms of its originating source and cause. In short, he still adheres to the classical tradition.

In order to justify these claims, I discuss below the relationship between the First Law of Motion and Definition III; important classical sources for the phrase *vis insita*, and its development in the writings on natural motion of representative medieval and Renaissance thinkers; and contemporary seventeenth-century literature (available to Newton) in which *vis insita* is used in explaining the causes and sources of natural change. It will become clear that Newton believes in the actuality of change and of the source of change, most particularily in *vis insita*, the determinate changer of what is changing.

1. *VIS INSITA* AND ITS CONCEPTUAL INTERRELATIONS

It might be claimed that Definition III anticipates the enunciation of the First Law of Motion, making that statement in part superfluous. There is of course a close connection in content between the two, but strictly speaking this claim is misleading. Definition III says: "The inherent force of matter is a power of resisting, by which each single body, so far as is in its power (*quantum in se est*), persists in its state either of resting or of moving uniformly straight forward."[2] This is a definition, and neither existential import nor presupposition is intended or implied. On the other hand, the First Law, which follows the definition, *is* enunciated by Newton with intended existential presupposition. It is, of course, a universal affirmative statement as understood in the Aristotelian syllogistic. Newton enunciates it in the belief that he is referring to bodily things that are independent of his perceptions. Accordingly, he makes the statement with existential presupposition, that is, with the assumption that the class of things to which it refers is not empty. And he also assumes that his readers do not need an additional statement of the existence of the class in question. Moreover, on the square of opposition, given a statement of the form "All *A*'s are *B*'s," it can be inferred that at least one *A* is *B*, namely, that "some *A*'s are *B*'s." Here, then, is a statement having existential import that is implied by the universal statement. Considered thus, Newton's First Law is consistent with the claim that there is at least one body of which it is true to say, "It is in a state either of resting or of moving along a right line." These assumptions and relationships were probably known to Newton from his undergraduate education and reading. In fact, his annotated copy of Robert Sanderson's *Logicae artis compendium* (Oxford, 1631) is in the Library of Trinity College, Cambridge, and contains a discussion of the existential commitments of syllogistic logic.

The concepts present in Law I and Definition III are interconnected. Law I uses the verb *perseverare* (literally, "to persist") in describing what bodies do naturally. The verb is invariably used in Newton's earlier formulations of natural motion, and is maintained by him in the three editions of the *Principia* produced in his lifetime. In the protodrafts of the law that immediately precede the publication of the *Principia*—as well as in that treatise itself—Newton employs the gerunds *quiescendi* and *movendi* to characterize the two states in which any body can "persist" in being. Thus, the verbal nouns "of resting" and "of moving" help to emphasize the active connotation already present in the verb "to persist." After all, Newton might well have written, "Every body continues in its state," using the verbs *manere* or *continere* to indicate that the gerunds are neutral and simply denote states of rest or motion.

It would be a mistake, however, to read too much, too soon, into the verbal resources of Newton's language. After all, there is nothing in the Law's enunciation to indicate whether "inertial motion" gives rise to a "force *of* motion," or is the manifestation of a "motive force" *in* bodies. Let us turn, then, to the wider context of Definition III, to Corollary I of the

---

[2] Ibid., 2. See note 4 for the phrase *quantum in se est*.

three Laws, and to Proposition I, Theorem I, Book I of the *Principia*. After stating Definition III (see above), Newton expands on its meaning:

> This [inherent force] is always proportional to the body itself, and never in any way differs from the *inertia* of mass, except in [our] manner of conceiving it. By means of the *inertia* of matter, each body is with difficulty put out of its state of resting or of moving. Whence also [this] inherent force (*vis insita*), by a most significant name, may be called force of inactivity (*vis inertiae*). In fact, a body only exercises this force in changes of state produced in it by another force impressed on it: and its exercise (i.e., the force called both *insita* and *inertia*) is, under different respects, both resistance and impetus: it is resistance in so far as the body, for conserving its state, opposes the impressed force: it is impetus in so far as the same body, by yielding with difficulty to the force of resistance of an obstacle, endeavors to change its state. Commonly, resistance is always attributed [to bodies] at rest and impetus [to those] in motion: but motion and rest, as commonly conceived, are distinguished only with respect to each other: nor do [those things] truly rest that are regarded as if they rested by ordinary people.[3]

We are told that the "inherent force of matter" (*vis insita*) is a "power of resisting." This power each body individually possesses in itself, so that the body is enabled to persist in its state "so far as is in its power." Consequently, the phrase *quantum in se est* simply denotes what the body is able to do "naturally," that is, to do in virtue of its own force (*sua vi*)[4] or inherent tendency. Thus, the body's ability to resist is commensurate with its mass. We are told, furthermore, that the body's *vis insita* (considered as a "power of resisting") is *only* exercised "in changes of state produced in it by another force impressed upon it." Therefore, this power is "excited" only when another body is acting to change the first body's state. And the measure of that change is the impulsive action of the other body, and not the prior and uniform momentum of the first body itself.

---

[3] Ibid., 2.

[4] See Cohen 1964, 131–35, for a discussion of the classical background of this phrase and its *fortuna* in the seventeenth century. The basic notion captured by the phrase *quantum in se est* is the idea that a body can move "by its own natural tendency" or of its own force. The Greek equivalent is the phrase ὅσον ἐφ᾽ ἑαυτῷ—literally, "so far as [depends] on it (if it could)." Thus, to say that something depends on itself conveys the idea that it behaves naturally according to its own power or ability. See Philoponus, *In Phys.*, 578.32–579.18 (Vitelli 1888), for a use of this Greek phrase in natural philosophical contexts. I have not been able to determine whether the Greek phrase occurs earlier than Lucretius's use of *quantum in se est* in *De rerum natura*. Newton first encountered this phrase, to denote the conception that each thing acts in accordance with its nature so far as it is able, in Daniel Stahl's *Axiomata philosophica*, a popular compendium of Aristotelian philosophy. He in fact copied a passage from Stahl into his Latin notes, which use the phrase in discussing the causal abilities of physical things. See McGuire and Tamny 1983, 17–19.

So far so good. But we are also told that this inherent power of resisting (that all bodies possess) is distinguishable only in conception from the body's "inertia of mass." Moreover, Newton also states that any body is not easily changed from a state of resting or of moving; indeed, thus considered, the *vis insita* of any body may also be named a *vis inertiae*—a "force of inactivity." Now, on the face of it, this raises a number of puzzles. It seems clear enough that Newton *intends* us to treat the notions of "inertial mass," *vis inertiae*, and *vis insita* as interchangeable names for equivalent conceptions of one and the same reality—that is, any body's ability to maintain its occurrent state. If we look beneath the surface of his rhetoric, however, conceptual tensions plainly lurk. A "power of resisting" is not equivalent in fact to the *inertia* of a body's mass; nor is a *vis insita* ("exercisable" only when one body is confronted by another) equivalent to a *vis inertiae* or a "force of inactivity." The conceptual overdetermination evident in Newton's rhetoric masks this fact to some extent.

As further evidence of this lack of equivalence, note that Newton further characterizes the power called either *vis insita* or *vis inertiae* as both a resistance and an impulse. It is a resistance "in so far as the body, for conserving its state, opposes the impressed force"; it is an impulse in so far as the *same body*, at the *same time*, "endeavors" to change the state of the other body. For Newton this is an absolute feature of bodies, since it obtains whether they are in motion or at rest. But a "power of resisting" is a passive disposition to react, whereas an impulse or "endeavor" to change the state of another body is a disposition to act that is actualizable. The two dispositions are evidently not equivalent, nor does Newton claim that they are.

We have, then, the following conceptions that must be kept separate. (1) To speak of a body's *vis insita* as a *vis inertiae* ("force of inactivity") is not at all the same as speaking of the *vis insita* as an active disposition exercisable only when the body is opposed. The conceptions of course differ (as Newton himself claims); but they also refer to different abilities that the body possesses. Moreover, the notion of a "force of inactivity" is ambiguous between two claims about resistance: To say a body is not easily put out of its state is consistent with saying it avoids change because of its "inertial mass." But to say that the body resists an impressed force by means of a *vis insita* only *exercised* under that circumstance involves quite a different conception of resistance. (2) In the same vein, to characterize the force called either *vis insita* or *vis inertiae* both a resistance and an impulse is to mobilize the language of disposition and of actualization in two quite different ways. Moreover, it is clear that the capacities for reaction and action are being attributed to one and the *same* body.

Newton also tells us in Law i that every body "persists," in the absence of opposing forces, in its intrinsic state. If it is moving, that state is conserved continuously along a right line, and is expressed by the absolute momentum of the body if it is regarded as moving with respect to absolute space. From Proposition I, Theorem I, we know that a body's ability "to persist" in a state is the manifestation of its "inherent force" (*vis insita*). There, as the prior condition of his proof of the areal law for the circle, Newton supposes that a body describes an initial right line "by its inherent force (*vis insita*)" alone.[5] In Definition IV and in Corollary I to the Laws we learn that *after* a body is acted on by impressed forces, it persists in a resultant right-line motion by its "*vis inertiae* only."[6] Thus, in discussing the notion of an impressed force in Definition IV, and its use in the constructed parallelogram of forces in the corollary, Newton states that an impressed force "consists in the action only, and remains no longer in the body when the action is over."[7] Consequently, a body's ability to be in a state of moving before and after being acted on by an opposing force is due uniquely to its own inherent force. Thus, it is clear that its inertial state is not maintained by a series of superimposed "impetuses" caused by the continual action of an external force.[8]

This means that a *vis insita*, understood as a "force of persistence," is ontologically prior in Newton's scheme to the action of an "impressive force" that may oppose that state. That a body by its *vis insita* is in a continuing state is a necessary condition for that state being changed. And together with the Second Law (which states that a body's "change of motion is proportional to the motive force impressed"), we have the necessary and sufficient conditions for determining a change of state along the right line in which the force is impressed.

In characterizing a body's ability to persist in a state of moving in virtue of its own inherent force, Newton is clearly referring to the continued presence of an "agency" operative in the body. As this "agency" is to be understood, however, it is not to be confused with a latent disposition in a body that can be actualized only when an external force is impressed upon it. In fact, in Definition III, there are two distinct ways in which a body's state is maintained: when a *vis insita*, understood as a "power of resisting," is excited to maintain the state; and when the *vis insita*, understood as a "force of persistence," maintains the body before *and* after it is affected by an opposing force.[9] Just as there are two distinct notions of resistance, there are likewise two distinct conceptions of how a state is maintained.

---

[5] Newton 1687, 37.

[6] "Per solam vim inertiae" (ibid., 2 and 13).

[7] "Consistit haec vis in actione sola, neque post actionem permanet in corpore" (ibid., 2).

[8] McMullin 1978, 36.

[9] As Proposition I, Theorem I, Definition IV, and Corollary I to the laws all clearly indicate, Newton does not reduce the role of *vis insita* as a "force of persistence" or as a "conserving force" to the disposition of a body to maintain its state when it is affected by another body.

In summary: there are three distinct ways in which Newtonian matter is in itself an intrinsic source of activity. First, all bodies possess an inherent "agency" that conserves the motion they already have. Second, they have the ability to persist in that motion, when opposed, in virtue of their internal "resisting power." Third, they have an internal disposition that, when actualized, "endeavors" to alter the motion of any external body that acts upon them. It is clear that Newton's thinking is an exercise in ontology, and a complicated one at that.

2. *VIS INSITA*: SOME IMPORTANT SOURCES AND USES

But what is this internal "agency"? Does it function as an internal efficient cause conserving the body's manifest state either of moving or of resting? And is it akin to the notion of a self-mover or an internal mover? Again, how is this "agency" or inherent force related to a body's disposition to be both reactive and active in the presence of an opposing body? As part of the answer to these questions I shall consider Aristotle and the Aristotelians on the *source* of natural change in inanimate bodies; Zabarella's treatment of the concept of an internal efficient cause in his *De rebus naturalibus*; and the Stoic notions of αἴτιος συνεκτικός (perfect or self-sufficient cause) and δι' ἑαυτοῦ (through itself) as they pertain to the motion of inanimate bodies. What will become evident are some significant connections between the Aristotelian notion of φύσις—in the sense of the inherent source of change in a physical thing—and the notion of *vis insita* understood as an internal cause of something's change. Below I shall consider some contemporary sources of these ideas that were available to Newton.

At *Phys.* II.1, 192b18, in discussing his doctrine of nature, Aristotle asserts that unlike natural things, manufactured artifacts (a bed, for example) "have no innate impulse for change." Moreover, he argues that all natural things possess this "innate impulse" for change or for remaining unchanged in themselves—as a constitutive fact of their individual natures. Thus, if nothing prevents it, a stone necessarily moves downward to its natural place, in virtue of a change defined by its intrinsic nature alone. Consequently, its "innate impulse" for a specific sort of natural change is manifested by the occurrence of just that change. Moreover, the occurrence exhibits an intrinsic relationship between what the stone *is* and what the stone is *able to do*.

The phrase "innate impulse" renders Aristotle's ὁρμὴ ἔμφυτος. In many medieval and Renaissance translations of *Phys.* II.1, the phrase "have no innate impulse for change" is translated *nullum mutationis impetum insitum habent*.[10] Thus the Greek ὁρμὴ ἔμφυτος is rendered by *impetus*

10 At *Phys.* II.1, 192b18, the original Greek is οὐδεμίαν ὁρμὴν ἔχει μεταβολῆς ἔμφυτον.

insitus ("innate impetus"), or alternatively by the phrase *impetus innatus*.[11] The term *insitus* occurs classically in Cicero and Horace, and is used to mean either that which is "implanted" in something or that which is "innate" or "natural" to something.[12] Noting the latter sense of the term, we are not surprised that Aristotle's Latin translators use either *insitus* or *innatus* to express the intrinsic character of the "impetus" that the Stagirite ascribes to the natures of things. And it is well to notice here that the term "impetus" is used traditionally in two different ways. In a strict sense it is equated with the notion of *vis impressa*—an internal force impressed from without. But in a wider usage the term refers to a force internal to a moving body, whether impressed or not. It is in this latter sense that the Latin translators employ the term to render Aristotle's conception. Accordingly, they reflect the practice of a large group of thinkers who use "impetus" (for either ὁρμή or ῥοπή) to indicate that inanimate things move in virtue of either an internal mover or a natural impulse.

Newton does not accept the Aristotelian ontology of simple bodies, that is, the view that heavy things move downward if not impeded, whereas light things move upward. On the contrary, a "Newtonian body," in the absence of external forces, can move indefinitely, multidirectionally, and uniformly along any right line according to its intrinsic nature alone; or it can remain at rest.[13] Nevertheless, there is a strong family resemblance between Aristotle's and Newton's ontological commitments. For both thinkers, inanimate things are naturally the *source* and *subject* of their characteristic behavior; in Newton's case a body will move with a uniform and rectilinear motion if not impeded. Moreover, in *Phys.* II.1 Aristotle refers to nature not only as a source of change and nonchange, but also as a *cause* of change that is in the thing it changes per se and not accidently (192b21). Although he gives no explicit account there of the sort of cause a nature qua source is, he seems to think of it as an intrinsic cause responsible for the sorts of change determinative of the thing in question. Thus, causes are sources, and natures are sources; but so, too, are powers and innate impulses. At *Meta.* Θ.1, 1046a10–11, a power (δύναμις) is defined, in its primary sense, as that which is the source of change. Accordingly, there are intrinsic links in Aristotle's mind between the notions of nature, cause, and

[11] See Vimercato 1564, 59; and Pacius 1608, 36. Vimercato and Pacius were well known in the seventeenth century as Aristotelian translators and commentators. See also Perion 1554, 22; Niphus 1569, 132; and Pendasius 1604, 323. Pendasius has a lengthy discussion of Philoponus's views on nature (see 348–49).

[12] See Pease 1955, 2:579–80 (commentary on Cicero's *ND*), for a discussion of the terms *insitus* and *innatus*. See also ibid., 1: 287–89, for an extended discussion of *insitus* and its relation to *vis*.

[13] Newton assumes that straight-line motion is the simplest, a view he probably assimilates from Descartes, who argues explicitly for it. He also holds that a body can move rectilinearly in any direction whatsoever in homogeneous space.

power. Given this, and the intrinsic relation between a thing's nature and what it *does*, Aristotle holds that the exercise of a natural power can be described as the operation of an internal efficient cause.

It is evident enough that Aristotle's analysis provides a framework of concepts relevant to Newton's position. Newton's writing does not reflect Aristotle's semantics of "natural-forced-upward-downward" motion, but it still reflects Aristotle's topical semantics or structure. That is, Newton's phrase *vis insita*, used to signify a body's inner source and cause of change, maintains a logic of "place" within the ordered components of the traditional topic of matter, directional change, and space. Although the extent to which Newton was fully aware of Aristotle's views is not clear, he does cite two interesting passages that indicate familiarity with some relevant texts.

Two references to Aristotle occur in a manuscript fragment, written by Newton between 1684 and 1694, in which he traces the genesis of the First Law back to Lucretius, Anaxagoras, and Aristotle. The first reference, though citing the *Meteorology*, is in fact to Aristotle's *De caelo*. Newton's Latin in translation reads:

> Aristotle was of the same mind, since he expresses his opinion thus in the third book of the *Meteors*, chap. 2: *If a body*, he says, *destitute of gravity and levity, be moved, it is necessary that it be moved by an external force; and when it is once moved by a source, it will conserve its motion indefinitely.*[14]

The translation is sound, and Newton quotes the Greek accurately. In this chapter (*De cae.* iii.2, 301b1–4), Aristotle is concerned to show that the simple bodies (air, fire, water, earth) have a natural motion that is caused neither by an outside force (βία) nor contrary to their nature (παρὰ φύσιν). The text Newton cites is quoted from a passage in which Aristotle argues that "some bodies must possess an inclination [to move] owing to their weight or lightness" (301a22–23). But if bodies do not possess a "natural impulse" (φύσει ῥοπή), they cannot move naturally either upward or downward. Aristotle's term here for "inclination" or "natural impulse" is ῥοπή, and it is used repeatedly in the *De caelo* to characterize the inner source of natural motion in bodies. The argument is in the form of a *reductio* in which Aristotle attempts to show that a weightless or an absolutely light body must traverse the same distance in the same time as bodies that are heavy and light. But in fact a weightless or an absolutely light body can only move laterally if it is impressed by an outside force (βία); given these conditions, such a force will result in indefinite motion over an indefinite distance, but not with infinite speed (301a20–b16).

In Aristotle's view, such states of affairs are physically impossible: for all

[14] Hall and Hall 1962, 310.

bodies move naturally according to their weights (and in an inverse proportion to the resistance of the medium) to a finite terminus. Moreover, Aristotle's argument shows that the constrained motion of a weightless body, however large, is incommensurable with the motion over the same distance of any small body with weight. By taking the passage out of its context, however, one can read it as an anticipation of the law of inertia, as Newton does. Now the second sentence of the passage is open to two interpretations: either the internal force, which maintains the body's motion, is impressed from without, or the external force initiates the motion, which the body's power alone conserves thereafter. In the light of his own conceptual framework, Newton would read the sentence in the second way. And he could scarcely fail to notice Aristotle's claim that the "natural inclination" (heaviness and lightness) of bodies is a positive cause of their downward or upward motion (301a3–4). That is, weight does not merely denote the *fact* that a heavy body moves downward if released; it also indicates that its "natural inclination" to do so is the internal cause of that motion. In other words, the Aristotle of *De caelo* holds that the heavy and the light "seem to possess in themselves (ἐν αὐτοῖς δοκεῖ ἔχειν) a source of change" (310b24–25). Thus, the *motus separati* of the simple bodies (that is, their motions when they are no longer in contact with a generator or a releaser) are caused by "inclinations" or "impulses" intrinsic to their natures. Given his commitments, Newton could well have detached the conception that natural motions are caused by internal movers from its embedment in Aristotelian theory while perceiving the relevance of Aristotle's discussion to his own conception that bodies move of themselves naturally and uniformly along a right line if not prevented. For there are clear affinities between the causal roles that ῥοπή and ὁρμή play in Aristotle's theory of natural motion in *De caelo*, and the causal role that *vis insita* plays in Newton's. Thus, given these affinities, Aristotle may well have influenced the development of Newton's thinking on the source and cause of natural motion.

The second passage from Aristotle that Newton cites in his manuscript fragment is from *Phys.* IV.8, 215a19–22. It occurs in an antiatomist argument designed by Aristotle to show that a void cannot exist (IV.8, 215a1–22). Newton cites the passage in Greek and then provides a Latin translation. If there were motion in a void, Aristotle reasons that "no one could say why a thing once in motion should rest anywhere; for why here rather than here? So a thing will either be at rest or must be moved indefinitely, unless something stronger impedes it."[15] For Aristotle, then, there is no sufficient reason why anything should rest at any particular "place" in a void, which is everywhere uniform and alike: quite simply, there is nowhere

---

[15] Ibid., 311.

for it to be, nor is there a terminus to which it can go. Thus, there can be no motion in a void, because there are no differentiations or places by which to judge a change in circumstance. Moreover, in Aristotle's view, forced motion in a void is impossible. It presupposes natural motion, which also cannot obtain, because the void lacks natural places. If we do suppose a forced motion in a void, however, it will be indefinite: for why should the body rest here as opposed to there?[16] For Newton, of course, a void is a real extension, so that motion through it is through an *actual* distance, not instantaneously, but in a determined time. He therefore construes Aristotle's statement that a body in a void could move indefinitely as a partial statement of inertial motion. It is important to notice that Newton also refers to Aristotle's argument in his *Quaestiones quaedam philosophicae* of 1664. This reference occurs in an essay in which he argues, by a thought experiment, for the possibility of the perpetual motion of a body along a right line in a void.[17] Moreover, Newton states explicitly that the continuing cause of the body's motion is its own "natural gravity" functioning as an intrinsic source of its own natural motion. Thus, from the outset, Newton attributes natural motion to the action of an internal mover or force. Some four years later (c. 1668), he continues to do so. In a lengthy metaphysical treatise now known as *De gravitatione*, Newton says that "inertia is an internal force of a body (*vis interna corporis*), lest its state should be changed by an external exciting force." In this text he also defines such terms as *conatus*, "impetus," "pressure," and "gravity." In Definition v, Newton gives a general account of force, telling us that "force is the causal source of motion and rest," which is either external and impressed or an "internal source by which existing motion or rest is conserved (*conservatur*) in a body, and by which any being endeavors (*conatus*) to persist in its state, and opposes resistance."[18] Thus natural motion is here explicitly linked with an internal force that acts causally to conserve motion and rest, and with a *conatus* for maintaining and resisting a change of state, in a manner reminiscent of Law i and Definition iii of the *Principia*. Moreover, Newton unambiguously identifies an internal force as a "causal source" of both motion and rest.[19]

[16] Aristotle is not arguing that motion through a void would be either instantaneous or with infinite speed. His point is rather that there can be no ratio between a speed in a void and one in a given medium. That is, there is no proportion between a zero and a finite magnitude. See Funkenstein 1986, 152–64, for a full discussion of this point.

[17] See McGuire and Tamny 1983, 209–15. Newton's argument is probably intended as a reply to Aristotle's *reductio* at *Phys.* iv.8, 215a1–216a26. He imagines three separated globes, partly emersed in a medium and partly in a void, and argues that the parts in the void move naturally in the same way and in the same time as the parts in the medium. The argument seems to be an attempt to turn Aristotle's *reductio* against itself.

[18] Hall and Hall 1962, 114.

[19] That is, Newton is explicitly treating "force" in the category of an internal cause. This

Newton's belief that the inertial motion of physical things arises from an internal cause or force puts him with those who conceive internal forces as causes of natural motions. Among important proponents of this view are Chrysippus, Philoponus, Avicenna, Albert the Great, Roger Bacon, Duns Scotus, Buridan, Oresme, and Jacopo Zabarella.[20] Opponents of this position are historically the strict Aristotelians. Basing themselves on texts such as *Phys.* ii.1 and viii.4, figures like Simplicius and Aquinas helped to shape an interpretation of natural motion that was canonical in many circles.[21] On this view, *Phys.* viii.4 tells us that animate things are candidates for self-motion, in that they alone possess two-way abilities, that is, the abilities both to sit and to stand or to start and to stop. Inanimate things, in contrast, possess a one-way ability, an "inclination" to move to their natural place if not prevented, since by nature they possess an internal and passive ability to be moved or "to suffer" motion. What they do not possess by nature is an inner source for making them come to rest prior to their arrival at their proper places.

But *Phys.* viii.4 is not without its expository tensions. Aristotle certainly wishes to preserve a clear distinction between natural movers (the simple bodies or elements) and self-movers (animate things). Accordingly, the picture he imparts is that simple bodies cannot initiate their own motion but will move necessarily to their natural places once the last inhibitor to their doing so is removed. So unlike self-movers, which can be said to initiate their own motion in the absence of prevention, simple bodies can only begin to move relative to the removal of the last impediment. This action, the removal of impediment, is the true initiator of their motion. But once a simple body is undergoing motion, and is no longer in contact with its initiating conditions, it is then actualizing its impulse to move naturally.

Aristotle's main argument in *Phys.* viii.4 is that any "continuous and naturally connected thing" (255a12), such as a simple body, cannot be said to move itself, because a real distinction between an active "moving part" and a passive "moved part" does not obtain. This, he seems to imply, is at least a necessary condition for a self-mover. There are two passages in

---

view he continues to make explicit as late as 1684 in one of the *De motu* drafts. There he says, "Every body by an inherent force (*vi insita*) alone moves uniformily and indefinitely along a right line, unless impeded by something extrinsic."

[20] For Chrysippus, see *De fato* 42, 43, in Ax [1938] 1965; for Philoponus, see Rasarius 1558, 67, and Dorotheo 1554, 31; Avicenna's views are discussed by Pines (1961, 21–54). For Albert the Great, see Albert (1494, bk. 2, 19–20), who says, *Est enim natura vis insita naturalibus.* For Roger Bacon, see Delorme 1938, 58–60; and for Duns Scotus, see Duns Scotus 1617, 167–77 and 722–31. John Buridan's view is found in *Liber* iv, *Quaestio* 4 (Moody 1942, 254–56); and Nicole Oresme's views are in Menut and Denomy 1968, 607–12 and 678–81. Zabarella's views are in *Liber de natura*, chap. 4, 1–9, and 117–26 of his *De rebus naturalis* (1604).

[21] Simplicius 1566, bk. 2, 91–95; Aquinas 1949, bk. 2, *lectio* 1, 259–63.

Phys. VIII.4, however, that indicate a certain expository tension in Aristotle's argument. Speaking of the most difficult class, the class of movers whose motion is natural yet derived, Aristotle says:

> Therefore none of these things moves itself (for each is connected), nor does anything else that is continuous, but it is necessary to distinguish the changer in each one (ἐν ἑκάστῳ) with regard to what is changed, as we see, for example, in the case of inanimate things when something animate moves them. (255a15–18)

This leaves open the possibility that even in the case of natural movers whose motion is derived, it is still necessary to distinguish in them, at least conceptually, the changer from the changed. Under this rubric a simple body (insofar as it is undergoing motion) can be considered the active source and subject of its own change. For the Aristotelians (Zabarella included), the distinction between source and subject of change is understood through the form/matter distinction. Although less clear in the case of the uniform and elemental bodies, Aristotle never suggests that the distinction does not apply. Futhermore, he also holds that the form, what a thing is for, and that from which its change originates, often coincide, although they differ in account (*Phys.* II.7, 198a21–31).

At *Phys.* VIII.4, 255a30–33 and 255b5–31, Aristotle says that simple bodies, once they are undergoing unimpeded and contactless motion, are actualizing their ability to move naturally. This ability he likens to the ability to exercise knowledge having first exercised a first potential in acquiring it. Just as one can be said to manifest a second potential in actually using the knowledge acquired if not prevented, so a simple body if not prevented can be said to be actualizing its innate (not acquired) ability when undergoing a change to its proper place. According to this analogy, a simple body can be construed as exercising its ability to move in virtue of itself. It is to such passages, and to similar ones in works such as *De caelo*, that the Stoics, Philoponus, and Zabarella appeal to extract from Aristotle the view that the inanimate motion of elemental bodies is actively caused by sources intrinsic to the thing moving and hence can be seen as a type of self-motion.

Of course, this is not the view of elemental natural change that Aristotle wishes to establish. Certainly he holds that the light and the heavy move up and down respectively because "they have a natural tendency to some place" (255b15–17); indeed, he tells us that an elemental thing both is and is not moved by that which removes what is blocking and preventing its motion (255b24). But he also tells us that though elemental things have their source of motion in them, they do not for that change themselves. What they possess is a passive source for change "not of changing something, nor of making something come about, but of suffering" (255b30–

31). So although elemental things can undergo change in virtue of what they are, they cannot initiate it. But this does not deny that they maintain and conserve those changes natural to them. Given that Aristotle does analogize their activity of changing to the exercise of a second potential and leave open the possibility of conceptually distinguishing a changer from what is changing, it is not surprising that an interpretive tradition should arise that construes that intrinsic source for change in an active causal sense.

Accordingly, there are two main interpretive positions historically: the view that the inanimate motion of the elements is caused strictly by causes intrinsic to the moving thing; and the view that such motion is caused by external agents, inanimate things being the passive recipients of the change that results. Those who support the second view emphasize one or more of the following agents: that which generates a natural motion, such as the heated fuel that produces the rising fire; either the absence of what prohibits a natural motion (the cause *per accidens*) or the proximate cause whose removal triggers it; and the role of the medium and of a thing's natural place interpreted as the final cause of a body's motion. Writers of the Hellenistic, medieval, and Renaissance periods address these issues extensively, and they are discussed well into the seventeenth century in Aristotelian and non-Aristotelian works alike.

Jacopo Zabarella devotes a full and detailed discussion to traditional views of the concept of nature, skillfully adjudicating between such notables as Avicenna, Averroes, Albert, Aquinas, Duns Scotus, and Aristotle himself. In his *De rebus naturalibus* he raises the standard issue of whether nature (as it pertains to inanimate things) is an active or a passive principle.[22] He notes that animate things are self-movers for Aristotle because they possess the "internal productive cause of their own motion."[23] He immediately points out, however, that there are many reasons for thinking that the individual forms of the elements "are the active (*activa*) principles of their natural motion."[24] He goes on to develop the view that the elements possess both an active factor and a passive factor, which are exhibited in their motion. They are active by nature in virtue of their intrinsic forms, but at the same time passive in motion in virtue of their nature understood as matter.[25] Thus, the elements are the source and the subject of their own motion, and for Zabarella there is a formal distinction *a parte rei* between their individual forms qua active principle and their individual informed matter qua passive principle: "For that reason, the active and

[22] Zabarella 1604, *Liber de natura*, chaps. 1–9, 117–26.

[23] *Internam habere causam effectricem sui motus* (ibid., chap. 6, 121).

[24] *Si elementa a formis suis moventur, ut multi putant; formae elementorum sunt activa principia motuum naturalium* (ibid.).

[25] Ibid., chaps. 6, 7, and 8, 121–25.

passive principles of motion cannot be separated" in the elements as such.[26] Moreover, Zabarella endorses Buridan's opinion that if what is natural has "per se in itself (*in seipsis*) a productive principle of motion, any element is indeed a natural body; therefore it ought to have *in se* an active principle of motion."[27] In Zabarella's view, this is its substantial form.

How does Zabarella understand the active principle of motion in the elements? Does it refer to the internal cause and source of their natural motion? It is one thing to castigate Simplicius for holding that nature is *principium patiendi, non principium agendi*,[28] but quite another to respond to the fact that Aristotle holds in *Phys.* VIII.4 that the elements, far from being self-movers, are natural movers able only *to be* moved. Zabarella's strategy is to argue that Aristotle's own explanatory principles, considered together, do not deny that there is a clear sense in which the elements are internal movers. Thus, in Zabarella's view, Aristotle "does not deny absolutely that the heavy and the light move of themselves, but denies [only] that animate things move *a se* in that manner."[29]

After stating that "nature is a cause of motion both immanently and transeuntly,"[30] Zabarella proceeds to clarify these terms and to argue that the elements possess an internal efficient cause that is responsible for their own proper motions. His first move is to argue that the strict cause of a heavy thing's natural motion downward is one that is simultaneous and commensurate with that actual effect, that is, the downward motion itself. In other words, since motion downward is "an actually existing effect, the cause ought to have some coexisting actuality."[31] This causal principle he attributes to *Phys.* II.1 (not unreasonably) and *Po. An.* II.12 (95a10–b1). Neither the generator of an element nor the removal of the impediment to its motion satisfies this principle: neither is co-present nor concomitant with the actually occurring effect, that is, the downward motion. Nor is the element's natural place a candidate. Because the proper function of the

---

[26] *Propterea, principium motus activum et passivum non possunt separari* (ibid., chap. 7, 123). See also the *De motu gravium, et levium*, bk. 1, chap. 9, 162; and chap. 12, 166–67. On p. 166, he says, *Ergo vult propriam elementi naturam esse principium activum sui motus naturalis*. Zabarella proceeds to develop his view in the context of a careful discussion of the nature and application of the real, the formal, and the conceptual distinctions.

[27] *In seipsis per se principium motus effectivum: elementum autem est corpus naturale; ergo debet in se habere principium motus activum* (*De motu gravium, et levium*, bk. 1, chap. 4, 159).

[28] Zabarella 1604, *Liber de natura*, chap. 3, 118, and chap. 5, 120.

[29] *Aristotelis absolute ibi negat gravia et levia moveri a seipsis, sed negat eo modo, quo a se moventur animalia* (ibid., chap. 9, 126).

[30] Ibid., chap. 8, 125. Immanent motion has its cause in the thing itself, whereas transeunt motion arises from a cause other than the thing itself.

[31] *De motu gravium, et levium*, bk. 1, chap. 4, 159: *Effectus actu existens debet habere causam actu existentem*. Zabarella goes on to argue that only an internal cause can satisfy this condition.

element's individual form is to act,[32] and because it is co-present with the element's motion, the form, not the external natural place, is the simultaneous cause of the element's actual motion.[33] In his view of natural place, Zabarella is probably endebted to Philoponus, a writer whom he cites often, and one who had a considerable influence on Renaissance natural philosophy. In his commentary on the *Physics*, Philoponus denies the teleology of natural places. For him, elemental bodies do not move upward or downward in relation to external causes. They move as they do because their internal causes drive them to establish a definite and positional order within an external space (Philoponus *In Phys.* 633.8–9; see note 45 below). Thus, only the form, that which is an internal active principle, can satisfy the requirement that the "cause necessarily and simultaneously exists in the same way" as the actuality of the continuing activity of an element in natural motion.[34] Nor is the element's downward motion *a seipso per accidens*. In Zabarella's view, the absence of the impediment is simply the removal of a hindrance to motion. In no way does its removal initiate the impulse to movement; rather, it is a negative condition, the removal of which allows the element to move by its own internal cause through the first as through all subsequent moments of its fall.[35]

Given the principle that strict causes are concomitant with their effects, and act continuously through the changes they produce, Zabarella introduces a distinction between two kinds of efficient cause. In the first sense, the cause acts on something other than itself to produce an effect in it, and is said to be an *efficiens transmutans* or *proprie efficiens*.[36] In the second sense, the internal cause produces an effect in itself and is called by Zabarella an *efficiens per emanationem*.[37] It is this second conception that Zabarella deems appropriate for understanding the motion of the elements in the absence of a generator or an impediment. Thus, in Zabarella's view, the motion of an *efficiens per emanationem* signifies the Greek verb ἐνεργεῖν—which in Latin is *agere* or *operari*, the very activity of an action itself. Thus, on this view, it is the power of an element's nature itself that actively carries it to its natural place after the effect of the generator or the removal of an impediment cease.[38] Moreover, there "cannot be a real

---

[32] Ibid., chap. 4, 159.

[33] Ibid., 159. Zabarella's considered opinion is that an elemental form possesses essentially the ability to ground motion in a thing if not prevented. The form itself does not move since it is an inner principle of motion, not a *motivum*.

[34] *Quare dum effectus existit, necesse est causam quoque simul eodem modo existere* (ibid., 159).

[35] Ibid., 161.

[36] Ibid., chap. 12, 166.

[37] Ibid. See Wallace 1978 for the influence of Zabarella's distinction in Italy.

[38] Zarabella 1604, chap. 12, 166.

distinction between the *agens per emanationem* and the patient."[39] After all, the form is both the formal and the efficient cause of the element's motion, and, as such, it and the matter it informs comprise a definite unity.[40] Thus, "the element is moved *per se* by its own form, as though by an agent *per emanationem*; for by that [agent] the natural motion in the element itself arises (*emanat*) immediately."[41] Accordingly, the agent operating *per emanationem* is prior in the *ordine naturae*, and the effect of the medium together with resistance is posterior.[42] Furthermore, as Zabarella uses the phrase *efficiens per emanationem*, it denotes something in an element's nature that springs from it naturally and enables it to underwrite its proper change. Thus it echoes the scholastic notion that natural change is a process of coming to be out of potency: an element educes its proper change from its own potentiality if unimpeded.

Reasonably enough, Zabarella's view that the simple bodies move by internal efficient causes is consciously developed within an Aristotelian framework. Moreover, he states explicitly that in an element, "the form in and of itself provides the motive force (*dat vim motricem*); but this is to say that the form is the motor (*motricem*) of the element."[43] Thus, the internal efficient cause that drives an element functions, in effect, as an internal force. This conception again indicates the probable influence of Philoponus on Zabarella.[44] In his emendation of Aristotle's classic definition of nature in *Phys.* II.1, Philoponus says that "nature is either life or power (δύναμις) that is diffused throughout bodies, completely formative and directive of them, being the source of change and remaining unchanged in that in which it belongs primarily of itself and not accidentally."[45] And he argues that the inanimate simple bodies move to their proper places by their internal force or power alone. Specifically, he holds that heaviness indicates a natural, intrinsic, and absolute power (δύναμιν φυσικήν) in a simple body itself, which is the productive cause of its motion.[46] Phi-

---

[39] *Sed agens per emanationem non potest esse re distinctum a patiente* (ibid.).

[40] Ibid., 167.

[41] *Movetur elementum a sua forma per se, tanquam ab agente per emanationem, ab ea namque emanat immediate motus naturalis in ipsomet elemento* (ibid.).

[42] Ibid., 168.

[43] *Formam, dat vim motricem sui ipsius; at hoc est dicere formam esse motricem elementi* (ibid., 166). Zabarella insists, however, that there is no real distinction between "the mover" and "the moved" in an elemental nature: *Patet in motu elementi non esse divisionem fieri in partem per se moventem et partem per se motum; quia per se movens est forma, per se est motum totum compositum quod eandem formam complectitur* (167).

[44] See Schmitt 1987.

[45] *In Phys.* 197.30–198.8 (Vitelli 1888); and McGuire 1985. For the influence of Philoponus on the Arabic and Latin cultures, see Pines 1961.

[46] *In Phys.* 499.12 and 678.23 (Vitelli 1888).

loponus's commentary on the first four books of the *Physics* was first translated into Latin by Gulielmus Dorotheo in 1554, and then by Baptista Rasarius in 1558. They both render Philoponus's statement as *Natura est quaedam vita sive vis quae per corpora diffunditur* ("Nature is a certain life or force that is diffused through bodies").[47] Nothing corresponding to *quaedam* is present in Philoponus's Greek, but it appears in most subsequent Latin versions of his statement. For example, Toletus in his commentary on the *Physics* writes: *natura est vita, seu vis quaedam per corpora diffusa*.[48] The source of the phrase might well be Albert the Great (himself influenced by Avicenna, who holds that in inanimate things nature is an internal *vis* and efficient cause of change), who writes that all natural things have a *quandam virtutem in seipsis sua sive vim*.[49] In any event, Philoponus's interpretation, in Latin dress, directed attention once again to the possibility of conceiving nature as a kind of force or cause internal to inanimate bodies. As discussed earlier, in line with this conception, Zabarella gives an account of how nature, conceived as an internal force, operates in bodies, and why it is necessary that the source of an element's actual motion is a cause that is co-present with that continuous effect.

Apart from his acceptance of the Aristotelian conception of simple, natural motion (either upward or downward), there is much in Zabarella's account that is relevant to Newton's commitments.[50] First, Zabarella argues that natural, inanimate motions have internal causes that are the efficient source of the change that occurs. That is, a natural motion (as such) is effected by an internal mover alone, and is not caused primarily by anything external. Indeed, he goes further. Not only can a superimposed impetus not be a source of a natural motion, but neither can anything that is in continuous contact with the body, such as the air. Thus, this schema provides some explanatory features that reemerge in Newton's thought. For Newton, a *vis insita* is an inherent force or mover, which is the sole efficient source conserving a body's motion in the *absence* of an opposing force. As in Zabarella's scheme, a body in natural motion is the source *and* subject of that motion, except that in Newton's case the motion is along a right line indefinitely. Accordingly, for Newton, natural motion *is* a continuous change caused by a body's internal force. In this regard, recall the important phrase "so far as is in its power" (*quantum in se est*), which characterizes the "power of resisting" by which each body conserves its continuing state of moving or of resting. The phrase indicates clearly that

[47] Dorotheo 1554, 31; and Rasarius 1558, 67.

[48] Toletus 1585, 46.

[49] Albert the Great 1494, bk. 2, 19.

[50] This is important. Aristotle holds that simple motions are of themselves simple absolutely and not just relative to other motions that are more complex. Many medieval commentators read Aristotle in the second way, Zabarella in the first.

the "power" of a *vis insita* is commensurate with the body in which it inheres, and is simultaneous in its action with the state that it maintains. Moreover, the phrase *quantum in se est* is equivalent to the phrase *sua vi*: "of its own force" or "by its own natural tendency."[51] This is clearly Newtonian usage. Thus, much in the manner of Zabarella's causal picture, Newton is claiming that any body acts naturally, according to its inherent force, to conserve its state of motion. This commitment brings into focus another feature of Zabarella's schema, namely the Aristotelian-based principle that a strict cause is simultaneous with, and proportional to, its effect. Recall that Newton conceives the continuity of natural motion as the manifestation of an internal force, the presence of which is the sole causal feature responsible for that motion. This is clearly an instance of the causal model of natural motion advocated by Zabarella. It treats natural motion as a *positive* change. Moreover, every effect, continuous and noncontinuous alike, has a concomitant cause, since any and every change requires a co-present cause. There is no evidence that Newton knew Zabarella's views directly. But they were widely read and discussed in Europe, as I explain in the next section.

Much has been written on the Stoic anticipation of inertial natural motion in virtue of their notion that all things strive for self-preservation. But there is a more specific piece of analysis pertinent to Newton's view of the causes of natural motion. According to Cicero, Chrysippus distinguished the role of external and internal causes in natural motion. The external cause gets objects moving by impulsion,[52] and thus contributes to the initiation of that motion. But once the cylinder is rolling by itself, the causation is internal, since "it is by its own nature (*suapte natura*), for the rest, that the cylinder rolls and the spin-top turns."[53] Chrysippus also holds a related distinction, the division of forces into those that are perfect and principal (*perfectae et principales*) and those that are auxiliary and proximate (*adiuvantes et proximae*). There are thus two sorts of *vis*: an external *vis* or antecedent cause, and an internal *vis*, which itself maintains, say, the rolling of the cylinder after the initial impulse. Both causes are active, and the latter is termed a perfect and principal cause.[54] Since the antecedent cause cannot initiate motion without the cylinder, whereas the cylinder is able to roll in virtue of its internal cause alone, the latter is a perfect and complete cause whose action is independent of anything else. Cicero's *causa perfecta* is the Greek αἴτιος αὐτοτελής, literally "self-sufficient cause." Clement of Alexandria, a reliable source on the Stoics, reports that "the complete cause and the self-sufficient cause they [the

---

[51] Bailey 1947, 1: 246 and 248
[52] Cicero, *De fato* 42 (Ax [1938] 1965, 18.237).
[53] Ibid.
[54] Ibid., 43 (19.237).

Stoics] name synonymously, since it is sufficiently productive through itself of its own end."[55] Here, then, is a theory relevant to Newton's view of natural motion, especially the conception that a body is the sufficient source of its motion independent of the initial effect of a *vis impressa*. Newton may well have known Stoic views, since he possessed a copy of the *Opera* of Cicero.

The notion of δι' ἑαυτοῦ ("through itself") in the Clement passage is worth comment. As Hahm indicates (in this volume), the Stoics developed an ontology that embraces three different sorts of self-mover: those that move "through themselves" (δι' ἑαυτῶν), inanimate objects; those that move "out of themselves" (ἐξ ἑαυτῶν), the plants; and those that move "from themselves" (ἀφ' ἑαυτῶν), the animals. Zabarella's *De rebus* often reflects these Stoic distinctions among self-movers, using the Latin *ex se* and *a se* to express the idea that elemental bodies move "through themselves." A probable source for Zabarella's terminology is Averroes' comments on *Phys.* ii.1 and vii.1. Averroes says there is "no doubt that they are moved through themselves (*ex se*) and not from an extrinsic mover, namely, the four elements and all bodies moved through themselves." He also tells us that "it is apparent to sense that some things are moved through themselves (*ex se*) without the mover being distinguished from the moved by sense, as in the four elements."[56] In my view (see note 45), Philoponus stands as much behind Averroes as he does behind Zabarella and Paduan naturalism. Moreover, there is no good ground to deny Averroes' direct influence on Zabarella and, through him, the naturalism of the ancient Stoics.

3. *VIS INSITA* AND NEWTON'S INTELLECTUAL ENVIRONMENT

There are many seventeenth-century writers who use the phrase *vis insita* to characterize the source of natural motion. In his widely used *Systema logicae* (Hanover, 1616), Keckermann says that a natural cause in physical things "acts from an inherent force of nature (*ex insita vi naturae*) without any deliberation."[57] In his popular *Lexicon philosophicum* (Frankfurt, 1613), Goclenius defines *vis* as either inherent or violent.[58] Moreover,

---

[55] Migne 1890, 8: 9.600.

[56] Averroes 1562, 8: 49C–D and 306B. Averroes' position appears to be inconsistent, however, inasmuch as he follows Aristotle's view in *Phys.* viii.4 that the simple bodies are only the passive source of their natural changes. For an interesting discussion of how Averroes' commentaries are to be reconciled, see Macierowski and Hassing 1988, 77–88.

[57] *Quae ex insita vi naturae agit sine aliqua deliberatione* (Keckermann 1616, *De causa efficiente*, bk. 1, chap. 15, 134). This definition he attributes to Philoponus with approval.

[58] *Vis: vis insita est, vel violenta insita ut naturalis potestas* (321).

under the heading *actiones*, he uses Zabarella's terminology, stating that "internal efficient causes (those that are in the same subject as the effect) or agents by emanation (*agentes per emanationem*) act by continuous action, as fire produces heat."[59] Zabarella's influence is also found in Francis Glisson and Emanuel Maignon. Glisson tells us repeatedly that in animate and inanimate things alike, nature is an *actio immanens*. And using the term *insita* to characterize the origin of natural changes, he states that "the nature of material substances is an internal source of motion."[60] Maignon holds that "any heavy thing, if it were considered by itself, is productive of its own motion by an innate force" so that gravity is an "innate source of downward motion."[61] In his Aristotelian *Physiologia* (a work from which Newton made extensive notes), Johann Magirus uses the phrase *vis insita* frequently to characterize the natural powers of both animate and inanimate things. For example, he says, "Motion is *per se* or proper, when a movable body moves by its own power (*sua virtute*): thus a man is said to move *per se* because he moves wholly and by his own inherent force (*insita vi sua*)."[62] Magirus also makes extensive use of Zabarella's ideas. Furthermore, there is a host of earlier writers (both Aristotelian and non-Aristotelian) who use the phrase (or cognate phrases) in speaking of the source of any type of natural motion: Toletus, Pendasius, Niphus, Nunnesius, Vimercato, Bartolomew Amico, Francis Wallis, Pererius, Pacius, and Vitelleschi.[63] Some of these writers, such as Pacius, Vimercato, and Toletus, were well known in the seventeenth century. Aquinas, in his well-known commentary on Aristotle's *Physics*, chides those who wish to correct Aristotle's definition of nature by defining it as "something absolute—saying that nature is an innate power (*vis insita*) in things or something of that sort."[64] Aquinas most probably has Albert the Great and Avicenna in mind as among those who speak of nature as a *vis insita*.

In his *Astronomia nova* (Prague, 1607), Kepler repeatedly uses the phrase *vis insita*. In the third part of his treatise, he entitles one of his chapters as follows: "Besides the common moving force of the sun, the

[59] *Atqui efficientes internae (quae sunt in eodem subjecto cum effectum) seu agentes per emanationem, agunt per continuatam actionem, sic ignis producit calorem* (43).

[60] *Assero igitur, naturam substantiae materialis esse internum motus principium* (Glisson 1672, chap. 17, 229).

[61] *Quodlibet grave si per se solum consideretur, esse ab innata vi effectivum proprii motus* (Maignon 1653, 1266). Cf. *Gravitatem vocamus principium innatum motus deorsum; levitatem autem principium innatum motus sursum* (1223).

[62] Magirus 1642, bk. 1, chap. 4, sec. 29, 59, and bk. 3, chap. 2, 163.

[63] Nunnesius 1554, bks. 3 and 4; and Amico 1620, *Tractatus* 7, *Quaestio* 7, 525–31. Amico discusses Zabarella's view that nature is an internal efficient cause. Wallis 1690, 18; Pererius 1579, chap. 15, 431–35. For Vitelleschi, see Wallace 1978.

[64]: *Unde deridendi sunt qui volentes definire conati sunt, dicentes, quod natura est vis insita rebus, vel aliquid hujusmodi* (Aquinas 1949, bk. 2, *lectio* 1, 261).

planets are endowed with a *vis insita*: and thus the motion of each single [planet] is composed from two causes."[65] This chapter is important. In it, Kepler argues that planetary motions demand for their complete explanation reference to the *vis insita* of each planet itself (an inherent and innate force that "resides in the body of the planet itself"),[66] and reference to the action of the sun directed toward each of the planets (the sun's extraneous force or *vis extranea*). Thus, the regular and natural motion of each of the planets is grounded in its individual *vis insita*. But the sun's continual action serves to perturbate their motions, causing them to move along enclosed paths. There are clear analogies with Newton's position. Just as Kepler views the motion of each planet as involving the combined effect of its own *vis insita* together with the sun's *vis extranea*, so Newton views the movement of each planet as resulting from the combined effect of its individual *vis insita* and the continual action of the sun's gravity affecting it (that is, the sun's *vis impressa*).

The significance of Leibniz's *On Nature Itself* (1698) should not be overlooked. Its Latin title is *De ipsa natura sive de vi insita actionibusque creaturarum*. Leibniz argues for an intrinsic connection between individual natures, understood in the Aristotelian manner as inner and determinate sources of directed change, and the notion of *vis insita*. His polemic is against Robert Boyle and Christopher Sturm, both of whom criticize Aristotelian conceptions of nature and natures. In his defense of an intrinsic and dynamic conception of individual nature, Leibniz discusses many seventeenth-century positions on the issue. His exposition is therefore a record of key terms used in the debate, among them *vis insita*.

I have traced Newton's view that bodies *causally conserve* their natural states of moving or resting in virtue of an inner force to a number of prevalent sources. We know that Newton took his principle of natural motion from Descartes' *Principia*, together with the notion (Descartes uses the phrase *quantum in se est*) that motion is a state preserved "so far as is in its [the body's] power."[67] It must be emphasized, however, that Newton's

---

[65] *Planetas praeter communem solis vim motricem praeditos esse vi insita: Et motus eorum singulorum componi ex duabus causas* (Kepler 1607, pt. 3, chap. 38, 184). See also p. 185 for the details of Kepler's argument, and pt. 4, chap. 57, 275 ff.

[66] *Virtutem—in ipso Planetae corpore residentem* (ibid., pt. 3, chap. 38, 186). See also chap. 33, 167–68, in which Kepler repeatedly uses phrases like *insit aut in ipso Planetae corpore, eique insita vi motrice*. Cf. also pt. 4, chap. 57, 275. Other possible sources of influence on Newton are writers who are concerned with occult phenomena. On this, see Bianchi 1987, 85–96. Bianchi has an interesting discussion of *vis interna*, as used by a wide range of authors. From my own limited knowledge, it seems that the phrase *vis insita* does not appear in these writers.

[67] See Herival 1965, 44–45; and Cohen 1964, 133–39.

strategy is different from Descartes'. The latter defines natural motion as a *real tendency* to move along a right line that can never be physically actualized in his plenistic universe. Newton, on the other hand, conceives natural motion along a right line as a physically possible condition of bodies that could and would obtain in the absence of opposing forces. In other words, the *vis insita* of bodies is an *absolute* feature of what they are, one that does not depend on their relationships to one another. Consequently, in Newton's view, if there were but one body alone positioned in absolute space, its state of resting or moving would be conserved by its inherent force. Thus Newton, unlike Descartes, conceives natural motion as an obtainable and actual change to be explained by the causal action of an inner force. Newton's conception is clearly actualist in scope. And the conceptual developments that make it possible show the differences between the Newtonian and Cartesian accounts. Unlike Descartes, Newton does not view natural motion as ideal and unrealizable, as a limiting case that stands proxy for the motions of actual phenomena. On the contrary, he conceives it as an absolute motion that can obtain, and its continuance as the manifestation of an inner force that bodies possess naturally. Thus, if a body moves uniquely with respect to absolute space, its inner force explains its continuance in that state along the right line. Moreover, it is the active causal ground that links the body's motion (together with its directionality) to the absoluteness of space. In Newton's view, the body's absolute and natural motion is an internal denomination that refers to the inner force that generates that motion.

It is clear that *vis insita*, considered both as a resistance to change and as an inner impetus disposed to change the state of an opposing body, is not reducible to the role of *vis insita* considered as a conserving force. The story I have told does not explain Newton's sources for this conception. Anneliese Maier has pointed out that *vis inertiae*, viewed as the manifestation of the passive resistance bodies have to being changed, is linked by Buridan and his school to the notion of a *potentia resistendi* (an in-dwelling passive force) that causes the state of a body to be disturbed with difficulty.[68] This appears to be cognate to Newton's conception in Definition III, and one that he extends to states of uniform motion as well as of rest. Of course, this conception is different from the notion that a body has an inner impulse to impress change on an opposing body. This is an active disposition, and is probably a legacy of Newton's earlier practice of conceiving bodies as possessing a *conatus* or endeavor to change anything that comes into contact with them.[69]

But what of Newton's attempt in Definition III to transform *vis insita* into a *vis inertiae*? And what of his claim that "force of inertia" and

[68] Maier 1960.
[69] Hall and Hall 1962, 114.

"inertia of mass" are "always proportional to" a body's mass? Recall that a "force of inactivity" (*vis inertiae*) is not at all the same as a *vis insita*. The former conception is consistent with a *vis motus*, which *results from* the body's momentum (mass conjoined with velocity); but the latter is a true *vis motrix*, an inner cause responsible for the body's preserving its state. Thus, in my view, Newton has, in effect, a two-tiered ontology, which I will call the "surface ontology" and the "inner ontology." The "surface ontology" denotes the manifest "state" of the body, and is characterized by its observable mass and momentum and by the change of these parameters through the action of external forces. It is in reference to these features that Newton speaks of the *vis inertiae* of matter as a passive force or principle "from which alone no motion could ever arise in the universe."[70] As he goes on in this passage to emphasize, the body can only be put into new motion by the *vis impressa* of an external and dynamic force. But when it is in its state of new motion, an internal force is required to conserve that motion, since an impressed force consists entirely in its external action on the body. This internal force—the *vis insita*—is the inner ontology, the cause that grounds the body's continuous change. Thus, the "state of inertia" of a body denotes such surface parameters as mass, which is the external measure of the body's resistance to either an impulsive or an accelerative force. It is this "surface ontology" that is assimilated into physical thought after Newton, together with a rejection of the ontology of *vis insita*.

John Herival has suggested that the protodrafts for Definition III of the *Principia* reveal a transition in Newton's thought regarding the status of *vis insita*. According to Herival, Newton comes to reject the idea that was "his previous, essentially medieval belief in the necessity of some interior force or impetus to maintain an inertial state of uniform motion." Far from continuing to warrant this belief, says Herival, Newton restricts the *vis insita* of bodies to being called into action only in changes of their states.[71] This is certainly one of its roles, and an important one at that. And certainly in Definition III Newton is concerned to stress that function of *vis insita*. In the light of my discussion, however, it clearly continues to play other explanatory roles in Newtonian thought that are not reducible to its dispositional role in a body's ability to act both to restrict a change in its state and to impress a change on an impinging body. Newton preserves two vocabularies throughout his work on dynamics: the vocabulary of dispositions signaled by his continued use of the term *conatus*; and that of intrinsic causes, which maintain the uniform motion of bodies, signaled by his use of the phrase *vis insita*. Unfortunately, *vis insita* functions in both

---

[70] Newton 1952, q.31, 39.
[71] Herival 1965, 26–28.

vocabularies. And it indicates that Newton did not put together coherently all that he was committed to by way of explanatory commitment. Moreover, it is evident enough that he had not transcended completely either his medieval inheritance or the classical tradition of the causes that informed him.

It is clear that Newton conceives natural motion as a species of self-motion. Furthermore, he conceives it as a true change. But in the notion of change as traditionally conceived, there is the changer or the mover, and something that is changed or moved—in short, both an active and a passive principle. Thus, every body in natural and uniform motion is conceived under two different aspects: under one description it is the source, under another the subject, of its proper change. *Vis insita* denotes the active description and *vis inertiae* the passive description of the body's behavior, the latter being the continuous state that manifests the action of the inherent force and cause. But the basis for this distinction lies in natural things themselves and is far from being merely conceptual. Moreover, it is no part of Newton's conception to hold that the exercise of a body's *vis insita* is to be likened straightforwardly to the action of an internal motor. But it is a *vis motrix*, an explainer of change. It is the exercise of an internal efficient cause insofar as the body is able "through itself" to educe its proper change from its own potency, both when impeded and when unimpeded. And this change is manifest through the reinforcing effect of the body's repeated acts.

Contributors

CYNTHIA A. FREELAND is Associate Professor of Philosophy at the University of Houston.

DAVID FURLEY is Professor Emeritus of Classics at Princeton University.

MARY LOUISE GILL is Associate Professor of Classics and Philosophy at the University of Pittsburgh.

DAVID E. HAHM is Professor of Classics at The Ohio State University.

LINDSAY JUDSON is Official Student and Tutor in Philosophy at Christ Church, Oxford.

PETER KING is Associate Professor of Philosophy at The Ohio State University.

ARYEH KOSMAN is Professor of Philosophy at Haverford College.

JAMES G. LENNOX is Professor of History and Philosophy of Science, Philosophy, and Classics at the University of Pittsburgh.

J. E. MCGUIRE is Professor of History and Philosophy of Science and Philosophy at the University of Pittsburgh.

SUSAN SUAVÉ MEYER is Associate Professor of Philosophy and Classics at Harvard University.

CALVIN G. NORMORE is Professor of Philosophy at the University of Toronto and at The Ohio State University.

CHRISTOPHER SHIELDS is Associate Professor of Philosophy at the University of Colorado.

MICHAEL V. WEDIN is Professor of Philosophy at the University of California, Davis.

Bibliography

Albert the Great. 1494. *De Physico auditu, Libri Octo*. Venice.

Algra, K. 1988. "The Early Stoics on the Immobility and Coherence of the Cosmos." *Phronesis* 33: 155–80.

Allan, D. J. 1936. *Aristotelis De caelo*. Oxford.

Alluntis, Felix. 1968. *Obras del Doctor Sutil Juan Duns Escoto: Cuestiones Cuodlibetales*. Edition and Spanish translation. Madrid.

Amico, Bartolomew. 1620. *In Aristotelis libros de caelo et mundo*. Venice.

Annas, Julia. 1982. "Aristotle on Inefficient Causes." *Philosophical Quarterly* 32: 311–26.

Anscombe, G.E.M. 1969. *Intention*. Ithaca, N.Y.

Aquinas, Thomas. 1882–. *S. Thomae Aquinatis Doctoris angelici opera omnia*. Vols. 4–12: *Summa theologiae*; vols. 13–15: *Summa contra gentiles*; vol. 46: *Quaestiones disputatae de veritate*. Edited by Leonine Commission. Vatican City.

———. [1852–73] 1948–49. *S. Thomae Aquinatis opera omnia*. Vol. 18: *De Physico auditu*. Parma. Reprint, Masurgia, N.Y.

Averroes. [1562–74] 1962. *Aristotelis opera cum Averrois commentariis*. Vol. 4: *De Physico auditu libri octo*. Vol. 8: *Metaphysicorum libri XIV*. Venice. Reprint, Frankfurt.

Ax, W. [1938] 1965. *M. Tulli Ciceronis scripta quae manserunt omnia*. Vol. 46: *De divinatione, De Fato, Timaeus*. Teubner ed. Reprint, Leipzig.

Bailey, Cyril. 1947. *Titi Lucreti Cari De rerum natura libri sex*. Prolegomena, critical text, translation, and commentary. 3 vols. Oxford.

Balić, P. Carolus. 1927. *Les Commentaires de Jean Duns Scot sur les quatres livres des Sentences*. Louvain.

Balić, P. Carolus, et al. 1950–. *Iohannis Duns Scoti Doctoris Subtilis et Mariani opera omnia*. Vols. 1–7, 16–18. Vatican City. [Vat.]

Barnes, J., and M. Minucci, eds. 1988. *Matter and Metaphysics*. Proceedings of the Fourth Symposium Hellenisticum. Naples.

Barnes, J., M. Schofield, and R. Sorabji, eds. 1975–79. *Articles on Aristotle*. 4 vols. London.

Berti, E., ed. 1981. *Aristotle on Science: The Posterior Analytics*. Proceedings of the Eighth Symposium Aristotelicum. Padua.

Bett, Richard. 1986. "Immortality and the Nature of the Soul in the *Phaedrus*." *Phronesis* 31: 1–26.

Bianchi, M. L. 1987. *Signatura rerum: segni, magia e conoscenza da Paracelso a Leibniz*. Rome.

Bogen, James, and J. E. McGuire. 1986–87. "Aristotle's Great Clock: Necessity, Possibility and the Motion of the Cosmos in *De Caelo* 1.12." *Philosophy Research Archives* 12: 387–448.

Boler, John. 1993. "Transcending the Natural: Duns Scotus on the Two Affections of the Will." *American Catholic Philosophical Quarterly* 67, 1: 109–26.

Bonaventure. 1882–1902. *S. Bonaventura opera omnia*. Vol. 1: *Commentarius in quattuor libros Sententiarum Petri Lombardi*. Edited by Collegium S. Bonaventure. Quarrachi.

Brentano, Franz. 1967. *Die Psychologie des Aristoteles*. 2d ed. Darmstadt.

Broadie, Sarah Waterlow. Typescript. "What Does Aristotle's Prime Mover Do?"

Brown, Steven, et al. 1967–85. *Guillelmi de Ockham Opera philosophica et theologica*. Franciscan Institute. St. Bonaventure, N.Y. [*OP* and *OT*]

Bruns, I. 1887. *Alexandri Aphrodisiensis praeter commentaria scripta minora: De anima liber cum mantissa*. Commentaria in Aristotelem graeca, suppl. vol. 2, pt. 1. Berlin.

―――. 1892. *Alexandri Aphrodisiensis praeter commentaria scripta minora: Quaestiones. De fato. De mixtione*. Commentaria in Aristotelem graeca, suppl. vol. 2, pt. 2. Berlin.

Buridan, Jean. [1518] 1964. *In Metaphysicam Aristotelis quaestiones*. Paris. Reprint, Frankfurt.

Burnet, John. 1900–1907. *Platonis Opera*. 5 vols. Oxford.

Bywater, I. 1894. *Aristotelis Ethica Nicomachea*. Oxford.

Carteron, Henri. 1923. *La Notion de force dans le système d'Aristote*. Paris.

Chisholm, Roderick. [1964] 1982. "Human Freedom and Self." The Lindley Lecture: Department of Philosophy, University of Kansas. In Watson 1982, 24–35.

Cleary, John J., and Daniel Shartin, eds. 1989. *Proceedings of the Boston Area Colloquium*. Vol. 4. Lanham, Md.

Code, Alan. 1987. "Soul as Efficient Cause in Aristotle's Embryology." *Philosophical Topics* 15: 51–59.

Cohen, Bernard I. 1964. "*Quantum in se est*: Newton's Concept of Inertia in Relation to Descartes and Lucretius." *Notes and Records of the Royal Society of London* 19: 131–35.

Cohn, L., P. Wendland, and S. Reiter. 1894–1915. *Philonis Alexandrini opera quae supersunt*. 6 vols. Berlin. Reprint, 1962.

Cooper, John M. 1975. *Reason and Human Good in Aristotle*. Cambridge, Mass.

―――. 1982. "Aristotle on Natural Teleology." In Schofield and Nussbaum 1982, 197–222.

―――. 1987. "Hypothetical Necessity and Natural Teleology." In Gotthelf and Lennox 1987, 243–74.

Corcoran, John, ed. 1974. *Ancient Logic and Its Modern Interpretations*. Dordrecht.

Corcoran, T. H. 1971–72. *Seneca: Naturales quaestiones*. 2 vols. Loeb Classical Library. Cambridge, Mass. and London.

Crouzel, H., and M. Simonetti. 1978–84. *Origène: Traité des principes*. 5 vols. Sources chrétiennes, vols. 252–53, 268–69, 312. Paris.

De Careil, A. Foucher. 1854. *Leibniz: Refutation inédite de Spinoza*. Paris.

Delorme, F. M. 1938. *Roger Bacon: Quaestiones supra libros quattuor inedita*. Vol. 8. Oxford.

Devereux, Daniel, and Pierre Pellegrin, eds. 1990. *Biologie, logique et métaphysique chez Aristote*. Paris.

De Wulf, Maurice, and J. Hoffmans. 1914. *Les philosophes Belges*. Vol. 3. (Godfrey of Fontaines, *Quodlibets 5–7*). Louvain.

Diels, H. 1879. *Doxographi Graeci*. Berlin.

————. 1892–95. *Simplicii In Aristotelis Physicorum libros octo commentaria*. 2 vols. Commentaria in Aristotelem graeca, vols. 9–10. Berlin.

Diels, H., and W. Kranz. [1903] 1972. *Die Fragmente der Vorsokratiker*. 16th reprint, 6th ed. 3 vols. Zürich. [DK]

Donagan A., N. Perovich, and M. Wedin, eds. 1985. *Human Nature and Natural Knowledge*. Dordrecht.

Dorotheo, Guillelmo. 1554. *Physicorum. Hoc est. De naturali auscultatione primi quattuor Aristotelis libri cum Ioannis Grammatici Philoponi commentariis*. Venice.

Dragona-Monachou, M. 1976. *The Stoic Arguments for the Existence and Providence of the Gods*. Athens.

Dretske, Fred. 1988. *Explaining Behavior: Reasons in a World of Causes*. Cambridge, Mass.

Duns Scotus, John. 1617. *In octo libri Physicorum Aristotelis*. Annotations by F. de Pitigianis. Venice.

Düring, I. 1961. *Aristotle's Protrepticus: An Attempt at Reconstruction*. Göteborg.

Durrant, M., ed. 1993. *Aristotle's De anima in Focus*. London.

Easterling, H. J. 1966. "A Note on *De anima* 413a8–9." *Phronesis* 11: 159–62.

Edelstein, L., and I. G. Kidd. 1972–88. *Posidonius*. 2 vols. in 3. Cambridge Classical Texts and Commentaries 13–14. Cambridge.

Effler, Roy. 1962. *John Duns Scotus and the Principle "Omne quod movetur ab alio movetur"*. The Franciscan Institute Philosophy Series. St. Bonaventure, N.Y.

Evans, Gareth. 1982. *The Varieties of Reference*. Oxford.

Festugière, A.-J. 1966–68. *Proclus: Commentaire sur le Timée*. Paris.

Fine, Gail. 1987. "Forms as Causes: Plato and Aristotle." In Graeser 1987, 69–112.

Franks, Joan. 1992. Review of Wedin 1988. *International Studies in Philosophy* 24: 146–48.

Frede, Dorothea. 1985. "Aristotle on the Limits of Determinism: Accidental Causes in *Metaphysics* E.3." In Gotthelf 1985, 207–25.

Frege, G. 1956. "The Thought: A Logical Inquiry." *Mind* 65: 289–311.

Freeland, Cynthia. 1982. "Moral Virtues and Human Powers." *Review of Metaphysics* 36: 3–22.

————. 1991. "Accidental Causes and Real Explanations." In Judson 1991, 49–72.

————. 1992. "Aristotle on the Sense of Touch." In Nussbaum and Rorty 1992, 227–48.

Funkenstein, Amos. 1986. *Theology and the Scientific Imagination from the Middle Ages to the Seventeenth Century*. Princeton.

Furley, David. 1967. *Two Studies in the Greek Atomists*. Princeton.

————. 1978. "Self-Movers." In Lloyd and Owen 1978, 165–79. Reprinted in Rorty 1980, 55–67; and in Furley 1989, 121–31.

————. 1989. *Cosmic Problems: Essays on Greek and Roman Philosophy of Nature*. Cambridge.

Geach, Peter. 1957. *Mental Acts*. London.

Geyer, Bernhard, et al. 1960. *Alberti Magni opera omnia*. Vol. 16, pt. 1. Westphalia.

Gill, Mary Louise. 1989. *Aristotle on Substance: The Paradox of Unity*. Princeton.

————. 1991. "Aristotle on Self-Motion." In Judson 1991, 243–65.

Glisson, Francis. 1672. *Tractatus de natura substantiae energetica*. London.

Goclenius, Rudolph. [1613] 1964. *Lexicon philosophicum*. Frankfort. Olms reprint, Hildesheim.

Görgemanns, H., and H. Kaarp. 1976. *Origenes vier Bücher von den Prinzipien*. Texte zur Forschung 24. Darmstadt.

Gotthelf, Allan, ed. 1985. *Aristotle on Nature and Living Things: Philosophical and Historical Studies Presented to David M. Balme on His Seventieth Birthday*. Pittsburgh.

————. 1989a. "The Place of the Good in Aristotle's Teleology." In Cleary and Shartin 1989, 113–47.

————. 1989b. "Teleology and Spontaneous Generation in Aristotle: A Discussion." In Penner and Kraut 1989, 181–93.

Gotthelf, Allan, and James G. Lennox, eds. 1987. *Philosophical Issues in Aristotle's Biology*. Cambridge.

Gould, Stephen J. 1977. *Ever Since Darwin: Reflections in Natural History*. New York.

————. 1982. *The Panda's Thumb: More Reflections in Natural History*. New York.

Graeser, A., ed. 1987. *Mathematik und Metaphysik bei Aristoteles*. Proceedings of the Tenth Symposium Aristotelicum. Bern.

Graham, Daniel. 1987. *Aristotle's Two Systems*. Oxford.

Gummere, R. M. 1917–25. *Seneca: Ad Lucilium epistulae morales*. 3 vols. Loeb Classical Library. Cambridge, Mass. and London.

Guthrie, W.K.C. 1933. "The Development of Aristotle's Theology, I." *Classical Quarterly* 27: 162–71.

————. 1934. "The Development of Aristotle's Theology, II." *Classical Quarterly* 28: 90–98.

————. 1939. *Aristotle: On the Heavens*. Loeb Classical Library. London and Cambridge, Mass.

Hahm, David E. 1977. *The Origins of Stoic Cosmology*. Columbus, Ohio.

————. 1991. "Aristotle and the Stoics: A Methodological Crux." *Archiv für Geschichte der Philosophie* 73: 297–311.

————. 1992. "A Neglected Stoic Argument for Human Responsibility." *Illinois Classical Studies* 17: 23–48.

Hall, Rupert A., and Marie Boas Hall. 1962. *Unpublished Scientific Papers of Isaac Newton*. Cambridge.

Hamlyn, D. W. 1959. "Aristotle's Account of Aesthesis in De Anima." *Classical Quarterly*, n.s. 9: 6–16.

————. 1968. *Aristotle's De Anima: Books I and II*. Oxford.

Hampshire, Stuart. 1959. *Thought and Action*. London.

Hartman, Edwin. 1977. *Substance, Body, and Soul: Aristotelian Investigations*. Princeton.

Hayduck, M. 1882. *Simplicii In libros Aristotelis De anima commentaria*. Commentaria in Aristotelem graeca, vol. 11. Berlin.

Heath, Thomas. 1981. *Aristarchus of Samos: The Ancient Copernicus*. New York.

Heiberg, I. L. 1894. *Simplicii In Aristotelis De caelo commentaria*. Commentaria in Aristotelem graeca, vol. 7. Berlin.

Heinaman, Robert. 1981. "Non-Substantial Individuals in the *Categories*." *Phronesis* 26: 295–307.

———. 1985. "Aristotle on Housebuilding." *History of Philosophy Quarterly* 2: 145–62.

Helmreich, G. 1894. "Galeni περὶ τῶν ἑαυτῷ δοκούντων fragmenta inedita." *Philologus* 52: 432–34.

Henninger, Mark G. 1989. *Relations: Medieval Theories 1250–1325*. Oxford.

Herival, John. 1965. *The Background of Newton's Principia*. Oxford.

Hicks, R. D. 1908. *Aristotle's De anima*. Cambridge.

Hierocles. 1992. *Corpus dei filosofici greci e latini*. Pt. 1, vol. 1.2. Accademica toscana di scienze e lettere La Colombaria. Florence. Pp. 296–366.

Hoffmans, J. 1921. *Les philosophes Belges*. Vol. 4 (Godfrey of Fontaines, *Quodlibet* 8). Louvain.

Hubbell, H. M. 1949. *Cicero: De inventione*. Loeb Classical Library. Cambridge, Mass.

Inwood, Brad. 1985. *Ethics and Human Action in Stoicism*. Oxford.

Irwin, Terence. 1980. "The Metaphysical and Psychological Basis of Aristotle's Ethics." In Rorty 1980, 35–53.

———. 1982. "Aristotle's Concept of Signification." In Schofield and Nussbaum 1982, 241–66.

Jaeger, Werner. 1948. *Aristotle: Fundamentals of the History of His Development*. 2d ed. Translated by Richard Robinson. Oxford.

———. 1957. *Aristotelis Metaphysica*. Oxford.

Jensen, Bernard. 1922–27. *Petrus Olivi: Quaestiones in secundum librum Sententiarum*. Quarrachi.

Joachim, Harold. 1922. *Aristotle: On Coming-to-Be and Passing-Away*. A revised text with introduction and commentary. Oxford.

Judson, Lindsay, 1987. "God or Nature? Philoponus on Generability and Perishability." In Sorabji 1987, 179–96.

———. ed. 1991. *Aristotle's Physics: A Collection of Essays*. Oxford.

Kahn, Charles. 1981. "The Role of *nous* in the Cognition of First Principles in *Posterior Analytics* II.19." In Berti 1981, 385–414.

———. 1985a. "The Place of the Prime Mover in Aristotle's Teleology." In Gotthelf 1985, 183–205.

———. 1985b. "On the Intended Interpretation of Aristotle's *Metaphysics*." In Wiesner 1985, 311–38.

Kalbfleisch, K. 1907. *Simplicii In Aristotelis categorias commentarium*. Commentaria in Aristotelem graeca, vol. 8. Berlin.

Keckermann, Bartholomew. 1616. *Systema logicae*. Hanover.

Kent, Bonnie B. 1984. "Aristotle and the Franciscans: Gerard Odonis' Commentary on the *Nicomachean Ethics*." Dissertation, Columbia University.

Kepler, Johannes. 1607. *Astronomia nova*. Prague.

Koetschau, P. 1899. *Origenes Werke*. Vol. 2: *Buch V–VIII Gegen Celsus: Die Schrift vom Gebet*. Die christlichen Schriftsteller der ersten drei Jahrhunderte, vol. 3. Leipzig.

———. 1913. *Origenes Werke*. Vol. 5: *De principiis*. Die christlichen Schriftsteller der ersten drei Jahrhunderte, vol. 22. Leipzig.

Kosman, L. A. 1969. "Aristotle's Definition of Motion." *Phronesis* 14: 40–62.

———. 1984. "Substance, Being, and *Energeia*." *Oxford Studies in Ancient Philosophy* 2: 121–49.

Kretzmann, Norman. 1974. "Aristotle on Spoken Sound Significant by Convention." In Corcoran, 1974, 3–21.

Kretzmann, Norman, Anthony Kenny, Jan Pinborg, and Eleanor Stump, eds. 1982. *The Cambridge History of Later Medieval Philosophy: From the Rediscovery of Aristotle to the Disintegration of Scholasticism, 1100–1600.* Cambridge.

Kühn, C. G. [1821] 1964. *Claudii Galeni opera omnia.* 20 vols. Leipzig. Reprint, Hildesheim.

Kuhn, Thomas. 1957. *The Copernican Revolution.* Cambridge, Mass.

Labarrière, Jean-Louis. 1984. "Imagination humaine et imagination animale chez Aristote." *Phronesis* 29: 17–49.

———. 1990. "De la *phronesis* animale." In Devereux and Pellegrin 1990, 405–28.

———. 1991. Review of Wedin 1988. *Philosophische Rundshau* 38: 225–29.

Lang, H. S. 1981. "Aristotle's Immaterial Mover and the Problem of Location in *Physics* VIII." *Review of Metaphysics* 35: 321–35.

Lear, Jonathan. 1988. *Aristotle: The Desire to Understand.* Cambridge.

Lee, H.P.D. 1952. *Aristotle: Meteorologica.* Loeb Classical Library. Cambridge, Mass.

Lefèvre, C. 1978. "Sur le statut de l'âme dans le *De anima* et les *Parva naturalia.*" In Lloyd and Owen 1978, 21–67.

Leibniz, Gottfried Wilhelm. 1960. *Die philosophischen Schriften.* Olms reprint. Hildesheim.

Lewis, E. 1988. "Diogenes Laertius and the Stoic Theory of Mixture." *Bulletin of the Institute of Classical Studies* 35: 84–90.

Liddell, H. G., R. Scott, H. S. Jones, and R. McKenzie. 1940. *Greek-English Lexicon.* 9th ed. Oxford. [LSJ]

Lloyd, A. C. 1969–70. "Nondiscursive Thought—An Enigma of Greek Philosophy." *Proceedings of the Aristotelian Society* 70: 261–74.

Lloyd, G.E.R., and G.E.L. Owen, eds. 1978. *Aristotle on Mind and the Senses.* Proceedings of the Seventh Symposium Aristotelicum. Cambridge.

Long, A. A. 1970. "Stoic Determinism and Alexander of Aphrodisias *De fato* (i–xiv)." *Archiv für Geschichte der Philosophie* 52: 247–68.

———. 1971a. "Freedom and Determinism in the Stoic Theory of Human Action." In Long 1971b, 173–99.

———, ed. 1971b. *Problems in Stoicism.* London.

———. 1982. "Soul and Body in Stoicism." *Phronesis* 27: 34–57.

Long, A. A., and D. L. Sedley. 1987. *The Hellenistic Philosophers.* 2 vols. Cambridge. [LS]

Long, H. S. 1964. *Diogenis Laertii Vitae philosophorum.* 2 vols. Oxford.

Lulofs, H. J. Drossaart. 1965. *Aristotelis De generatione animalium.* Oxford.

McGuire, J. E. 1985. "Philoponus on *Physics* II.1: Φύσις, Δύναμις, and the Motion of Simple Bodies." *Ancient Philosophy* 5: 241–67.

McGuire, J. E., and Martin Tamny. 1983. *Certain Philosophical Questions: Newton's Trinity Notebook.* Cambridge.

Macierowski, E. M., and R. F. Hassing. 1988. "John Philoponus on Aristotle's Definition of Nature." *Ancient Philosophy* 8: 73–100.

Macken, R., et al. 1979-. *Henrici de Gandavo Opera omnia.* Vol. 13: *Quodlibet 9;* vol. 14: *Quodlibet 10;* edited by J. Decorte. Louvain.

Mackie, J. L. 1965. "Causes and Conditions." *American Philosophical Quarterly* 2: 245–64.

McMullin, Ernan. 1978. *Newton on Matter and Activity.* Notre Dame, Ind.

Maggiòlo, P. M. 1965. *S. Thomae Aquinatis in octo libros Physicorum Aristotelis expositio.* Turin.

Magirus, Johann. 1642. *Physiologiae peripateticae libri sex.* Cambridge.

Maier, Anneliese. 1960. "Ergebnisse der Spatscholastischen Naturphilosophie." *Scholastick* 35: 161–87.

Maignon, Emanuel. 1653. *Cursus philosophicus.* Toulouse.

Mandonnet P., and M. F. Moos. 1929–56. *S. Thomae Aquinatis Scriptum super Sententiis.* 4 vols. Turin.

Marache, R. 1967–89. *Aulu-Gelle: Les nuits attiques.* 3 vols. Budé ed. Paris.

Marshall, P. K. 1968. *Aulus Gellius: Noctes Atticae.* Oxford.

Menut, A. D., and A. J. Denomy. 1968. *Nicole Oresme: Le Livre du ciel et du monde.* Madison, Wis.

Meyer, Susan Sauvé. 1992. "Aristotle, Teleology, and Reduction." *Philosophical Review* 101: 791–825.

———. 1994. *Aristotle on Moral Responsibility: Character and Cause.* Oxford.

Migne, J. P. 1890. *Patrologiae cursus completus: Series graeca.* Vols. 8–9: *Clemens Alexandrinus: Stromata.* Paris.

Minio-Paluello, L., et al., eds. 1958–. *Aristoteles latinus.* Vols. 16–17: *Metaphysics.* Edited by G. Vuillemin-Diem. Paris. [AL]

Modrak, Deborah. 1987. *Aristotle: The Power of Perception.* Chicago.

Moody, Ernest A. 1942. *Johannis Buridan: Quaestiones super libris quattuor de caelo et mundo.* Cambridge, Mass.

Morani, M. 1987. *Nemesii Emeseni De natura hominis.* Teubner ed. Leipzig.

Moravcsik, Julius. 1974. "Aristotle on Adequate Explanations." *Synthese* 28: 3–17.

Mras, K. 1954–56. *Eusebius Werke.* Vol. 8: *Die Praeparatio evangelica.* Die griechischen christlichen Schriftsteller, vol. 43, pt. 1–2. Berlin.

Mutschmann, H., and J. Mau. 1912–54. *Sexti Empirici opera.* 3 vols. Teubner ed. Leipzig.

Newton, Isaac. 1687. *Philosophiae naturalis principia mathematica.* London.

———. 1952. *Opticks.* New York. Dover reprint of 4th ed., 1730.

Niphus, Augustinus. 1569. *Expositio super VIII libros de physico auditu.* Venice.

Normore, C. G. Forthcoming. "Anselm on Choosing between Goodness and Rightness." *Proceedings of the Ninth Annual Conference of the Societé pour l'étude de la philosophie medievale.*

Nunnesius, Johannes. 1554. *Institutionum Physicarum libri IV.* Valensia.

Nussbaum, Martha. 1978. *Aristotle's De motu animalium.* Text with translation, commentary, and interpretive essays. Princeton.

Nussbaum, Martha, and Amélie Rorty, eds. 1992. *Essays on Aristotle's De anima.* Oxford.

Oltramare, P. 1929. *Sénèque: Questions naturelles.* 2 vols. Budé ed. Paris.

Owens, Joseph. Typescript. "The Problematic of the Active Mind's Causation in Aristotle, *De anima* 3.5."

Pacius, Julius. 1608. *Aristotelis stagiritae, peripateticorum principiorum naturalis auscultationis libri VIII.* Hanover.

Palmer, Robert P., ed. 1971. *Philomathes: Studies in Memory of Philip Merlan.* The Hague.

Pegis, A. C. 1945. *Basic Works of Thomas Aquinas.* New York.

Pendasius, Fredericus. 1604. *Physicae auditionis texturae libri VIII.* Venice.

Penner, Terry, and Richard Kraut, eds. 1989. *Nature, Knowledge, and Virtue: Essays in Memory of Joan Kung. Apeiron* 22. Edmonton, Alberta.

Pease, A. S. 1955. *Cicero: De natura deorum.* Cambridge, Mass.

Pererius, Benedictus. 1579. *De communibus omnium rerum naturalium principiis et affectionibus.* Paris.

Perion, Joachimus. 1554. *De natura aut de rerum principiis libros VIII observationes.* Paris.

Pines, S. 1961. "*Omne quod movetur necesse est ab alique moveri*: Alexander of Aphrodisias and the Theory of Motion." *Isis* 52: 21–54.

———. 1963. *Moses Maimonides: The Guide of the Perplexed.* Chicago.

Pohlenz, M., and R. Westman. 1959. *Plutarchi Moralia.* Vol. 6, pt. 2. 2d ed. Teubner ed. Leipzig.

Préchac, F., and H. Noblot. 1969–85. *Sénèque: Lettres à Lucilius.* 5 vols. Budé ed. Paris.

Rackham, H. 1968. *Cicero: De oratore III. De fato. Paradoxa Stoicorum. De partitione.* Loeb Classical Library. Cambridge, Mass. and London.

Rasarius, B. 1558. *Aristotelis physicorum libri quattuor cum Ioannis Grammatici cognomento Philoponi commentariis.* Venice.

Rieth, O. 1933. *Grundbegriffe der stoischen Ethik: Eine Traditionsgeschichtliche Untersuchung.* Problemata 9. Berlin.

Rodier, G. 1900. *Aristote: Traité de l'âme.* 2 vols. Paris.

Rorty, Amélie, ed. 1980. *Essays on Aristotle's Ethics.* Berkeley.

Rose, V. 1886. *Aristotelis qui ferebunter librorum fragmenta.* 2d ed. Teubner ed. Leipzig.

Ross, G.T.R. [1906] 1973. *Aristotle: De sensu and De memoria.* Cambridge. Reprint, New York.

Ross, W. D. 1924. *Aristotle's Metaphysics.* A revised text with introduction and commentary. 2 vols. Oxford.

———. 1936. *Aristotle's Physics.* A revised text with introduction and commentary. Oxford.

———. 1955. *Aristotle: Parva naturalia.* Oxford.

———. 1957. "The Development of Aristotle's Thought." *Proceedings of the British Academy* 43: 63–78. Reprinted in Barnes, Schofield, and Sorabji 1975–79, 1: 1–13.

———. 1961. *Aristotle: De anima.* Oxford.

Russell, Bertrand. 1912. *The Problems of Philosophy.* Oxford.

Sandbach, F. H. 1985. *Aristotle and the Stoics.* Proceedings of the Cambridge Philological Society, suppl. vol. 10. Cambridge.

Sanderson, Robert. 1631. *Logicae artis compendium.* Oxford.

Sapegno, N. 1976. *Dante Alighieri: La divina commedia.* 3 vols. Florence.

Sauvé, Susan. 1987. "Unmoved Movers, Form, and Matter." *Philosophical Topics* 15: 171–96.

Schenkl, H. 1916. *Epicteti dissertationes ab Arriano digestae*. Complete edition. Teubner ed. Leipzig.

Schmitt, Charles. 1987. "Philoponus' Commentary on Aristotle's *Physics* in the Sixteenth Century." In Sorabji 1987, 210–27.

Schmitt, F. S. 1946. *Sancti Anselmi Cantuariensis Archiepiscopi opera omnia*. Vol. 2. Edinburgh.

Schofield, Malcolm. 1978. "Aristotle on the Imagination." In Lloyd and Owen 1978, 99–140.

Schofield, Malcolm, and Martha C. Nussbaum, eds. 1982. *Language and Logos: Studies in Ancient Philosophy Presented to G.E.L. Owen*. Cambridge.

Seeck, G. A. 1965. *"Nachträge" im achten Buch der Physik des Aristoteles*. Abhandlungen der Geisterung Sozialwissenschaftlichen Klasse, Akademie der Wissenschaften und der Literatur. Mainz.

Sharples, R. W. 1978. "Alexander of Aphrodisias *De fato*: Some Parallels." *Classical Quarterly*, n.s. 28: 243–66.

———. 1983. *Alexander of Aphrodisias On Fate*. Text, translation, and commentary. London.

Simplicius. 1566. *Commentaria in octo libros Aristotelis de Physico auditu*. Venice.

Skemp, J. B. 1978. "Ορεξις in *De anima* 3.10." In Lloyd and Owen 1978, 181–89.

Solmsen, Friedrich. 1960. *Aristotle's System of the Physical World*. Ithaca, N.Y.

———. 1971. "Plato's First Mover in the Eighth Book of Aristotle's *Physics*." In Palmer 1971, 171–82.

Sorabji, Richard. [1971] 1975–79. "Aristotle on Demarcating the Five Senses." *Philosophical Review* 80: 55–79. Reprinted in Barnes, Schofield, and Sorabji 1975–79, 4: 76–92.

———. 1980. *Necessity, Cause, and Blame: Perspectives on Aristotle's Theory*. London and Ithaca, N.Y.

———. 1982. "Myths about Non-Propositional Thought." In Schofield and Nussbaum 1982, 295–314.

———, ed. 1987. *Philoponus and the Rejection of Aristotelian Science*. London and Ithaca, N.Y.

———. 1988. *Matter, Space and Motion: Theories in Antiquity and Their Sequel*. London.

Stahl, Daniel. 1645. *Axiomata philosophica*. Cambridge.

Stählin, O., L. Früchtel, and U. Treu. 1960–70. *Clemens Alexandrinus*. Vols. 2 (3d ed.) and 3 (2d ed.). Die griechischen christlichen Schriftsteller, vols. 52 (new numbering 15) and 17. Berlin.

Susemihl, F. [1884] 1967. *Eudemi Rhodii Ethica*. Teubner ed. Leipzig. Reprint, Amsterdam.

Sutton, E. W., and H. Rackham. 1942. *Cicero: De oratore I–II*. Loeb Classical Library. Cambridge, Mass. and London.

Taylor, Charles. 1964. *The Explanation of Behaviour*. London.

Thillet, P. 1984. *Alexandre d'Aphrodise: Traité du destin*. Edition and translation. Budé ed. Paris.

Tieleman, T. 1991. "Diogenes of Babylon and Stoic Embryology." *Mnemosyne* 44: 106–25.

Todd, R. B. 1976. *Alexander of Aphrodisias on Stoic Physics*. Edition and translation of *De mixtione*. Leiden.

Toletus, Franciscus. 1585. *Commentaria in octo libros Aristotelis de Physica auscultatione*. Cologne.

Van der Ejik, Ph. J. 1989. "Divine Movement and Human Nature in *Eudemian Ethics* 8.2." *Hermes* 117: 24–43.

Verardo, R. A., R. M. Spiazzi, and M. Calcaterra 1954. *Thomas Aquinas: Compendium theologiae. Opuscula theologica*. Turin.

Vimercato, Francesco. 1564. *In octo libros Aristotelis de naturali auscultatione commentarii*. Venice.

Vitelli, H. 1888. *Philoponi in Aristotelis Physica commentaria*. 2 vols. Commentaria in Aristotelem graeca, vols. 16–17. Berlin.

Von Arnim, H. 1903–5. *Stoicorum veterum fragmenta*. 3 vols. Vol. 4: *Indices*, edited by M. Adler [1924]. Teubner ed. Leipzig. Reprint, 4 vols. Stuttgart, 1979. [*SVF*]

———. 1906. *Hierokles: Ethische Elementarlehre (Papyrus 9780)*. Berliner Klassikertexte 4. Berlin.

Wachsmuth, C., and O. Hense. 1884–1912. *Ioannis Stobaei anthologium*. 5 vols. Berlin.

Wadding, Luke. [1639] 1891–95. *Joannis Duns Scoti Doctoris Subtilis Ordinis Minorum opera omnia*. Lyon. Republished, with only slight alterations, by L. Vivès. Vols. 1–26. Paris. [WV]

Wallace, William A. 1978. "Causes and Forces in Sixteenth-Century Physics." *Isis* 69: 400–415.

Wallis, Francis. 1690. *Synopsis Physicae tam Aristotelicae*. London.

Waszink, J. H. 1962. *Calcidius: In Timaeo*. Leiden.

Waterlow, Sarah. 1982. *Nature, Change, and Agency in Aristotle's Physics*. Oxford.

Watson, Gary, ed. 1982. *Free Will*. New York.

Wedin, Michael V. 1985. "Tracking Aristotle's ΝΟΥΣ." In Donagan, Perovich, and Wedin 1985, 167–97. Reprinted in Durrant 1993, 128–61.

———. 1988. *Mind and Imagination in Aristotle*. New Haven, Conn.

———. 1989. "Aristotle on the Mechanics of Thought." *Ancient Philosophy* 9: 67–86.

———. 1993. "Content and Cause in the Aristotelian Mind." Spindel Conference 1992: Ancient Minds. *Southern Journal of Philosophy* 31 suppl.: 49–105.

Wiesner, Jürgen, ed. 1985. *Aristoteles und seine Schule*. Berlin.

Williams, C.J.F. 1982. *Aristotle's De generatione et corruptione*. Clarendon Aristotle Series. Oxford.

Wippel, John F. 1981. *The Metaphysical Thought of Godfrey of Fontaines*. Washington, D.C.

Wolff, M. 1988. "Hipparchus and the Stoic Theory of Motion." In Barnes and Minucci 1988, 471–545.

Wolter, Alan B. 1966. *John Duns Scotus: A Treatise on God as First Principle*. 2d ed. Chicago.

Woodfield, Andrew. 1976. *Teleology*. London.

Woods, Michael. 1982. *Aristotle's Eudemian Ethics. Books I, II and VIII*. Oxford.

Zabarella, Jacopo. 1604. *De rebus naturalibus, libri XXX*. Tarvisia.